Hutterite Studies

Essays by Robert Friedmann

EDITED BY HAROLD S. BENDER
SECOND EDITION

© 1961 by The Mennonite Historical Society.
Reprinted with kind permission by the Hutterian Brethren Book Centre.

Box 40 • Macgregor, MB • R0H 0R0 • Canada
P. 204-272-5132 • F. 204-252-2381

Cover photo: © 1996–2010 The Global Anabaptist Mennonite Encyclopedia Online (GAMEO). All rights reserved. Used by permission.

Cover design: Yvonne Parks

Habaner motif: © Jan Glaysteen. Used by permission.

Photo with biography: Mennonite Church USA Historical Committee and Archives, Goshen, Indiana.

Translation of Astrid von Schlachta's foreword: Karin James, Das bunte Fenster, Winnipeg, Manitoba.

The publisher is grateful to Patrick Murphy, Jennifer Waldner and Lucas Waldner for their kind assistance with this project. Astrid von Schlachta (Innsbruck, Austria) and Leonard Gross (Goshen, Indiana) enthusiastically provided an afterword and foreword. The errata of the previous publication was implemented to minimize error, but facts and details that reveal the dated nature of the original remain intact.

ISBN 978-0-9865381-0-0

Library and Archives Canada Cataloguing in Publication

Friedmann, Robert, 1891-1970
    Hutterite studies / essays by Robert Friedmann ;
edited by Harold S. Bender. -- 2nd ed.

Includes index.
Celebrating the life and work of an Anabaptist scholar.
ISBN 978-0-9865381-0-0

    1. Hutterite Brethren. 2. Hutterite Brethren--Biography.
I. Bender, Harold Stauffer, 1897-1962 II. Title.

BX8129.H8F74 2010   289.7'3   C2010-900845-6

Printed and bound in Canada.

TABLE OF CONTENTS

Foreword to this Edition — III
Preface — IX

I. Anabaptism

Conception of the Anabaptists — 1
Recent Interpretations of Anabaptism — 23

II. Hutterite History

The Hutterian Brethren — 41
Anabaptism in Moravia — 59
Anabaptism in Transdanubia — 65
Sobotiste — 67
The Habaner — 71
Hutterite Mission Work and Missioners — 75

III. Hutterite Doctrines

The Christian Communism of the Hutterite Brethren — 79
Peter Riedemann on Original Sin and the Way of Redemption — 91
The Doctrine of the Two Worlds — 97

IV. Hutterite Life

Bruderhof — 107
Gemeindeordnungen — 111
Diener der Notdurft — 115
Economic Aspects of Early Hutterite Life — 119
Hutterite Marriage Practices — 127
Medicine Among the Hutterites — 131
Hutterite Physicians and Barber–Surgeons — 135
Hutterite Education — 145
Hutterite Pottery, or Haban Fayence — 149

V. Hutterite Writings

Hutterite Chronicles	157
Epistles of the Hutterian Brethren	163
Hutterite Sermons	191
Hutterite *Taufreden*	195
Die Lieder der Hutterischen Brüder	197
The Hutterite *Article Book*	201
Jakob Hutter's Last Epistle to the Church in Moravia, 1535	205
The Oldest Church Discipline of the Anabaptists	219
Brüderliche Vereinigung of 1556–57	225
The Anabaptists Answer Melanchthon: *Handbüchlein wider den Prozess*	227
Peter Reidemann's *Rechenschaft*	231
An Anabaptist Ordinance of 1633 on Nonresistance	237
Concerning the True Soldier of Jesus Christ	249

VI. Hutterite Biographies

Leonhard Schiemer and Hans Schlaffer: Two Tyrolean Anabaptist Martyr–Apostles of 1528	261
Shorter Sketches of Outstanding Leaders	273
Peter Riedemann	273
Ulich Stadler	277
Hans Schmid	280
Klaus Felbinger	282
Kaspar Braitmichel	284
Peter Walpot	285
Johannes Waldner	288
Elias Walter	289

VII. Hutterite Research

The Oldest Known Hutterite Codex of 1560: A Chapter in Anabaptist Intellectual History	293
A Comprehensive Review of Research on the Hutterites	305
Afterword	319
Key to Symbols and Abbreviations	323
A Chronological Bibliography of the Chief Writings of Robert Friedmann, 1927–1961	325

FOREWORD TO THIS EDITION
Robert Friedmann – Searching for the Meaning of Faith for the World

On July 2, 1961, about three weeks after his 70th birthday, Robert Friedmann writes a letter to Otto Bauer, his old friend and companion from his days back in Austria. Both had to emigrate to the United States during the Nazi regime. Friedmann details the many surprises he experienced on his birthday—among which was the "completely unexpected" publication of most of his essays regarding Hutterite history in the work "Hutterite Studies." Friedmann appeared just as moved about this "wonderful honour" as he was about the large sum of money that was raised mostly by his son John in order to publish the work: in excess of $ 1,000. At the same time, he expressed confidence that the first edition could be sold "easily."

The Hutterites and Otto Bauer—they represent the two poles that characterize Robert Friedmann's life from the early days in Vienna, Austria to his spiritual and professional experiences on the other side of the Atlantic, in Goshen and in Kalamazoo. Otto Bauer was one of the spiritual leaders of the religious socialist movement, popular in Europe during the 1920s and 30s. Friedmann came in contact with religious Socialists in the 1920s after his conversion to Protestantism which was only one station on his spiritual journey. Soon, he began to search for alternatives to German Lutheran Protestantism which he perceived as "rather weak."

He interpreted the spiritual climate of Vienna as difficult and not hope inducing—he deemed the majority of all people as "indifferent" and "lethargic" as well as rather unreceptive to dedicate themselves to the "difficult problems of mission." He saw some hope within the small circle of religious Socialists around Otto Bauer who wanted to use Socialist ideas combined with a decidedly religious conviction to work in the political and social arena. Robert Friedmann identified in Otto Bauer and his circle a "true integrity" and felt it was "full of rare energy."[1]

Robert Friedmann found a second alternative to Protestantism in the Anabaptist movement. During the course of his studies at the University of

---

1 Letter by Robert Friedmann to Leonhard Ragaz, Feb. 24, 1929, 1, 3, in: Woodcrest Archives, Church Communities International, Rifton, NY.

Vienna in a seminar with the Austrian historian Alfons Dopsch, Friedmann turned his interests to the history of the Austrian Anabaptists which he found increasingly fascinating. In retrospect, he repeatedly refers to the importance of the Anabaptist example for his conversion, since the letters by the Austrian Anabaptist martyrs were responsible for truly "converting" him.[2]

In 1945, he describes his enthusiasm for the letters of the martyrs to his partner in correspondence, Otto Bauer, in more detail. The letters conveyed a deeply felt "consolation in suffering"—a consolation that Friedmann himself had never experienced and that, as Friedmann suspected, would likely only be experienced in the very last hour. In fact, that Friedmann left his old Jewish faith behind and converted to the Lutheran faith resulted mainly from very few positive perceptions of his old faith whose spiritual and institutional development he repeatedly described as much too institutionalized. Finally, Friedmann was baptized, however, despite this deliberate association with the Christian faith, he always remained connected to his Jewish roots. In 1930, Friedmann declared himself a "Jew who sides with Jesus Christ."[3]

All his life, Friedmann was concerned with the search for community and the question of which path would best realize the Christian idea of community. After World War II, when all the "demonic nature" of war and of National Socialism came to light, he hoped for a renewal of Christianity as the consequence to the exponentiated rise of evil. This hope combined with a confidence that in the future a large percentage of the population would live life more consistently according to God's will. He counted on the masses to feel the urge to live more communally, to give up their own desires and to subordinate their will to God's will.

"During times of an abundant rise in spirituality 'one' simply knows what God's will is and the disciple fulfills it. Yes, he joyfully fulfills it, even if this discipleship includes the danger of martyrdom. There simply is no other way. This is true for all great 'rebels of God'"[4]—such were Friedmann's expectations and his wording in 1955. Again, the model of the Anabaptists formed the basis and historical reference point for this hopeful perspective since exactly this would have been the principle for the very first Anabaptists.

His own experiences of emigration, as well as the political and societal events during the Second World War, have led Friedmann to increased awareness of and attention to suffering that have culminated in the insight that suffering is necessary. According to Friedmann during the years following the war, there are no "freebies" in life. Given the evil, the suffering and

---

2   Letters by Robert Friedmann to Otto Bauer from June 17, 1954, 2 (all information regarding letters by Robert Friedmann refer to copies in the archive Michael Benedikt, Vienna, unless otherwise specified). Re: Friedmann's interest in the Anabaptists of the 16th Century see Leonard Gross, "Conversations with Robert Friedmann", *Mennonite Quarterly Review* 48, 1974, 141-173, esp. 148 f.

3   Letter by Robert Friedmann to Leonhard Ragaz, Dec. 29, 1930, 1, in: Woodcrest Archives, Church Communities International, Rifton, NY.

4   Letter by Robert Friedmann to Otto Bauer, Jan. 26, 1955, 3.

the wickedness connected to war we have to bid adieu to the God of the Old Testament who lets things happen and who punishes, especially when considering the question: "Why does God let this happen?" Friedmann states that the God of the New Testament himself has died on the cross and suffered there, has experienced suffering and misery.[5] This suffering on the cross was, according to Friedmann, not simply "vicarious suffering," but "original suffering"—an endurance of pain. In Friedmann's reflections, the insight that Jesus Christ appeared to destroy the devil's work (1 John 3:8) became the basis supporting his theological idea structure and his "classical position." With this, he turns his back on his earlier period when Tolstoi was the major thinker on his path to Christianity. The important statements of the Sermon on the Mount recede, as he realizes, and the cross itself which he had previously regarded simply as a symbol for a private salvation gains importance. It combines with the central idea that Jesus Christ came to this Earth to destroy evil. With this, Friedmann finds his own Christian answer to the experience with the atrocities of war and of persecution and to the social injustices of his time that only increased with the technological advances of the post-war era and the experiments with the atomic bomb.[6]

Again, the Anabaptist martyrs' letters are Friedmann's reference point to hope for suffering as an effective societal function. To him, the consolation in the suffering was a powerful message in these letters that would recognize the function of suffering mostly in the need for it to happen in order to destroy the devil's work. By "enduring all suffering" Jesus "crush the snake's head" and thereby left an inheritance from which to learn to follow his example. In their "unprovoked" suffering, i.e. suffering that was not intended in advance, the Anabaptists presented the world with a challenge. The world reacted to the Anabaptists out of an "awareness of the challenge…something the world could not handle."[7] "It is part of God's kingdom on Earth to be persecuted, to not be tolerated by the world."[8] This is the church under the cross. According to Friedmann, this martyrdom is affecting the church in its entirety and encompasses a communal experience. Friedmann is convinced that for the Anabaptists this was something "almost inevitable" which is why they accepted it in patience and humility.[9]

"Do not merely listen to the word, and so deceive yourselves. Do what it says." Robert Friedmann quoted this verse from the New Testament (James 1:22) to introduce his essay "Das täuferische Glaubensgut" (Anabaptist

---

5   Letter by Robert Friedmann to Otto Bauer, 1945; letter of Robert Friedmann to Otto Bauer, Sept. 12, 1942.

6   Letter by Robert Friedmann to Otto Bauer, Apr. 13, 1945, 1f., Leonard Gross, "Conversations with Robert Friedmann", *Mennonite Quarterly Review* 48, 1974, 141-173, here 146.

7   Letter by Robert Friedmann to Otto Bauer, 22.5.1953, 2.

8   Robert Friedmann, Das täuferische Glaubensgut. Versuch einer Deutung, *Archiv für Reformationsgeschichte* 55, 1964, 145-161, here 148.

9   Robert Friedmann, Das täuferische Glaubensgut. Versuch einer Deutung, *Archiv für Reformationsgeschichte* 55, 1964, 145-161, here 147.

Body of Faith).[10] This verse represents an important differentiation that Robert Friedmann made in his theological ideas and his interpretation of Anabaptist history. For him, there could be "no 'simple saved by faith alone'"—salvation without deeds is Lutheran thinking. The path of the Anabaptists, however, was "existential, real," the Kingdom of God as experienced in a life of community and in which "the power of evil has been conquered" by "each and everyone who follows Jesus Christ in love and suffering."[11] According to Friedmann, Anabaptists follow a true inner rebirth and acceptance of baptism on faith by a life change: "Do not sin anymore (or fight against it) and increase the extent of brotherly love as much as that is possible in weak humans." In a letter to Otto Bauer in May 1968, Friedmann declares that Anabaptists, as "carriers of the light" have paid a high price for their orthopractical approach to faith, namely the deaths of many. They had consistently "left behind our so-called civilization" which could not contribute to the Kingdom of God anyway.[12] Friedmann recognizes Anabaptist history as an active union of faith and life that simultaneously produces a brotherly form of Christianity, as he explains in an 1964 article in the *Archiv für Reformationsgeschichte*. In this new social order created by the Anabaptists there is no salvation outside of community, only a salvation "hand in hand" with brothers and sisters in faith. A brotherhood is "not only an integral part of Christian life" but has a "central function" in Christian life.[13] For Friedmann, the Anabaptists therefore are direct descendents of the apostolic community—both communities had followed an "existential form of Christianity," which meant a life of faith in dissociation and the highest possible purity.

Despite this clear decision to follow a life of community that could best be lived in dissociation from the world, it becomes clear that Robert Friedmann struggled with the dilemma between "world" and "Kingdom of God"—in 1952 he described himself as positioned between religious Socialists and Anabaptists. This tension between the wish to make the Christian faith effective for the world, to make changes in society on the one hand and the "sectarian" attitude, to segregate oneself from the world, thereby loosing any chance to broadcast this on the other hand cast him into ambivalence. On the one hand, he was deeply affected and moved by this "Anabaptist matter," on the other hand, he knew that as a Christian, one should not withdraw from the world, but had to touch it with the "matter of Jesus Christ" and a Christian political view.[14] However, after the Second World War, Friedmann increasingly doubted that "politics out of faith" could be possible. In-depth study of the New Testament made it clear to him that Christian faith and

---

10 *Archiv für Reformationsgeschichte* 55, 1964, 145-161.
11 Letter by Robert Friedmann to Otto Bauer, 18.7.1951, 2.
12 Letter by Robert Friedmann to Otto Bauer, 22.5.1968.
13 Robert Friedmann, Das täuferische Glaubensgut. Versuch einer Deutung, *Archiv für Reformationsgeschichte* 55, 1964, 145-161, here 148.
14 Letter to Otto Bauer, 5.6.1952.

politics cannot form a good union. Politics do not exist in the "Kingdom of God." Friedmann compared this to the relationship of two people who love one another. Each wants what is best for the other, each wants consensus, not the "right use of power."

Robert Friedmann's quest was to discover the Kingdom of God in Anabaptist history. The many essays in the "Hutterite Studies" bear witness to this quest and in this new edition they will be available to a larger audience. Friedmann's analyses of the Hutterite portion of the "Anabaptist Story" became the basis for the historical account of Anabaptist history and for the interpretation of confessionally deviant faith and life in Early Modern times. Robert Friedmann's merits regarding the research into Hutterite history are diverse and of permanent relevance. Together with Rudolf Wolkan, he is a pioneer in Hutterite research who helped this Anabaptist group gain appropriate attention in the scholarly world. The topics in "Hutterite Studies" range from Hutterite history to the foundation of faith, life and written works of Hutterites and biographies of important Hutterite leaders.

The works emphasize how Robert Friedmann's personal life was touched by the research topic and how history enriches life. The correspondence with Otto Bauer provides the religious Socialist counter evidence for the importance of Anabaptist history. As early as 1927, Otto Bauer referred to the Anabaptists as "Christians of deep faith" and "blood witnesses of faithful Socialism" in the foreword to his "Erläuterung des Linzer Programms" (Annotation to the Program of Linz) and dedicated this piece to them. Bauer saw Socialism substantiated mainly in those Anabaptists who "tried to revive the primitive Communism of early Christian communities." In their dissociation they had been the "first fighters for segregation of church and state" and had to pay for their convictions with their lives.[15]

Dr. Astrid von Schlachta
Universität Innsbruck, Austria
February 2010

---

15 Otto Bauer, *Sozialdemokratie, Religion und Kirche. Ein Beitrag zur Erläuterung des Linzer Programms*, Vienna 1927, 3 f.

PREFACE

Robert Friedmann stands in the line of the great interpreters of Anabaptism, the line of Cornelius, Keller, Beck, Bossert, Wolkan, Loserth, Hege, Neff, and Horsch. These were the scholars who pressed beyond a correction of the false image of the Anabaptists, which was the legacy of the sixteenth century confessional historiography, into a thoroughgoing reconstruction of the history of the movement on the basis of objective research in the sources. His particular field has been the Hutterite Anabaptists; and in this field he is the acknowledged master. With sound historical method, combined with sympathetic understanding, he has explored every aspect of Hutterite life and sought to expound their faith in fullness. For a third of a century, beginning with his first publication in Vienna in 1927, an almost constant flow of scholarly articles on this unique Christian communal brotherhood has marked his career, first in Austria, then in the United States, climaxed by his contribution of almost two hundred articles to the *Mennonite Encyclopedia* on the Hutterian Brethren as well as other Anabaptistica. That we know so much about the Hutterites is due not only to the extraordinary source material which has become available, but also to the profound learning, penetrating interpretative skill, and unflagging energy of Robert Friedmann.

Professor Friedmann has also contributed significantly to major advances in the knowledge and interpretation of Anabaptism as a whole and, beyond sixteenth-century Anabaptism, of Mennonitism in the following centuries. The bibliography of his writings is a testimony to the scope and depth of his contribution. But the writings alone do not tell the whole story. His colleagues, and the students and friends who have sat in his lectures or shared with him in seminars and study conferences, and enjoyed delightful hours of scholarly and engaging conversation, will be forever grateful for the enlightenment and stimulation which they have received and continue to receive from him.

The Mennonite Historical Society is proud to honor the revered scholar on the occasion of his seventieth birthday anniversary, June 9, 1961, by the collection and publication of his most significant historical essays in the field of Hutterite Anabaptism. Together with his family, who by a generous contribution to the cost of publication have made this anniversary volume possible, it extends heartiest congratulations and best wishes to Robert Friedmann. May this volume be a visible token of the esteem and affectionate regard with which he is held by his many friends and colleagues.

Harold S. Bender, President
The Mennonite Historical Society, Goshen, Indiana
June 6, 1961

CONCEPTION OF THE ANABAPTISTS

Who is an Anabaptist? There seems to be a certain amount of confusion with regard to this term and its conception, and a lack of objectivity is still here and there to be met. Emotional prejudices, misleading tradition, insufficient research material, and a mixture of different groups and attitudes prevented church history scholars almost to the present time from reaching a just judgment of these Christian radicals in Europe of the sixteenth and seventeenth centuries. To find out the right place of Anabaptism in history it might be useful to begin with some negative statements.

What an Anabaptist Does not Stand for

There are several misunderstandings to be cleared up before starting to define the right conception.

1. The practice of adult baptism is not peculiar to our group. It is a matter of fact that the idea of adult baptism (or the decline of infant baptism) was widespread in the sixteenth century, especially among the various radicals, as a sign of differentiation; but its justification was not at all uniform. We sometimes find Biblical reasons for it and sometimes only formal reasons (as with the Antitrinitarians). And sometimes there is a complete absence of interest in ceremonies at all, e.g., with Thomas Müntzer or David Joris. It is obvious that Collegiants (practicing adult baptism), for instance, are far more distant in their Christian pattern from Anabaptist groups than men like Sebastian Franck or Hans Denck, although these did not care much about baptism. On the other hand antipedobaptism is nearly as old as the Christian church itself. The Donatists are a famous example, and we find adult baptism practiced later on not only by the English Baptists but also sometimes by the eighteenth century Pietist–Separatists in Germany.

   Furthermore, we know that in the beginning even the Reformers (especially Zwingli) considered infant baptism as unbiblical. Its establishment is due only to the need for a general sign of a national or territorial church (*Volkskirche*). To group all opponents to such a conception of the church under the term "Anabaptist" would not be correct, as it unites highly moral movements with extravagances and rebellions of a rather low order. Accordingly, this term as a negative characteristic needs a positive reason for the practice of adult baptism.

2. Luther disparaged all those who could endanger his church in the making by labeling them *Schwärmer*, without considering their differences. They were against him; consequently they were of the type which he named "enthusiasts" (like the "prophets" of Zwickau), according to his first experiences with opponents. It is strange that this point of view continued in official church history in Europe. Even in our time it is to be found, especially in the large work by Karl Holl, *Luther*.[1] In his essay "Luther and the Enthusiasts,"[2] he rejects very definitely the distinctions of Troeltsch and others, and repeats in modern manner the sixteenth-century reproaches. Whoever is unwilling to accept the idea of an institutional church, every nonconformist and separatist, belongs to these *Schwärmer*.[3] Of course, this expression involves vilification which forestalls the reconsideration of the basic arguments. No doubt such confused groups have appeared and will appear in history, especially in periods of excitement, but they do not represent Anabaptism in its strict sense, and their mistakes must not be charged to the real representatives of that group.

Schwärmer were mostly people with their own visions and revelations, prophets (like Joris), "dreamers" (like those whose deeds are recorded in the Brandenburg *Wiedertäuferakten*, edited by Schornbaum). *Schwärmer* were also certain foolish people in Holland and England, like the naked-runners (because of Isaiah 20:3) and some antinomian groups with a mystical background (like the Family of Love of Henrik Niclaes). They have never belonged to the Anabaptists. It is significant for the enthusiasts that they either neglected the Bible altogether or gave it fantastic interpretations, while the Anabaptists were strong biblicists of a sober or more spiritual fashion.

3. Close to this misleading conception of Anabaptism as enthusiasm is its understanding as the typical "eschatological rebellion" of the sixteenth century. This is the most important and lasting misinterpretation of the historical facts. To find the right judgment it might be useful to distinguish the eschatological standpoint of the Gospel from the millenarian teaching of the Revelation of St. John. Surely everyone in the beginning of the Reformation was eschatologically disposed, even Luther

---

1 Karl Holl, *Gesammelte Aufsätze zur Kirchengeschichte* (Tübingen, 1923), I, *Luther*.
2 Holl, *Luther*, 420–67.
3 This word does not mean today only "an enthusiast," as it did in the sixteenth century, but also in general "confused people," or, in short, "an emotionalist," without sober judgement.

himself.[4] And that is very understandable, since a religious revolution requires in a certain measure this general outlook of the imminence of the great change: "Be awake, be prepared, change your life now, risk the great step," and so on. That is the basis of any evangelical radicalism. Even among some gentle Pietists of the eighteenth century one can find this expectation (e.g., Bengel, Oettinger). Very different from this soundly evangelical outlook is the millenarian position—the companion of every excited period. The predilection to apocalyptic speculations leads to impatient outbursts of violent and preposterous actions in order to speed up the coming of the new era.

There were two significant phenomena of that kind in the sixteenth century: Thomas Müntzer and the Münsterite upheaval. It would not be enough to describe Müntzer under this pattern only. He, the fiery mind of his time, a typical German with his agony but without self-control, united nearly all the different ideas of his time, ran through manifold positions and presented to his contemporaries a multitude of slogans and formulae. Only in his last year was he under the influence of a violent millenarianism. It became his fate! Yet it would be historically wrong to derive all later nonconformist developments from him. This was unfortunately the idea of Heinrich Boehmer and his seminar.

Boehmer suggested a good many valuable research publications along that line, like K. Ecke, *Schwenckfeld, Luther und der Gedanke einer apostolischen Reformation* (Berlin, 1911); W. Neuser, *Hans Hut* (Bonn, 1913); C. Sachsse, *Balthasar Hubmaier als Theologe* (Berlin, 1914); Lydia Müller, *Der Kommunismus der mährischen Wiedertäufer* (Leipzig, 1927); and finally Annemarie Lohmann, *Zur geistigen Entwicklung Thomas Müntzers* (Leipzig, 1931). They all argue that Müntzer was the real originator of Anabaptism, claiming that this movement was but an explication of Müntzer's ideas, which were, "as evidence shows," millenarian and revolutionary. This is an improper simplification prompted by the old Lutheran fiction. There is no room for a full refutation. I mention only the well-known letter by Conrad Grebel to Müntzer of September 5, 1524, containing the admonition to avoid the use of arms in order to establish the kingdom of God.[5]

The other occurrence of that nature was the deplorable upheaval in Münster, with all its extravagances. It is true that the Münster group practised adult baptism; but this episode had nothing to do with the quiet and sober Anabaptist movement. It is well known that afterwards this movement was defamed by those events which gave an obvious and easy justification for persecutions. And the prejudice still adheres to the

---

4 Cf. Johannes Köstlin; "Ein Beitrag zur Eschatologie der Reformatoren," *Theologische Studien und Kritiken* (Hamburg, 1879), LII.

5 H. Boehmer–P. Kirn, *Thomas Müntzer's Briefwechsel* (Leipzig, 1931), and Otto H. Brandt; *Thomas Müntzer, Leben und Schriften* (Jena, 1933).

word "Anabaptism." That was also a reason for choosing other terms like Täufer, *Doopsgezinde*, Mennonites, or simply Brethren. The Münsterites were extremely millenarian and convinced that risks had to be taken in inaugurating the new era. After the fall of Münster, the Batenburgers tried to carry on this ideology; but at the Conference at Bocholt (1536), David Joris succeeded in soothing them by saying: "The time of the 'kingdom of the elect' has not yet come. You have to leave the power to the infidel magistrates up to that time."[6] It was a mediation intended to postpone the use of force until the right day—an enunciation which is unique in Anabaptist history. All the other groups declined absolutely the use of any force at any time, and the suspicion of the princes and magistrates against Anabaptists was completely unfounded, since evangelical discipleship excludes violence.

Finally, a revival of this kind of millenarian spirit occurred in Cromwell's time under the Fifth Monarchy Men and the followers of Harrison, but nobody would justly call these groups "Anabaptist." I think that Troeltsch is right in naming this type "Taborites," and describing it as a phenomenon in itself. Unfortunately, in many textbooks of history in England as well as elsewhere the evil repute of the Münsterites still is applied to the whole body of Anabaptism.

4. In the last place, a certain misunderstanding might arise from calling the Anabaptists "Antitrinitarians," as is mostly done in Italian treatises. It is more difficult to clear up this point than the former ones. What are the facts? On the average, no doubt, Anabaptism accepted the Apostles' Creed and the orthodox teachings concerning the Trinity. But, as it was primarily a pragmatic movement, it was not much concerned with dogmatic issues. I agree completely with a statement of Roland H. Bainton that "Antitrinitarianism was simply an aversion to speculation— first shared even by Luther and Calvin. This movement cuts across all groups." The more spiritualistic or mystical a thinker was, the more averse he was to the propounding of an explicit scholarly theology. That is true of men like Franck and Denck and Ludwig Haetzer, but their connection with Anabaptism was very tenuous. It is misleading when F. L. Weis in his new biography of Haetzer calls him an antitrinitarian Anabaptist and a forerunner of the Unitarians of today.[7] There is too little evidence for it, and such interpretation is rather strained. On the whole, I cannot find that Haetzer had any important influence on the movement, with the exception of some of his canticles.

---

6 F. Nippold, "David Joris von Delft," in *Zeitschrift für Historische Theologie*, XXXIII (1963), 52; and Roland H. Bainton, *David Joris, Wiedertäufer und Vorkämpfer für Toleranz im 16. Jahrhundert* (Leipzig, 1937), 25; Rufus M Jones, *Studies in Mysical Religion* (London, 1909).

7 Frederick L. Weis, *The Life, Teaching and Works of Ludwig Hetzer* (Lancaster, Mass., 1930). The best information on the question is found in the enlightening article by Christian Neff, "Ludwig Hetzer," *ML*, II (1937), 225 ff., especially 231, where the arguments are discussed.

It is a matter of fact that the Italian Anabaptists in Venice (1555) had a definite antitrinitarian attitude, like other Italian dissenters. But they disappeared after a few years. As for the Socinians in Poland, they also have sometimes been called Anabaptists. But the charge was not well grounded and was designed only to give them an evil repute. Actually, there is only one definite antitrinitarian Anabaptist known in history, Adam Pastor, for a short time collaborator with Menno Simons and Dirk Philips, but in 1547 excommunicated because of his convictions. Stanislaus von Dunin–Borkowski[8] calls him the genuine father of Antitrinitarianism and gives a full account of his teachings, which were in many respects very different from the common Anabaptist tenets.[9] Pastor prepared indeed the way for the reception of Socinianism in northern Germany and Holland. In the middle of the seventeenth century, the Mennonites suffered a serious schism on account of the activity of Galenus de Haan who, it was said, called himself a "Socinian" but derived his convictions really from the Collegiants.[10]

So far the facts. I think it would not be significant to group the Anabaptists under the caption "Antitrinitarians," whether they were sympathizers or not. It was not their main concern. We have, therefore, to look for a more striking and positive definition of this movement which, in spite of separation into many groups, represents a united whole with a common spirit.

We do not understand the issue by reducing one less known phenomenon to another more popular one, or by simplification. So it has happened very often that a nickname of old standing continues through the centuries, perpetuating prejudices, notwithstanding the progress of research and objectivity.

This is a typical case. Was it not the same with the Cathari or the Albigenses in the Middle Ages? The name of a relatively small group became general for all "heretics" without searching the particulars of their convictions. They were not Catholics—then they must surely be one of those "Middle Ages Bolsheviks," even if they confess an extreme pacifism. Nobody would believe otherwise save some simple people. And was there not the same situation in England of the sixteenth and the seventeenth centuries? The collective name for nonconformists was partly Anabaptism (without any concrete background) and partly Puritanism. Whoever was against the king's prerogatives on behalf of the church was a "Puritan." The meaning of this term is just the same as the meaning of Cathari: it points out the intention to stress more purification than edification.

---

8   *Scholastik*, VII (1932).
9   A. H. Newman, "Adam Pastor," *American Society of Church History Papers*, 2nd Series, V (1914), 74–99, and John Horsch, *Menno Simons* (Scottdale, 1916), 194–203.
10 See the very clear and sympathetic report in H. E. Dosker, *The Dutch Anabaptists* (Philadelphia, 1921).

It was a mockery on the part of the churchmen similar to that of the *Schwärmer* in Germany. There is an obvious reason for such a usage; the history of the present time was and is always partial—a kind of apology for one's own standpoint—as long as the will to mutual understanding is lacking. And once coined, a name perseveres with all its confusion.

What an Anabaptist Could Stand for

Modern church history has begun to emancipate itself from this defect and trace the lines more properly adapted to the facts. Especially the peaceful cooperation of all denominations in America makes it much easier to get a true insight into the different pattern of religious movements than does the contest in Europe.

1. It was a great step forward when Ernst Troeltsch first so clearly distinguished church and sect—although primarily from a sociological point of view. Church is the institution of salvation for all baptized members; sect is the brotherhood of the regenerate, the congregation of saints, a gathered church of true Christians either for the celebration of the Lord's Supper alone or for a collective life according to the Sermon on the Mount. As this Sermon had not found any place in the Reformation itself, the disappointed groups necessarily caused a division within Protestantism. While the Middle Ages had monasteries for those who strove toward a pure and holy life, the modern times engendered the Protestant sect, with discipline, aloofness from the world, general priesthood of believers, separation from the state—a congregation of volunteers on the basis of a strong biblicism. Finally, Troeltsch identifies Anabaptism with this Protestant type of sect as a whole, and distinguishes it from the Church, and from mysticism and spiritualism, because of their different social appearance. His main point throughout is the contrast between the absolute and radical natural law of the sect, e.g., the individual law of every person according to the Sermon on the Mount on one hand, and the relative law of office or the morality of a worldly life on the other.

   I am afraid that this conception of Anabaptism, as well as the description of the sect in general, is too broadly shaped. Not every sect of modern times has this high moral pattern of the "evangelical" Anabaptists whose picture Troeltsch draws so sympathetically. There were other groups based on the study of the Revelation of John and groups of antinomian or enthusiastic character without any reference to the Bible or the Sermon on the Mount. Anabaptism disappeared in Germany toward the end of the sixteenth century—save for some small and little significant minorities—but the sect has remained within Protestantism up to the present.

According to his new distinction, Troeltsch classifies and groups the facts of modern church history in a very remarkable but somewhat controversial way. In the chapter on "Anabaptism and the Protestant Sects," he includes not only all English movements of the seventeenth century, but also Pietism in Germany and Methodism in England. On the other hand, he puts under the headings, "Spiritualism" and "Mysticism," Thomas Müntzer, Sebastian Franck, Cornheert, David Joris, as well as Caspar Schwenckfeld, whose idea of apostolic reformation lies just between Anabaptism and Pietism.

Nevertheless, it was a great advance to recognize Pietism as the sect-type within the church, although it is not based on the Sermon on the Mount. It is a very significant fact that as soon as Anabaptism became settled or established, it changed from the sect type to the church type. But as it continued to cherish its old heritage, this little church developed a pietistic pattern. Many a church in the United States gives evidence of that fact.[11]

2. It was somewhat the same intention of grouping the facts justly and with a better understanding of their character, that led Roland H. Bainton to coin the remarkable expression for our subject of "Left–Wing Protestantism."[12] What Luther once contemptuously called "*Schwärmer*" without any differentiation and what Troeltsch sociologically called "sect," Bainton sums up as the "Left–Wing movement" in general, meaning the radical reformation. Is it really identical with Anabaptism as he states, only because all those who rejected the established national church practised adult baptism? Is that summary under a single caption of any real help?

First, let us see how one could define "Left–Wing," a word derived from the political sphere, in church history. "Left" (i.e., radical) could refer either to the interpretation of the sacraments, or to the church organization, or to the doctrines (Trinity); but Bainton prefers as the principle of his division the relation between church and state. Whoever rejected the civil arm in matters of religion was a "leftist." Usually those groups were also leftist with regard to other points, such as organization, sacraments, and creeds. Were they spiritualistic, mystical, rational, enthusiastic, or Biblical? That is not essential for this picture. "Nonconformity" would be the right term in English church history; "*Ketzer*" in the positive sense of Sebastian Franck is probably the best correlative term in German historiography. So Bainton fits in a remarkable line of historians which started with Sebastian Franck's *Chronica, Zeitbuch und Geschichtsbibel* (1531, with its "*Ketzer–chronik*" in its third part), continued with Gottfried Arnold's *Unpartheyische Kirchen– und Ketzerhistorie* (Frankfurt

---

11 Cf. Robert Friedmann, "Anabaptism and Pietism," *MQR*, XIV (1940), 2 and 3.
12 In an unpublished paper which I had the privilege to study.

am Main, 1699), found an anonymous continuator in Gottfried Arnold's *Fortsetzung und Erläuterung* (oder 3. und 4. Teil) *der unpartheyischen Kirchen– und Ketzerhistorie* (Frankfurt am Main, 1715), and an imitator in Johann Lorentz von Mosheim, the author of *Anderweitiger Versuch einer vollständigen und unparteiischen Ketzergeschichte* (Helmstädt, 1748). In Switzerland we find Otte's *Annales Anabaptistici* (Basel, 1672) as a representative of that kind of literature and later Johann Conrad Fuesslin's *Neue und unpartheyische Kirchen– und Ketzerhistorie der mittleren Zeit* (1770–1774). Erich Seeberg in his *Gottfried Arnold*[13] has stimulatingly analyzed this attitude.

These Left–Wing groups (this expression is better, of course, than "*Ketzer*") have a definite conviction of the fall of the official church since the early days of Constantine; it is an attempt at rehabilitation of Christian radicalism on the basis of a Biblical pattern. There remains only the question whether one can justify in this way the whole "Left–Wing" movement, or whether one would degrade the finer groups by putting them together with rough or even debased movements.

Left Wing, it is true, could be called the fourth reformation, besides Luther's, Zwingli's, and Calvin's. It is highly important to give due consideration to this aspect of history neglected by scholars for so long a time and misunderstood in its purposes and effects. Left Wing means in any case democracy in church (or sect) government, religious toleration, and absolute independence. It has different branches: an ethical or "Donatist" (the evangelical Anabaptists, for instance, though the comparison with Donatists is not absolutely fitting); an eschatological, and a branch described by Bainton as "Christian primitivism," including the prophets of the spirit and the Biblical extravagants like Joris. Negatively, these groups were all disappointed with the official Protestant churches and were full of intellectual accusations or even aggressive activities against them. Positively, they believed in personal rebirth as the basic condition of membership and in "restitution" of the original Christianity as the mold of their new life.[14] Nearly all these groups practised adult baptism, not as a sacramental act but mostly as a sign of differentiation. That is why Bainton calls these Left–Wing groups "Anabaptists" without further asking whether they referred to the Sermon on the Mount (as pacifists), or to the Revelation of John (as rebels), or to neither (as prophets). That is why the Quakers, on the other hand, did not find a place in his picture, although they were at least as leftist as the evangelical Anabaptists.

However, the aim to treat fairly all these opponents of state churches and of established or institutional Christianity under a common term

---

13 Erich Seeberg, *Gottfried Arnold, Studien zur Historiographie und zur Mystik* (Berlin, 1923), 257–534.

14 Bainton gives in his treatise, "Changing Ideas and Ideals in the 16th Century," *The Journal of Modern History*, VIII (1936), 428, a list of books with the title *Restitutio*.

is highly important. They were persecuted in the sixteenth century and burned at the stake, but most of their ideas remained and found a belated but full recognition in the seventeenth and eighteenth centuries, especially in New England. And their starting point is still stirring humanity: should the Church be thought of primarily in terms of leaven (for but few) or of light (for all)?

3. Troeltsch and Bainton generalize consciously in placing the phenomena in the great context of the trend of events. And so, because of the reasons mentioned above, it still remains our duty to look for sharper distinctions. Are Anabaptists *sui generis*, not comparable at all to any other groups? Or are they to be reduced to the better known groups of earlier times? It depends on which aspect of Anabaptism we look for: the millenarian (a well-known attitude throughout the centuries), or the prophetic (also a rather frequent occurrence in history), or those quiet and evangelical qualities modeled upon the Sermon on the Mount.

It was Albrecht Ritschl, the famous historian of Pietism, who first raised the question.[15] Surprisingly, he found a striking likeness between the Franciscan tertiaries, the (evangelical) Anabaptists, and the Pietists of the seventeenth century. He starts with a glimpse of what he calls the Franciscan idea of church reform: restitution of the early form of Christianity by renunciation of the world, personal purity, poverty and, finally, expectation of the Kingdom of God. Asceticism within the world and a prevailing religious emotionalism in practising brotherly love are said to be the main features of this group. The *ordo tertius* was especially designed to cultivate these qualities. Anabaptism—of which Ritschl gives a fairly good picture, though his main source is Bullinger—appears to him as a revival of the Franciscan reformation, a worldly monasticism. A direct derivation from the tertiaries could not, of course, be traced—but on pages 31 ff. Ritschl gives detailed and interesting parallels between the two movements. Because the dominant idea of the Kingdom of Christ is understood by both groups as a feasible way of Christian life, underscoring the importance of work, Ritschl calls the Anabaptists (from his Lutheran point of view) "mediaeval" and "catholic." Also the eschatology affords analogous views, especially if one looks more on the Spiritual Franciscans than on the tertiaries.

On the other hand, Pietism renewed within the Protestant churches the Anabaptist tendencies of "reform," in the meaning of Romans 12:1, namely, renunciation of the world and discipline. Ritschl also quoted Luther to the effect that sometimes he also had this idea of a pure congregation, but—alas! "*Wir Deutsche sind ein wildes, rohes, tobendes Volk, mit dem nicht leichtlich ist etwas anzufangen....*"[16] In the

---

15   Albrecht Ritschl, *Geschichte des Pieismus* (Bonn, 1880), I, 1–100.
16   Martin Luther, *Deutsche Messe* (1526); cf. Ritschl, *Geschichte des Pietismus*, 73 ff.

Netherlands, J. v. Lodenstein is said to be somehow near to both tertiaries and the Anabaptists.

In criticism, there are two points to be rectified. If Franciscans and Anabaptists are to be compared, then a recourse to the Spiritual Franciscans would be more proper than to the tertiaries. The Fraticelli are far more a Protestant sect than a Catholic order directed toward a genuine Christian primitivism.[17] On the other hand, the Pietists may be compared more easily with Caspar Schwenckfeld's movement toward an "apostolic reform of the church"[18] than with the Anabaptists. And Schwenckfeld did not belong to the Anabaptist movement at all. But however the picture might be corrected, Ritschl's thesis is a suggestive one and in some ways certainly influenced Troeltsch's theory.

4. While Ritschl sought the ideological roots of Anabaptism in mediaeval Franciscanism, another scholar of his time, Ludwig Keller, looked for the same roots in the Waldensian movement of about the same mediaeval period. So Keller became the counterpart to Ritschl. He advocated a hypothesis of the continuity of primitive Christian brotherhoods throughout the centuries, like Franck's *"Ketzer."* Stimulated by a remark in Tieleman van Braght's *Martyrs Mirror*, Keller coined for these congregations the expression "old evangelical brotherhoods." He thought that they had never died since the very days of the early church, but invisibly handed over the perennial fire of pure faith from one group to another. As nobody was concerned to record the ways of intellectual influence by means of spoken word, pamphlets or letters lost long ago, the silence of the surviving historical material is not decisive. Accordingly, Keller constructed a history of the "Christian idea" from the early "Puritan" sects like Paulicians and Bogomiles to the Cathari and Waldenses, and then partly to the Bohemian Brethren and partly to the Anabaptists. Further, he traced the line up to recent movements like the Free Masons, or his own "Comenius Society." It is remarkable that Keller's main book on the subject, *Die Reformation und die älteren Reformparteien*, was published in Leipzig in 1885, only five years after Ritschl brought forth his hypothesis.[19] Both hypotheses are rather arbitrary simplifications of historical developments although they are grounded on a right intuition and give incentive to new research. It is a fact that there are immediate links between the Waldenses and the Bohemian Brethren,[20] but one must not confuse the Bohemian movement with the Anabaptist. The Bohemians had sacraments, hierarchy, confessions and

---

17　E. Benz, *Ecclesia Spiritualis, Die Idee der franziskanischen Kirchenreform* (1934).
18　K. Ecke, *Schwenckfeld, Luther und der Gedanke einer apostolischen Reformation* (Berlin, 1911).
19　Keller's books are well known and were once much discussed. His biography of Hans Denck (Leipzig, 1882) marks a real epoch in our field; but also his other books, essays, and lectures were stimulating even if some conclusions were wrong. He discovered new facts, and the reading is worthwhile.
20　J. Th. Müller, *Geschichte der böhmischen Brüder* (Herrnhut, 1922), I.

Lent, like the Waldenses or the Donatists, while the Anabaptists lived according to the more Protestant pattern. Therefore there was never any serious approach or important disputation between these groups. They went on untouched by one another, and it is obviously wrong to speak so generally of "evangelical brotherhoods" without finer distinctions.[21]

Nevertheless, Keller has focused attention on hitherto little known facts, books, and so on, and he found followers who made valuable contributions. The outstanding controversy was prompted by A. Nicoladoni in his book *Johannes Bünderlin von Linz* (Berlin, 1893). He thought he had proved some connection between the Waldenses and the Anabaptists in Upper Austria, e.g., in the town of Steyr. J. Jäkel has refuted this statement,[22] rightly calling the Anabaptist movement there independent, due to the missionary work of Hans Hut, but the fact remains that the Waldenses lived in this part of Austria and may have prepared the soil for the new seeds even if there is no record to prove it. That is the general trouble with this kind of historiography; a certain amount of vagueness remains.[23] Anyhow, there exists a similarity between all these nonconformist groups, and it would be helpful to refer to it for understanding and orientation. It is the old idea of Sebastian Franck that the "*Ketzer*" or "Puritans" have been persecuted and defamed by church and state, but that their ideas have been finally victorious.

5. Another classification of interesting and positive judgment comes from Rufus M. Jones. In his fine book, *Studies in Mystical Religion*, he gives a very noble treatment of the evangelical Anabaptists as far as their spiritual pattern was known at that time. Of course, there exists also a mystical element in their literature which has not yet been investigated thoroughly. We know, for example, that they favored especially the term *Gelassenheit*, but it must be noted that they did not get this expression directly from the mediaeval mystics, but either from Thomas Müntzer or from Sebastian Franck. And, furthermore, they used it not in a quietistic but in a more practical and ethical meaning which changed the whole conception. Accordingly, the connection with mystical religion is not very striking. And in his later book, Jones deals only with some outstanding individuals of that time—like Hans Denck—as the predecessors or intellectual fathers of Quakerism, and wholly omits the Anabaptists as a group. In fact, Quakerism is a unique synthesis of mysticism or spiritualism on the one side and evangelical activism like Anabaptism on the other. England never had a movement closer to the evangelical

---

21 That becomes clear by the inclusion in this category of the Free Masons, who are very far from our groups. As for the distant relations between the Bohemians and the Anabaptists, see Robert Friedmann, in *MQR*, XIV (1940), 112–13.

22 In several papers published in local periodicals, 1888–95.

23 The same situation was repeated when some ten years later Heinrich Boehmer launched his thesis of the origin of Anabaptism as a whole in Thomas Müntzer. Although this statement was wrong, it has prompted valuable research in many new directions.

Anabaptists of the Continent than the Quakers. This statement is valid also in regard to their social background in the early days. That is why H. Richard Niebuhr rightly states: "Quakerism is the Anglo–Saxon parallel to Anabaptism."[24]

6. Generalization, simplification, or reduction of other or earlier forms can give only a part of the truth. Anabaptism as a lasting and effective phenomenon is a fact *sui generis* and requires recognition as such. As far as I know, Johannes Kühn in his book, *Toleranz und Offenbarung* (Leipzig, 1923), was the first to adopt this standpoint in productive elaboration of Troeltsch's ideas and give it a historical grouping which can be considered as fairly definite. His fine attempt—full of understanding and knowledge of both Continental and British movements—is an advanced *geistesgeschichtlich* and psychological one. It grants Anabaptism for the first time an equal rank with many other collective phenomena of church history. Though he focuses his study on the attitude of the groups toward the toleration issue (with some general restrictions), his descriptions are accurate and clear. He discerns in Biblical Protestantism (or as he calls it *offenbarungsgläubigen* Protestantism) five types or motives: the prophetic, of which Luther is an example; the spiritualistic, with Schwenckfeld and Roger Williams as examples; the *täuferische Nachfolge*, with Anabaptists and Quakers as illustrations; the mystic, under which caption he discusses David Joris as well as Jakob Böhme; the motive of ethical and rational religion, illustrated by Castellio, Acontius, and Arminius, and controversial, also with Spener as an example.

It may be that these examples would have been different if Kühn had not followed the thread of the toleration issue. But at any rate, the attempt to classify and describe the multiplicity of Protestantism in this way is very successful and marks a real progress in classification.

As for the first type: for the prophetic attitude, the main duty is felt to be the announcement of the revealed divine will. This is an absolute objective well recognizable in the Holy Scriptures and requiring pure faith. The establishment of a church on this basis is possible. (Note the contrast to Troeltsch's sociological conception of "church" as a comprehensive institute of salvation.)

As for the second type: for the spiritualistic thinker or believer this objectivity of the divine will does not exist any longer, and Scripture is more freely interpreted according to the spirit. But at least this "spirit" is still concrete, religious, genuine, and not identified with reason or the *lumen naturale*. Kühn does not care very much about the sociological outcomes and puts Schwenckfeld—who was more a churchman than a sectarian—together with Roger Williams, the typical leader of a

---

[24] H. Richard Niebuhr, *The Social Sources of Denominationalism* (New York, 1929), 39.

"gathered" congregation or sect. I do not know why Kühn does not mention men like Franck or Denck, perhaps he judged them too far from a positive Biblical background.

As to the fourth type: the contrast to the mystics is obvious. The spiritualist does not seek and never gains that unity with God which is the center of mystical life. Now here is an interesting point: Rufus M. Jones discusses Jakob Böhme as the most important Continental forerunner of Quakerism, but classifies him as a "spiritual reformer," while Kühn rightly calls him a mystic. On the other hand, the latter puts the Quakers in the neighborhood of the Anabaptists, while Jones has treated them as a "mystical group." As for David Joris, the mystical is only one side of his intellectual personality. Roland H. Bainton, in his fine biography, *David Joris* (1937), discusses this issue fully (pp. 34–36), saying that Joris' mysticism has softened the Messianism which was his dominant feature. I do not know whether one may call the idea of the "key of David," by which to open the Book with Seven Seals, mystic or spiritualistic, or something else. In any case it is rather different from Jakob Böhme's Christian theosophy.

As to the fifth type: with the beginning of rationalism in religion the *concretum* is more and more dissolved. The Holy Spirit is replaced by reason or emotion or even by sentimentality. "The world of the religious concrete is definitely abandoned, the Christian religion becomes a general religion of Idealism." But, on the other side, it is the most effective type in the fight for religious freedom, comparable only to the Anabaptists, though their motives for tolerance are different. Rationalism was present throughout the centuries, but became universal in the era of Enlightenment. It afforded probably also the background for Spener and his Pietism, which as a type stands between rationalism and prophetism (in Kühn's terminology).

Mystics, spiritualists, and religious rationalists are either single individuals or loose groups or congregations. The social relation is in no case essential for their convictions. Quite different is the third religious type, the *täuferische Nachfolge*, including also the Quakers, though they do not practise adult baptism. The description of Kühn is excellent and very proper.

To translate adequately the German expression *Nachfolge* offers some difficulty, as there are different conceptions as to what Christ meant by saying "take your cross and follow Me." *Imitatio Christi*, the usual Latin term for it, has often been falsely given the meaning of "copying" the holy way. Who is a true disciple or follower? Was it St. Francis, the lover, or Thomas à Kempis, the mystic, or John Bunyan's Pilgrim with his hard and precise work of self-control and self-conquest? Discipleship in any case means the great freedom of conducting one's own life in the spirit of the Gospel. And that is why I would suggest the translation of *Nachfolge* as "emulation." That cannot be ambiguous even if one should emphasize one part of Christ's life more than another.

In the main, the pattern of that life means two things: love and the cross. They belong together, as real love meets everywhere in this world opposition, suspicion, and even persecution. Kühn carries out this thesis very finely throughout the different historical phenomena. *Nachfolge* as love means brotherhood, social community, and sometimes even community of goods (Hutterians). It is not the question at the moment how far such an aim can be realized with our "corrupt" body, but at least one has to strive toward this end and to learn *Gelassenheit*. That is another German expression of mystic derivation, the translation of which is difficult. "Unresponsiveness" (the stoic *ataraxia*) does not correspond to the Anabaptist conception, which as the right attitude of love demands response to the call of the neighbor.[25] "Resignation," on the other hand, has a flavor of submission or renunciation of inner freedom without which love is not possible. "Conquest of selfishness" would probably be an apposite rendering. The Anabaptists' concept of love is very different from the cheerful love of St. Francis to all creatures or the philanthropic love among the Quakers. But they are all bound together by the seriousness of their attempt in a true Christian life which requests more purification than edification, and which often leads to the cross and martyrdom.

No other group has so strongly underscored the truth of the cross as the evangelical Anabaptists. Neither St. Francis nor Thomas à Kempis centers his realism on this point.[26] Suffering—it is to be read and reread in Anabaptist tracts—is the unavoidable fate of a true Christian on this earth. "*Die Dornenkrone steht über dem Glorienschein.*"[27] Whoever seeks seriously to put Christian love into action meets inevitably the opposition of worldly powers.

It was Ethelbert Stauffer in an outstanding treatise on *Märtyrertheologie und Täuferbewegung*[28] who, independently of Kühn, gave evidence of this general Christian foundation of Anabaptism and confirmed the above statements with new material. So Anabaptism—in the specific sense of modern German church history usage—became the proper martyr sect type more than any other.

---

25 Cf. Robert Friedmann, "Concerning a True Soldier of Christ, a Hitherto Unknown Tract of the Philippites in Moravia," *MQR*, V (1931), 91, 94. It deals with a very significant tract from about 1534–35.

26 Bunyan's teaching of the cross is in some regards akin to Anabaptist tenets, but he does not derive it primarily from social attitudes. Even he was not really convinced of nonviolence, the genuine demand of Christian love.

27 Pilgram Marpeck's *Verantwortung* (1542), ed. Loserth (Vienna, 1929), 160 and *passim*.

28 *Zeitschrift für Kirchengeschichte*, XV (1933), 545–98.

If that is so, it is not allowable to lump together these emulators of Christ with Millenarians, Enthusiasts, Taborites, and other excited revivalists who had nothing in common with them except the not very significant practice of adult baptism. But it must be conceded that there is a great temptation, just for these evangelical Anabaptists, to ease a bit their conception of discipleship of Christ either in the direction of a dominating emotionalism leading to Pietism, or in the direction of rationalizing the ethics of the Sermon on the Mount, or finally by a far-reaching spiritualizing, as with Denck or Haetzer. But, in general, Anabaptism as a fact of historical significance remained faithful to its principles and withstood those subtle and sometimes imperceptible temptations.

As a criticism of Kühn's outline or classification we may point out that these five types by no means exhaust the fullness of religious phenomena of modern times. For instance, there is no place for the "enthusiasts" like Thomas Müntzer or David Joris. And after all there is no mention of the millenarian group (with revolutionary attitude) for which Troeltsch has generalized the name "Taborites." It is understandable, of course, that they are absent in a study on tolerance, but nevertheless they are very definite types.

Secondly, the main criticism is directed to the point that no attempt at classification can be satisfactory in the face of historical reality. There are no pure types. Many of our men or groups or movements were inspired by different motives, either at once in competition to each other or combined in new forms or in chronological succession. It is well known that all these men, eager for true reform, ran through manifold varieties of religious attitudes, especially in the stirring decade of 1520–1530. Thomas Müntzer is probably the best example of this phenomenon, but Luther's mutations may also be mentioned. And the same happened with most of the spiritual reformers who changed from Anabaptism to spiritualism and from there finally to a kind of mysticism.

7. In spite of this criticism we have to recognize the high value of Kühn's statements and to agree with his discriminations to a great extent. But one must not forget that his scheme was made for a special purpose which could not exhaust all possibilities; accordingly, another starting point for general historical treatment needs to be found. This could supplement the first one and more strongly emphasize the fundamental antithesis of evangelical and revolutionary Anabaptism. This new starting point may be formulated as a question: what attitude does one take toward the Holy Bible and especially toward the New Testament? What does one think of it, or which part of it has been chosen as the definite truth and pattern of one's life? This seems to be the core of the religious problem and is well adapted to our thesis as it aims directly at the fundamental

position. Of course every attempt at such classification has its limitations, and must not be pressed too far. Nevertheless, the advantage of a survey will prevail and lead us to new insights. The theological question as to whether we have to understand the Scriptures as a uniform whole or not need not be discussed, but rather our task is to look for the fact that the New Testament contains different elements which allow very different interpretations of life and redemption.

There are first the Synoptics: the original teaching of Christ of the imminent Kingdom of God, toward which we must ceaselessly strive in love and suffering and purity; there are the Epistles of St. Paul with their teaching of justification and redemption by grace only, the basis of all Christian churches; there is the Revelation of John, quite different in its intention from the other parts and the cause of many queer phenomena in history. And finally, we may distinguish the Johannine Prologue with its Greek mysticism of light—the real start for many a theosophical speculation outside of pragmatic Christianity. Struggle for the Kingdom of God is the idea of Puritan sects and brotherhoods. Redemption by faith in Christ's sacrificial death is the basis of churches and pietist groups. Expectation of the new era leads sometimes to revolutionary upheavals. Neoplatonic or Gnostic speculations lead to spiritualist interpretations of the Christian facts. These are the main and very distinct lines which develop from the New Testament. But there is still a fifth group, which has no concern for the written word at all: the new prophets and dreamers. They like quotations from the Scripture, but the gist of their teaching is a new revelation and religion. In times of excitement one can meet them in many places. Usually they are also antinomian.

The summary of this survey is given in the accompanying chart (found at the end of the article). We omit the description of the particular differences within one column. It may also be that this picture is too simplified, but on the other hand, it gives the expression of a genuine religious concern more systematically than Kühn does. The graph also shows distinctly the contradiction between evangelical Anabaptists and Münsterites and the like. It becomes clear that there is more relation between evangelical Anabaptists, Franciscans, Waldenses, and so on, than between evangelical Anabaptists and revolutionary ones—not primarily because of the question of the sword but because of the different religious orientation in the fundamentals. Controversial in our graph is the right place of the Quakers, whose ethic brings them near to the Anabaptists, but whose reference to the "inner light" more than to the Scriptures would justify a place nearer to the new prophets. Quakerism as a whole is really a unique fact in its combination—as mentioned above. Finally, the graph needs one additional remark: there is no room in it for the Antitrinitarians. With Bainton I would accept for this group the characterization as "Left–Wing theology."

So far our attempt has concerned itself with description by classification. But there remains still a second task, the discovery of the right and unequivocal term for our group. There is a misleading confusion of words and facts derived from certain national differences. As an example, I quote a very enlightening passage from the newest English treatment of our subject:

> There is difficulty in ascertaining the extent of Anabaptism in England during the sixteenth and seventeenth centuries since the name 'Anabaptist' was evidently employed as a generic term to designate separatists or any persons of irregular or fanatical religious opinions. There was great confusion as to its use: Independents and other sectaries usually applied it to Baptists alone; Royalists, foreigners and sometimes Presbyterians made it include the Fifth Monarchy Men and all other extreme sectaries, and sometimes it was used yet more loosely as a mere term of reproach. [29]

The name was vague and lent itself to misuse. In recent church history scholarship there is an obvious endeavor to clarify the situation, in America as well as in Germany. While recognizing the inaccuracy of the term *Wiedertäufer*, once used consciously for debasing the movement, one restricts it now mostly to the Münsterite episode. The *Verein für Reformationsgeschichte* adopted generally the term *Täufer* for the evangelical or *stille* Anabaptists, while the Mennonites in their historical essays use for all nonviolent groups of that kind the name "Mennonite." The Dutch name *Doopsgezinde* is also sometimes in use for that purpose, especially in Dutch literature. In English and American treatments, the terminology is quite different. Since the translation of *Täufer* would give "Baptists," this simplest way is apparently not practicable, to avoid confusion with the other denomination of that name. So it became customary to call even the Mennonites in Holland "Anabaptists," and this led then easily to misunderstanding. Enthusiasts were confused with sober Christians, revolutionaries with martyrs of nonresistance; and the reputation of the genuine religious group became vilified by the evil repute of others. England did not have the *stille Täufer* as Germany did, but only Quakers as the nearest analogy, and these Quakers practiced no baptism at all. A. H. Newman used the term "Antipedobaptists,"[30] but it is neither fitting nor accurate.

I would suggest the use of the composite expression "evangelical Anabaptists" for the German word *Täufer*. They alone were influential in the subsequent centuries, especially in America's struggle for tolerance and human rights,[31] while the "revolutionary millenarians" could probably affect

---

29 R. Smithson, *The Anabaptists* (London, 1935), 193.
30 A. H. Newman, *A History of Anti–Pedobaptism to 1609* (Philadelphia, PA., 1897).
31 George Jellinek, *The Declaration of the Rights of Man and Citizen, a Contribution to Modern*

the world for a short time but never change it. The following survey gives briefly the main historical analogies:

Germany, Austria, Holland	England
Stille Täufer	Quakers
Mennonites (established)	Baptists
Münster Wiedertäufer	Fifth Monarchy Men
(*Chiliasts*)	Millenarians

The question whether there were genuine English Anabaptists is still open and on the whole unlikely. The few real "Anabaptists" mentioned in some English places seem to have been Dutch refugees, either Melchiorites (Hofmannites) or probably Mennonites. So the expression "Anabaptists" occurs in American and English church history almost solely with reference to German nonconformity.

Spread of Anabaptism

This conclusion leads us to an affiliated question in the whole issue, namely, the spread of the so-called Anabaptism in the sixteenth and seventeenth centuries, in contrast to other "Left-Wing" (radical or primitive) Christian groups. I am surprised that this question of national determination of the different Christian patterns has never been earnestly discussed.

Though the true fellowship of Christians is of an international character, the rise of special groups depends largely on national dispositions and heritage. I agree thoroughly with Smithson when he writes, "Anabaptism made no strong appeal to the English mind.[32] That is true; and we could add that religious Left-Wing movements as a whole never found any considerable roots in French Protestantism. The Calvinist Huguenots caught up all radical forces, although the movement was not an exclusively religious one. Beyond the Vosges there never sprang up primitive Christian sects after the time of the Waldenses. In Italy the trend of religious activities was primarily directed to dogmatic disputations, especially in Antitrinitarianism. Even the Italian Anabaptists at their Council of Venice (1555) showed this predominant concern.[33] From Italy, a popular movement of this theological character was started in Poland. As for England, her real religious Left-Wing activity did not begin much earlier than the seventeenth century, and was then more interested in a struggle for externals, e.g., church government, than in the fundamentals. The Netherlands, on the other hand, with its readiness for

---

Constitutional History (New York, 1901). Jellinek shows very clearly the thread which led from the Dutch Mennonites to Roger Williams and to the Declaration of Rights.
    32 R. Smithson, *The Anabaptists*, 203.
    33 Karl Benrath, "Wiedertäufer im Venetianischen, um die Mitte des 16. Jahrhunderts," *Theologische Studien und Kritiken*, LVIII (1885).

religious liberty, was the theater of Left–Wing movements which very soon turned into established forms, as the Dutch Mennonites (or *Doopsgezinde*) or the Remonstrants. Even the Collegiants slowly developed the character of a settled church group, due to the absence of persecution.

We perceive that the spread of evangelical Anabaptism in its proper sense—as a real leaven for the propagation of the Kingdom of God on earth—is mainly restricted to the German-speaking peoples. It was the greatest attempt to realize the idea of love and of nonviolence in these countries.

To get a better view of what has occurred along these lines and to recognize the miscellaneous structure of the movement, a second graph is given, though it shows only a rough epitome of the facts. But it may furnish a better picture of all the varieties of forms and a more strict circumscription of our issue than a long description might afford.

SOURCE: *Church History*, IX (1940), pp. 341–65.

The Christian refers to the New Testament as his proper basis, but mostly chooses only one part of is a decisive for his life. He chooses:				The New Test. is not needed in the main for religious guidance.
Synoptics	Johannine Prologue	St. Paul's Epistles	Revelation of St. John	
1	2	3	4	5
"Old evangelical brotherhoods" Franciscans (*Fraticelli*) Waldenses Evangelical Anabaptists (love and cross)	Mystics, Christian Theosophy (Böhme, Paracelsus ------ Neo–Platonism ------ Spiritualism (single)	Teaching of grace and redemption. Theology of salvation ------ All churches ------ Majoriy of sects (even Donatists) ------ Pietism, has some evangelical tones but remains Paulinistic, Methodism too	Millenarians (Eschatology Apocalyptic) Taborites Münsterites Harrison (Fifth Monarchy) Mostly antinomian	"*Schwärmer*" Enthusiasts, New Prophets, Dreamers, (Müntzer, David Joris, etc.) Mostly antinomian.
Quakers Combine 1, 2, and 5			
Humanistic ethics (rationalism, Tolstoy)			

Recent interpretations of Anabaptism

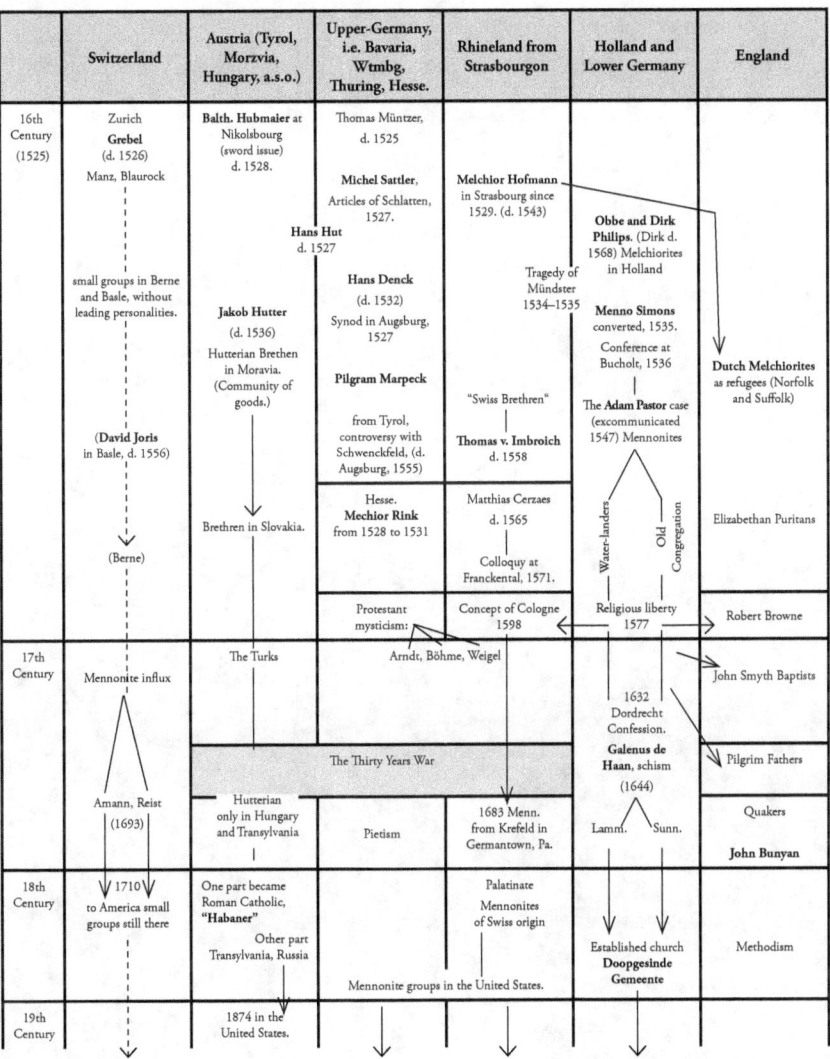

RECENT INTERPRETATIONS OF ANABAPTISM[1]

When in the process of historical research the step is taken from a mere collecting of facts to a meaningful interpretation of these facts, we may speak of the maturity of this historical research. If that is true in general history, it is even more significant in the field of church history, where ideas and spiritual principles dominate the scene. But the difficulties in this area are even more conspicuous than elsewhere. A perfectly objective church historiography is almost impossible due to the inevitable bias of the writer, his sympathies and his restricted ability to appreciate phenomena in widely different fields. In fact, no historiography can do without a set of categories and concepts of a specific nature, and the choice of these is definitely the work of the particular research person and his preferences. Whether such a person is a Catholic or a Lutheran, a Liberal or a Neo–Orthodox will certainly influence his picture and his conclusions, if ever so slightly, no matter how hard he may strive for scholarly objectivity.

The story of the Anabaptists is a good illustration of this situation. Most official church historiographies missed, either completely or in significant parts, this unfamiliar subject. It was understood either as the fanatical fringe of Protestantism, or as a self–meritorious and moralizing experiment which was bound to fail sooner or later. Its place in the total history of the Christian Church has never been clearly defined, and our textbooks insert, at best, one chapter on it out of organic connection with the rest. That in–group research often does not improve on this picture is true enough, due to the natural bias of the research persons.

So it happens that Anabaptism still presents to us an oscillating phenomenon: on the one hand it is understood as a "Left–Wing" experiment of the Reformation, interesting though soon fading out, and on the other hand it is looked at as an experiment in the realization of genuine though radical Christianity whose problems apply to some extent to everyone and reach far beyond mere historical interest. The claim would go that principles are involved which challenge the mind of any earnest Christian. If that is correct, then Anabaptism takes a unique place in the picture of the sixteenth–

---

1 Read, in part, before the American Society of Church History, Evanston, April 24, 1953.

century struggle for new patterns of Christian realization. It becomes apparent here that interpretation may become a truly controversial issue.

For a long time an excuse was at hand on both sides of the controversy; namely, that we do not know well enough the facts proper, the events and the ideas behind them. This, fortunately, is no longer true. A wealth of source material has become available in recent years which greatly changed the picture. The *Täuferakten Kommission* (TAK), an organization for the publication of all available sources (in the German language), has done an admirable job: five volumes are on hand, covering main areas of the Anabaptist movement and also some major testimonies (*Glaubenszeugnisse*). Independently of these TAK–publications, one such volume came out recently on Hesse and another one on Switzerland, the latter dealing with less than the first decade of the movement. The collection is to be continued. One volume on Alsace is nearly ready, another volume of testimonies likewise. Austria and Moravia. are just now being worked upon, more is in the stage of planning. Still more important are other source publications such as the two Hutterite chronicles edited by the late Professor A. J. F. Zieglschmid; the English version of Riedemann's great *Confession of Faith* of 1540–45; smaller Anabaptist tracts translated by Professor John C. Wenger (in the *Mennonite Quarterly Review*); and a new Menno Simons edition in English, now in preparation. Admirable though this is, much more is still needed to familiarize scholars with the almost inexhaustible source material extant. The new series of *Christian Classics* (Westminster Press) will include a volume of Anabaptist sources in English translation. The writer of this paper has been commissioned to bring out a volume of Anabaptist epistles. Other promising materials are in preparation at various centers of research.

But the time has now come to go beyond a mere collecting and confirming of factual data. Interpretations of the meaning and essence of this so intriguing "Left–Wing" movement of the sixteenth century have been attempted time and again. Earlier claims that the Anabaptists were just a mild but perfectly orthodox branch of Protestantism (John Horsch belonged to this group) cannot be considered successful any longer. It was an interpretation from the position of American Mennonitism around the turn of the century when it was strongly felt that the church had long become a Protestant denomination like any other in this country. Other attempts by liberal out–group historians were not much more successful. They recognized the moral seriousness of these sectarians, and this moved them either into the neighborhood of Erasmian Christianity or perhaps even nearer to Calvinist patterns. No better, that is, no new categories were available for a reinterpretation of the historical phenomenon of Anabaptism.

In the last decade and a half, things have changed a great deal. Of these changes, and of a few new categories introduced into modern church historiography, the present paper will try to give a brief account. It will fall into two parts: first, the account proper, and second, the attempt toward a systematic analysis of basic problems and answers. Since the writer had already once, in 1940, tried such an analysis,[2] which listed all the then available aspects, it seems advisable not to go further back but to study what has been achieved between 1940 and 1954.

Interpretations 1940–1954

In 1943, Dean Harold S. Bender of Goshen College gave as his presidential address to the American Society of Church History his revealing paper, *The Anabaptist Vision*,[3] one of the most felicitous formulations ever attempted. He sees the essence of Anabaptism in three basic elements:

1. a new concept of the church as a "brotherhood of committed disciples,"
2. a new concept of the essence of Christianity as discipleship, and
3. a new ethic of love.

This paper was so successful that it has been reprinted many times and also been published in Dutch, French, German, and Italian. In 1949 the present writer published his volume, *Mennonite Piety Through the Centuries*,[4] in which the tension between Anabaptism and Pietism was studied in great detail. As we shall come back to this issue later on, it might be left undiscussed at this place. In 1950, Harold S. Bender brought out his long expected work on Conrad Grebel[5] (who died as early as 1526). Valuable to us is particularly the last chapter of the book, "Things Most Surely Believed." The core of these is the idea of the "suffering church," whose members are to face persecution for conscience's sake simply by dint of their absolute nonconformity to the world. In the same year 1950, the "Anabaptist Theology" issue of the *Mennonite Quarterly Review*[6] presented a number of significant papers which found wide attention. In 1951, John C. Wenger of Goshen College (to whom we owe much for his translations of Anabaptist tracts and for his Marpeck studies, one of which was published in *Church History*) published a helpful small book, *Doctrines of the Mennonites*.[7] Though not fully systematic it yet helps a great deal toward clarification of (as he puts it) "some unique emphases in Anabaptist–Mennonite doctrine." The formula: "the church as a fellowship of committed disciples," first used by Bender, seems to be

---

2 Robert Friedmann, "Conception of an Anabaptist," *Church History*, 1940, 341–64.
3 In *Church History*, 1944.
4 Published by the Mennonite Historical Society, Goshen, Indiana, 1949.
5 Harold S. Bender, *Conrad Grebel, 1498–1526, The Founder of the Swiss Brethren, Sometimes called Anabaptists* (Mennonite Historical Society, Goshen, 1950).
6 *MQR*, XXIV (1950) (contains: C. Krahn, "Prolegomena to an Anabaptist Theology"; R. Friedmann, "Anabaptism and Protestantism"; H. S. Bender, "The Anabaptist Theology of Discipleship"; Franklin H. Littell, "The Anabaptist Doctrine of the Restitution of the True Church"; L. Verduin, "Menno Simons' Theology Reviewed"; John C. Wenger, "The Doctrinal Position of the Swiss Brethren as Revealed in Polemical Tracts"; Don E. Smucker, "Anabaptist Theology in the Light of Modern Theological Trends").
7 Published by Mennonite Publishing House, Goshen, Indiana, 1950.

particularly fortunate and is most likely here to stay. Surprising enough for the outsider is the paucity of Anabaptist–Mennonite material concerning the doctrines of salvation, justification by faith, and atonement, elsewhere in Protestantism the very core of theology. We must reflect on this negative factor more in detail in our systematic part.

In 1952, Dr. Franklin H. Littell, former Dean of the Boston University Chapel, brought out his excellent book, *The Anabaptist View of the Church*.[8] As a piece of out–group research in this field it deserves special attention. The idea of "restitution" of the true, i.e., apostolic church, looms large in it, also the idea of Christian primitivism, by which modern term Littell wants to interpret the spirit and essence of Anabaptism. In the same year a Viennese doctoral dissertation was published for the first time (in an English translation), Franz Heimann's paper, "*The Hutterite Doctrine of Church and Common Life, a Study of Riedemann's Confession of 1540.*"[9] In the opinion of the writer it is one of the best studies in this field. Here we learn of the hidden (Biblical) spiritualism of the Brethren and the unique combination of it with a practical organization of the brotherhood. Without the latter, to be sure, Anabaptism would not be what it actually is. The idea of the "Fellowship of the Lord's Table" as the very center of the Hutterite church idea is a real gain for the ongoing discussion.

Two more out–group publications of high value came out in the same year (1952): Wilhelm Wiswedel's third volume of his excellent *Bilder und Führergestalten aus dem Täufertum*,[10] in which he utilizes, as no one else has done, the previous material of the "Beck Collection" in the state archive of Brno, Moravia, one of the richest mines of Anabaptistica in the world.[11] It is planned to have all three volumes published in an English version which may become a real eye opener to many. Wiswedel is a Baptist minister in Germany, now in his seventies, who has dedicated a great deal of his life to this kind of research. His book is both scholarly and narrative in character. Another piece of narrative–analytical historiography of first rank is a study by Fritz Blanke, Professor of Church History in Zürich, Switzerland, concerning "The First Anabaptist Congregation: Zollikon, 1525.[12] It is based on source material recently made accessible in the Switzerland volume of the *Täuferakten*.

In 1953, Bender published a fine study of a topic never broached before: "The Anabaptists and Religious Liberty in the Sixteenth Century,[13] in which he gives ample proof that the Anabaptists were among the earliest champions

---

8 Franklin H. Littell, *The Anabaptist View of the Church, an Introduction to Sectarian Protestantism* (American Society of Church History, 952).

9 In *MQR*, XXVI (1952), 22–47, 142–60.

10 Published by J. G. Oncken Verlag, Kassel, Germany, 1952.

11 H. S. Bender, "Anabaptist Manuscripts in the Archive at Brno, Czechoslovakia," *MQR*, XXIII (1949), 105 ff.

12 Fritz Blanke, "Zollikon 1525, Die Entstehung der ältesten Täufergemeinde," *Theologische Zeitschrift*, VIII, Basel (1952), 241–61; English translation in *MQR*, XXVII (1953), 17–33.

13 In *Archiv für Reformationsgeschichte*, 1953, 32–51.

of religious liberty, although for reasons very different from those of humanist defenders like Castellio.

Not very much has been done thus far to clarify the theological ideas of these Anabaptist brethren. This might be due, in part, to the fact that most sources are of a nontheological nature (as is fitting to a sectarian movement), and in part because the problem has not yet been fully visualized in this area. What was the very idea of salvation and redemption among Anabaptists, what do they teach concerning atonement and justification, and what, finally, do they teach about free will and predestination? Actually there is much material available already, but it will require a great deal of empathy for its proper interpretation and placement.[14] Quotations alone would hardly satisfy.

A highly challenging study of this interpretive nature is A. Orley Swartzentruber's paper, *The Piety and Theology of the Anabaptist Martyrs in Van Braght's Martyr's Mirror*.[15] The author observes a marked change in emphasis between the earlier period (to 1560) and the later period (to 1600) of Anabaptist history. The earlier phase is characterized by three key words: revelation (a pneumatic experience), discipleship (brotherly love in practice), and kingdom (martyr–mindedness with an eschatological orientation). The later period, mainly in the North where persecution had ceased, is characterized by the key words, obedience (acceptance of the New Testamental commandments as the new order) and heaven (the place of rest). Grace as a personal charismatic experience, so strong in the first period and leading to courageous witnessing, is now more and more lost as the brotherhoods become formalized and well established.

Quite helpful is also the predominantly theological paper by Hans G. Fischer, a Lutheran minister of Vienna, Austria, entitled, *Lutheranism and the Vindication of the Anabaptist Way*,[16] in which the concepts of justification and sanctification are discussed in their mutual tension. For the Anabaptists the way to conquer sin as far as humanly possible had at all times the precedence over the concern for salvation. But such a way, to be sure, is possible only *sola gratia*, and must never be understood as a type of work—righteousness or perfectionism.

Some Major Categories of These Interpretations

As we now turn to a scanning of the results of these recent endeavors, we may group these formulations of the "essence of Anabaptism" into those by out–group scholars and those by in–group scholars (the term I have borrowed from Franklin H. Littell). In 1935, Professor Arthur Lovejoy of Johns Hopkins

---

14 Frank J. Wray in an unpublished 1953 Yale Dissertation, "History as seen through the Eyes of Sixteenth Century Anabaptists," has also a good chapter on the Free Will issue. The theology of atonement in the Anabaptist understanding is very well represented in an early anonymous tract, "Concerning the Satisfaction of Christ," translated and edited by John C. Wenger, *MQR*, XX (1946), 243–54.

15 *MQR*, XXVIII (1954), 5–26, 128–42.

16 *MQR*, XXVIII (1954), 27–38.

University introduced the term "primitivism" into the history of ideas. Some years later Roland H. Bainton of Yale Divinity School applied it generally to the "Left Wing of the Reformation."[17] Franklin H. Littell devotes a whole chapter (Ch. III) to this idea of "Christian Primitivism," using as his subtitle "The Fall of the Church." Anabaptism is thus considered as a form of "religious primitivism." Littell underscores the particular concept of the "church" as the very essence of Anabaptism. This contention was challenged in a paper by Harold S. Bender of Goshen College. I am not so sure, either, whether "Christian primitivism" is too helpful a term. It is true that Anabaptists do speak of the corruption of the church after it made its peace with the Roman State under Constantine the Great. But in this criticism they do not stand alone. It seems to me that Anabaptism is more than simply Christian primitivism, although some of it enters the picture, too, without doubt. As to the supplementary idea of "Restitution" or "Restoration" of the primitive church here and now, it has to be said that the source material does not fully bear out this claim. Do its defenders (generally speaking the school around Bainton[18]) mean to say that the evangelical Anabaptists actually planned such a restoration? Frank J. Wray in a recent paper admits that "the term restitution was used more frequently by those on the fringe of Anabaptism than by the representatives of the main stream of the movement."[19] But he adds that this does not mean that, among the Anabaptists at least, the characteristic "attitude" of restoration was also not much alive—which to a certain extent is correct. If attitudes are considered, however, it would still be more correct to say that what concerned these Brethren was not so much a historical reestablishment of something previously lost, but rather obedience to the divine will without any reservation. In other words, they think in terms of a continuation of the "true church," the timeless and perennial community of genuine believers. That the Brethren sometimes refer to the church of the apostles, so-to-speak as their model, does not really indicate their restitution-mindedness but should be understood rather as a way of illustration of their own intent, and perhaps also as an encouragement to continue in their difficult endeavor. Restitution has too strongly an historical connotation to fit perfectly to the idea of discipleship and the imitation of Christ.[20]

---

17 Roland H. Bainton, "The Left Wing of the Reformation," *Journal of Religion* (1941), 127.

18 The idea of "restitution" within the Left Wing of the Reformation was for the first time discussed by Roland H. Bainton in his study, "Changing Ideas and Ideals in the Sixteenth Century," *Journal of Modern History*, VIII (1936), 417–43.

19 Frank J. Wray, "The Anabaptist Doctrine of the Restitution of the Church," *MQR*, XXVIII (1954), 186–96.

20 In a letter to this writer, Roland H. Bainton makes a fine differentiation concerning this principle of Restitution. "The ideal of restitution or restoration was common in the age of Reformation, and all parties desired to restore something. The difference was only as to what, and how far back to go. Luther wished to restore the church of the early Middle Ages; for him the great corruption was the rise of the temporal power of the papacy in the eighth century. The Anabaptists went back further than any of the other groups, and turned exclusively to the New Testament. Even within the New Testament they tended to neglect Paul and push back to Jesus. That is why the ideal of Restoration tends to coincide with the ideal of the imitation of Christ."

Occasionally, Littell uses also another descriptive term for the Anabaptists: he calls them the "covenant people" (borrowing this term most likely from Champlin Burrage, *The Church Covenant Idea*, 1904). I would welcome the wider acceptance of this term as it stresses the absolutely obligatory nature of membership in these brotherhoods. Through adult baptism, members enter a covenant, to be sure not among themselves but between God and themselves. Although Littell does not quote it in his book, one of the most often repeated verses in Anabaptist writings is I Peter 3:21, "Baptism [of adults] is the covenant of a good conscience with God."[21] To me this appears as one of the key ideas in Anabaptism, and it becomes particularly revealing if one thinks of the position of Luther, who had little use for the term "good conscience" in view of man's sinfulness. Peter Riedemann, however, speaks in his great confession, the *Rechenschaft* of 1540, of this covenant as a "covenant of childlike freedom." "We are the children of it," he says, "if we let ourselves be sealed by this covenant and submit and surrender ourselves to its working."[22]

Many a scholar has claimed that Anabaptism was "Biblical literalism," thus creating anew the "legalism" which Luther had abolished in opposition to the Roman Church. Truly enough, the New Testament (more than the Old) revealed to the Brethren the norm and direction of all their seeking and finding. They declined any spiritualism other than a Biblical one, claiming that only the man with a spirit akin to the Scriptures can understand the latter. Nevertheless, it was only in later centuries, when the original fervor had died out, that the Bible became "the letter" to the last item, an attitude which has often led to formalism and sometimes rigidity (as is the case with today's Hutterites and Amish). In the sixteenth century such letter–worship was nearly unknown. True, the Brethren were Scriptural in everything, but only by virtue of their inner, i.e., spiritual understanding. It is the "living word," as they called it, "that pierces the soul," never the dead letter.[23]

Professor Blanke called Anabaptism a genuine revival movement (*Erweckungsbewegung*), and that it certainly was. Inner rebirth is emphasized as the very beginning of a Christian life of this kind and as its precondition. Since neither Luther nor Zwingli stressed such revival or conversion, Anabaptism might be justly called "the awakening movement of the sixteenth century." The difference lies only in the proper understanding of this term. Revival movements and awakenings have occurred many times in church history and belong, for instance, also to the very nature of American Christendom. Obviously the idea of "revival movement" contains a certain ambiguity which becomes particularly evident when we think of the ease with which later Anabaptism changed into a pietistic form of Christianity. Apparently, a

---

21 According to Luther's translation.
22 Robert Friedmann, "Peter Riedemann on Original Sin and the Way to Redemption," *MQR*, XXVI (1952), 214.
23 *MQR*, XXVI (1952), 43 (in the study quoted in note 8). Compare also the excellent study of Wilhelm Wiswedel, "The Inner and the Outer Word, A Study in the Anabaptist Doctrine of Scripture," *MQR*, XXVI (1952), 171–91.

revival movement in the sixteenth century was very different in kind from a revival movement in the eighteenth century or later. Also the often applied term "sanctification of life," which is traditionally contrasted to "justification from sin," will need further clarification. Certainly, Anabaptism as a "way" rather than a theology emphasized sanctification of life to such an extent that life in its totality became almost one great sacrament. Nevertheless, also the Pietists and their Anglo–Saxon counterpart, the Methodists, speak often of such sanctification side by side with justification, and the confusion of terms becomes obvious.

From here we now turn to some formulations nearer the center of the actual phenomena. Ethelbert Stauffer spoke in 1933 of an "Anabaptist Theology of Martyrdom"[24] as most characteristic for the life of the Brethren. Bender, who himself emphasized the idea of a "suffering church" with Conrad Grebel and his successors, rejects Stauffer's term "theology" in this connection. The idea of martyrdom, he contends, is the background of the picture rather than the content of the faith for which the Anabaptists bled and died. Although this criticism is correct, it is yet good to put the spotlight on this issue, for only such a martyr–mindedness makes it bearable for the victims to face so much suffering and to bear it "with a laughing mouth," as the Hutterite Chronicle once reported on such an occasion. The idea of the "bitter Christ," who requires complete self–surrender, in opposition to the "sweet Christ," who would not burden man with such requirement (it was Thomas Müntzer who once contrasted in this way his own idea of Christ with that of Luther) is certainly present also in the Anabaptist outlook, and makes the readiness to suffer "for the sake of the Kingdom" better understandable. One of their violent opponents, the Dominican preacher Johannes Faber of Heilbronn (d. 1557), even wrote a small tract in 1550 on this fact with the characteristic subtitle, "Whence it Cometh that Anabaptists Suffer the Pain of Death so Cheerfully and Confidently."[25]

The next and last of our interpretations is most likely the best of all, the one which explains more than any earlier named attempt. And it is one which eliminates ambiguity and misunderstanding to a very large extent. It is the idea of "discipleship," or in German *Nachfolge Christi*. It was first Johannes Kühn who in his book, *Toleranz und Offenbarung* (1923), described this type of *Nachfolge*, presenting Anabaptism on the one side and Quakerism on the other side as best representatives of this type of Christianity. Bender then continued this thought both in his book on Grebel and in his paper "Theology of Discipleship."[26] Such discipleship means that the commandment of Jesus Christ, "Take up thy cross and follow me," be taken absolutely seriously. That

---

24 Ethelbert Stauffer, "Täufertheologie und Märtyrertum," *Zeitschrift für Kirchengeschichte*, LII (1933), 545–98; English trans. "The Anabaptist Theology of Martyrdom," *MQR*, XIX (1945), 179–214.

25 A copy of the pamphlet in Goshen College Library. Cf. the article "Faber (Fabri)" by Neff in *ML*, I, 624.

26 Harold S. Bender, "The Theology of Discipleship," *MQR*, XXIV (1950), 25–32.

it implies separation from the world, nonconformity and consequently the narrow path which might end in martyrdom, is only too obvious. It is also obvious that all the other qualities previously discussed root in this central and most profound idea. Above all, I am inclined to agree with Bender that the church concept of the Brethren, although one of the most distinctive features of Anabaptist life, is yet a *derivative* idea, and can therefore not be called "the" essence of Anabaptism (as for instance Littell claimed). We have not yet arrived at the heart of the matter when we stop with the idea of the "church." At the heart we discover one idea only, and that is the idea of faithful and free voluntary discipleship which the Anabaptist is resolved to accept without faltering. Discipleship and new life mean about the same; that under this aspect a "theology of salvation" recedes somewhat into the background should not surprise us any longer.

It might, however, be argued that discipleship is merely a way and not a theology (as Bender claimed in his paper) and that therefore the same criticism could be raised against the term "theology of discipleship" which Bender himself offered against Stauffer's term "theology of martyrdom." Although there is some point to this argument we might yet interpret Bender's phrase in a way which makes it acceptable at once. What he had in mind was obviously the vision of a "theology" in which discipleship becomes a regulative or normative idea. Under this restriction his thesis becomes very fruitful although further specifications are still needed.

The Nature of Anabaptism, a Suggested Reformulation

Here then let us stop our survey. That it was not in vain will be readily admitted, likewise that it deals with most central Christian issues which go far beyond the interest in sectarian peculiarities. In brief, the issue posed by the Anabaptists is whether it is possible to realize such a life of discipleship or not. In other words, whether Christ's commandment to follow Him was meant for practical realization or only as a distant ideal hardly ever to be approximated within earthly life.

On this question the ways part. It is well known that Luther had his doubts whether a "brotherhood of committed disciples" is possible, or—neglecting a general church—is even desirable.[27] Thus he decided for a *Volkskirche* which would comprise both saints and sinners. The Anabaptists, on the other hand, decided exactly for the opposite way, that is, for the "church holy" rather than for the "church universal" (Bainton's terms).[28] That such a "church holy" is not only a distant ideal but a distinct possibility for man was demonstrated by the Anabaptists, at least in their first period (to 1560), with much dedication

---

27 Luther, *Deutsche Messe*, *Werke, W. A.*, XIX, p. 75; cf. also Albrecht Ritschl, *Geschichte des Pietismus*, I (Bonn, 1880), 73, and Roland H. Bainton, "The Development and Consistency of Luther's Attitude toward Religious Libery," *Harvard Theological Review*, XXII (1929), 130–31.

28 See note 17.

and vigor. It meant, of course, complete separation from the world and nonconformity to it, with all the consequences implied. To embark upon this way was certainly not simple, but those who actually embarked did so out of a great "must" which genuine rebirth carries with it, no matter how high the price.

To give a dramatic picture of such an almost New Testamental conversion together with all its consequences, let us now briefly look at Blanke's masterly description of the first Anabaptist congregation at Zollikon near Zürich.[29]

On a January day of 1525, a peculiar incident happened near this place. At a public fountain two men stopped, and the one said to the other, "Well, Hans, you have taught me the truth. For that I thank you, and request now the sign." The other man did not hesitate, and by sprinkling him with water from the fountain he performed the rite of baptism on his companion. On the same evening a number of men assembled in the house of the one who had baptized his fellow believer, and here they broke bread together in a most simple, yet impressive, communion service. Blanke calls this Lord's Supper an event which includes both the obligation to a Christian way of life, of love to God and to all fellow men, and a celebration of those who know that they are saved. There is nothing in these two acts, baptism and Lord's Supper, which would make these men feel rebellious; in fact they proceeded with the greatest calm as if they had full authority to do so. Needless to say, there was nothing emotional in these acts either. The ordinances were to them symbols of grace, and of divine grace they knew something ever since they had renounced their old life, sin and world. One of the men present, but not yet baptized into the new covenant, could not find sleep during that night. He knew no way out but to ask God to give him right understanding, which finally broke upon him with convincing force. Early in the morning of the next day he got up, wakened some Brethren and engaged in a pastoral conversation, the result of which was his baptism upon faith. They later reported that they all had prayed to God for recognition of sin. They knew that not only forgiveness of sin, but already that awareness of sin is a gift of God. Now these men went forth to become missioners of their new faith and their new way. After a very short period they all stood before a court. Asked by the judge whether they in future leave Anabaptism, one of them gave the following most revealing answer: "I am God's servant and have no longer authority over myself. I have enrolled under the captain Jesus Christ and would go to death with Him. Whatever He commands and reveals I would be obedient to and do the same." According to Blanke, it was here in Zollikon that a new type of church had begun to differentiate itself, the Free–Church type.

This story is the earliest on record, if we omit the night event of a few days earlier when Conrad Grebel first baptized Jörg Blaurock in a room in Zürich, whereupon the latter baptized all the rest of those present. The same

---

29 See note 12.

story repeats itself from now on time and again; with a high consciousness of authority, in an almost Gospel–like fashion, such new brotherhoods spring up everywhere in Switzerland, South Germany, Austria, Tyrol, Moravia, and likewise in the North, in the Netherlands and adjoining German territories. The story of the Austrian Hutterites is somewhat better known due to their two published chronicles and needs no repetition here. Repentance, rebirth, baptism on faith, and a full dedication to a life of discipleship and obedience—this sequence will be experienced henceforth in innumerable cases throughout the sixteenth century.

As we now enter into the more systematic discussion of the nature of Anabaptism, a number of questions suggest themselves which require analysis and clarification. First and foremost is the issue of Anabaptism and Pietism. Do not all these stories which we have heard sound almost like pietistic, Methodistic, revivalistic events, only too well known from later periods both in Europe and in America? The only difference would be that these awakening–movements later on were no longer looked upon as dangerous, and therefore did not provoke persecutions. But could it not be, we ask, that this difference is due only to the fact that in the meantime a more tolerant mood had come up which allowed dissent without punishment? Or is there rather a difference "in kind" between the Anabaptist way of the sixteenth century and that of pietistic movements of later centuries? If we decide for the latter interpretation, then the burden is upon us to establish the specific difference between these two externally so similar phenomena. First we will readily admit that the temptation was always at hand to slip away from the narrow and difficult path of discipleship to the easier pietistic pattern. Pietism in a strict sense, to be sure, did not exist in the sixteenth century. Nevertheless Caspar Schwenckfeld (who died in 1561, the year in which Menno Simons also died) is often termed as a "pietist before Pietism,"[30] and his type of Christian teaching ought to be considered in the present context. It is very significant that Schwenckfeld openly and in a most outspoken manner attacked the Anabaptists,[31] to which the Brethren then passionately reacted, quite in contrast to their usual self–restraint. Pilgram Marpeck[32] wrote an

---

30 Joachim Wach, "Caspar Schwenckfeld, a Pupil and a Teacher in the School of Christ," in his *Types of Religious Experience, Christian and Non–Christian* (Chicago, 1951), 135–70, in particular note 19.

31 Karl Ecke, *Schwenkfeld, Luther und der Gedanke einer apostolischen Reformation* (Berlin, 1911), and by the same author, *Caspar Schwenckfeld* (Stuttgart, 1952; a condensation of the earlier book). Both books deal extensively with Schwenckfeld's reaction to the Anabaptist way. He calls the Anabaptists false apostles for "they do not know the true way of salvation, and have no living experience of salvation.... They know little of sin and forgiving grace [i.e., of the *sola fide* theology]. They do not know anything essential about man's basic corruption and do not teach the power of sin. Hence they are ignorant of the true justifying faith. They have an unbiblical genius of judging and self-righteousness (*Richtgeist*), and show spiritual arrogance. The sacraments they dispose of lightly. Marpeck in particular has a very superficial judgement concerning original sin and salvation. In short: The Anabaptists represent a new type of Judaism [i.e., legalism]...." These remarks show impressively that Schwenckfeld was unable to grasp the genius of Anabaptism, due most likely to his own *sola fide* approach, and they show at the same time the deep gulf between the latter and the Anabaptist vision. It was much easier for a spiritual Reformer like Sebastian Franck to appreciate the positive qualities of Anabaptism without, however, ever identifying himself with it.

32 See John C. Wenger, "Pilgram Marpeck, Tyrolese Engineer and Anabaptist Elder," *Church History*,

elaborate polemical book against him in 1542–43[33] which most clearly states the differences. In chapter 47, for instance, we read: "He (Schwenckfeld) teaches only the inward and glorified Christ in Heaven, but not the suffering one on earth; he teaches but the word of his glory and magnificence, but not the word of his Cross and tribulation, as Christ had to bear before his ascension and as it is befitting to bear for his untransfigured body still today." The crown of thorns (the symbol of the Anabaptist type of Christianity) and halo of glory (the symbol of the pietistic vision of Christianity); the "sweet Christ" as the ideal of the latter versus the "bitter Christ" as the ideal of the Anabaptists. In spite of great external similarities, a deep gulf seems to prevail which separates these two types.

The difference seems to center around the idea of man's sinfulness and the way of overcoming it. Pietism is principally characterized by the subjective experience of the fact that the sinner, though incapable of doing anything good, is yet saved through the atoning death of Christ, and the subsequent joy which goes with such an experience. The pietist knows of his sinfulness, but in a struggle of repentance he overcomes it and now rejoices in his feeling of being saved and accepted by the Lord. A quiet moralism usually goes along with it, together with a conventicle type of church life (which, by the way, is not the same as a brotherhood). The world, apparently, does not feel challenged or endangered by this attitude, and the result is an absence of persecution.

With the Anabaptists things seem to be quite different. The rebirth is a radical one, and with it the resolution to a new way in obedience to the "law of Christ." No conventicles but brotherhoods (*koinonia*) are established in order to build or to promote the Kingdom of God on earth. Once embarked on the path of obedience, little concern is shown regarding the question of one's own salvation. "We teach and try to establish the obedience of faith," writes Peter Walpot, a Hutterite bishop, around 1560, "and with it the true free and voluntary surrender unto God. Upon this we baptize...."[34] "Disobedience is the mother of all sins," writes succinctly Peter Riedemann, another Hutterite leader, around 1540. The brother who endeavors to be obedient does not worry any longer about his redeemed status. No rejoicing, therefore, is experienced in connection with man's awareness of salvation. In fact, very little theology on this point was ever developed by the Brethren; their extensive writings are rather poor with regard to a theology of salvation. The reborn Anabaptist knows that "inherent" (*anklebende*) sin still prevails in his body as a sort of inclination toward that which is not divine, and Riedemann teaches even that this kind of sin is the first cause of man's physical death. But he denies

---

IX (1940), 24–36.

33   *Pilgram Marpecks Antwort auf Kaspar Schwenckfelds Beurteilung des Buches der Bundesbezeugung von 1542*, edited by Johann Loserth (under the heading: *Quellen und Forschungen zur Geschichte der oberdeutschen Taufgesinnten des 16. Jahrhunderts*), Vienna und Leipzig, 1929; a volume of nearly 600 pages in folio. The 47th chapter on pp. 153–62.

34   Quoted by Robert Friedmann, *Archiv für Reformationsgeschichte* (1931), 109.

very outspokenly any total corruption which would make obedience to the Word of God impossible. Man, thus he claims, can resist evil and temptation to evil, can avoid sinful works and can die unto actual sin. Only by this way may he hope to follow Christ in true discipleship. *Sola fide* theology hardly ever entered into his mind (at least not in the form which was taught by Luther), and therefore the enjoyment of the fruits of such justification (as in Pietism) is more or less foreign to him. It was only about one century later, when the basic attitude of the Brethren became weakened or almost lost, that pietistic emotionalism took the place of the former *Nachfolge* or discipleship motive, and with this change (hardly ever noticed) the genuine Anabaptist spirit faded away.

Apparently, then, Anabaptism represents a new type of Christianity, different from the traditional patterns of Protestantism in general. It is certainly not a creedal (i.e., theological) church in which the idea of salvation takes the center of concern, nor is it a pietistic church in which the fruits of salvation may be enjoyed. Thus the question is not without meaning whether Anabaptism may still be considered as a part of the great Protestant family (aside from the merely negative fact of separation from Rome).[35] But in what other way then could this Anabaptist movement be classified or characterized, in order to give it its proper place in church history?

Here I venture a new interpretation which might be quite helpful in the understanding of the movement even though it is not completely free of a certain vagueness. That is the interpretation of Anabaptism as an outstanding example of *existential Christianity*. This term is, of course, no longer new today. What is new at this place is perhaps only its application to the subject of our study. The term "existential" means here, above all, an extreme concreteness of the Christian experience. Such an experience is neither of an intellectual nature (doctrinal understanding) nor is it emotional. For lack of a better description we will call it "total," something most typical with all conversion experiences. In this total or concrete Christianity the distinctions between doctrine and ethics, belief and practice, no longer exist. Life becomes here a great "yes" to the call, something which goes far beyond both mere speculation and mere moralism. Spirituality and obedience become one and the same in such a Christian existence, an unreserved surrender and dedication to the divine will. That such Christian existence has also very little in common with emotionalism becomes likewise clear by now and should make us alert not to confound these two fundamentally different kinds of experience.

The best demonstration of this "existential" quality may perhaps be attained by an analysis of the phenomenon of faith, the very center of all Christianity. Faith may mean two very different things: trust or confidence on the one side, knowledge and vision on the other. With the main stream of Protestantism, faith is above all a trust, the confidence that God is true and

---

35 Robert Friedmann, "Anabaptism and Protestantism," *MQR*, XXIV (1950), 14.

that His promises therefore will come true. It is not mere chance that Harry E. Fosdick quotes Luther to demonstrate just this point. "Faith means not so much a believing about God as a lively, reckless confidence in the grace of God."[36] This gives the believer comfort and satisfaction. Man, to be sure, is and remains a sinner but at the same time he is also justified and reconciled in God by such faith alone.[37]

With the Anabaptists faith appears to be of a different kind. It is less a trust than an awareness of a new, spiritual reality known only to the one who experiences an inner birth or conversion. Here faith means a certain possession or a knowing, a new horizon and the acknowledgment of a call. The well known formula, *simul justus ac peccator*, is not shared by the Anabaptists, in fact it is very much against their particular understanding of the Christian message. To them faith and life are basically and very concretely one and the same: the believer simply cannot do otherwise than he is actually doing. No threat of martyrdom will influence him to deviate in any way.

A person who in this way has experienced something of the genuine Gospel–spirit now becomes a disciple in the most natural fashion; there is no other way possible to him. If we read any of the great testimonies of sixteenth century Anabaptism, this kind of genuineness and existential realism at once becomes apparent. With Paul these men could say, "Not I, but Christ liveth in me" (Gal. 2:20). They would say it with greatest simplicity and without any sophistication, giving them a strange, but obviously genuine, charismatic authority.

Brotherly love is the most conspicuous sign of such an existential type of Christianity: where it is practiced we might also speak of a work at the Kingdom of God. It is obvious, moreover, that the Kingdom cannot exist for the "single one" in his isolation but only for those who have united in the *koinonia*, the *Gemeinschaft* or *Gemeinde*. Earlier we called it the fellowship of committed disciples. Kingdom–mindedness is a phenomenon not too often encountered in church history. We might refer, however, to the Waldenses or the Fraticelli (Franciscan Spirituals) as similar phenomena, perhaps also to the oldest form of the Bohemian Brethren, whose spokesman was Peter Chelchitzki (1390–1460). In any case, this kingdom–mindedness works for group building, in fact it could not possibly actualize outside a group.[38] Only through genuine fellowship does the single one find his way to God. Thus the

---

36 Harry Emerson Fosdick, *Great Voices of the Reformation* (New York, 1952), 542.

37 A good illustration of this situation may be also drawn from the following Luther quotation: "When God speaks and gives signs [sacraments], man must firmly and wholeheartedly believe that what God says and signifies is true.... Then God, in turn, will count this faith unto our righteousness, good and sufficient to salvation." Martin Luther, *Works*, ed. Jacobs (Philadelphia), III, 20f.

38 It is true that the Pietists also speak of promoting the Kingdom of God, but it seems to me that their idea of the Kingdom is rather of a sentimental (non–"existential") nature. We meet here a similar difference in shade (perhaps in kind) as with the contradistinction of conventicle and *koinonia*, the Anabaptist brotherhood. The difference, however, is too subtle to be discussed in a brief footnote.

principle of love (*agape*) becomes here the very core of Christian existence, by resolving both theology and ethics into the new life of discipleship.

Existential Christianity and kingdom–mindedness are here suggested as new descriptive categories, differentiating Anabaptism from other forms of religious realization or expression. They both support the theory that discipleship is actually the essence of Anabaptism. It gave Anabaptism that concreteness and convincing power which made it so strong and capable to survive for so long. Rebirth[39] belongs to it, too, that inexplicable change in spiritual levels with its tremendous uplift, which enables the believer actually to walk the narrow path of following Christ. Thus the realization of love is no longer a mere paradox but something very much alive—the very norm of man's spiritual existence.

Quite naturally, this type of kingdom–mindedness produces also a new kind of eschatological thinking. The Brethren are deeply aware of the coexistence of two worlds: this world and the world of the Kingdom. They understand without much explanation the "in–breaking miracle of the eschatological order,"[40] as Rudolf Otto calls it, that is of the kingdom here and now. Absolute separation from the world and nonconformity to it easily follow as corollaries. Occasionally we read in Anabaptist tracts phrases like this, "In these latter and dangerous days…," but almost nowhere do we find apocalyptic speculations.[41] Their eschatology is strictly evangelical: the Christian has "to fight the good fight" (I Tim. 6:12), and to prevail over the great enemy, the tempter; in other words, he has to resist sin with all his strength. Discipline and the ban are but two means to this end within the brotherhood. That such an attitude very tangibly challenged or provoked the world at large is quite evident, and the Brethren recognized it as their fate that love and cross always go together. In this connection, a quotation from Sebastian Franck, the sixteenth–century spiritual Reformer, is very revealing. In his *Chronica…Geschichtsbibel* of 1531, he writes about these Brethren as follows: "They taught nothing but love, faith and the cross. They showed themselves humble and patient under much suffering. They broke bread with one another as an evidence of unity and love.… And they died as martyrs, patiently and humbly enduring all persecution.[42]

Another term of great significance in Anabaptist thought is "obedience." An early Anabaptist tract expressly emphasized this thought by distinguishing between "childlike obedience in freedom," and "servile (*knechtisch*) obedience"

---

39 What in Biblical terminology is called "rebirth" (John 3:3), Kierkegaard calls "the leap", that is, the sudden change in spiritual levels.

40 Compare Rudolph Otto, *The Kingdom of God and the Son of Man* (London, 1943; Germany, 1932), p. 312, a book which helped me greatly to understand not only the apostolic church, but also the Anabaptist genius with its great inner kinship to that apostolic church.

41 The only exception from this general rule is perhaps Melichior Hofman (1495–1543), the beginner of evangelical Anabaptism in the Netherlands. Tragically he saw all his expectations come to naught. He died after many years of imprisonment in Strasbourg. See Neff's article in *ML*, II, 326–35.

42 Sebastian Frank, *Chronica, Zeytbuch, und Geschychtbichel* (Strasbourg, 1531), folio 444b.

which but leads to false legalism.⁴³ Further, a letter of 1571 by a Hutterite bishop to a Unitarian inquirer in Poland offers a fine example of this obedience motive. He begins by quoting Paul (II Cor. 10:5), "Bring your reason into the captivity of the obedience of Christ." In this spirit he continues, "We establish the obedience of faith.... The servant who knows his Lord's will is obliged not to stand around too long but to go ahead and to do it." Obedience and faith become here almost identical terms. "Mere knowledge and learning," he assures us, "are not enough." Those who claim to believe have first to be tested and proved through tribulation, etc. "Hold fast to God and look out to Him with a humble and staunch heart.⁴⁴ That is typical Anabaptist style. As can be readily seen there is nothing emotional or sophisticated in it. It is rather a spiritual realism which knows of the difference of the two worlds.

Obedience then is the Anabaptist term for "discipleship." They would not often speak of the latter but simply insist upon the former. They did not worry whether such obedience and discipleship are actually possible or not. Did not Paul himself speak of "the obedience unto righteousness" (Rom. 6:16)? It requires but the right commitment and the right fellowship.

Two ordinances help to strengthen these two, and they are baptism and the Lord's Supper. Baptism they call occasionally with Paul "the bath of rebirth" (Tim. 3:5, Luther's version). It is understood as a most solemn event. It does not bestow graces upon the receiver but means rather a sealing (*Versiegelung*) of the new life and commitment. In character such baptism might perhaps best be compared with a monastic vow. Whoever demanded baptism upon faith and, after due inquiry, received it will no longer deviate from his new path. Basically it means the determination to resist sin in all its subtle temptations. As a presupposition, however, the Brethren taught a genuinely felt self-surrender unto God (in German, *Gelassenheit*, i.e., self-abandoning, yieldedness), the very qualification for the entrance into the new covenant of grace.

Once this stage is reached, the brother is accepted at the Lord's Table. Franz Heimann, in his earlier mentioned dissertation, states quite correctly that such a "Unity of the fellowship of the Lord's Table must exist prior to the celebration of the Lord's Supper proper."⁴⁵ This concept of a "fellowship of the Lord's Table" (*Abendmahlsgemeinde*) is very helpful indeed, symbolizing the close inner relatedness and unity of all brethren within the group. It is much more than a mere "assembly of saints" (as for instance in pietistic conventicles), and might best be considered as an expression of "the unity of the spirit in love and faith." At the celebration of the Lord's Supper the Brethren liked to recite the old parable of bread and wine, first mentioned in

---

43 "Two Kinds of Obedience, An Anabaptist Tract on Christian Freedom," translated and edited by John C. Wenger, *MQR*, XXI (1947), 18–22; also in Fosdick, *op. cit.*, pp. 296–99.
44 Robert Friedmann, "Reason and Obedience: An Old Anabaptist Letter of Peter Walpot, 1571, and its meaning," *MQR*, XIX (1945), 27–40.
45 See note 9.

the *Teachings of the Twelve Apostles* (the "Didache") of about A.D. 120. In one of our texts it runs about as follows:

> As the grain kernels are altogether merged and each must give its content into the one flour and bread, likewise also the wine, where the single grapes are crushed under the press and each grape gives away all its juice and all its strength into one wine. Whichever kernel and whichever grape, however, is not crushed and retains its strength for itself alone, such an one is unworthy and is cast out. This is what Christ wanted to bring home to his companions and guests at the Last Supper as an example of how they should be together in such a fellowship.[46]

That from such an experience of unity occasionally a sort of communion of goods resulted should not surprise us any longer. With the Hutterites it was a full communion of both consumption and production (as in monasteries), with the other groups it was what Troeltsch called a "communion of love," a sharing in that which was needed.

This Lord's Supper was of course a most solemn affair, like baptism, and it was often celebrated under greatest dangers at some remote mountain glens or forest retreats, quite often at night. When we consider the meaning of the original Supper in the Upper Room and compare it with these Anabaptist ceremonies, we are at once impressed by the similarity of the spirit. According to Rudolf Otto, the original Supper was "a consecrated meal of a fellowship of religious brethren.... It was a fraternal meal with sacramental character, a real sharing in the means of expiation. The meaning of this meal was definitely eschatological: the experience of the eschatological order itself here and now. By participating in this meal a power was experienced which released the members from the burden of guilt and made them aware of the miracle of atonement."[47] The parallels with the Lord's Supper and its interpretation among Anabaptists is at once striking. I would, however, not call these parallels "primitivism" as has been done (though there is something of it apparent) but rather the result of a unique similarity of the basic spiritual experiences.

The Brethren never developed binding creeds, and this is another feature typical of this type of Christianity. Our sources abound in "Confessions of Faith," "Accounts of our Religion," and the like. But these statements are no creeds in the conventional ecclesiastical sense; they are rather personal documents, testimonies so to speak, which every brother produced for himself. Their existential character is recognized by the frequent introduction, "This I do confess" or "This we do believe." That such confessions were never binding

---

46 Andreas Ehrenpreis, *Ein Sendbrief...*, 1652 (reprinted Scottdale, PA., 1920). Menno Simons has a similar quotation; cf. Cornelius Krahn, *Menno Simons* (Karlsruhe, 1936), 142. It is noteworthy that also Martin Luther once quoted this parable, in his 1519 sermon "Von dem hochwürdigen Sakrament des heiligen wahren Leichnams Christi," yet without further applications. Most remarkably, this parable is still in use among the Old Order Amish in their communion sermons.

47 Rudolph Otto, *loc. cit.* (note 44), 312.

for the group as a whole, and likewise not conducive to the establishment of ecclesiastical bodies, is readily understandable. These testimonies are usually very simple, abounding in Bible quotations and short declarations. Theology was not intended and will hardly be found in them. Nevertheless, these documents are of a very high standard, and regularly surprised interrogating commissions, judges or priests bent on the conversion of Brethren held in prison. The way in which these Brethren bore their trials and defended their faith with dignity and expertness is truly amazing. It might be considered as another evidence of the existential nature of Anabaptist Christianity, and also of the vitality of their Gospel–spirit.

And finally the church. Is its meaning that of a "church universal" comprising saints and sinners, or is its meaning to be a "church holy" whose light shines on the hill?[48] Peter Riedemann in 1540 had this to answer: "The church is a lantern of righteousness in which the light of grace is borne and held before the whole world. The true church is completely filled with the light of Christ in the same way as the lantern is illuminated and made bright by the light in it."[49] Those who live in it as true members not only experience salvation as "liberation from sin" but also as a new covenant of grace, or, as it was occasionally called, as a "covenant of childlike freedom." This remarkable self–interpretation agrees, of course, also very well with our earlier more sociological interpretation according to which the church was understood as a "fellowship of committed disciples."

As we now look back to our analysis, it becomes rather clear that all the features discussed in the first section fit beautifully to these *new descriptive categories* such as: existential Christianity, kingdom–mindedness, discipleship, obedience, and fellowship of the Lord's Table. Theology of martyrdom, Christian primitivism, restitution of the church, sanctification of life,… they all round up one and the same picture. That this picture is quite different from that of the state churches (in Europe) or from that of the large denominational bodies (in America) becomes evident at once. It explains also the great difficulty of mutual understanding and appreciation. It might, perhaps, bring us somewhat further in this endeavor if we apply the new typology suggested earlier in this paper, namely the distinction between creedal (theological), pietistic and existential Christianity.

SOURCE: *Church History*, XXIV (1955), pp. 132-51.

---

48 Roland H. Bainton, see above note 17.
49 MQR, XXVI (1952), 37 (in the article quoted in note 9).

THE HUTTERIAN BRETHREN

The Hutterian Brethren, also called Hutterites, were the Austrian branch of the great Anabaptist movement of the sixteenth century, characterized by the practice of community of goods, as first established in Moravia in 1529 and reestablished on more solid grounds by Jakob Hutter in 1533. In contradistinction to the other Anabaptist groups, the Hutterites had the unique chance to develop their communal life in comparatively peaceful Moravia where, due to a predominantly Slavic surrounding, they lived in relative isolation from the rest of the world. Thus a rich group life developed with a strong sense for their own history. Remarkable is also their extensive manuscript literature (devotional and historical), which made it possible that their teachings and their history, particularly of the beginnings, should become better known than those of any other group of the Anabaptist movement except the Dutch.

The 1520's saw a lively spread of Anabaptism throughout the Hapsburg territories, Tyrol, Austria, Carinthia, etc. In Tyrol in particular Anabaptism was by far the strongest trend, and remained so until far into the second half of the sixteenth century, in spite of a government which ruthlessly fought all "heretics" wherever they could be ferreted out. It was here that Georg Blaurock of Switzerland worked successfully as a missioner until his early martyrdom in 1529. Persecutions were extremely bloody. One major source, indeed, claims that prior to 1530 no less than one thousand had been executed, and that the pyres were burning all along the Inn Valley. Yet the number of Anabaptists only grew. Soon the news became known that Moravia (and in particular the manorial estate Nikolsburg of the lords of Liechtenstein) was a haven for all sectarians. Here Hubmaier could freely write and print his new ideas concerning adult baptism. In fact, one of the Liechtensteins himself accepted baptism upon faith. Also other manorial lords showed sympathy and toleration, perhaps due to the fact that this country had seen the Hussites (now called Piccards) for nearly a century, and allowed complete freedom of conscience to practically all sorts of beliefs. Naturally from now on a continuous stream of Anabaptists moved toward this "promised land," from Tyrol as well as from other Hapsburg lands, but also from South Germany, Bavaria, Württemberg, Hesse, and even from Switzerland.

In 1528 the nonresistant group, called *Stäbler* (staff–bearers), were expelled from Nikolsburg, then the center of the opposing group, the *Schwertler* (sword–bearers, the Hubmaier followers), who, however, soon died out. Compelled by the emergency situation, the need of taking care of the many indigent Brethren, they pooled all their possessions and money in the manner of the first church in Jerusalem. But this act was at first not understood as a definite step toward complete community of goods comprising both consumption and production. This development came but slowly, step by step. Jakob Wiedemann, the "one-eyed one," was the first leader; later leaders were Siegmund Schützinger, Jörg Zaunring, and Gabriel Ascherham. The groups around 1529-33 lived by no means in brotherly harmony; local quarrels over leadership and form of community–life mar these first years in Moravia. Jakob Hutter, an Anabaptist from Tyrol who had visited the Moravian brotherhoods in 1529, and who worried much about these conditions, first sent his emissary, Jörg Zaunring, but eventually decided to leave Tyrol and to try for himself to settle these disputes and rivalries, and to establish more evangelical foundations. Details of this intricate story cannot be told here, but it soon became obvious that Hutter was by far the strongest leader of all. In 1533 the evangelical (nonresistant) Anabaptists of Moravia broke up into three groups:

1. Those who accepted Jakob Hutter's leadership and (according to his organization) complete community of goods, called themselves from now on *Hutterische Brüder*. Hutter, himself a very strong prophetic and charismatic leader, had given to this group such definite foundations that it could survive and, in spite of many ups and downs, preserve its basic principles through more than four centuries.

2. The Philippites, named after Philipp Plener or Blauärmel, a Württemberger. This group left Moravia already in 1535 during the first bitter days of persecution. They returned through Austria to South Germany. On their way many were imprisoned in Passau, while others decided to stay in Upper Austria where still in the 1530's Peter Riedemann visited them and managed eventually a merger with the Hutterian Brethren. This group stressed the suffering church in particular and with it *Gelassenheit*.

3. The Gabrielites, named for Gabriel Ascherham. They, too, soon moved out of Moravia back to Silesia, Ascherham's home country. But soon they became disappointed with their leader, who tended more and more toward a vague spiritualism. Between 1542 and 1545 most of these Gabrielites returned and likewise merged with the Hutterites. The doctrinal basis for this is contained in a document inserted in Wolkan, *Geschicht–Buch*, pp. 197–200, "Der Gabrieler Vereinigung mit uns." Other groups of evangelical Anabaptists in Moravia who did not accept community of goods were given the

general name "Swiss Brethren," even though they did not come from Switzerland. Also a small group of followers of Pilgram Marpeck were found in Southern Moravia under the leadership of a son of Leopold Scharnschlager. Yet these groups later disappeared, while the Hutterian Brethren managed to maintain themselves through all the early hardships and local persecutions.

This may have been due to a large extent to a remarkable number of outstanding leaders: Ulrich Stadler from the Tyrol, Hans Amon of Bavaria, Peter Riedemann of Silesia, Peter Walpot from the Tyrol, Klaus Braidl of Hesse, not to mention the long array of other Brethren, most of whom died as martyrs or suffered long years of imprisonment. Although "expelled" from Moravia more than once upon mandates by Ferdinand (the later emperor), they somehow succeeded in finding the sympathy of the manorial lords, who quickly recognized their value as craftsmen and tillers of the soil. Many of these lords were either Protestants or at least in sympathy with the Reformation, and proud of their quasi–independence from the government in Vienna. And thus, Moravia remained the one tolerant place in this century of intolerance and suffering. In 1546 the Brethren also moved east across the border into adjacent Slovakia (then a part of Hungary) where the influence of the Hapsburgs was still weaker, and where a good many of the lords belonged to the Reformed faith.

Jacob Hutter was a leader for only two years (1533-35); he returned to Tyrol where he too eventually fell into the hands of his persecutors. In February 1536 he was martyred. Hans Amon thereupon became the *Vorsteher* or head bishop of the brotherhood, 1536-42, being a strong and inspiring leader. In this time organized missionary activities of the brethren set in, perhaps the first such in all of Europe. Missioners (*Sendboten*) were sent out to many places (knowing quite well the fate ahead of them; eighty per cent of them died a martyr's death), and those in the throes of death were comforted by epistles and visiting Brethren (e.g., the case of the 140 Falkenstein Brethren who were sent to Trieste to become galley slaves, 1539–40). One of the strongest missioners of this time was Peter Riedemann, who went more than once to Upper Austria and to Hesse. While in jail in Hesse (1540–42), he drew up that outstanding document which from now on became the very symbolic book of the brotherhood, the *Account of Our Religion* (*Rechenschaft*), 1540 (printed 1565, and again in the nineteenth and twentieth centuries). In 1542–56 he shared the leadership of the brotherhood with Leonhard Lanzenstiel or Seiler.

While elsewhere persecution intensified (Anabaptism had died out by the middle of the sixteenth century in the Hapsburg domains except Tyrol; it declined in Bavaria and other German lands), in Moravia on the contrary it now experienced a kind of flowering. This was particularly true during the reign of Emperor Maximilian II (1564–76), himself rather in sympathy with Protestantism, hence averse to any harsh measures. The Brethren speak of the "Good Period" (ca. 1554–65) and of the "Golden Period" (1565–90 or 95). Although the Jesuits had been admitted in Hapsburg territories since about 1550–60, they did not find full influence in Moravia until the end of the century. It is true that Nikolsburg had changed hands; the Dietrichsteins bought it in 1575, but even though these were more in sympathy with the Counter–Reformation, the Brethren could still persist here, too, relatively peacefully, until the coming of the Cardinal Franz von Dietrichstein in 1599, the very head of the Catholic party.

During its Golden Age, the brotherhood, now well established all over southern Moravia and Slovakia, found a particularly strong leader in Peter Walpot, a Tyrolean, who led the group in 1565–78, and whose activities added much to further consolidate the brotherhood. A number of regulations were drawn up, both for the general conduct of the brotherhood and for the different crafts or trades. The schools of the Brethren were organized on better defined grounds. Doctrinal and polemic writings (mostly anonymous) were drawn up (such as the *Great Article Book*, the *Handbüchlein*, the book called *Anschläg und Fürwenden*, etc.). A rich correspondence with missionaries all over the countries of German tongue came in and went out (carefully recorded in a *Schreibstube* or *scriptorium*); the great *Geschicht–Buch* was then begun by Caspar Braitmichel on the basis of archival material collected almost from the very beginning. In short, it was the peak of Hutterite history. It has been estimated that in Moravia and Slovakia together there existed at that time about one hundred Bruderhofs or farm colonies, with a population estimated at between 20,000 and 30,000. (Certain estimates go as high as 70,000, but that figure is most unlikely). While Anabaptism elsewhere (except for the Netherlands and Prussia) was on a sharp decline, in fact nearly disappeared as an articulated movement in the latter half of the sixteenth century, in remote Moravia and Slovakia it was almost on its way to becoming a distinct denomination (were it not that the sect–principle, i.e., brotherhood living, continued to be dominant).

Very remarkable of that time are also contacts with the antitrinitarian Polish Brethren (Socinians), who in Racov (Poland) tried to set up their "New Jerusalem," somewhat along lines which they had been studying at the Moravian Hutterite communistic colonies. Visitors and correspondence witness to this contact which, however, never became very warm due to basic differences both in doctrine and intellectual background.

Contacts with Swiss Brethren, in Switzerland and elsewhere, continued to be intensive; missioners were sent out and a good number of Anabaptists from Switzerland and South Germany joined the church in Moravia. (The bishop Ulrich Jausling, serving 1619–21, had been such a Swiss newcomer.) Of particular interest here is a long letter (almost a tract) which the *Vorsteher* Claus Braidl sent to a Swiss Brother Christian Raussenberger in 1601 defending on Biblical ground the principle of community of goods. Also with the Prussian Mennonites around Elbing and Danzig contacts were obtained around the turn of the century. Even a settlement was attempted in Elbing though without success. In the meantime the peaceful period had come to an end, and severe trials were in store.

   a. The Counter–Reformation now became the cry of the day. Whoever would not be converted to the Roman Church was to leave Moravia. Cardinal Franz von Dietrichstein gave the lead in that movement, supported by a most vigilant government in Vienna and two priests, Christoph Erhard and Christoph Andreas Fischer in southern Moravia, who supplied the Catholics with polemical material (gross slanders), and cast suspicions of all kinds. They incited the hatred of the poor peasant population all around who naturally could not compete with large–scale rational farm economics. In short the situation became precarious. Yet, until 1622, the Brethren somehow managed to come through, although on a declining scale.
   b. Turkish wars and invasions added to these internal troubles. Emperor Rudolph II asked for war contributions, and Dietrichstein was to extort them from the Brethren (at one time no less than 20,000 fl. was asked). Needless to say, the Brethren very decidedly declined, accepting all the consequences. In 1605 Turks and their Hungarian allies plundered southern Moravia and many Brethren were killed or dragged away into Turkish captivity.
   c. Eventually, the event later called the Thirty Years War, 1618–48, brought the Moravian establishments of the Brethren to a complete end. After the success of the Catholic forces at the White Mountain in 1620, all restraint was dropped; complete expulsion was ordered by Vienna. The *Geschicht–Buch* (570–71) reports that what they lost in inventory (corn, wine, cattle, linen and woolens, groceries, equipment, and furniture) amounted to about 364,000 florins not assessing any houses and grounds. And all this after only one year earlier (1621) a sum of 30,000 fl. had been taken away from the Brethren by methods of extortion and downright robbery.

With these events the brotherhood begins to show a sharp decline in activities and also in loyalty to the old principles, and even in number of members and colonies (in Slovakia there were only fifteen colonies). Although Moravia was now lost, the Brethren could still withdraw to their Slovakian colonies, and since 1621 also to their new Bruderhof in Alvinc, Transylvania (today Rumania). In spite of continued great hardships, mainly through Turkish marauders, the Brethren carried on, and visitors were amazed by their industriousness and diligence. The brotherhood was fortunate enough in getting once more a bishop of outstanding qualities in leadership and spirituality, viz., Andreas Ehrenpreis, 1639–62, the real leader already since 1630. He was born in a Moravian colony. His work was an effort to revive the brotherhood in many regards: the last mission work in Silesia (contacts with Schwenckfelders) and Danzig (the Socinians were contacted) was carried out, although with rather moderate success. A short–lived colony was established in Mannheim in 1664. Internal discipline was reestablished by strict regulations. Also a rich literature was produced. Of particular value for posterity was also the new custom of writing down all sermons (called *Lehr und Vorred*). The amount of such manuscript material is amazing; there are about 250 such *Lehren* (some quite voluminous books about most books of the New Testament, and many of the Old Testament, mainly prophets, psalms, also about many apocryphal books and pseudepigrapha), and about as many *Vorreden* (shorter sermons). The *Klein–Geschichtsbuch* (204–21) brings excerpts from these sermons. One may safely say that the Hutterian Brethren of today continue the Ehrenpreis tradition at least as much if not more than any earlier tradition (e.g., that of Jakob Hutter). Ehrenpreis' *Gemeinde–ordnung* of 1651 is still in use, and the sermons of that period are the backbone of all spiritual life of the Brethren today.

After Ehrenpreis' death more tribulations made life in community of goods more difficult until this core element of the Hutterites was partly abandoned, and a semiprivate or semicooperative form of economy was accepted (1685, 1695). The great misery of Turkish invasions with its looting (which the nonviolent Brethren could not stop in any way) impoverished the brotherhood to such an extent that they had to turn to their Dutch Mennonite "cousins" to ask for financial aid. The Great Chronicle ends with the letter which Johann Riecker, the successor of Ehrenpreis, wrote to the "Gemeinden in Holland," April 20, 1665. It is known that the *Doopsgezinde* most generously responded (*Inv. Arch. Amst.*, II, 419, a letter of thanks). Yet also this help could not prevent further troubles.

After the defeat of the Turks before Vienna (1683) and their expulsion from Hungary (1700), the Hapsburg government also gained strength in this newly conquered territory. And even though the eighteenth century is known as one of religious toleration, this was not the case for Hungary. Empress Maria Theresa (1740-80) allowed the otherwise forbidden Jesuits to exert all means to convert non-Catholics back to the Roman Church. And what torture, dungeon, and executioners could not achieve in the sixteenth century, the Jesuits achieved, at least partly, in the eighteenth, mainly in Slovakia. Their old manuscript books were confiscated (1757-63, 1782-84); children were taken away from their parents; and the more important male members were put into monasteries until they either accepted instructions and were converted, or until they died. Catholic services were established at the Bruderhofs and everyone was compelled to attend. In short, externally the Hutterite population now turned Catholic, although in secret they continued to practice their old beliefs, likewise maintaining their cooperative enterprises. From now on the nickname *Habaner* became the general name for these people.

In Transylvania the Brethren had dwindled to scarcely more than a small group of perhaps thirty or forty souls. Then Lutheran transmigrants from Carinthia to Transylvania (they arrived in 1756) came into contact with this remnant of Hutterite life, and felt immediately attracted by this form of Christian communism. They joined the brotherhood, and thus brought about a rejuvenation of and rededication to the old principles. Naturally, persecutions, mainly by Jesuits, quickly set in here too. After a number of attempts to find other places the Brethren finally decided to flee Transylvania (1767, after a stay of 146 years), across high mountain passes almost without trails, and to enter Walachia (now Rumania), where conditions looked favorable. Another Turkish War (against Russia) again brought hardships, and the great trek continued after three years. In 1770 at the Dniester River the Brethren were received by the Russian general Count Rumyantsov, who offered them an asylum on his own estate in the Ukraine (then a rather sparsely populated area). At Vishenka the Brethren finally settled down for about one generation. In 1802 the colony was transferred to Czarist crown land at Raditchev, ten miles north. It was Johannes Waldner (born in Carinthia) who was then the most outstanding *Vorsteher* of the brotherhood (1794-1824). It was he who between 1793 and 1802 wrote the second big chronicle of the Hutterites, the *Klein–Geschichtsbuch*, a work of great charm and refinement. Loserth called Waldner a genuine historian. He was also a genuine disciple of Jakob Hutter, who with all his strength opposed the threatening abandonment of the principle of community of goods, which one group under the leadership of Jakob Walter (formerly of Slovakia) carried out in 1818. This new Walter group then settled down in southern Russia (Molotschna district, under the sponsorship of the Mennonite Johann Cornies), where for about forty years it practiced private property. In 1859-60 some leaders dared to reestablish communal life as of old, and soon the new Hutterite villages began to thrive. Then in 1870 universal military conscription in Russia brought an end to all former privileges, and the Brethren saw no other way out than again to migrate—in this case to emigrate to America.

The story of this migration is too long to be retold here in detail. After a trip of inspection and scouting (1873), all the Brethren decided to come to the United States, where they chose the prairie land of South Dakota for settlement (in scenery so similar to the steppes of Russia). They arrived in 1874, 1877, and 1879, settling down in complete community of goods in three colonies near Yankton. According to these three settlements they are still today divided into the *Darius–Leut* (named after Darius Walter, their leader), *Schmiede–Leut* (after Michael Waldner, a blacksmith, their leader), and *Lehrer–Leut* (named after Jacob Wipf, called the *Lehrer*). The last group when still in Russia did not practice community of goods, but began to do so in South Dakota. Those of their members who were disinclined, however, to accept this new-old form of living and wanted to stay in private ownership, later joined the group now called Krimmer Mennonite Brethren or also the General Conference Mennonites.

The colonies soon grew again under the favorable conditions of American democracy and its freedom, until new suffering occurred during World War I. Then superpatriots could not understand the nonresistant attitude of these Anabaptists, and a number of young Hutterite conscientious objectors went through almost unbelievable hardships in federal prisons. Two young men died there on account of exposure and privations. At that point the Brethren decided to move on to Canada where exemption from military service was granted. They located in southern Alberta, and south central Manitoba. However, one colony, the original one at Bon homme, remained in South Dakota, and several new ones have been reestablished there, while others were established in north central Montana from Alberta.

Today, the brotherhood is still growing, and in general their young people stay loyal to their group. In 1954 they have close to 120 farm colonies (Bruderhofs) with almost 10,000 souls (between 50 and 150 souls per colony). Community of goods is practiced everywhere, rather strictly, and seems to result in thrift and general health, both physical and moral. By and large, the customs of old are observed, and this reminded the visitor occasionally of similar Amish attitudes. Although the young people learn English in their schools (on each Bruderhof), they speak exclusively German at home. Since the days of Ehrenpreis (seventeenth century), mission work was abandoned. At their services they read the sermons of old, and would not allow any new ones. The use of farm machinery, cars, telephone, and electric light is accepted, but otherwise they share very little in modern American civilization. They continue to copy their manuscript books by hand (in fine penmanship). By 1950, only the two Chronicles and their hymnbook have been printed, together with Riedemann's *Rechenschaft* of 1540 and Ehrenpreis' great *Sendbrief* of 1652.

The story of the new Hutterite group (Eberhard Arnold–Leut), originating in Germany in the 1920's, which joined the brotherhood around 1930, and now is settled in Paraguay, England, and recently (1954) also in New York State at Rifton (Woodcrest), cannot be told in this article.

LIST OF HUTTERITE BRUDERHOFS

1. Moravia, 1529–1622

(According to Ernst Crous, *ML*, III, 420-22. For location of the Bruderhofs see the numbers 1-85 on Hutterite Map II.)

1. Alexowitz (Alexowitz, Olkowitz)
2. Altenmarkt (Zierotin, 1545)
3. Auspitz
4. Austerlitz
5. Bergen (Pergen)
6. Bilowitz (Billowitz, Pillowitz) (1545)
7. Birnbaum
8. Bisenz (Bisentz) (Zierotin, 1545)
9. Bogesch (Bogesitz/Bogenitz)
10. Bohntitz (Bohutitz/Bochtitz–Pochtitz) (1546)
11. Boretitz/Borzetitz (Paraditz) (1545)
12. Budespitz/Butschowitz (Bucovic, Pudespitz) (1536)
13. Budkau (Budkaw)
14. Czermakowitz (Schermankowitz)
15. Damborschitz/Damborzitz (Dämberschitz) (Kaunitz, 1550)
16. Eibenschitz (Lipa)
17. Eibis
18. Frätz/Wratzow (Niary von Bedek, 1547)
19. Frischau (1581)
20. Gobschitz/Gubschitz (1545)
21. Göding (Hodonin) (Lipa, 1545)
22. Gurda/Burdau
23. Herspitz (Gerspitz)
24. Hosterlitz
25. Hrubschitz (Rupschitz) (1546)
26. Jamnitz
27. Jemeritz (Jemeritz/Jaronowitz)
28. Kanitz
29. Kobily/Kobyli (Kobelitz)
30. Kostl/Kostel (Gostal) (Zierotin)
31. Kreuz (Creutz) (Lipa, 1565)
32. Kromau (Lipa, 1540)
33. Landshut (Zierotin, 1565)

33a. Lettnitz/Letonitz (Lettonitz)
34. Lundenburg (Breclav)
35. Milotitz/Millotitz
36. Mistrin/Mistrin
37. Moskowitz (Maskowitz)
38. Muschau
39. Napagedl (Napejedl) (Zierotin, 1545)
40. Nembschitz/Klein Niemtschitz (east of Auspitz)
41. Nembschitz /Klein Niemtschitz (near Prahlitz) (1562)
42. Nemschau/Niemtschau (Neimtscha) (Kaunitz, 1560)
43. Neudorf near Lundenburg (Zierotin, 1570)
43a. Neudorf, Hungarian–Ostra district (Liechtenstein, 1570)
44. Neumühl (Liechtenstein, 1558)
45. Nikolsburg (Mikulov) (Liechtenstein, Maximilian II, Dietrichstein, 1556)
46. Nikolschitz/Nikoltschitz (Zierotin, 1570)
47. Nusslau (Nuslau) (Zierotin, 1583)
48. Paulowitz/Pawlowitz (Lipa, 1545)
49. Pausram (Zierotin, 1538)
50. Pohrlitz (Zierotin, 1581)
51. Polau/Pollau
52. Polehraditz (Bellerditz, Pellertitz) (1559)
53. Popitz/Poppitz (1537)
54. Pribitz/Przibitz (Zierotin, 1565)
55. Pruschank/Pruschanek
56. Pulgrams/Pulgram (1538)
57. Puslawitz/Bohuslawitz (Postlawitz) (1546)
58. Rackschitz/Rakschitz (Lipa, 1545)
59. Rakowitz (Räkowitz/Rakwitz) (Lipa, 1540)
60. Rampersdorf (Zierotin)
61. Rohatetz
62. Ropitz/Rossitz (Pernstein, Lipa, Zierotin)
63. Saitz (Lipa, 1540)
64. Schaidowitz/Ziadowitz (1553)
65. Schaikowitz (Schaickowitz/Ceikowitz) (1545)
66. Schäkowitz (Schäckowitz/Schakwitz) (Lipa, 1533)
67. (Klein-) Selowitz/Kl. Seelowitz
68. Skalitz (Gallitz) (1563)

69. (Klein– or Gross–) Steurowitz
69a. Stigonitz /Stignitz
70. Swatoborschitz /Swatoboritz
71. Swetlau
72. Tannowitz (Abtei Kanitz, Thurn)
73. Taykowitz/Taikowitz
74. Tracht (1558)
75. Tscheitsch/Ceitsch (Schenkhof)
76. TurnitzlDurdenitz
77. Urschitz/Uhrzitz (Kaunitz)
78. Voit (e)lsbrunn (1557)
79. Watzenowitz (Wacenowitz) (Zierotin)
79a. Weisstätten
80. Welka–Hulka (Zierotin, um 1560)
81. Wernslitz (Wemslitz/Weimis(ss)litz)
82. Wessely (1546)
83. Wischenau
84. Wisternitz
85. Wostitz (Thurn, 1567)

2. Slovakia, 1545–1762

(According to Ernst Crous, *ML*, III, 423. For location of the Bruderhofs see the numbers I–XIV on Hutterite Map III.)

I. Broczko (Protzka; Neutra) (1547)
II. Dejte (Dechtitz; Oberneutra)
III. Dobravoda (Gutenwasser, Oberneutra)
IV. Egbell (Neutra)
V. Farkashida (Farkenschin; Pressburg) (1622)
VI. Holics (Holitsch; Neutra)
VII. Kosolna (Kesselsdorf; Pressburg)
VIII. Kuty (Glätte; Neutra) (1550)
IX. Lévàrd Velky–Levary (Gross–Schützen, Lewär; Pressburg) (1588)
X. Pobudin (Popadin, Popodin; Neutra) (Bakisch de Lák)
XI. Rovenszko (Rabenska; Neutra) (1622)
XII. Soblaho (Soblahov, Zobelhof; Trentschin) (Illésházi, 1622)
XIII. Sobotiste (Freischütz, Sabatisch; Neutra) (1546)
XIV. Unter–Nussdorf (Deutsch–Nussdorf; Pressburg) (1548)

3. Moravia, by manorial estates, 1619–22

(According to Fr. Hruby, *Die Wiedertäufer in Mähren*, Leipzig, 1935).

1. *Lundenburg–Billowitz*: Lundenberg, Altenmarkt, Gostal (Ober- and Niederhaus), Pillowitz, Rampersdorf
2. *Seelowitz*: Eibes (auch Meubes), Nikolschitz, Nusslau, Pausraum, Pribitz, Poherlitz
3. *Austerlitz*: Austerlitz and Gerspitz
4. *Nikolsburg*: Nikolsburg and Tracht
5. *Steinitz*: Dämberschitz
6. *Kanitz*: Klein–Niemtschitz (Ober– and Unterhaus)
7. *Landshut*: Landshut
8. *Lettonitz*: Lettnitz
9. *Skalitz*: Gallitz
10. *Wischenau*: Wischnau and Stignitz
11. *Tscheikowitz*: Schläkowitz (Schaikowitz) and Prutschan
12. *Bochtitz*: Pochtitz
13. *Frischau*: Frischau
14. *Göding*: Göding and Koblitz
15. *Mähr. Kromau*: Maskowitz and Oleckowitz
16. *Milotitz*: Wäzenobis
17. *Uhritz*: Urschitz
18. *Wesseli*: Wessela
19. *Ziadowitz*: Schädewitz
20. *Ungarisch–Ostra*: Neudorf
21. *Eisgrub*: Neumühl
22. *Ober-Tannowitz*: Tannewitz
23. *Tulleschitz*: Schermankowitz
24. *Wostitz*: (Wostite), Weisstätten
25. *Polehraditz*: Pellertitz
26. *Tawikowitz*: Teikowitz

4. Transylvania

1. Alvinc, 1621–1767
2. Kreuz, 1761–67
3. Stein, 1761–67

5. Ukraine

1. Vishenka (1770–1802)
2. Raditchev (1802–42)
3. Hutterthal (1842–57)
4. Hutterdorf (2) (1859–74)
5. Johannisruh (1864–77)
6. Sheromet (1868–74)
7. Neu-Hutterthal or Dabritcha (1866–75)

6. Germany
Rhönbruderhof (1920–37)

7. Liechtenstein
Almbruderhof (1934–38)

8. England
Cotswold (1936–40)
Wheathill (1942–)

The first exhaustive list of Hutterite Bruderhofs in Europe with locations (concerning Moravia and Slovakia, however) is that prepared by E. Crous and published in 1953 in connection with the article *Rabenska* in the *Mennonitisches Lexikon* (Installment 39, pp. 418–23) where two maps are also given, prepared by Dr. Herhard Wöhlke of the Geographical Institute of Göttingen on the basis of the Austrian Spezialkarte 1:75,000, published 1869–88 by the K. K. Militärgeographisches Institut. The Crous lists are here reproduced, but new maps have been prepared by Dr. Robert Friedmann, two of which are based on the *Mennonitisches Lexikon* maps. The first two lists contain all known Bruderhofs of the sixteenth and seventeenth centuries, without indication as to the date of dissolution. They therefore do not reveal how many were in existence at any one time, although most were in existence in the "Golden Age," ca. 1590. The only such list is the third one which names the Bruderhofs in existence in Moravia, 1619–22, 1622 being the date when all were expelled from the country.

J. Loserth published the first list of Bruderhofs in his *Communismus* (1894) p. 246. This list he published in *Mennonitisches Lexikon* (1931) "Haushaben," slightly revised, where eighty-eight locations are named. Fr. Hruby published a list of forty-three Bruderhofs in existence in Moravia in 1619–22, in his *Wiedertäufer in Mähren* (Leipzig, 1935), which is reproduced as list no. 3 above. He reports that a considerable number of Bruderhofs were destroyed in 1605. According to Hruby most of the Bruderhofs were in Czech nationality areas; only nine of the forty–three listed Bruderhofs were in German nationality areas.

Zieglschmid's list of North American Bruderhofs (*Klein– Geschichtsbuch*, 677–80) contains only sixty–four, although it was not quite exhaustive. He reports (p. 471) the growth in numbers as follows: 1878 (3), 1900 (10), 1915 (17), 1926 (29), 1944 (57), 1947 (64). Before 1918 all American Bruderhofs were in South Dakota. The first Canadian Bruderhofs were established in Manitoba and Alberta in 1918, when a mass migration occurred. Zieglschmid (p. 472 f.) gives a genealogical chart of the origin of the North American Bruderhofs of the Schmiede–Leut and Darius–Leut in existence in 1947.

SOURCE: *Mennonite Encyclopedia*, II, pp. 854–65.

Map I.

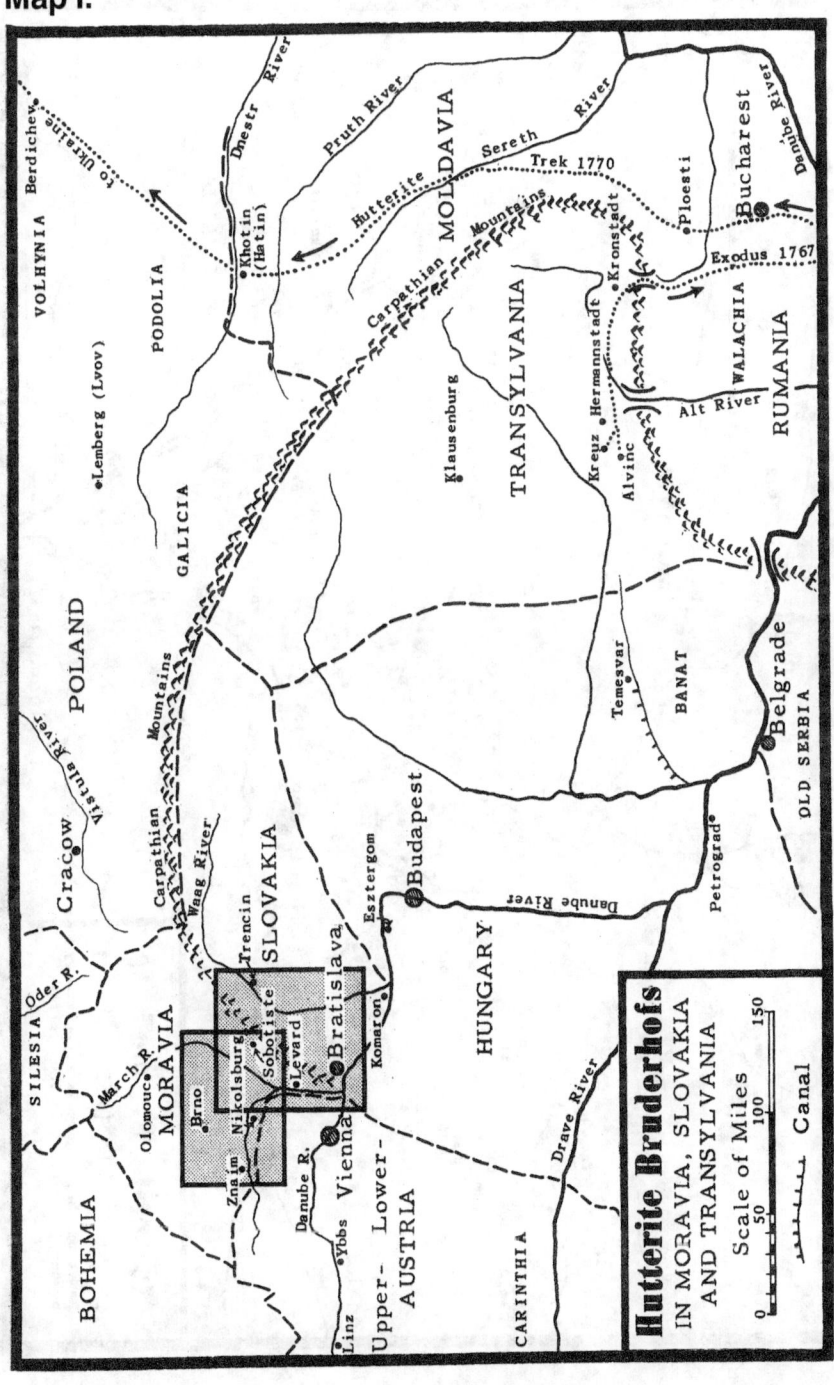

Map II.

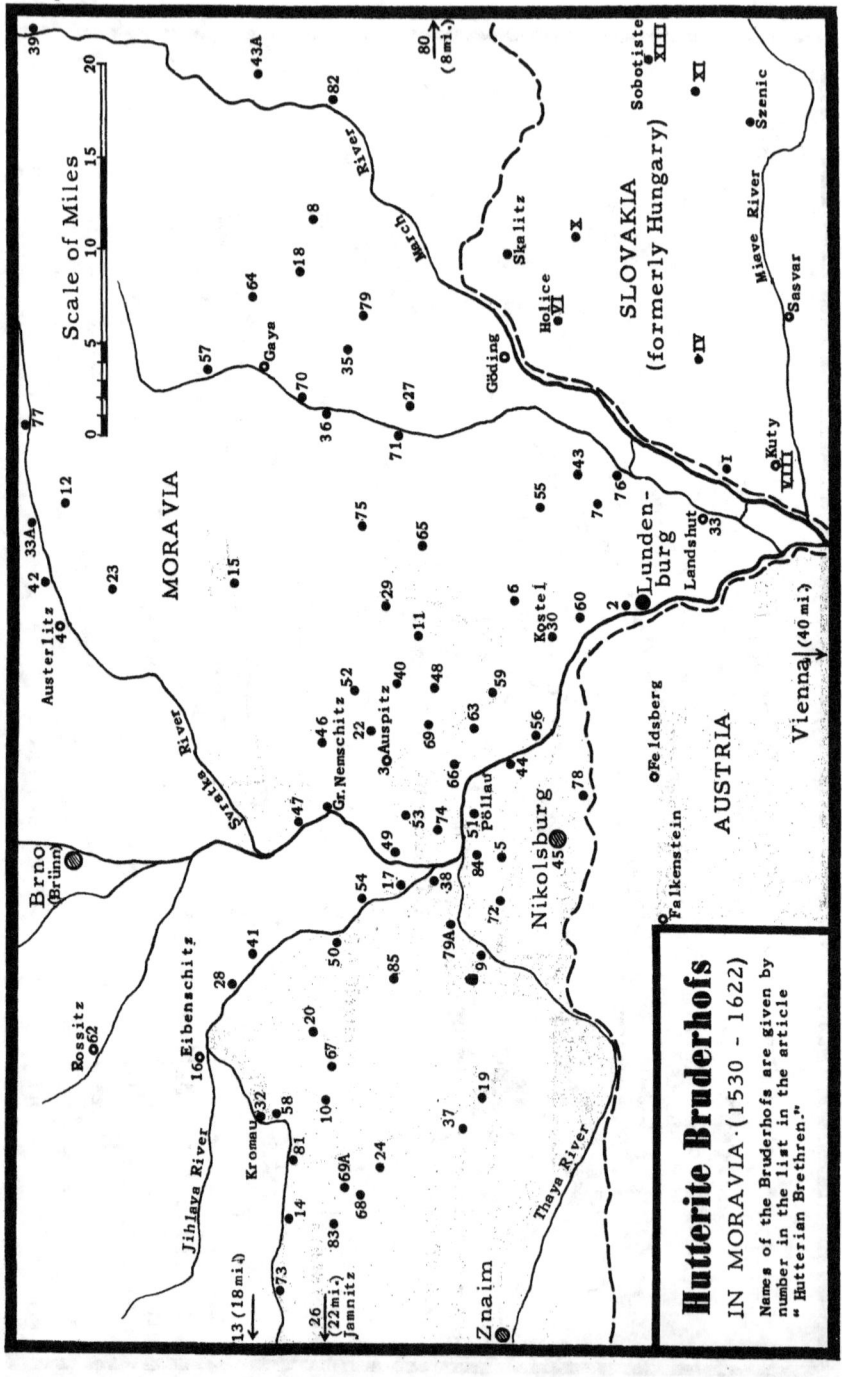

Map III.

Map IV.

ANABAPTISM IN MORAVIA

Moravia, in the sixteenth century often called "the Promised Land" of the Anabaptists, was during the Middle Ages a margravure and part of the Kingdom of Bohemia. As such it experienced also the rise and spread of Hussitism in the fifteenth century. When this pre–Protestant movement settled down to become a quiet sectarian church, several names appeared for it, such as Bohemian Brethren and Picards (a nickname erroneously derived from Beghards). Under this last name the movement was widely spread also in Moravia during the sixteenth century, to be sure among the Czech–speaking population only and with practically no contact with the German–speaking people of that land.

In 1526 the last king of Bohemia (and incidentally also king of Hungary) fell in a battle against the Turks, and Archduke Ferdinand of Hapsburg, his brother–in–law and later emperor, became King of Bohemia and of (a small part of) Hungary. Being a staunch Catholic he naturally tried to make Bohemia and Moravia thoroughly Catholic, an endeavor in which, however, all the Hapsburgs failed up to 1620. The provincial estates (*Landstände*) were exceedingly jealous of their local autonomy and resented all aggressive interference from the government in Vienna, Austria. They elected (and the Hapsburgs approved) a governor (*Landeshauptmann*) from their midst as head of the provincial (thoroughly feudal) government and also as their spokesman in Vienna at the Hapsburg court. On the other hand King Ferdinand was never certain whether his orders to this governor were actually carried out or not; thus he often sent his orders instead to the Bishop of Olmütz (Olomouc), the ecclesiastical ruler of Moravia. Moravia had three "royal" cities: Olmütz, Brno, and Znaim (Znojmo); provincial diets were held alternately in these three cities, with proceedings in the Czech language. Until 1636 Olmütz was the capital of Moravia; after that year Brno became the capital. There were many smaller cities, too, such as Nikolsburg or Austerlitz, but they had the character of centers of large manorial estates rather than the cities in the modern sense. Here the lords could act more or less as they pleased.

It was these lords (some of them Protestants) who practiced such a degree of religious toleration that this country rightly stands out in the sixteenth century as a unique area of refuge for those fleeing religious persecution. Perhaps only Poland could compete with it to any extent; the rest of Europe knew nothing but persecution of those who did not conform. Franticek Hruby discusses at great length the roots of this liberal attitude. He is certain that it was by no means derived from economic motives only (sectarians being usually good and reliable workers); perhaps the Hussite–Picard tradition of more than half a century had something to do with it, and likewise the old feudal pride in independence. In short, not only Anabaptists of all shades but many other "left–wing" groups of the age of the Reformation found a welcome refuge in Moravia for shorter or longer periods. As far as the records go, there was only one execution for reasons of nonconformity in Moravia, namely, the burning at the stake of the Anabaptist brother Thoman Waldhauser in Brno in 1528. But at that time Brno had a city government and was rather cool to manorial or feudal tradition.

Perhaps the earliest report on sectarian activities is found in a printed book of 1526 by Oswald Glaidt, which records a religious debate in Austerlitz in March 1526, sponsored by a nobleman John Dubchansky, who wanted to achieve a sort of unification of all non–Catholics (Utraquists, Lutherans, and independent groups, one of them called Habrovans). Oswald Glaidt, the recorder, was at that time not yet an Anabaptist. A few weeks after this debate, Balthasar Hubmaier, since May 1525 an Anabaptist preacher, arrived in Nikolsburg upon the express invitation of the nobleman Johann von Liechtenstein, lord of Nikolsburg and himself a sympathizer with Hubmaier's views. Most likely Liechtenstein was later baptized by his illustrious guest. From that time on Anabaptism found a foothold in Moravia. Glaidt also went to Nikolsburg, as did Hans Hut, Ambrosius Spittelmaier, Jacob Wiedemann, and many more. Soon Anabaptism experienced its first split: Hubmaier and Spittelmaier defended the use of the sword (*Schwertler*), while Hut, Glaidt, and Wiedemann opposed it, hence were derisively called *Stäbler* (staff–bearers). As persecutions intensified elsewhere, a stream of refugees now poured into Moravia, coming from Tyrol and other Hapsburg areas, as well as from South Germany, Bavaria, Württemberg, etc. In the 1530's three main groups are observed: Hutterian Brethren (destined to survive all the vicissitudes of history), Gabrielites, who first left for Silesia but around 1545 joined the Hutterites, and Philippites, some of whom likewise joined the first–named group, while others returned to Germany, when for a few years even Moravia attempted to expel its Anabaptists. Besides these three main groups there were also "Swiss" Brethren, i.e., Anabaptists who did not practice community of goods. Whether they were actually Swiss is not known, but it is certain that small groups of them existed as late as 1591 and even 1618. There were also the Pilgramites, apparently the followers of Pilgram Marpeck. Leopold Scharnschlager was for a while their leader (in the 1530's). But the number of independent groups other than Anabaptists was far greater.

Anabaptism in Moravia

Several published lists and other reports show that at certain places such as Austerlitz, there existed at least thirteen or fourteen sectarian (non–Catholic) groups. The earliest list, of 1556, enumerates twenty such sects. DeWind published several such lists (of 1567 and later) which name, besides Picards, Lutherans, and Calvinists, various Anabaptist groups (one called Austerlitzer Brüder), then "Arians, Samosatenes, and Sabbatarians," apparently all three names for the antitrinitarian Socinians, all of whom were immigrant Italians), then Adamites and similar marginal groups, practically all of them (except the Socinians) German–speaking people now living in Czech surroundings. DeWind also names some of the more outstanding manorial lords who made the opportunities for these groups available. Besides the lord of Nikolsburg (Liechtenstein), there was the lord of Austerlitz, Ulrich von Kaunitz, who was perhaps the most broad–minded of all (Austerlitz was said to have been at times a "Babel"), then Johann von Lipa, the lord of Kromau and Schäkovitz (incidentally the man who also offered a safe refuge in 1537 to Paracelsus, the famous physician of that day), Heinrich von Lomnitz, lord of Jamnitz, who is said to have ransomed Anabaptist Brethren from the dungeon of Passau and, strangely enough, also the Abbess of Maria–Saal near Brno, the mistress of Auspitz, another well–known center of Anabaptism. Apparently she needed reliable tillers of the soil and skilled craftsmen more than anything else. Somewhat later the lords of Seelovitz, the Zierotin family, became outstanding as protectors of the Hutterian Brethren and broad–minded lords. Three of these Zierotins, Friedrich (d. 1598), Karl, and Ladislaus Velen (1619–21), were also governors of Moravia and exerted a beneficent influence on behalf of the Anabaptists.

Only twice did it happen that King Ferdinand had his way and the lords had to yield; viz., 1535–36 and 1547–51. These were hard times for the Anabaptists (and most likely also for other "left–wing" groups). In 1535 Ferdinand came for the first time personally to a provincial diet, and prevailed upon the reluctant lords to expel all "heretics." It was then that the Philippites left Moravia for good (except a few remnants), and that Jakob Hutter addressed his famous letter to the governor Johan Kuna von Kunstadt, to be sure without success. The Brethren had no choice and began wandering hither and thither. Fortunately, the stern measures did not last for very long, and in 1537 new Bruderhofs could be established again on various estates. In 1546 Ferdinand came again to Moravia. Things looked favorable for the Hapsburgs; the Turks had been defeated (at least for the moment) and Ferdinand's brother, Emperor Charles V, held the Protestants in check in the Schmalkaldian War. Now the danger for the Brethren was even more serious than a decade earlier. They began new settlements in near–by Slovakia, then belonging to Hungary, where the Hapsburgs had not yet gained much influence. But even here the situation became somewhat critical in 1548–53. Thus the brotherhoods shuttled back and forth between Moravia, Lower

Austria, and Slovakia. Nowhere did they find a place of rest. It may have been in these dark years that they began to dig out the underground tunnels found all over that area and called in Czech *Lochy*, i.e., *Löcher*, meaning holes. They are pathetic witnesses of persecution. The Hutterites, however, tried again to write to the governor (Wenzel von Ludanitz) in 1545, with no success, as could have been expected.

But the political scene changed again; the Turks threatened again from Hungary, and Charles V was defeated by the Schmalkaldians. Thus, around 1551–52 peace came for the Brethren, making it possible for them to develop permanent settlements (Bruderhofs). From 1551 until about 1600 the peace was but very little disturbed. The Hutterian Brethren called this period the "Golden Era." Their number multiplied now by leaps and bounds, mainly because of newcomers from many countries (Germany, Switzerland, Austria, etc.); their activities were so successful that the jealousy of the surrounding population was aroused. Jesuits arrived in Nikolsburg in the 1570's, but neither they nor other priests (Erhard or Fischer) could do much harm to the brotherhood which was so powerfully protected by the nobles.

The Hutterites were, however, not the only Anabaptists in Moravia, although they are the only ones of whom there is a continuous record. It is known that until the end of the sixteenth century Swiss Brethren also lived in Moravia (though in small numbers) and Pilgramites, the Marpeck group. As for the Swiss Brethren (besides what Beck had to say; see above) a remarkable event is known through a Dutch booklet, *Het Brilleken* of 1630, which tells of the visit of "Greek Brethren" from Thessalonica to these Brethren in Moravia around 1550, and also of the flight of one of these Swiss Brethren (who later tells this story) around 1620. As for the Pilgramites, one of their most precious possessions, Marpeck's *Verantwortung* (1542), was copied in Moravia (now preserved in the library in Olmütz). This manuscript contains a letter of 1571 by a certain Wernhard Riepl of Klein–Teschau, Moravia, concerning certain theological arguments among these brethren, referring back to a tract by Leopold Scharnschlager. This is apparently the latest reference available for the existence of the Marpeck group in Moravia and elsewhere.

One of the "administrative" centers of the Hutterites between 1565 and 1620 was the Bruderhof at Neumühl, ten miles east of Nikolsburg, which became the residence of four successive head bishops or *Vorsteher*, viz., Peter Walpot, Hans Kral, Klaus Braidl, and Sebastian Dietrich. It was here that the Great Chronicle was written, where all the outgoing and incoming correspondence was handled and filed away, where some of the famous codices (*Epistel–* and *Artikel–Büchlein*) were written, and where the important community regulations (*Gemeindeordnungen*) were formulated. It was also here that Polish antitrinitarian visitors were entertained. All practical and doctrinal decisions of the second half of the sixteenth century seem to have originated at this place.

Unfortunate conditions brought this flowering to a bitter end. A Turkish–Hungarian war brought the invasion of undisciplined hordes, who inflicted severe tribulations upon the brotherhood: murder, rape, torture, arson, carrying away of women and children, war in its worst aspect, coming upon people who were nonresistant and therefore helpless in the face of such dangers. Three hymns in the Hutterite hymnal tell of those terrible years (the "Botschkai Lieder"). The detailed story is also told in their chronicles. In addition to all this tribulation came intensified demands from the Emperor Rudolph II (residing in Prague) for money (actually war loans), which the Brethren emphatically refused to give, thus provoking renewed threats. And then the Catholic Counter–Reformation came into full swing in the formerly liberal margravure of Moravia. The number of Bruderhofs declined but they still were strong spiritually and in organization.

Then, once again, it appeared that good fortune would make it possible for the Brethren to continue their work, internally by building up their brotherhood, externally by sending out missioners to the farthest corners of the German–speaking territories (such as East Prussia). When in the Bohemian Rebellion of 1618–19 the Hapsburgs lost their old kingdom, and Frederick, the prince–elector of the Palatinate, became the ruler (later called the "Winter–King," 1619–20), things looked somewhat hopeful again. Frederick himself was a Calvinist, but for the moment he was definitely graciously inclined toward all sectarians. When he came to visit Moravia he also stopped at some Hutterite colonies (such as Kromau), where he was given presents, and promised his royal protection (Hruby). This did not last longer than one winter, however. In 1620 Frederick lost the battle at the White Mountain (near Prague) and had to flee; with it the fate of the Protestants (and Anabaptists) in the Hapsburg lands was sealed. Emperor Ferdinand II, supported by Cardinal Franz von Dietrichstein, now insisted upon total expulsion of all non–Catholics. No lord could any longer protect the Hutterian Brethren, who thus suffered both from the unrestrained military hordes (e.g., Dampierre's cavalry), and the ruthless orders of the authorities. The severity of this suffering through war can still be felt in reading the moving three "Pribitz hymns" of 1620–22. Lives were lost and goods destroyed or confiscated. And then one *Vorsteher*, Hirzel, betrayed a number of hiding places of their savings, thus leaving the Brethren nearly penniless.

After 1622 no Anabaptist could remain in Moravia any longer. A few lords tried still to employ some single individuals on their estates, but as the Thirty Years' War progressed these also had to be sent away. Slovakia promised, at least for a while, safe refuge. As for the non–Hutterites, there is no knowledge at all concerning their fate.

And yet the crafts of the Brethren even after that tragic war continued to attract the interest of Moravian nobles. As Hruby proved, the famous Habaner ceramics were found throughout the seventeenth century in the inventories of Moravian castles and manor houses. The same is true regarding the Hutterite cutlery (knives) and their beautifully worked clocks, to be found on many a tower. But otherwise Moravia like Bohemia had been thoroughly reconverted to Catholicism. The old feudal independence faded away and the great period of Moravian history was over.

SOURCE: *Mennonite Encyclopedia*, III, pp. 747–50.

ANABAPTISM IN TRANSDANUBIA

Transdanubia is an old name for the western–most part of the former kingdom of Hungary, roughly the *comitat* of Sopron–Ödenburg, today in the main the Austrian province of Burgenland. It has long been known that Anabaptists existed here in the sixteenth and seventeenth centuries. Since, however, the Hutterite Chronicle mentions this area but slightly, and pertinent research has been carried out exclusively in the Magyar language, Western scholars have much neglected this entire area. The country was settled primarily by German frontiersmen (history speaks of the *Militärgrenze*, i.e., a strip of land on the Turkish border where every farmhouse was at the same time a small fortress). Because of the Turkish invasion of Balkan countries, many Croatian peasants sought refuge here too. Popularly they were known as Krovoten or Krabaten. Finally, here as elsewhere, the greater part of the land was in the hands of Hungarian manorial lords, and of them is known that they were rather friendly toward the Anabaptists because of their good craftsmanship and husbandry. Thus, it is no small wonder that the archives of these noble families contain many references to Anabaptist craftsmen (mainly potters and barber–surgeons).

Alexander Payr in his book, *Protestant Church History of Ödenburg* (in the Magyar language), claims that city records mention Anabaptist craftsmen on and off from 1547 to 1635. Of course it could be argued that these men were but "loaned out" single brethren from Slovakia who went to work elsewhere, without however establishing Anabaptist colonies. But at least in one instance this seems to be contradicted by a message in the Hutterite Chronicle itself which, for the year 1632, records the death of one brother Lorenz Putz, "Diener des Wortes," at Gissingen, who had served the congregation beyond the Danube in "Krabatenland" for about one year. Gissingen is to be identified as today's Güssing in Burgenland; a brotherhood settlement must have existed there for some time. Incidentally, the name Putz is well known for the continued craftsmanship of the family in the field of ceramics.

Local research has also proved the existence of Anabaptists in the small town of Güns in the same general area around 1660. Noteworthy is also a remark by the late Professor Loesche (1926) that the Lutheran minister of the city of Schlanning, Burgenland, once found in the hands of playing children an old Anabaptist codex of 1612, incomplete and poorly preserved, which contained eleven Anabaptist hymns and several medical recipes. The book is definitely of Hutterite origin and points again to a former presence of these Brethren in Transdanubia. A Hungarian scholar informed this writer that at least three places mentioned in the Hutterite Chronicle were erroneously identified by scholars as Moravian or Slovakian, in reality being Transdanubian villages, thus indicating the existence of Bruderhofs in this area. The names are Freischütz, Kreutz, and Gätta; documentation will be given in forthcoming publications. Most important of all, however, the same expert claims that many of the beautiful ceramic tablewares for the nobles (now in museums) were produced in potteries in Transdanubia, as can be gathered from inscriptions on these pieces.

All this seems to indicate that Anabaptists (obviously of the Hutterite variety) were more widely spread in Eastern Europe than was formerly known, mainly in the century 1550–1650. No doubt both pottery and archive records will yield still more information as research in this area proceeds and becomes better known.

SOURCE: *Mennonite Encyclopedia*, IV, p. 1130.

SOBOTISTE

Sobotiste (German, *Freischütz*; in Hutterite sources *Sabatisch*), is a town in Slovakia near the Moravian border, the site of a large Hutterite Bruderhof which is still inhabited by descendants of the Hutterites, the only Bruderhof which continued in existence throughout the entire period of Hutterite history in Central Europe (1546–1762). In the sixteenth century this market village belonged to the manorial nobleman Franz Niary of Bedek, lord of the castle of Branc. Since he needed good tillers of the soil and tenders of the vineyards he invited the Hutterites from nearby Moravia to settle on his estate in 1546. Soon times of great hardship set in, but in 1554–1605 the peace was not disturbed. Then followed a Turkish invasion, and it was not until 1613 that the Brethren began anew to build a Bruderhof. From then on until today this Bruderhof has existed nearly unchanged. All the *Vorsteher* or "bishops" of the Hutterite brotherhood lived here, including particularly Andreas Ehrenpreis. The lords gave the Brethren a charter of privileges (*Hausbrief*) in 1613 and another in 1640; the latter is still in the possession of the Hof and was reported in 1937 and 1938. In 1621, Franz Walter started an exodus of some 180 Brethren from here to Transylvania. The best time was the Ehrenpreis period, 1630–62, which might be called the high point of the Sobotiste congregation.

In 1665 a marked decline set in. A delegation was sent to the Mennonites in the Netherlands for material help, but even though this was granted it could not stop the rapid deterioration of the Sobotiste group, both economically and spiritually. Eventually the practice of complete community of goods was given up, although many elements of it still remained. The eighteenth century saw the coming of the Jesuits and with it a real crisis set in. The brotherhood was no longer strong enough to resist the aggressive manipulations of both the Jesuits and the governmental authorities. The last *Vorsteher* was Zacharias Walther, a descendant of the oldest still living Anabaptist family. In his days the congregation numbered about 220 souls, and in 1753 they built a clock tower and in 1754 a "Bet–Haus" (i.e., a meetinghouse; picture in Lydia Müller). Beck found records of these years showing that Hutterite, or more correctly now Habaner, midwives were very popular and much in demand with the local population. In 1748 and again in 1752, Walther wrote to the

Mennonites in Amsterdam, apparently hoping again to receive both material and moral support in the hard struggle of the time. (All the correspondence both of 1665 and of 1748 and 1752 is found in the archives of the Mennonite Church of Amsterdam.) But in 1761 the Jesuits decided to act: a number of Brethren were taken into custody, including Zacharias Walther, who was sent into a monastery in Budapest where eventually he yielded and became Catholic in 1763, Heinrich Kuhn who turned Catholic in 1762, and Tobias Pullman (or Polman) who did the same in 1763 in the city of Neutra.

These conversions, however, were of little value. Privately these Sobotiste people continued in their old Hutterite faith as far as possible (infant baptism was obligatory now), and thus, much hypocrisy developed. The Brethren knew of course of the new settlements in the Ukraine which had been started by the Transylvanian group, and there was much discussion about whether or not to leave everything behind and try to join these Brethren. One of the strongest in character among the men of Sobotiste was a Jakob Walter, of whom the *Klein-Geschichtsbuch* relates an interesting story. In 1782 he left Sobotiste alone, and traveled via Herrnhut (the German center of the Moravian Brethren Church) to Vishenka (Wischenka), Ukraine, where the new Bruderhof had been started about 1770. The next year he came back in order to take his wife and child along to these Brethren; one daughter had to be left behind as she had married a Catholic. With the help of several other Brethren who were sent back from Russia to assist Sobotiste, eleven families managed to escape the surveillance of the clergy, and some fifty-six souls eventually reached the new Ukraine Bruderhof, 1782-83. The last visit of these Vishenka brethren in Sobotiste occurred in 1795, but after 1782 no further transfers took place. Those who decided to stay in Sobotiste were resigned in their new religion (Catholicism), glad that the clergy allowed them at least to continue most of their old communal institutions.

In 1937 two American Hutterite brethren visited this place, and from the unpublished diary of David Hofer we learn the following details. The Bruderhof buildings had survived essentially unchanged since 1613, consisting all in all of thirty-nine straw-thatched houses, dominated in the distance by the ruins of the former castle of Branc. Some of the names of the inhabitants were Baumgartner, Pullmann, and Tschetterle (Ceterle, Tschetter), all well-known Hutterite names. All in all, there were some forty families who still lived in this large-scale Hof or colony. All of them spoke German besides the native Slovakian. In 1937 the mill, the dye house, the inn, the wine cellars, and the woods were still held as communal property by the present-day Habaner. The mill, erected in 1739, was still working. The Chapel was still standing, but the clock and bells had been removed from the old clock tower during World War I. In the Town Hall the visitors found an old clock of their forefathers. In the cemetery most tombstones had disappeared except one of 1755, for Tobias Seidel. The once famous pottery workshop no longer existed, but some people had started digging and had found in the ground potsherds and a few fine specimens of this lost art. (Most of the Habaner fayence that has survived is found in museums in Bratislava, Budapest, and elsewhere.) In the houses and in the Town Hall the visitors found ancient heavy oak tables of Hutterite origin and other household goods, even old books. The charter of 1640 (*Hausbrief*) was likewise shown to the guests from America, who were received with warm hospitality by these Catholic Habaner. But, naturally, they showed little interest in their own history and the tradition of a time long gone by. Nothing of the old things described was for sale, hard as the American Brethren tried to buy a few souvenirs.

In 1945 in the wave of anti–German feeling following the war, most of the German–speaking people were expelled from Czechoslovakia, and it must be assumed that this fate also hit most of the Habaner of Sobotiste, unless they declared themselves openly as Slovaks.

SOURCE: *Mennonite Encyclopedia*, IV, pp. 557–58.

THE HABANER

"Habaner" was originally a nickname for the Hutterites in Slovakia, used by the Slovakian peasants; later it became the general name for those Hutterites who, after about 1760, turned Catholic and, as such, were permitted to continue to live in their existing Bruderhofs on a semi-community or cooperative principle. These Habaners are still living in a few villages of western Slovakia today; in 1925 the older people were still speaking German. Today they have become almost completely Slavicized, and their old traditions, customs, and skills are nearly gone, although remnants of their former community organization still exist. The name "Habaner" has been differently explained: as deriving from "Haben," a section of Velky-Levary (the former Gross-Schützen), or from "Haushaben" (another term for Bruderhof), which the neighbors abbreviated into Haben. The latter interpretation would correspond to the usage of neighbors in America who call the Hutterites "the colony people."

History

The violent conversion of the Brethren by the strengthened absolutistic government under Maria Theresa (1740–80) and the greater Jesuit missionary activity then permitted in Hungary is graphically described in the Hutterite *Klein-Geschichtsbuch* (pp. 230–39). Around 1700 their former community of goods was widely abandoned, yet the Bruderhof organization still remained under a central leadership, with communal bakeshop, blacksmith shop, slaughterhouse, school, and common pastures and ponds. After 1726, infants were generally, although not always, baptized. The last active *Vorsteher* of the brotherhood was one Zacharias Walter, 1746–61, but eventually he could no longer stand the brutalities of his persecutors, and turned Catholic. The next *Vorsteher*, Heinrich Müller, died steadfast in a monastery 1762. After 1757–58 all Anabaptist books were confiscated by Jesuits and later sent to Bratislava, Esztergom, and even Budapest. In 1769 the entire population of the Bruderhofs in Sobotiste, Velky-Levary, St. Johann, and Trenchin were compelled to attend Catholic services. The methods used were rather brutal: children were taken away from their parents and put into Catholic orphanages, and the men were dragged into monasteries until they accepted the Catholic faith. In the 1780's (time of Joseph II) a second wave of book confiscation set in. Recent reports, however, show that, never-the-less, a good number of their precious handwritten books were kept and hidden. In the 1890's, when an old house was torn down, books were found behind the plaster of the walls. It was not until 1863 that all fields were completely parceled out into individual lots. But, even in 1925, they had something like a community chest and a few other cooperative activities on their Hofs.

Many Brethren tried to emigrate to the Ukraine (Little Russia), where those Brethren who had lived in Transylvania had found a new refuge. But this was more difficult than anticipated, with the authorities being extremely vigilant and permitting no emigration whatever. Strangely enough, Emperor Joseph II (1780–90), generally known as an "enlightened" ruler, who issued the famous Toleration Edict of 1781, and who in 1782 had a long conversation with a group of petitioning Brethren, still refused to give the Brethren freedom of worship, and demanded that they stay in their new Catholic faith. During the 1780's the Brethren in the Ukraine five times sent missionary teams to Slovakia to induce emigration, but in spite of the desire of nearly all Habaners to return to their former faith, the results were rather poor. The *Klein–Geschichtsbuch* (p. 374) lists a total of eleven families with fifty–six souls who actually managed to reach the Ukrainian Bruderhofs. Among them was also one Jacob Walter, of probably the oldest Hutterite family in existence (since the 1590's). After the promulgation of the Toleration Edict in 1781, many Habaners declared themselves no longer willing to go to a Catholic church, but their resistance soon broke down. In 1793 another team arrived from Russia, but it failed completely in its purpose. One hundred years later the Brethren now in America again invited the late descendants of these Brethren in Slovakia to come over and begin anew a life in the brotherhood. One Ignatz Pullman came in 1892, bringing a number of rare codices and books along (no longer of value to him) but soon left again. Today the Habaners have almost completely lost knowledge of their own earlier history as Hutterites. Occasional visitors (Dutch Mennonites in 1910, Hutterites from America in 1936, also a few interested scholars like Beck and others) told them their own history, yet hardly awakened any reaction to it.

Description of the Habanerhofs

Today there exist only two such Hofs in Slovakia, namely, in Sobotiste and in Velky–Levary. They represent closed settlements with handsome white–washed, one–story houses (built of sun–baked clay brick), arranged in a square around a central courtyard, very clean and so solidly built that most of these houses still stand as they were built soon after 1621. Remarkable are their high thatch roofs which are almost fireproof because the straw on the inside of the roof was worked through and covered with clay so that no straw is visible at all (a good protection also against heat and cold, and even dirt). At the ground level are found all those rooms which once served brotherhood activities such as worship, eating, cooking, children's and sick rooms. The floor of this level is of stamped clay covered with yellow sand—a practice which the Brethren also continued even in their American houses the first half of the 20th century. The attics have two stories with the bedrooms, called *Oertl* or *Stuben*. Besides the square, around the courtyard there are other buildings such as the mill, the forge, butcher shops, and in Sobotiste also a remarkable clock tower.

Famous were the crafts of the Habaners. Still today one house in Velky–Levary shows the tiled sign of a potter's "firm," J.H. 1781, which stands for Joseph Hörndl, the *Krüglmacher*, a man known for his stubborn allegiance to the old faith, who wrote to the Ukraine for help. Their ceramics, called "Habaner–fayence," were of the highest quality and still are the pride of museums.

Today this craft is no longer practiced. Their other outstanding craft was the making of fine steel knives; it, too, is dead today. Only minor crafts such as shoe making, tanning, etc., have survived and found a good market both in Slovakia, and before 1918 in Lower Austria.

The most remarkable fact is that in spite of re-Catholization and de-Germanization, a skeleton organization still has survived to this day. In 1936, when two Hutterite elders from Canada visited these places, they were warmly received, shown around, and even some faint memories of old stories came to the surface. In fact, in one chest some old books were still discovered, and a few of them were even taken to America.

SOURCE: *Mennonite Encyclopedia*, II, pp. 618–19.

HUTTERITE MISSION WORK AND MISSIONERS

While it is characteristic of Anabaptism in general that its very existence is preconditioned by the mission idea (as over against the state and national churches with their comprehensive constituency), this is in particular true of the Hutterites, perhaps the most active and aggressive missioners of the entire sixteenth century. They acted out of a strong sense of being called to spread the Gospel, to call people to repent and to change their life in a spiritual rebirth, and to invite men and women to follow Christ as true disciples. They "sent Brethren every year to lands near and far according to the commandments of Christ and the practice of the apostles, to teach and to preach and to gather for the Lord God's people" (Ehrenpreis, *Ein Sendbrief,* 1652, reprint 1920, 122 ff., *Von der Sendung in die Länder*).

The established churches in Germany contested the right of the Brethren to send out missioners on the ground that they had not been ordained by God to do so. For instance the Calvinist superintendent of Alzey in the Palatinate asked the Hutterite missioner Leonhard Dax, imprisoned in 1567, who had given him the right and authority to come into the Palatinate to confuse the people. Dax replied that he was not sent to confuse them but rather to lead everybody from error to the right way of Christian discipleship. The Brethren owed it to the world to bring it the pure and unadulterated Word of God. And those who were sent by the brotherhood were properly ordained as "apostles" (*Sendboten*), and must be considered as commissioned by God Himself. Otherwise also the apostolic church would not have done right. (He quoted Philippians 2; Colossians 4; II Timothy 4; Titus 3; Acts 11, 12, 13, and 18.) Dax had also been chosen to this service by an orderly established Christian church (*Gemeinde*), whose duty it was to preach faith in Christ and to testify both to repentance and forgiveness of sins in His name, and that not only at one specified place, but to the ends of the earth.

In order to be able to fulfill the task laid upon them by the Lord, the congregation semi-annually (usually in the spring and fall) chose from the preachers a number of Brethren to perform a widespread missionary service in all directions, to preach the Gospel in accordance with the commandment of Christ, and to lead the converts to the "promised land" or Moravia.

The departure of these missioners was always a most solemn occasion, as everyone was fully conscious of the extraordinary responsibilities laid upon these itinerant preachers, and also of the real dangers involved in this task. We find in one Hutterite codex of 1628 (in Esztergom) two descriptions: "How the Brethren who go into foreign lands take leave from the brotherhood" and "Response of the elders to the Brethren who are about to leave."[1] Words of encouragement, of wisdom, and of trust in God and His guidance are exchanged, and the parting Brethren are then assured of the intercessory prayers of the entire brotherhood while they are away on their dangerous task. At the end, a hymn composed especially for this occasion was sung, "Ein Lied wöllen wir singen und fürher bringen tun" (1568); Wolkan (*Lieder*, pp. 206–9) printed the entire hymn, and the *Lieder der Hutterischen Brüder* (pp. 650–52) borrows from him.

Each missioner had his field assigned to him; thus brethren went out to all parts of Germany (Bavaria, Württemberg, Hesse, Thuringia, Rhineland, also Silesia and Prussia), to Switzerland, to Poland, and in two cases also to Venice, Italy. A few even came as far as Denmark and Sweden, but that was hardly their actual field of work. Each brother had epistles and tracts in his knapsack. The home congregation supported its missionaries not only by prayers but also by writing them letters and, in case of imprisonment, by dispatching brethren to maintain contact, bring them these letters and receive their replies, also to bring home all news of importance. The missionaries, on the other hand, never tired of writing letters home about their success or, if arrested, their trials and their good cheer and unshaken trust in God.

As a rule the brethren held their meetings at night in remote places, often in forests or mountain glens, in lonely mills, barns, stone quarries, and the like. It was not as their opponents asserted (Menius, for example), that they only "sneaked" around in corners because they feared the light of the day or despised church buildings, but merely because they were safer in such places. By chance we learn also how they called such meetings and how they came into contact with possible listeners. T. W. Röhrich published a "letter of invitation" (which by chance was found in the Strasbourg church archives) in which those who arranged the meeting wrote to a couple to come then and there ("in the house where one has been before") and not to be late and also to invite "the old man" to come too.[2]

As to the exact contents of their message and preaching we do not know too much. We may assume that it was about the same as what we read in their epistles and tracts. In the *Handbüchlein wider den Prozess* we read: "An evangelical missioner shall use the sword of the Spirit which reveals to men the sin of their heart, separates them from the wrong, revives the soul and gives assurance of eternal life in the faith of Christ."

---

1 A full description may be found in Loserth, 228-231, and Wiswedel, *Archiv für Reformationsgeschichte* 1948: 119 f.)

2 Röhrich, T. W. "Zur Geschichte der Strassburger Wiedertäufer." *Zeitschrift für Historische Theologie* (1860): 115 n., note 73.

Hutterite Mission Work and Missioners

"We believe in Jesus Christ," writes Riedemann in his *Rechenschaft*, "and although men cry against us that we seek to become pious and saved by our own works, we say no to that." And Hans Hut confessed at his trial that he taught nothing but first repentance, then believing, and finally baptism upon faith. But this baptism imposes also the obligation to live as the Word of God indicates. Without such a life of obedience, faith does not save. Above all they stressed discipleship—a message which people could not hear anywhere else. There is no God–fearing life without the "fruits of the Spirit." Hence, it is deemed necessary to leave this worldly life and join the brotherhood. People may see for themselves in Moravia how genuine disciples of Christ actually live.

The result of this message was truly amazing. A continuous stream of Brethren moved from all parts toward Moravia, from Tyrol, from Switzerland, and also from Württemberg, and the Rhineland, including the Palatinate. It made the authorities of these countries uneasy, and almost everywhere laws were enacted specifying that those who left for Moravia should lose all claim to their parental inheritance. But the price of these achievements was also no small one. Very few of the missioners died a natural death. Most of them ended their lives as martyrs, being burned, beheaded, drowned, or imprisoned for life. "Thus fare the messengers of God who seek to help people out of ruin," remarks the *Geschicht–Buch*. The memory of these blood witnesses is retained by the brotherhood by word, song, or writings. Time and again we find remarks of that kind in the Chronicle.

The execution of these brave men was quite often a public event shared by a crowd "of thousands." As these Brethren went to the place of martyrdom with shining eyes, admonishing people to remain loyal to their faith in God and to follow His commandments, people were profoundly touched, and many turned Anabaptist as a consequence of such an event. And this the Brethren knew and were unafraid of trial and suffering. There was a time, Loserth contended, when almost all of Tyrol and Styria were in sympathy with Anabaptism. It was about the same everywhere in southern Germany.

The missionary zeal lessened somewhat toward the end of the sixteenth century when the situation in Moravia began to deteriorate, hence the incentive to come thither grew weaker. But we still hear of mission work done in Prussia (Joseph Hauser) and in Silesia in the early seventeenth century. Even after the Brethren had been expelled from Moravia and moved to Slovakia, they tried to continue their mission work although on a reduced scale. The last mission work was done around 1650–54 in Danzig, where individuals of the Polish (Antitrinitarian) Church were contacted.

Perhaps the most successful of all Hutterite missioners was the brother Hänsel Schmidt or Raiffer, who was burned at Aachen in 1558.

Source: *Mennonite Encyclopedia*, II, pp. 866–67.

THE CHRISTIAN COMMUNISM OF THE HUTTERIAN BRETHREN[1]

In recent years more and more attention has been paid to that strange group of Christian sectarians in northwestern United States and Canada called the Hutterites, who are living there in great farm colonies with complete community of goods, and who are healthy, economically successful, and increasing in number in spite of a rigid austerity. The amazing thing is that they have been living this kind of life for 425 years, a phenomenon truly unique in social and religious history. Were it not that they emphasize married life, the nearest comparison of their communities would be with monasteries where similar principles of organized communal living prevail. However, the difference in spirit and motivation is too great to allow any further comparison.[2]

Social scientists have tried to study and understand these people, interpreting them sociologically, economically, and genetically. But it is obvious that they all have missed the central point, the deep Christian foundation upon which the Hutterites have built and still continue to derive their strength and courage. Only by a thorough study of the rich Hutterite manuscript literature of the sixteenth and seventeenth centuries can we discover the underlying principles which motivated these people in the first place and made possible a survival through all these centuries. This paper is an attempt to make just such an interpretation. But before we can enter upon it, two points must be discussed: first, a brief outline of the history of the Brethren, which in itself is a subject of great interest; and, second, a description of the pattern of such communal life, both of four hundred years ago and of today.

The great movement of the evangelical Anabaptists of the sixteenth century was by no means uniform in character. Three distinct groups developed, which may be distinguished as follows:

---

1 Paper read at the annual meeting of the American Society for Reformation Research, New York City, December 29, 1954.

2 Roland H. Bainton is inclined to compare these Brethren with the Franciscan tertiaries, who also accepted a married status. I would admit that there actually exists some similarity, which, however, should not be carried too far.

1. the **Swiss Brethren**, from 1525, led by Conrad Grebel, Felix Manz, and Jörg Blaurock, whose spiritual descendants in America are the Mennonites;
2. the **Dutch Mennonites**, led from 1536 by Menno Simons and Dirk Philips, today represented by the *Doopsgezinde* of the Netherlands and the Mennonites of North Germany and Prussia, some of whom later emigrated to Russia and some descendants of whom are now settled in the western parts of the United States and Canada; and
3. the **Hutterian Brethren** in Austria, particularly in Moravia, from 1529, or, more specifically, from 1533, when Jakob Hutter became their leader. Only the Hutterite group developed a remarkable system of communal living which should be called "Christian communism."

I. Historical Development[3]

If we say that the Hutterites represent the Austrian branch of the Anabaptist movement, that is only correct in a broad sense. It means that these Brethren originated in part in the Hapsburg lands, in particular Tyrol, and that some of them found a haven of relative peace and security in another of the Hapsburg territories, Moravia, where perhaps the tradition of the Hussites made the manorial lords more tolerant than elsewhere. And here, in basically Slavic surroundings, they not only conceived but carried out their new ideal of Christian brotherhood in the form of a close living together in unity of spirit and complete community of goods both in consumption and in production. The earliest beginnings in 1529, partly born out of an emergency situation, can be omitted here, for the real founding did not begin until the coming of Jakob Hutter, a truly charismatic and prophetic leader. In 1533 he established the communal type of brotherhood on such solid foundations that the group could somehow survive the vicissitudes of their history through all the centuries. From now on they called themselves the Hutterites, or Hutterian Brethren. Hutter was leader for only two years (1533–35); early in 1536 he was martyred in the Tyrol. Other strong and inspired leaders followed throughout the sixteenth century, such as Ulrich Stadler, Peter Riedemann, and Peter Walpot; the communities multiplied and grew by the addition of newcomers from many lands, mainly of the German tongue. That was, by the way, the fruit of a great and vigorous missionary campaign (one of the first of modern times) which reached as far as Holland, Italy, and East Prussia. During their best period, roughly between 1560 and 1590, more than one hundred such farm communities, called Bruderhofs,

---

3 Basic literature for this section includes Loserth, *Communismus*; Wolkan, *Die Hutter* (Vienna, 1918); Lydia Müller, *Der Kommunismus der mährischen Wiedertäufer* (Leipzig, 1927); John Horsch, *The Hutterian Brethren* (Goshen, 1931); Fr. Hruby, *Die Widertäufer in Mähren* (Leipzig, 1935); also all the articles in the *Mennonitisches Lexicon* and the *Mennonite Encyclopedia* (Scottdale, Pa.). Basic sources are the *Geschichts–Bücher*, edited by Beck; the *Geschicht–Buch*, edited by Wolkan (Vienna, 1923); *Die älteste Chronik*, edited by Zieglschmid; and the *Klein–Geschichtsbuch*, edited by Zieglschmid.

existed both in Moravia and adjoining Slovakia, which would account for approximately 25,000 persons, including both baptized members and children.

But then wars, a strengthened Counter-Reformation, and, from the beginning of the seventeenth century, a better organized Hapsburg government, brought this flowering to an abrupt end. In 1622 the Brethren were expelled from Moravia, leaving all their farms with their rich inventory behind. They now concentrated in Slovakia (still tolerant under Hungarian lords of the Reformed faith) and, from 1621, also in Transylvania (then under the suzerainty of the Turks). For the Brethren this was the time of the third and fourth generation of Anabaptists, who were no longer as vigorous and prophetic as their predecessors. Once more, under the inspired leadership of the bishop Andreas Ehrenpreis, a revival was started about 1640–60; but then a sharp decline set in. The eighteenth century saw intensified activity on the part of the Jesuits in Hungary, and the majority of the Brethren turned Catholic.

Then something unexpected took place. A group of convinced Lutherans of Carinthia, expelled about 1750 from their homeland for the sake of their Protestant faith, were transferred to Transylvania. There they came into contact with the last poor remnants of the Hutterites. It was like a miracle: within a few years they themselves became Hutterites and staunchly embraced the principle of communal living. New persecutions drove the small flock of approximately two hundred determined Brethren across mountain passes into Rumania in 1767, and thence three years later on to Little Russia (Ukraine). Here they again began their settlements, though on a reduced scale. Half a century later communal living was given up altogether, but about 1860 dedicated leaders tried it again, and soon with obvious success. Military conscription in Russia, however, made the Brethren seek another land. Between 1874 and 1877 they all came to the United States, where they first settled in three farm colonies in the prairie land of South Dakota, so similar in scenery to the steppes of Russia. During World War I new sufferings at the hands of superpatriots occurred which prompted an exodus of the greater part of the Brethren into Alberta and Manitoba. In both the United States and Canada, we count nearly 120 colonies with a population of nearly 10,000, and today they are still growing rapidly. To be sure, they have lost much of their former spiritual vigor, they do little missionary work, they no longer write their sermons but read the old and time-honored ones, but in their convictions and principles they are as strong as ever, and most of their communal organization has been preserved almost unchanged. Above all, their young people continue loyally their traditional forms of living, and it appears that the group will continue its Christian communism for a long time.

II. Description of Communal Life

Let us visit for a moment one of these Bruderhofs, not one of today, but one of four hundred years ago, one in Moravia or in Slovakia. One may still see some of these former Bruderhof establishments with their thatch-roofed and whitewashed houses around a central courtyard or square, almost unchanged by the passing of time.[4]

In the *Great Chronicle* of the Hutterites, a book of unique charm and value, we read of the "Golden Age" about 1560–1590, when they lived and worked together in a joyous brotherly fashion. "It was like a big clockwork," says the Chronicle, "where one wheel drives the other one, promotes, helps, and makes the whole clock function." Or still more graphically, "It is like a beehive where all the busy bees work together to a common end, the one doing this, the other that, not for their own need but for the good of all."[5] Each Bruderhof was supposed to be self-sufficient, comprising between two hundred and three hundred souls. The entire brotherhood was guided by one bishop or *Vorsteher*, while each separate Bruderhof had one or more preachers (*Diener des Wortes*) and a head manager with several assistants (*Diener der Notdurft*). All buying and selling was done by specially appointed men who took care of these duties for the entire community in a most efficient fashion. No one was to be idle. Everyone had to learn a craft or to do some ordinary manual labor as assigned by the manager (the *Haushalter, Wirt,* or, in modern America, "the boss"). Not only the men worked in this way, "as if they were being paid," as Grimmelshausen states in his *Simplizissimus*, describing such Slovakian Bruderhofs, but the women likewise were organized into work teams for cooking, spinning, sewing, caring for the children, and similar work. Due to an extremely ascetic outlook on life, hard and steady work, six days a week, was accepted as a matter of fact, while consumption was restrained to the absolute needs of the body. Accordingly, these colonies were soon thriving and highly successful, economically speaking. In the sixteenth century such large-scale, efficient enterprises were otherwise almost unknown—hence the temptation for the neighboring poor peasants to slander the Brethren and to spread false stories of their secret wealth. Later these stories were used by Counter–Reformation leaders.

The crafts of the Brethren were outstanding. Above all, their beautiful ceramics and cutlery. They were also skilled in carriage-making and in the production of a new kind of steel bedsteads. Occasionally we hear of intricate clocks produced for the nobility. Likewise unique were their bathhouses, to which even the nobles flocked from far and near, as they also availed themselves of the excellent services of the Hutterite barber–

---

4   In 1925 I visited these colonies in Slovakia and reported about them in *Wiener Zeitschrift für Volkskunde*, 1927 ("Die Habaner in der Slovakei"). Cf. article "Habaner" in *ML*.
5   *Älteste Chronik*, 435–36 (for the year 1569). Also *Geschicht–Buch*, 334–35.

surgeons and physicians.[6] Strict regulations were set up for all these crafts and activities, particularly after the end of the sixteenth century. Ordinances and regulations, called *Gemeinde-Ordnungen*, drawn up by the bishops, set up rigid standards both for the general conduct of the life of the Brethren and for the operation of their crafts. The most outstanding of these regulations (reminiscent of monastic *regulae*) is the one of 1651, by Andreas Ehrenpreis, which is still in use today.[7] Among other things it reminds the Brethren that no form of private property was allowed, not even that of their beautifully handwritten books, otherwise their most precious possession. Naturally all forms of inheritance are abolished. All earnings gained by outside work are to be placed into a common purse; and even if someone should find a coin on the road, it also must go into this purse.

Concerning the upbringing of children and the education of the young people, it is characteristic of this kind of communal living that family life was minimized as far as possible. Thus, the little ones stayed in the parents' room only until they were two or at the most three years old. Then they were put into the *Kleine Schul* in each Bruderhof, a kind of nursery school, kindergarten and boarding school (unique, by the way, for the Europe of the sixteenth century), where teachers, schoolmothers, and attendants cared for the entire group day and night. There they learned praying, proper behavior, a high degree of cleanliness, and, above all, living together in peace and cooperation. Later they attended the *Grosse Schul*, the elementary school, again combined with complete board. The school was said to be so well run that even nobles sent their children to it, although they learned hardly more than reading and writing.[8]

At twenty or twenty-one years of age, after thorough instruction, the young people were baptized. Sometimes this took place even later, just as each one felt capable of accepting such a solemn *covenant with God* which would bind one as much as a monk was bound by his monastic vows. Baptism was interpreted (according to I Peter 3:21 in Luther's translation) as "the covenant of a good conscience with God." It meant the acceptance of an obligation and the promise never to deviate from the prescribed path of the brotherhood.

To the middle of the nineteenth century the practice of choosing mates was rather peculiar. Romance and courtship were completely condemned as the product of an individualistic and secular civilization. Even today such emotional motives are reduced to a minimum. The elders more or less chose the spouses, and this selection was accepted silently presumably often with

---

6   Cf. Friedmann, "Hutterite Physicians and Barber-Surgeons," *MQR*, XXVII (1953), 128–36, and John L. Sommer, "Hutterite Medicine and Physicians in Moravia in the Sixteenth Century and After, *ibid.*, 111–27.

7   Now published by A. J. F. Zieglschmid in the appendix to the *Klein-Geschichtsbuch*, 519–32. See also the article "Ehrenpreis, Andreas," in *ML*, I, 530–32.

8   Incidentally, the penmanship of their manuscript books is still today an object of amazement. Two examples can be seen in the *ML* article, "Geschichtsbücher der mährischen Täufer," II, 94–95.

quiet resignation.[9] After all, the purpose of married life was exclusively the procreation of children according to God's command to the patriarchs of old. That alone vindicated the institution of marriage. As one early Hutterite brother said, "God winks at our marital work ... on behalf of the children, and does not reckon it upon those who act in fear and discipline." And then, somewhat mournfully, he adds, "The spirit of God sighs in all His children because it is not quite possible that this marital work can be performed absolutely purely, denying all evil lust, as the blessing of God to multiply and be fruitful."[10]

Finally, all meals were taken in one common eating room, all men sitting at one side and the women at the other side. Any mingling of the sexes was more or less frowned upon. Even at wedding festivals bridegroom and bride sat at separate tables.

III. The Motives and Arguments for this Christian Communism

The central theme of this study concerns the analysis of the underlying spirit or genius of the brotherhood which brought it into existence and enabled it to survive. Since all human actions have many and often contradictory motives, such an analysis is by no means a simple matter; hence the following discussion is submitted merely as an essay in interpretation, although its basic orientation at least is undoubtedly correct.

It might be useful to look briefly at other attempts of interpretation. There is above all the sociological explanation that the Hutterites were primarily simple peasants, who as such were unsympathetic to our entire civilization as it had developed since Renaissance and Reformation, with its urban and highly individualized spirit. It is true that an antagonism of this kind actually existed, however not so much because of a sociologically determined hostility of one class against another,[11] but rather because of a radical biblicist outlook, emphatically dualistic, in which the Kingdom of God and its righteousness was contraposed to the "world," our secular civilization. Thus the reference to

---

9   We have several objective descriptions of these marriage customs: first, a letter by Stephan Gerlach, Professor at the University of Tübingen, who in 1578 visited his sister in the colonies of Moravia; Gustav Bossert, *Quelle zur Geschichten der Wiedertäufer, I. Herzogtum Württemberg* (Leipzig, 1930), 1107; second, a letter by the Polish nobleman Andreas Rey de Naglovitz, who visited the Brethren in 1612. Fr. Hruby, *Die Wiedertäufer in Mähren* (1935), 128 (or *Archiv für Reformationsgeschichte*, 1935, p. 8), also 73–74. In 1643 Andreas Ehrenpreis issued a special ordinance concerning the proper way of "matching," lamenting the rise of individualistic choosing and the weakening of the old customs. He admonished strongly to return to the old ways. Cf. *Klein–Geschichtsbuch*, 214–18. According to the *Klein–Geschichtsbuch*, 437f., it was mainly Johann Cornies, a leading Mennonite in southern Russia around 1840–50, who exerted all his influence to soften this old custom.

10   Lydia Müller, *Glaubenzeugnisse oberdeutscher Taufgesinnter* (Leipzig, 1938), 228, Ulrich Stadler's Sendbrief "Von der Erbsünde," 1536. Ulrich Stadler was one of the most profound "theologians" among the Brethren of the first generation. His tracts are found in many codices.

11   In the sixteenth century by no means were all Brethren peasants. Compare P. Dedic, "Social Background of the Austrian Anabaptists," *MQR*, XIII (1939), 5–20.

sociological determinism fails to a large extent to explain this particular way of life, so hard and full of sacrifice.

The same holds true for what Kautsky and other socialists claim to see in these communities, namely, the early beginnings of socialism. Nothing is farther from the truth. Where the Bible rules, there is no room or need for social utopianism.

Likewise unsatisfactory is the reference to certain economic emergency conditions during the earliest period of Anabaptism. True, a need of taking care of the many indigent among the Brethren, reminiscent of the situation of the primitive church at Jerusalem, did actually exist and led to the pooling of goods in 1529.[12] But such an emergency motivation would never have produced survival for any protracted period of time. The primitive church in Jerusalem itself soon abandoned its experiment in communal living. Above all, it was not such a situation in 1529, but Jakob Hutter's radical reorganization in 1533, that actually established the new communistic pattern and point of view. It went far beyond the vague experimentation prior to this year 1533.

When we consult the Hutterite writings of the seventeenth century (by Claus Braidl, Joseph Hauser, and Andreas Ehrenpreis) or of present-day members of the Hutterite brotherhood, we almost uniformly meet but one answer: the reference to the primitive church as described in the Book of Acts, chapters 2, 4, and 5, plus some further texts interpreted in the light of these chapters. The Brethren understood themselves as obeying to the letter the Holy Scripture, following strictly the model of the first church without any further questioning.

Although this explanation comes nearer to the center of our problem because of its strong Biblical orientation, it does not really explain how this great venture in communal living began and throughout its first century maintained such a strong attraction for many seekers. After all, the mere reference to a historical antecedent lacks that spiritual vigor which alone makes such a sectarian movement possible and capable of growth and survival. Hence we must seek further to find a more satisfactory answer. Fortunately, the earliest writings of the Brethren allow us to gain deeper and more adequate spiritual insight. And it is this early period alone which matters and reveals a power and charismatic authority never again reached in later generations.

The epistles and confessions of faith and the tracts by Jakob Hutter, Peter Riedemann, Ulrich Stadler, Peter Walpot, and all the lesser known Brethren, the countless martyrs and witnesses to their faith, clearly disclose three major motives which produced the facts here discussed.

---

12 The Great Chronicle of the Brethren, written by Caspar Braitmichel (around 1560–70), reports this event, thoroughly in the style of the Bible, as follows: "At this time these men spread out a coat before all the people, and everyone put upon it his possession, with a willing and unconstrained mind, and they did so for the support of the needy according to the teachings of the prophets and the apostles." *Geschicht–Buch*, 63 (or *Älteste Chronik*, 87).

Motive one is brotherly love in action, the strong longing of Christians for brotherly sharing and togetherness.

Motive two is *Gelassenheit*, a term derived from the mystics and almost untranslatable. It means yielding absolutely to the will of God with a dedicated heart, forsaking all selfishness and one's own will.

Motive three, finally, is obedience to the divine commandments, understood as the inevitable consequence of the attitude of Gelassenheit. As one gives up one's own will, one naturally accepts God's commandments as the basis and guidepost for all further actions.

Motive one: the idea of love—brotherly togetherness and mutual giving and sharing—was present among the Brethren at all times. It was the very center of Jakob Hutter's work. He visualized the brotherhood as a great family. Since in such a family all material things are shared as a matter of fact, this should also be the case in a true *Gemeinschaft*, or community. And so we read throughout our records confessions like this: "Love is the tie of perfection…. Where she dwelleth she does not work partial but complete communion. It means having everything in common out of sheer love for the neighbor."[13] "Where Christian love of the neighbor does not produce community in things temporal, there the blood of Christ does not cleanse from sin."[14] In short, "Private property is the greatest enemy of Christian love." In love all men are considered equal and united in the oneness of the Spirit. The reference to the Book of Acts in these early tracts, however, serves not as a motivation but rather as an undergirding of this love–motive, as an exemplification of how it works, and as an assurance that this way is the right one. It was never to be understood as a strict commandment of God to be followed in obedience without any further questioning.

The **second motive** is *Gelassenheit*, a term of great richness, meaning self–surrender, yieldedness, the giving of one's self to God's guidance, even unto death. Among the Hutterites it also means the forsaking of all concern for personal property, thus leading almost naturally to a complete community of goods. At the earliest period this idea of *Gelassenheit* almost dominates the thought of the Brethren. "To have all things in common, a free, untrammeled, yielding, willing heart in Christ is needed," writes Ulrich Stadler about 1536.[15] "Whosoever is thus inwardly free and resigned (*gelassen*) in the Lord

---

13 This quotation is taken from the confessional document called "The five Articles of Our Greatest Quarrel with the World…," (Die Fünf Artikel des grössten Streits zwischen uns und der Welt) contained in the Great Chronicle, and inserted for the year 1547. The third article deals with "Von der wahren Gelassenheit und christlicher Gemeinschaft der Güter." (Cf. *Älteste Chronik*, 285–96).

14 Andreas Ehrenpreis, *Ein Sendbrief… brüderliche Gemeinschaft, das höchste Gebot der Liebe betreffend* (written 1650, printed for the first time 1652), *Aufs neue herausgegeben von den Hutterischen Brüdern in Amerika* (Scottdale, 1920), 49. The entire "Epistle" (actually a long tract) is a great defence of the principle of community of goods as the true expression of Christian love. In 1954 this epistle was reprinted by the Brethren in Canada.

15 This and the following quotation is taken from a beautiful meditation of the already mentioned brother Ulrich Stadler, entitled "Von der Ordnung der Heiligen in ihrer Gemeinschaft und Leben" (about 1536–37). published by Müller, *Glaubenszeugnisse* (1938), 225–26, also by Wolkan, *Die Hutterer* (1918), 153–61.

is also ready to surrender all temporal possession." To the rejoinder that such a community of goods is not a commandment of the Lord, the same brother answers as follows: "To serve the saints in this way with all one's possession is true and genuine *Gelassenheit*, and it is also the way of brotherly love. In summa: one brother should serve the other, live and work for him, and no one should do anything for himself." Elsewhere we read, "If you want to become a disciple you must resign to such a *Gelassenheit* and must renounce all private property."[16] At this place it might be good to stress that this attitude leads to the establishment of complete community of goods, while other Anabaptist groups, likewise intent on practicing love, were satisfied with a "community of charity," a caring for the needy without the demand of giving up private property altogether. Such a community of charity was typical among the Swiss and Dutch Brethren.

The Hutterites, however, in their strict biblicism, became extremely sensitive and alert to the pitfalls of "mammon" in all its forms. "As the beetle lives in the dung, and the worm in the wood, so avarice (or greed) has its dwelling place in private property"[17] (1599). Whosoever refuses communal living, they taught, shows obvious sympathy for avarice (or greed). And then they quote the example of the rich young man in the parable who could not enter the Kingdom of God because he was not willing to sell all that he had and give it to the poor. Avarice, the demon of possession, must therefore be overcome if true *Gelassenheit* is to be achieved. But once it has been overcome, there follows complete community of goods in brotherly togetherness and sharing. The ready acceptance of such complete community, incidentally, became the very touchstone of the regenerate. In particular it was also an indication whether or not a brother was capable and worthy of becoming a leader.

Taken all in all, the Hutterites represent a most original type of "theocratic society" or "theocratic communism," as it was once aptly called,[18] a venture otherwise rather foreign to the Western world. The Brethren were aware of this antagonism to world and culture, but affirmed time and again that no other way to salvation was possible. "It is but through *Gemeinschaft*, that is

---

16 *Das Grosse Artikelbuch* of 1577, sometimes also called *Ein schön lustig Büchlein* (its author was most likely Peter Walpot, the bishop of the brotherhood, 1565–78). It is an elaboration of the "Five Articles" mentioned in note 13. This quotation, taken from the original codex is quoted by Robert Friedmann, "Eine dogmatische Hauptschrift der Hutterischen Täufergemeinschaften in Mähren," in *Archiv für Reformationsgeschichte*, 1931, p. 210.

At this place a general remark may be inserted, namely the need for a distinction between genuine *Gelassenheit* (which by no means means passivism in life) and "Quietism" (as taught, e.g., by Madame Guyon), which shirks any activity in order to be as passive a vessel of divine influence as possible. Anabaptism never went to such extremes as it never was in such a way individualistically–minded.

17 *Communismus*, 240, quoted from a manuscript of 1599.

18 Franz Heimann in his excellent study, "The Hutterite Doctrine of Church and Common Life, a study of Peter Riedemann's Confession of Faith of 1540," in *MQR*, XXVI (1952), (English version of a Vienna Ph.D. thesis of 1928, translated by Friedmann).

communal living, that the blood of Christ may cleanse sinful man. Christ cannot help us unless we follow him all the way, without any reservation."[19]

This concept of "theocratic communism" naturally implies also the **third motive**, the principle of unconditional obedience by which we "bring into captivity every thought to the obedience of Christ" (II Cor. 10:5, as quoted now and then in Hutterite tracts). It means what the Brethren never tired of repeating, that what really is needed for a true disciple is this: walking the "narrow path," breaking the self-will, and subsequently submitting to the will of God, whatever He may command.

It is quite obvious that this principle of obedience involves a certain paradox: on the one hand, it is the most profound and most spiritual principle imaginable where the individual surrenders completely to divine guidance and asks nothing for himself, doing only that which he feels is required of him, even if it should lead to martyrdom. "Not my will be done, but Thine." That means genuine discipleship. It is the spirit of the first generation of Anabaptists, in particular Hutterites, who gave up everything in order to obey God. Suffering was accepted almost gladly as the inescapable consequence of such acts of obedience.

On the other hand, such prophetic conditions hardly persist in the long run, and among the second, third, and fourth generations of Anabaptists this principle becomes more and more formalized and external. "This is the time-honored rule and regulation," and the individual must conform to it. Occasionally such "obedience" can become a real burden and a dependence upon the leader (bishop) and his bigness or smallness in matters of the spirit. Moreover, the danger is at hand that those who now meticulously obey these rules laid down by the forefathers readily believe that they are the righteous ones and consider all nonconformists unrighteous. In the long history of the Brethren, this danger of legalism was not always avoided. But it should be said that the Brethren in the beginning were well aware of this pitfall. In one of the finest tracts of early Anabaptism, called "Two Kinds of Obedience," a clear distinction is made between "childlike" and "servile" obedience, and a warning is given to beware of the latter. The tract, although not of Hutterite origin, is found in several Hutterite manuscripts.[20]

Although this new life in perfect community of goods did bring a certain external security through mutual help and service, it meant a hard, daily internal struggle with that part of man's nature which insists upon self-will and personal possession. The Brethren by no means belittled this desire. In fact, they liked to quote in this connection a jingle which in the *Great Article Book* of 1577 concludes the third article "Concerning Community of Goods":

---

19   This is a statement made to the writer by one of the elders of the present-day Hutterites in Alberta, Canada (fall of 1954). It expresses a general conviction of the entire brotherhood.

20   "Two Kinds of Obedience: An Anabaptist Tract on Christian Freedom," translated and edited by John C. Wenger, *MQR*, XXI (1947), 18–22; see also Fosdick, *Great Voices of the Reformation* (1952).

Die Gemeinschaft wär nit schwer
Wenn nur der Eigennutz nit wär.

Or in a free English translation:
Communal living would not be hard
If there were not such self–regard.[21]

Source: *Archiv für Reformationsgeschichte*, LII (1955), pp. 196–208.

---

21   John Horsch, *The Hutterian Brethren, a Story of Loyalty and Martyrdom* (Goshen, 1931), 74.

PETER RIEDEMANN ON ORIGINAL SIN AND THE WAY OF REDEMPTION

Of Peter Riedemann, the outstanding Hutterite leader and teacher, and of his great confession of faith of 1540, called *Account of our Religion, Doctrine and Faith*, the *Mennonite Quarterly Review* recently published a valuable study by Franz Heimann, which afforded a profound insight into the doctrinal and theological thinking of genuine Anabaptism.[1] Most appropriately Heimann centered his attention in the main upon two points only, namely the teachings concerning the church and the common life (*Kirche, Gemeinschaft*), in which fields the Anabaptists distinguished themselves so signally from the great Protestant bodies. It is, however, obvious that these two points by no means exhaust the specifically Anabaptist views and teachings, and further inquiries into the *Account* are called for. The theology of the Anabaptists, a matter long neglected or misunderstood, is perhaps the most urgent problem at present in our research; it demands greater clarification of specific concepts and viewpoints. Although Heimann's study has much to offer in this line, one particular problem has been completely neglected in it, namely that of "original sin" and redemption. Has Riedemann, have the Hutterites, something essential to say concerning these two theological issues? Did they accept the general Protestant viewpoints, or did they ignore these questions altogether as did, for instance, the *Schleitheim Articles* of 1527? No doubt this is a central problem which might decide much regarding the "orthodoxy" of the Anabaptists and the question whether they may be classified as a strictly Protestant group or not. If not (and the present writer tends to incline to this position), Anabaptism would represent a distinctive type of Christian witnessing alongside of Catholicism and classic Protestantism.[2]

---

1 The recently published English version of the *Account*, ect., prepared by the Society of Brothers known as Hutterians, at Bromdon, Bridgnorth, England, 1950, reviewed MQR, XXVI (1952), deserves widest attention wherever the Anabaptist genius and vision is under discussion.

2 It has been pointed out that the later Lutherans and especially Lutheran "orthodoxy" of the seventeenth and eighteenth centuries misunderstood and even perverted Luther's position on major points. See for instance Aulen's great study of the history of the doctrine of the atonement (*Christus Victor*, 1931) in which he claims that later Lutheranism misunderstood Luther's doctrine of justification by faith, and that Luther actually conceived of the atonement as Christ's victory over sin by which the believer is also delivered from the actual bondage of sin and not just "justified." Dietrich Bonhöffer in his *Cost of Discipleship* (*Die Nachfolge Christi*) has severely castigated the Lutheran Church for its perversion of the doctrine of justification and the use of "cheap grace" whereby the sinner is in effect justified *in* his sin instead of *out* of it.

The doctrines of original sin and of justification by faith alone, pillars of Luther's theological edifice, find their main roots in a particular interpretation or emphasis of parts of the Epistle to the Romans and related Pauline writings. It is therefore of major interest to study what Anabaptists, and now especially Riedemann, were discovering in the same Scriptural sources. If a different reading of the same texts was possible, or at least a different emphasis as to their place in the total understanding of redemption, then the move toward the "radical" Christian way was inescapable. In the latter case "justification by faith alone" should not be the major concern of an earnest Christian. Rather, of him is the passionate rejection of sin altogether. The new birth, the sanctification of life and the preparation of God's kingdom on earth are then more in the center of concern than the aforementioned doctrines with their inherent temptation toward spiritual relaxation. "Obedience unto righteousness" (Rom. 6:16) is then more central than justification by faith. And original sin, though not denied (on the contrary recognized as the very cause of physical death) is reinterpreted as an inherited inclination and tendency to sin, which the regenerated man can and must fight.

In the great doctrinal tract of Riedemann, whose first and more important part covers about 130 pages, the section on "original sin" covers not more than three pages;[3] the term "justification by faith" does not appear at all (one might assume that the Brethren did not read Luther's tracts), and the classical *loci* for it, such as Rom. 3:28; 4:5; 11:6, and Gal. 2:16, etc., are quoted nowhere. Immediately following this part (pp. 56–59), a chapter appears entitled, "How Man May Again Find God and His Grace" (pp. 59–68), subdivided into the sections, "Concerning Remorse"; "Concerning Repentance"; "Man is Grafted into Christ"; and finally "Concerning the Old and the New Covenant." A reproduction of the entire section here seems to be appropriate; it will make possible a more concrete discussion of the issue and will help towards a better understanding of the specific "Christianity of the Anabaptists," insofar as we accept Riedemann as a good representative for it.

What Sin Is

Sin is, in essence, the forsaking of obedience to God, or disobedience (Gen. 3:6), and from this all else that is wrong hath come, as branches grow from the tree. Evil hath now taken the upper hand in the world, and still increaseth daily, so that men proceed from iniquity to iniquity, because they have yielded and committed their members to serve sin.

Now all unrighteousness is sin, as John saith, but disobedience is the mother of all sin. For as, through obedience, all the righteousness of

---

[3] Most Anabaptist sources do not mention original sin at all.

God cometh through Christ (Rom. 5:16–19), so also cometh all sin and unrighteousness from disobedience to and the forsaking of God's command.

Concerning Original Sin

Just here there ariseth oft very much quarreling and strife, for the one wanteth this and the other that; from which strife cometh more destruction than betterment, for since God is not a God of quarreling but a God of peace and love, He hath no pleasure in strife, neither hath He aught to do with the same, hence there is naught therein save destruction.

Now, therefore, we confess and teach that all men save Christ only have a sinful nature which they inherit from Adam, as it is written, "The imagination and desire of man's heart is evil from youth" (Gen. 8:21). David saith likewise, "Behold, I was shapen in iniquity; and in sin did my mother conceive me." Paul speaketh clearly, and saith, "By one man sin entered into the world and passed upon all men." Because then it hath come upon us all from him, it is thereby clear that we have inherited it from him.

What Original Sin Is

But the inheritance that we all have from our father Adam is the inclination to sin; that all of us have by nature a tendency toward evil and to have pleasure in sin (II Esdras 3:21–22). This inheritance manifesteth and showeth itself in all the children of Adam, and removeth, devoureth, and consumeth all that is good and of God in man; so that none may attain it again except he be born again (John 3:3–5).

This inheritance Paul nameth the messenger of Satan, who striketh him on the head or buffeteth him with fists, and speaketh thereby of the movement of the sinful inclination which stirreth in him, as in all men. Therefore saith John also, "He who saith he hath no sin, deceiveth himself, and the truth is not in him," and speaketh thereby of the inheritance which we all have from Adam, which he calleth sin; as also David saith in the book of Psalms: "In sin was I conceived and born." Thus through Adam we have all become sinful and must be justified through Christ, if we would have life with Him.

The Harm Wrought by Original Sin

Original sin, we say, is first the cause of physical death for men, for originally they were created and placed in life, so that there was naught corrupt in them. For God did not make death. Since, however, we all inherited sin, all, both young and old, we must taste of death. In truth, if Christ were not sent and come into the world there would be no more hope of life. Because, however, it was planned from the beginning by the Father, and because Christ hath come into the world and become the reconciliation not only for us but also for the whole world (I John 2:1–2), we believe that he hath brought it about that original sin before it stirreth within man leading to further sin now causeth physical death only and not eternal, that the word might be fulfilled: The children shall not bear the iniquities of the fathers (Ezek. 18:20, also 33:10–19), but he who sinneth shall himself die. Accordingly, we say that God also accepteth little children, as such, for indeed Christ is also their reconciler (I John 2).

Secondly, we say that original sin is also the cause of eternal death to man, in that it leadeth, guideth, and bringeth man into all sins, and through it we do much sin; for this is the sin, that stirreth up, rouseth, and bringeth to pass all other sins within us, as Paul declareth when he saith: "Sin, that it might appear sin, worketh death in me by that which is good, that it might become exceedingly sinful by the commandment" (Rom. 7:13).

Thus, therefore, all men have died in Adam, fallen away from God and forsaken him, as it is written, "There is none righteous, no not one, there is no fear of God before their eyes" (Rom. 3:10–18). Thus we show men how far they have estranged themselves from God and submerged themselves in their sin.

We show them also that all sin hath its source and origin in wrong taking, that man taketh what he should not and what is not his, and leaveth what he ought to take, loveth what he ought to hate and hateth what he ought to love. Thus man is turned aside and led away from God by that which should point and lead him to God, teach him to know God, and show him God. Thus, if one would come to God he must leave and deny what he hath previously wrongly taken, that is, all that is temporal and transitory, to cleave to God alone. This is true repentance that the Lord demandeth and desireth.

Now Followeth How Man May Again Find God and His Grace

Concerning Remorse

But he who would truly repent with all his heart must first feel real remorse for his sin.... For true remorse followeth the recognition of sin (II Samuel 12:13–17).

Now he who is sorry for his sin and regretteth having obeyed it ought and must henceforth all the more diligently guard himself against it, and flee from it as from a serpent....

Concerning Repentance

Thus remorse leadeth to true repentance, that is real humiliation and abasement before God because of the transgression...which shame bringeth a real turning point (*eine rechte Wiederkehr*), so that the man runneth with haste, calleth, crieth, and prayeth to God for forgiveness and grace, and beginneth at the same time to bring the flesh into subjection.... (I Cor. 9:24 f.) As David saith, "I lifted up mine eyes unto the hills to see from whence help would come to me, even so cometh my help from the Lord...." Every anxious, troubled, fearful, broken, and contrite heart, if it flees to Him, will find with Him peace and comfort....

We point out also thereby that no such "deathbed remorse" and repentance as the world hath (which saith today, "I am sorry for my sin" and yet doeth the same again tomorrow) can stand before God and receive grace; but only that which proceedeth from a sincere heart. To such, will God draw nigh and will both begin and bring to perfection His work in him (James 4:1–10).

Man Is Grafted into Christ

...We teach further that Christ came into the world to make sinners blessed (I Tim. 1:15).... Now because Christ is the root and the vine, and we are grafted into Him, through faith, even as the sap riseth from the root and maketh the branches fruitful (Rom. 11:16), even so the Spirit of Christ riseth from the root, Christ, into the branches or twigs to make them all fruitful....

God made His covenant firstly with Adam, and then also with Abraham and his seed, and now hath made it with us through Christ (Heb. 7:18) and established and confirmed it through His death...that we, redeemed from death through Him, might be children of His covenant (Acts 3:17) and that the same might be ours eternally.

Concerning the New Covenant

...God hath established, revealed and brought to light a covenant that is perfect, that abideth unchanged throughout eternity... (Heb. 7:18; Jer. 8:1–3).

This covenant is a covenant of grace, the revelation and the knowledge of God.... This knowledge, however, cometh alone from the receiving of the Holy Spirit....

This is the covenant of childlike freedom; of which we also are the children if we let ourselves be sealed by this covenant and submit and surrender ourselves to its working.... Therefore saith Paul, "Stand fast therefore in the liberty wherewith Christ hath made us free, and let not yourselves be entangled again with the yoke of bondage." (Gal. 5:14) For if ye let again yourselves be led into the yoke of bondage, then are ye led from the Spirit to the letter, and Christ profiteth you nothing. For which reason those who have not the Spirit are not the children of this covenant.

It cannot be denied that this is a genuinely Christian document of high originality. That it proposes an interpretation of the doctrine of original sin not found in the reformers is likewise obvious. Riedemann's main locus for an understanding of this doctrine is, surprisingly enough, Ezek. 18:20, which refers back to Deut. 24:16. There can be no "hereditary guilt" (from which no human being could ever escape) for we have the promise of God that "the children shall not bear the iniquities of the fathers." It is perhaps for this reason that the Old Testament never emphasizes the idea of original sin yet rather prepared the soil for the doctrine of the changed heart, the new birth. As the doctrine of original sin loses its crushing gravity (which Luther so painfully felt) it is quite in line that no theology of the atonement appears in these pages.[4] Man is called to active co-operation with God (I Cor. 3:9), to be sure, however, only after he has entered the state of rebirth. It is this state, therefore, which man has to search and to long for. The way to redemption leads through remorse and repentance to the point where the believer is ready to enter the "new covenant" of grace. It is "the covenant of childlike freedom," as Riedemann says; and it is granted to the believer only after he has submitted and surrendered to the working of this covenant. A modern Christian author has called this way to redemption, very graphically, "costly grace."[5] It is quite clear that such a way has nothing pietistic in it, nothing sweet or emotional, nothing to be only enjoyed. It is but a natural consequence of such a vision that it implies also a new form of human relationship, a new thought concerning the brother and fellow believer, a uniting with him at the Lord's Table and in life at large.

Source: *Mennonite Quarterly Review*, XXVI (1952), pp. 210–15.

---

4   There is a short tract by and unknown early Anabaptist entitled, "Concerning the Satisfaction of Christ," translated and edited by John C. Wenger in *MQR*, XX (1946), 243–54, but upon careful study one will discover that actually it does not deal at all with the doctrine of atonement as taught by the great Protestant theologians.

5   Dietrich Bonhöffer, *The Cost of Discipleship* (New York, 1949), 37 ff.

THE DOCTRINE OF THE TWO WORLDS

It has often been asked whether one may properly speak of an Anabaptist theology as such, or whether the Anabaptists simply aimed to follow the footsteps of the Master in a simple and unsophisticated manner without 'theological speculation' or foundation. As to the basic doctrines of Christianity, it is certain that they were orthodox, teaching nothing foreign to the Apostles' Creed. Since the center of their concern lay elsewhere, however, they have often been described as theologically naive. A deeper search, however, makes one wonder whether such a judgment is tenable. A movement of such strength is unthinkable without a definite theological foundation, without specific ideas concerning man's relationship to the divine and the meaning of earthly life. Even if these foundations were not expressed in a systematic way, one must assume that they were implied in all the doings and witnessing of the Anabaptists. The rediscovery of these presuppositions is a challenge to present–day research.

Several years ago Harold S. Bender, almost casually and without elaboration, proposed a possible answer to this question. Musing about the deeper motivations of the Anabaptists for their pacifistic stand, he made the following highly suggestive remarks:

> The answer is to be found rather in their [the Anabaptists'] doctrine of the two worlds. The new Kingdom of God which is being established in their terms and through them…is of necessity distinct from the world order which is dominated by Satan. That the church and state join in persecuting the true church is only one more bit of evidence of the wickedness of the world order, they concluded. The old church (both Roman Catholic and Protestant) has failed particularly in its mixing of the two kingdoms, hence the true church must be, and is being, reestablished separate from the world. This true church is the present Kingdom of Christ which is being established in the midst of and alongside of the kingdom of this world; it is not to be deferred to some millennial future.[1]

---

1 Harold S. Bender, "The Pacifism of the Sixteenth Century Anabaptists," *Church History*, XXIV (June 1955), 128 (a paper read before the American Society of Church History, New York, December 28, 1954). See also *MQR*, XXX (1956), 15.

Here then is a challenge. Is it true that this "doctrine of the two worlds" represents the deepest layer of the Anabaptist theological outlook, and if so, what constitutes its difference from the main stream of Protestant thought? Furthermore, what are the implications of this doctrine for faith and practice? These are questions which deserve more careful examination than they have hitherto received.

The main line of Protestant theology is a kind of one-sided interpretation of the Pauline teaching on justification by faith. Although including this doctrine in its foundation, sixteenth-century Anabaptism shows definitely a different orientation, emphasizing above all the commandment of discipleship. As Roland H. Bainton so appropriately put it:

> The Anabaptists went back further than any of the other groups of the age of the Reformation. They tended even to neglect Paul and to push back to Jesus. That is why the ideal of Restoration (common to all groups of that age) tends to coincide now with the ideal of the imitation of Christ.[2]

Certainly, Luther himself did not overlook Christ's teaching concerning discipleship, but unfortunately there was no organic place for it in his differently slanted system of Pauline-Augustinian theology. Thus, even though both the Reformers and Anabaptists alike claim to be strict Biblicists, a noticeable tension prevails in their way of reading the Holy Scriptures. The Anabaptists paid more attention to Christ's commandment concerning *Nachfolge*, being certain that if it was commanded it can also be carried out under proper conditions, while the Reformers focused nearly all of their attention upon man's sinful nature which makes him utterly helpless in the pursuit of the good. Consequently they came to rely almost exclusively upon the Pauline teachings regarding salvation of the individual sinner by faith, disclaiming even James's admonition to be doers of the Word, as well as hearers.

In connection with Anabaptism, Bender has introduced the term "theology of discipleship." The idea of discipleship or *Nachfolge*, however, does not yet constitute a theology in the proper sense of the word. It is rather an element of that implied theological system which enabled the Anabaptists to carry on so forcefully, and in which discipleship assumes but a constitutive character. The numerous confessions of faith and confessional tracts of the different Anabaptist groups do not give much help in the further elucidation of the question since, as stated above, they simply affirm their formal orthodoxy in the acceptance of the doctrine of the Trinity and of the Apostles' Creed, plus the call to unconditional obedience to the divine commandments: "Christ said so,... hence we have to do it."

It is certainly true that in the New Testament a theology in the more formal sense of the word is most explicit in the writings of Paul; but that does not mean that the teachings of Christ Himself, as recorded in the

---

2 Roland H. Bainton in a personal letter to the writer, November 23, 1953.

The Doctrine of the Two Worlds

Synoptic Gospels, are lacking in theological foundations. It has been only in recent decades that we have come to recognize this "implied" theology of the Synoptics, so long by-passed and overlooked, as exactly the one which became so central for the Anabaptists in the sixteenth century. The teachings of Paul are essentially not different from those of Christ, but the emphasis and the categories applied are different, or at least could be so interpreted. In any case it is possible to speak of a Pauline tradition, elaborated later by Augustine, and of a Synoptic tradition, preserved in the main by those groups which Ludwig Keller once called old evangelical brotherhoods.

As we now study this Synoptic tradition or emphasis, we find that central for it is the teaching of the two kingdoms, together with the message of what the Kingdom of God actually means and implies. I think it is justified to call these doctrines a genuine theology in the proper sense of the word, even though its forms of expression are different from the above-mentioned more sophisticated Pauline-Augustinian tradition. It is proposed to call this teaching "Kingdom theology." In a certain sense it is a continuation of the teachings of the Old Testament Prophets, in the main of Isaiah, where this basic dualism of the two realms already appears. Most important in this connection is the idea that the "other kingdom" is not merely something transcendental, something of another aeon, or something to be experienced only after death, but a reality to be expected and experienced in this life, even though in a sort of metahistorical situation.

As a matter of fact, the kingdom theology (as we see it, the very center of Christ's message and witnessing) is to be distinguished from a theology whose primary concern is personal salvation (the Protestant interpretation of Paulinism). These two theologies are complementary to each other and of equal importance. The Reformers knew this fact very well.[3] In fact, their outlook on history was decidedly Kingdom-oriented, but they had their reasons for underemphasizing this two-facet content of the New Testament theology. The Pietists a century and a half later revived the Kingdom idea, but being themselves the offspring of traditional Protestantism, they interpreted it in a non-Synoptic way. The real representatives of the Synoptic Kingdom theology have always been the old evangelical brotherhoods, but none were more outspokenly Kingdom-oriented, hence none more true to the spirit of the Master Himself, than the Anabaptists.

In the Pauline teaching the idea of original sin has a central position, making personal salvation and justification by faith a most urgent matter, while the Kingdom comes to occupy apparently a secondary position. In the teaching of Jesus, on the other hand, the sense of urgency seems to be

---

[3] Compare, for instance, the most recent treatment of this subject, Franz Lau, *Luthers Lehre von den beiden Reichen* ("Luthertum," Berlin, 1952). The traditional interpretation, however, reduced the dualism of "this world" and the Kingdom to the simplified dualism of Law and Gospel. This is certainly not the understanding of the Anabaptists.

associated predominantly with the Kingdom,[4] which, of course, includes the certainty of personal salvation. To be sure, Jesus taught by means of parables and pictures rather than by way of concepts and theories, and parables allow no easy translation into a system. And yet, the doctrine of the two worlds—the Kingdom of God which is to come here and now, and the kingdom of darkness which rules over all those who do not see the light—this doctrine represents definitely a very specific outlook or theology. As will be shown below, it has its own characteristic (1) value system; (2) view of history; and (3) social ethic. In short, it implies a real theology although of a character rather different from that of the Pauline tradition as interpreted by Augustine and the Reformers.

While Paul by no means taught only a theology of justification by faith *alone* (as the Reformers, in particular Luther, have done),[5] he gave enough attention to it to make possible the development of a one-sided theology at the hands of the Reformers, running something like this: The law has come to an end; all men have inherited original sin; Christ died for us; and thus the individual can and will be saved (i.e., justified before God) if only he puts all his confidence and faith in the atoning quality of Christ's supreme sacrifice. The essential element here is faith, not works, however the latter may be interpreted. This one-sided emphasis in a fully developed Protestantism, which tended to ignore both the remainder of Paul's teaching and the Gospels as well, produced a theological system which assumed an extremely individualistic outlook. The individual, a sinner through and through who cannot do good, craves for salvation and eventually finds it by believing.[6] The neighbor, the brother, important though he is, is in no way constitutive to this outlook on salvation. Love, we learn, is the fruit of faith, but such love adds nothing essential to the drama of completely unearned and even undeserved redemption, else it would assume the quality of works. No specific social implications could be deduced, and both Lutheranism and Calvinism became exceedingly individualistic in their teachings, while civilization at large went on independently and autonomously.

Kingdom theology is essentially of a different kind. The outlook is dualistic as throughout the New Testament. Yet while Paul preferably contraposes *spirit* and *flesh*, categories suggesting above all a conflict in the personal and private sphere, Kingdom theology distinguishes two other concepts in polarity. These concepts are *the world* (being ruled by "the prince of this world," i.e., Satan), and *the other world*, the Kingdom, which is God's world. Two possibilities are

---

4 Cf. Albert Schweitzer, *The Mystery of the Kingdom of God* (See note 9 *infra*).

5 The term "alone" was added by Luther to the text of the epistle to the Romans in order to make the idea more understandable and emphatic. Paul would have turned it down.

6 A good illustration of this type of thinking may be drawn from the following quotation from Luther: "When God speaks and gives signs [i.e., sacraments], man must firmly and wholeheartedly believe that what God says and signifies is true.... Then God, in turn, will count *this* faith unto our righteousness, good and sufficient to salvation," *Martin Luther's Works* (ed. Jacobs, Philadelphia), iii, 20f.

here to be contemplated: either that these two realms are coexistent, although on different levels, and the Kingdom of God is already present in or among those who have been born again or who are united in the name of the Master ("where two or three are together in my name..."); or the Kingdom of God is to come, in fact its coming is imminent, and one ought to prepare himself for this imminent coming by purification and a new life. The latter idea was present already in the teaching of the Essenes, of John the Baptist, and of some Ebionites. This second interpretation of the Kingdom idea we may call eschatological,[7] while the first has no special systematic name, yet is more closely associated with the idea of rebirth and conversion. These two views, the kingdom present in every reborn Christian (or present where two or three are assembled in the Master's name), and the kingdom as the new order to be expected at any moment and for which proper preparation is needed, are intermixed in Anabaptist thought just as they are in the original source of that teaching, the Gospels. But the eschatological hope was subdued and never dominated the thinking of the Anabaptists, just as in the Gospel the implied eschatology was never to outdo the positive teachings concerning the Kingdom as the newly revealed other–reality which is within the reach of everyone who earnestly longs and desires to enter the same.

As suggested earlier, the Kingdom theory implies first a new set of values. Certainly, the Sermon on the Mount is the best illustration: love, forgiveness, self–surrender, hating not even one's own persecutors, these values are so radically different that they seem paradoxical and unrealizable to an unregenerate mind. Certainly they go far beyond mere ethics. Rather they imply a different dimension, the world of the pure Spirit, in contrast with all secular this–worldly valuations. In fact, these new values are unobtainable except through rebirth and a radical change of mind, concept's not too much at home in orthodox Protestantism, the religion of the many. Historically, this has produced within Christendom what the sociologists of religion like to call sectarianism, meaning that the disciples, the *Nachfolger*, the citizens of the Kingdom, intentionally separate themselves from the "world," in order to share as little as possible in the affairs of the natural realm and of its citizens. They are highly suspicious of the values of this world, including even that which is usually called "culture," and they sense in it the working of destructive, non–divine forces in the background. All cathartic or puritanical tendencies have their roots in this new value system.

In the second place, Kingdom theology has its own specific outlook on history, a fact much forgotten today but very much alive even in the age of the Reformation. The two realms, the Kingdom of God and the kingdom of darkness, are engaged in a perennial struggle, a world drama, in which each

---

7   It might be well to compare at this point the eschatological outlook of the Gospels (such as Matt. 24, Mark 13, and Luke 21) with that of the Book of Revelation (Rev. 20). The latter never received much emphasis among the old evangelical brotherhoods.

person must choose and take his side. In the end the Kingdom of God will triumph over the powers of darkness. This is the eschatological expectation.[8] Hence, the sectarian feels a high sense of responsibility in this cosmic–historic process, and therefore accepts suffering and martyrdom without flinching. Only by witnessing to the Kingdom of Light can the latter even become full reality. That this outlook, although prominent in the New Testament, especially in the Gospels, recedes with the Reformers' interpretation of Paul hardly needs further elaboration.

Thirdly, the Kingdom theology includes also a social ethic, different, to be sure, from what usually goes by that name. A lack of "social ethics," or at least of what may better be called a concern for the social order of this world, was often observed in the teaching of the New Testament. The absence of any doctrine of "natural law" was observed at an early date in church history, but it was soon supplied from Stoic philosophy to promote a more adjustable foundation of church life. Thus far, however, very little attention has been given to the genuine social ethic of the Gospel message of the Kingdom of God, most likely because it does not fit too well into the ways of the world at large and into the social exigencies of civilization. We mean here the brotherhood idea, the idea of the *Gemeinde*, the *ecclesia* in its first meaning, the idea of the *koinonia*, a closely knit fellowship of believers and disciples, not in the form of the brotherhoods as we know them in the early church, and in all old evangelical brotherhoods including the Anabaptists. All individualism and individualistic concern for personal salvation is ruled out. No one can enter the Kingdom except together with his brother. The old saying that "there is no salvation outside the church" does not exactly express the underlying idea of this brotherhood ideal; actually, that doctrine belongs to a different frame of reference. And yet, it simply is so that the Kingdom of God means, from its very beginning, a togetherness, else it is no kingdom. The mere aggregation of saved souls, as in Pietism, does not constitute the Kingdom; it remains just an aggregation, nothing else. The horizontal man–to–man relationship belongs to the Kingdom just as much as does the vertical God–man relationship. In fact, the belief prevails that one cannot come to God (that is, attain salvation) except as one comes to Him together with one's brother. The brethren, the body of believers, constitutes the realm; hence brotherly love, *agape*, is more than mere ethics. It is one of the basic qualifications of the kingdom in the here and now.

Kingdom theology is hostile to *Kultur*, man's autonomous creation and setting of values. Actually *Kultur* or civilization is a Graeco–Roman and a Renaissance concept, not a Christian one; hence the apparent coolness of the Anabaptists toward human achievement and cultural advancement. Since

---

8 This particular outlook on history is actually much older than the New Testament. According to N. Söderblom, "Ages of the World," in Hastings' *Encyclopedia of Religion and Ethics*, I (1928), it is found in Iranian (Zoroastrian) ideas which entered later postexilic Judaism. Of course, the New Testament Kingdom theology gave this outlook a new and different significance.

the latter does not belong to the system of values embodied in the Kingdom theology they meet it with suspicion, fearful lest it contain elements of destruction, elements of despondency and non-salvation, in short, that it miss the essentials of Christ's message and world outlook. The Middle Ages, being steeped in the philosophy of history of the two realms, knew more about this tension between man-made civilization and God's Kingdom than has any time since the fifteenth century.

The Kingdom theology is concerned with the concrete, the life in the here and the now, although in a dimension other than the material. By no means does it teach that the Kingdom is found in heaven only, and attainable only after death. This is a post–New Testament interpretation. Kingdom theology does not mean merely a glorious expectation of life after death to be reached by the pious and the ascetic; it means a radical turn in life itself, the breaking in of a new dimension into the physical existence of man. Due to its new system of values, so highly challenging to anything known to "natural" man, the group life of the disciples has always been misunderstood and disliked, in fact persecuted by the world. Hence a "theology of martyrdom" developed among the Brethren, an understanding that the citizens of the kingdom of God will necessarily meet suffering in this world. This suffering, however, is of a redemptive character and represents a necessary element in the building of God's Kingdom. It was this way in the early centuries after Christ, and all through history. The Anabaptists in particular accepted the idea of the suffering church in an almost mater-of-fact fashion, and every member of this group understood it without much explanation. In fact, we often discover even a kind of longing for martyrdom, a desire to be allowed to testify for the new spiritual world through suffering and supreme sacrifice.

This martyr-mindedness is usually mellowed by a restrained eschatological outlook: God will soon change the world altogether. Wait but a little while, and yours will be the triumph. Save for a few exceptions, such as that of Melchior Hofmann, the Anabaptists did not calculate the end of the world, being mindful of the words of Christ that no one knows the day, not even the Son, but the Father alone. Nevertheless, they frequently speak of "these last and dangerous times," and of the "last fury of the beast." Here they use a figure from the Book of Revelation which is otherwise little used and quoted. Beyond this, however, eschatological expectations were seldom talked about. After all, is not the kingdom realized even now through the brotherhood of the reborn? Thus, although the kingdom theology always has an eschatological slant, implying a philosophy of history, it nevertheless does not lead to unbalanced expectations such as chiliasm, adventism, millennialism, and the like.

The question may be raised whether or not the Anabaptist sources actually support this thesis of their Kingdom theology. The Kingdom theology was never systematically formulated by the Anabaptists; implicitly, however, it is very much there. Even as Jesus spoke mainly in parables, thus revealing His theological ideas but indirectly, so it is also with the Anabaptists. Very clear, even radical, is their dualism concerning the two realms. Their disparagement, and even fear of the world goes beyond that opposition which we would find in Paul's derogation of the flesh. While the latter leads to asceticism and celibacy, the Anabaptist dualism is of a rather different kind, requiring complete separation from the world as the realm of the prince of darkness. The Anabaptists, however, were not puritans. The mere practice of purity of morals would mean little to them even though the idea of a "church without spot and wrinkle" is quite common with the Anabaptists. The Puritans certainly had one element of the Kingdom theology, the strictness of discipline; but they lacked certain other elements, due to their Calvinistic outlook.

The terms most often used by Anabaptists are *Nachfolge* (discipleship) and *Gehorsam* (obedience); that is, the acceptance of Christ's leadership and that spirit which permeates His teachings. In short, their way of thinking and of evaluation is that of the kingdom theology, even though an explicit theology of this kind might not be so easily demonstrable. They felt absolutely certain that they were citizens of that other (spiritual) world here and now, and accepted the values, the outlook on history and the social consequences which follow with this position as a matter of course.

This theology, however, needs one further analysis to exclude misunderstanding. Frequent attempts have been made to integrate kingdom theology and the typical Protestant theology of salvation, i.e., justification by faith alone. The outstanding attempt in this direction is Pietism, which likewise speaks of God's kingdom and its building up, mainly through intensive mission work. As in so many other areas, Anabaptism and Pietism have certain similarities also at this point. The Anabaptists, too, were intent on mission work and they were aware that by this work they were instrumental in building God's kingdom here and now. Likewise the Pietist emphasis upon the new birth is quite similar to that of Anabaptists, although the accompanying methodic struggle of repentance (the *Busskampf*) of Pietism is totally foreign to Anabaptism. In spite of all these similarities the concept of the kingdom in Pietism is yet basically different from that in Anabaptism. To Pietism of all shades the kingdom means the assembling of all those who have passed through the *Busskampf* experience and know themselves now as the reborn; they represent then the citizens of that kingdom, the conventicle of the saved who now enjoy their state of salvation in quiet withdrawal and devotional uplift (edification). The world outside is not challenged, and accordingly does not react against the Pietist. In Pietism, the dualism of the two realms is never dynamic, and the world is not decried as darkness, but is marginally accepted. Above all, the brotherhood idea is not present, at least not in the sense of the old evangelical brotherhoods with their togetherness and sharing.

To the Pietist the kingdom is the assembly or society of the redeemed, who join in a sort of conventicle; to Anabaptism it is a closely knit, non-individualistic brotherhood where the brother is *constitutive* to the idea of the Kingdom and its realization, and where the concern with one's own salvation from original sin is but marginal, and any thought of its "enjoyment" completely foreign. Obedience stands here in opposition to enjoyment (edification). In Anabaptism the Kingdom idea is the primary concern, and thus becomes dynamic, challenging, and extremely other–dimensional. With Pietism individual salvation is the primary concern, and the Kingdom idea assumes a non–dynamic and only mildly dualistic character, thus leading to less tension with the kingdom of this world. In Pietism, the idea of the cross becomes more emotional than existential, just as the idea of the Spirit is further reduced to a psychological uplift without the existential "I cannot do otherwise" of the Anabaptists. Finally, Pietism places undue emphasis on death and dying, as if the Kingdom of God were synonymous with heaven or paradise. Nothing is farther from Anabaptism than that. Thus, although the Kingdom idea and even a kind of kingdom theology occurs also within the respected circles of Protestantism, namely, the pietistic wings of Lutheranism and of Calvinism, the difference between this and the Kingdom theology of Anabaptism is nevertheless very real and tangible, and forbids any confusion between Anabaptism and Pietism.

It was only in fairly recent times that a more adequate appreciation of this Kingdom theology was promoted and, with it, a new understanding of the life and work of Christ and the meaning of discipleship. Two men were primarily instrumental in this regard: Albert Schweitzer, whose first book on this subject was published 1901,[9] and Leonhard Ragaz, the Swiss theologian, whose magazine *Neue Wege* began to appear in 1907 and whose major books were published between 1922 and 1925.[10] Unfortunately, neither of these two men was too successful in his endeavor as they challenged too strongly the traditional viewpoints of most Protestant theologians. This is particularly true of Ragaz, whose work was an unceasing "prophetic" fight for the recovery of the original meaning of the Kingdom theology and its consequences. In this connection he likes to speak of *die Sache Christi*, that is, loyalty or devotion to that which Christ stands for and is most concerned with, instead of "Christian religion" with its concentration on institutional church bodies. He also urges a "going back from Paul to Jesus," very outspokenly connecting discipleship with the Kingdom idea.

---

9 Albert Schweitzer, *The Mystery of the Kingdom of God; the Secret of Jesus' Messiahship and Passion* (*Das Messianitäts– und Leidensgeheimnis: Eine Skizze des Lebens Jesu*) was written in 1901 (translated into English in 1913; new edition with an introduction by Walter Lowrie, 1950).

10 Leonhard Ragaz, *Weltreich, Religion und Gottesherrschaft*, 2 vols. (Zürich, 1922); *Der Kampf um das Reich Gottes in Blumhard, Vater und Sohn, und Weiter* (Zürich, 1922); and the magazine *Neue Wege* (Zürich 1907 ff.). See also his *Gedanken aus vierzig Jahren geistigen Kampfes, ausgewählt von Freunden*, 2d ed. (Bern, 1951), with exhaustive bibliography by Lejeune.

From a historical viewpoint we might also mention the work of Rudolf Otto, who, in his *The Kingdom of God and the Son of Man*,[11] offers perhaps the finest scholarly treatment of the ideas here discussed, helpful also in the reinterpretation of Anabaptism. In contradistinction to the work of Ragaz, it remains a strictly historical analysis. I myself have likewise tried to clarify the issues in my *Mennonite Piety Through the Centuries*,[12] discussing the idea of the Kingdom and its difference from the doctrine of justification by faith alone. But then I was not yet prepared to carry the analysis as far as in the present paper. Very little has been said concerning the consequences of this theology of the Kingdom for the outlook on history. Otto Piper's *God in History*[13] emphasizes rightly the difference between secular history and holy (sacred, redemptive) history, but the consequences as to withdrawal and opposition to secular civilization are not clearly drawn.

The meaning of the present paper is to propose a comparatively new viewpoint and to invite further discussion and exchange of thoughts and research. I hope that our younger friends and co–workers will answer, correcting or setting aright whatever was said above. They should remember, however, that the idea of salvation by faith alone looks very different from this point of view than from that of the official Protestant interpretation. To be concerned with one's own salvation first and foremost is not the same as to feel a burning passion to serve the *Sache Christi* through *Nachfolge* and obedience, through the creation of a nucleus of the Kingdom here and now. The latter is the never–ending concern of those who have a vision of that other dimension which alone is the place where Spirit may truly become flesh.

Source: G. F. Hershberger, ed., *The Recovery of the Anabaptist Vision* (Scottdale, 1957), 105–18.

---

11   Rudolf Otto, *The Kingdom of God and the Son of Man* (published in German, 1930; first English edition, 1938; revised 1943).
12   Robert Friedmann, *Mennonite Piety Through the Centuries* (Goshen, 1949), 85–88.
13   Otto Piper, *God in History* (New York, 1936).

THE HUTTERITE BRUDERHOF

Bruderhof, also called Haushaben, was the name for the community settlements of the Hutterites in Moravia and Slovakia, found today in similar fashion also in South Dakota and Canada. Since community of goods is one of the main principles of the Hutterian Brethren, it was quite natural that from the very beginning of their settlement in Moravia they established such "collective farms" (if it is permissible to use this modern term, forgetting for a moment the great difference in the ideology of Anabaptist communism and Soviet Communism). The Bruderhofs were a unique undertaking without any model before them, yet highly successful and for that reason still practiced among the Hutterian Brethren. These Bruderhofs were quite elaborate establishments consisting as a rule of several larger and smaller houses (one such farm in Slovakia had no fewer than forty–seven buildings), usually around a village common or square. The ground floor of the buildings was used for community living: dining hall, kitchen, and rooms for nursery, school, laundry, spinning, weaving, and sewing, and also for maternity rooms. The roofs (thatch mixed with clay to make them fireproof, a much–discussed invention of the Brethren) were high and steep so that the attics contained two stories of small chambers (*Stuben*, *Oertel*) where the married couples lived with their small children. These houses must once have distinguished themselves from the poor shacks of most of the peasants of the sixteenth and seventeenth centuries. "They have the most beautiful houses," exclaimed even the archfoe of the Brethren, the Catholic priest Christoph Andreas Fischer, in 1605. A few of these houses are still standing in Slovakia. Some of the Bruderhofs in America are not unlike those of the far–off origins. A very graphic picture of these sixteenth–century houses may be found in a contemporary woodcut on the title page of the polemical book by Christoph Erhard, *Gründliche kurtz verfasste Historia...* (Munich, 1589). It shows a house with the thatched roof and two stories of windows in it, and in front of the house a man, woman, and child in the typical Hutterite garb. (This is perhaps the only original picture of the old Hutterites in existence.)

Each Bruderhof tried to be as self–sufficient as possible. It had not only its own fields, woods, ponds, mills, on the estates of the nobles, but also a great number of workshops, some of them of great renown. There were the shops of the black– and locksmiths, of the saddlers and shoemakers, of the carpenters, potters, cutlers (*Messerschmiede*), wagon–makers, and furriers. They had also well–known breweries (the Hutterites still drink beer), and occasionally wineries. Their *Kellermeister* (both stewards of the vineyards and of the revenues of the wineries, also keepers of the feudal wine cellars) were most in demand as masters in their field. Each household was managed by one responsible brother elected for this office, the *Diener der Notdurft*, the steward or keeper of the house. He had to purchase all that was needed— wool, cotton, and hemp, iron and other metals, wine and salt. His purchases were made with the proceeds of all the trades and crafts, and the material distributed as needed. He also organized the work on farm and shop, and directed everyone to his job according to the needs of the entire group. In North America the unlovely title of "boss" became the English designation for this office.

The afore–mentioned Fischer gives not only a very lively description of these community houses, but on the title pages of one of his pamphlets, entitled *Der Hutterische Taubenkobel* (1607), he has also a woodcut to illustrate his contention that the Brethren lived in these houses like doves in a dovecote. In another of his angry pamphlets, entitled *54 erhebliche Ursachen...* (1605), he mentions over seventy such households in southern Moravia, in each of which from 500 to 600 persons (including children) were said to be living, and in a few even as many as a thousand or more. (These statements are probably exaggerated.) He warns the authorities about the increase in number of these places, and pleads that the Brethren should not be tolerated any longer in Moravia. It was the climax of the Austrian Counter-Reformation; one should also keep in mind that these Bruderhofs were truly thriving, and that they were the object of much envy among the surrounding peasant farmers. The landed nobles, however, gladly availed themselves of the unusual skill and industriousness of these "heretics."

The number of these Bruderhofs is a much–discussed theme. Loserth counts around ninety such settlements in Moravia, while Fischer claims but seventy. F. Hruby, *Die Wiedertäufer in Mähren* (1935), is much more conservative in his well–documented estimates. He reports (for Moravia only) twenty–one such Bruderhofs in 1545, which number almost trebles to fifty–seven in the "Golden Age" around 1589. Then came bad times, a Turkish War (1605) with its devastations, and the preliminaries of the Thirty Years War, the high point of the Catholic Counter-Reformation. By 1619, only forty–five such collective farms are reported, and by 1622 not more than twenty–four. The number of Bruderhofs in Slovakia is nowhere reported, but one may assume that there were hardly more than twenty altogether. Some of the buildings there are still standing.

Each household had between 200 and 400 persons, one third roughly of this number not yet baptized children. The number of 1,000 inhabitants or more seems to be exaggerated—except for times of great disaster. Taking an average of 300 per unit, we arrive at the following approximate figures of Anabaptist population in Moravia (according to Hruby):

YEAR	COUNT
1545	6,300
1589	17,100
1619	13,500
1622	7,200

(In 1622, all these more than 7,000 Brethren were expelled from Moravia, and no Bruderhof was spared. It was the final end of the communal life in that country.) Sixteenth-century authors give quite different figures, varying between 20,000 and 70,000 and Johann Amos Comenius even claims that each Bruderhof held a population of between two and three thousand. This information has to be taken with caution; Hruby's calculations sound much more likely.

Today the Hutterite census, according to Joseph W. Eaton (*MQR*, January 1951), shows ninety-six Bruderhofs with a population of 9,211.

As to the economic value of the Bruderhofs in the Golden Age of Hutterite history (late sixteenth-century), the estimates are likewise somewhat vague. Loserth draws conclusions from a remark in the Chronicle that one single household was taxed 100 florins (gold pieces) and even more. Hruby found in one letter of Emperor Ferdinand II that up to 1620 at least 30,000 florins were confiscated from the Hutterites in southern Moravia. (He had very little power in Slovakia.) This is a tremendously large sum considering the devaluation of the currency at the time of the outbreak of the Thirty Years' War. Since the Brethren could still salvage some means when fleeing into Slovakia, their total fortune is estimated by Hruby as possibly more than 60,000 florins. Hence the repeated urge of the emperor (himself in never-ending need of money) to press the Brethren for all their hidden savings. Hruby's account of this topic is highly informative and well documented.

Varying are also the reports concerning the hygiene in these collective housings. Some reports stress their great cleanliness, unusual for the standards of sixteenth-century peasantry. Particularly the concern for the healthful upbringing of the children in nurseries and schools is emphasized time and again. Yet, a foreign visitor in 1612 has this to report (translated from the Latin): "For their education they crowd together 200 to 300 children in great filth and stench. Hence a great number of them die early." Of course this is a report of the declining years, but it could be stated fairly generally that, in spite of their excellent physicians, the knowledge of fighting epidemics was yet too poor to prevent a high infant mortality, particularly in the houses that were overcrowded with children. It is doubtful, however, whether it was worse than at any other place of the sixteenth century. Today the Bruderhofs in America have both cleanliness and good health.

The Bruderhof was also the place of worship since there was no separate chapel. It was in the common dining-room that they celebrated the Lord's Supper at certain intervals, coming together from the entire Bruderhof or even from several in the vicinity. It is understandable that this type of living together, working, caring and suffering together, produced a very closely knit fellowship. Mutual aid existed as a matter of fact, as well as a spirit of togetherness unknown anywhere else.

Source: *Mennonite Encyclopedia*, I, p. 445.

GEMEINDEORDNUNGEN

Gemeindeordnungen are the ordinances and regulations of the Hutterite brotherhood, also their church disciplines (although different in character from the conventional type of such documents, since church activities and everyday living were identical for the Brethren). They were issued by the bishop (*Vorsteher*) of the brotherhood. Some thirty such Ordnungen are known from 1561 to 1665, and again of 1762, 1793 and later. They are among the most original creations of the Hutterites and are in many ways unique documents, revealing the strong consciousness of the Brethren that they had to follow a very strict and austere way of life, the "narrow path," and that deviations must be prevented.

These Ordnungen are spiritual and moral as well as practical in nature (to the minutest detail). They are hortative, yet never threatening, admonishing all members of the church to cooperate most carefully and soberly in the great enterprise of brotherly living in community of goods, both in consumption and production, in the way which Christ and the apostles established. In this sense it is not incorrect to call the Anabaptist church in general, and the Hutterite brotherhood in particular, a "church of order," i.e., a disciplined and regulated church in which this order is voluntarily accepted by all. God speaks through the bishops, who thus assume a charismatic authority.

In many regards these ordinances suggest the rules and regulations of medieval monasteries, with which the Hutterite organization has many traits in common (the principle of merit is, however, completely absent here). In some other regards these ordinances are reminiscent of the medieval guild regulations, although their outspoken Christian emphasis distinguishes them again from these secular documents.

The Ordnungen may be classified into two kinds:
a. those dealing with the general organization and discipline of the community (*Gemein*, Bruderhofs), its morals and its spiritual guidance, also the formulation of the general genius of the group;
b. regulations dealing in particular with the special functions of the various members of the group, with the administration of crafts and other occupational tasks and their most careful and economical fulfillment. In this group, regulations for millers, cutlers (*Messerer*), barber–surgeons, potters (*Hafner*), the various kinds of smiths,

buyers, stock clerks (*Ausgeber*), stewards, and farm foremen (*Weinzierl*) appear more often than for other occupations. It seems that in these areas temptations were particularly strong to indulge in self-interested extra activities which could easily injure the group and spoil its good name.

The main tenor of all the Ordnungen is the battle against *Eigennutz* (selfishness, greed, profit-motive) and the admonition to live up to the requirements of a life in perfect community of goods. Austerity, puritanical simplicity, even a degree of ascetic living were enjoined time and again, and thus inculcated in the mind of every member. The education of the youth dared not be soft in any way, for they were to be trained for trying times and must then know why to suffer and be able to bear such situations. The reading of the old writings (epistles, confessions, hymns) was advised as helpful. All handiwork was to be diligent, solid, and reliable, carefully done without waste. Work should be done every day including Saturday, without haste but also without loafing; luxuries must not be allowed, likewise no private possessions of any kind. Ehrenpreis declared expressly, "Inheritance shall remain abolished as of old; if someone dies, everything he has used shall revert to the community, even his books (*Klein-Geschichtsbuch*, p. 526)." It should be remarked, however, that the latter point is no longer in practice today; books are now the only possession of a brother or sister which may be left to one's children.

The Ordnungen offer an extremely valuable insight into the inner life of the brotherhood from 1561 on, when the first ordinance of this kind was laid down by the *Vorsteher* Lanzenstiel. Before that year we have only Riedemann's *Rechenschaft* of 1540 and the epistles, mainly by Jacob Hutter, and the oral tradition.

In the main, four great *Vorsteher* distinguished themselves in the drawing up of *Gemeindeordnungen*: Peter Walpot 1565–78, Klaus Braidl 1583–1611, Sebastian Dietrich 1611–19, and Andreas Ehrenpreis 1639–62 but actually leading the brotherhood since 1633. Although the first-named two men contributed much to this tradition, the great Ordnungen were yet to come: Dietrich's general ordinance of 1612 (which fills twenty-two leaves in one manuscript) and Ehrenpreis' general ordinance of 1651 (which fills fourteen pages folio size small print of the *Klein-Geschichtsbuch*, pp. 519–32). That we are so well informed about all these writings is due to the tradition-mindedness of Ehrenpreis and his unusual sense for the orderly collection of all rules existent before his days, together with the contributions of his own spiritual government. In one handwritten book of 1640 (Codex III, 198 of Esztergom, apparently Ehrenpreis' own copy), with additions up to 1650, this *Vorsteher* put together nearly everything that had been said before and also that which he himself had presented to the brotherhood since 1633. There is, to be sure, also some repetition, but always with some new angles not stressed before. This codex has never been published; one copy of it is in the Beck collection of Brno, Nr. 87, another, also done by Beck in longhand, is deposited in the Mennonite Historical Library of Goshen College. Beck in his *Geschichts–Bücher* prints only the *Bader–Ordnung* of 1653 (ordinance for the barber–surgeons, actually a repetition of an earlier ordinance of 1633 in Beck, pp. 485–87); and a *Weinzierl–Ordnung* (order for the farm managers) of 1650 (Beck, pp. 478–79).

A number of hitherto completely unknown Ordnungen were made public for the first time when A. J. F. Zieglschmid's edition of the *Klein–Geschichtsbuch* came out in 1947. Not only does the Johannes Waldner text contain two remarkably strong instructions by Ehrenpreis: (a) concerning absolute non–resistance (1633; *Klein–Geschichtsbuch*, pp. 168–72), and (b) concerning the mating of young people, also against the bad practice of unchecked match–making (*Kuppelei*), which recently entered the brotherhood (1643; *Klein–Geschichtsbuch*, pp. 215–8). But the most outstanding Ordnung of all is the great ordinance of 1651, which Zieglschmid prints in an appendix from a copy still preserved and in use by the Brethren today (*Klein–Geschichtsbuch*, pp. 519–32). It contains a comprehensive instruction which touches practically every aspect of life, stern in character and yet with a loving concern. Among other things also the idea of shunning (*Meidung*) is enjoined; it must not be allowed to be taken lightly or to be denied altogether. The Ordnung of 1651 contains actually a complete "philosophy of life" in the minutest detail, and for that reason deserves particular attention. A footnote says that it was read before the assembled Brethren in Slovakia as well as in Transylvania year after year, and that it was reread to the brotherhood for the last time as late as 1734. Besides this Ordnung, the *Great Chronicle* of the Brethren, the *Geschicht–Buch*, contains also two letters to the Brethren in Transylvania of 1642 and of 1649, again by Ehrenpreis and with similar advice and admonitions.

"Be faithful and loyal, even unto the smallest detail," that is in a nutshell the message of Ehrenpreis, by which he wanted to strengthen the somewhat weakened brotherhood of his time, imbuing it with the spirit of the founding fathers. The scope of his concern is amazing. In retrospect we may say that his work has been fairly successful, even though a certain formalism became dominant as the living spirit faded out more or less.

The organization and the genius of the Hutterites today is to a certain extent based on those *Gemeindeordnungen*, which give to the brotherhood such directions that temptations will be met and as far as possible reduced. And yet, these regulations are by no means dictatorial in character; they are presented with a generally accepted authority of the bishops, and they breathe the spirit of brotherly love and concern in maintaining the way which the Brethren considered the true form of Christian discipleship.

Source: *Mennonite Encyclopedia*, II, pp. 454–55.

DIENER DER NOTDURFT

Diener der Notdurft was the title used by the Hutterites for their elected and ordained managers or stewards of their Bruderhofs who took care of all temporal needs of the community of each colony. (The title was also used to some extent by the Swiss–South German Anabaptists for the deacon.) Since the Hutterites lived and still live by the principle of community of goods, an elaborate organization of their establishments became necessary. It was based on the idea of Christian brotherhood, which means voluntary cooperation in all work, absence of "bossism" or paternalism, trusteeship, and acceptance of responsibilities for one another. For this organization to be efficient, it had to operate smoothly, economically, and above all cheerfully. At one place the Great Chronicle compares these Bruderhofs with the work of the bees. In spite of all good will there was still much need for alertness against selfishness (*Eigennutz*), lust for domineering, and the tendency toward laziness. Much exhortation was needed.

From the very beginnings in the days of Jakob Hutter, the main principles of such an organization were established: there were first the *Diener am Wort*, who took care of the spiritual needs, and then the *Diener der Notdurft*, who were responsible for the smooth functioning of the Bruderhofs in all practical regards. Peter Riedemann states in his great *Rechenschaft* of 1540 the basic organization of the leadership in the chapter on "Differences of Ministries" (p. 82 of English edition): "...There are rulers (*Regierer*) who order and arrange the house or church (*Gemein*), putting each in his place that everything may go properly and well. They also see that the church is cared for in temporal distribution, and are also called ministers of temporal needs." The Chronicle, too, once describes in detail the functioning of the church, and here again we learn something about this office of stewardship. The main source, however, for all further details is found in but one manuscript of 1640, containing a summary of all previous *Gemeindeordnungen* (regulations or ordinances,) with added new material; its author is the *Vorsteher* Andreas Ehrenpreis, who was eager to have his people stay strictly in the old tradition. Later Ordnungen of this kind were published by Zieglschmid in his edition of the *Klein–Geschichtsbuch* (1947), pp. 519–65, but they are less elaborate than the one yet unpublished manuscript of Ehrenpreis (a transcript in the

Goshen College Library). The following description is based exclusively on this document.

In general the *Diener der Notdurft* were active in four different functions or offices:

1. the most important office was that of *Haushälter*, general manager or steward of the house;
2. other brethren were *Einkäufer* (buyers);
3. again others were *Fürgestellte* or foremen of the different trades and shops; while
4. a last category, the *Meier*, were overseers or heads of the farms.

Actually, still more subdivisions were named under the title *Diener der Notdurft*; for instance, there was the *Weinzierl*, who was the assistant to the *Haushälter* and in his absence his deputy; and then the *Kellner*, originally the manager of the vineyards and its revenues, later about the same as *Meier*, general steward. Another helper of the steward was the *Kastner*, originally the caretaker of the flour bins, and so on.

Each office had its distinct duties.

1. The *Haushälter* managed, so to speak, the Bruderhof on the top level. He took care of all material needs of the brethren and sisters, including even the clothing and bedding, he distributed all work and supervised it, and he was also in charge of the general demeanor and discipline of the group, mainly at work. For smooth functioning of the whole, the brethren had to submit to his orders and arrangements. He assigned each person to his place, be it workshop, farm, or home duty. He had to be the first up in the morning and the last to bed at night. He kept an eye on the fireplaces to prevent harm. The sick, the old, and the children were under his general care. He was responsible that everybody got what he needed, and yet that nothing be wasted. If any major purchase was due, a committee of elders and the chief steward made the decision. He had to watch the economy of the Bruderhof, to be careful in the administration of the money, and to keep an account of all transactions. From the craftsmen and shops he claimed revenues about every other week, and he watched also that they supplied the Bruderhof with all things needed. If one considers the rather large size of most of these Bruderhofs (200 to 400 persons), it becomes quite obvious that this office of *Haushälter* was a difficult and responsible one, and that he certainly was in need of an assistant (the *Weinzierl*). To fulfill these duties with tact and modesty a high standard of Christian character was needed, and only the best fitted were elected and ordained (after a time of probation) to this office. The flowering of the entire church depended, at least

partly, upon his work, and thus he was in need of spiritual support by the bishop and the *Diener am Wort*.

2. The *Einkäufer* or buyer was, so to speak, the liaison man with the "world" with which he had to deal. He, too, had to be careful with all his purchases, and "should not fall into the tricks of the traders, butchers, and Jews." When in doubt he was to ask the counsel of the elders. The funds which were entrusted to him he did not dare leave with the women but he might deposit them with the elders or the general steward.

3. The *Fürgestellten* or foremen of the shops and the different trades (smiths, cloth makers, tanners, shoemakers, cutlers, etc.) took care of their particular business, bought whatever material they needed, and sold on the market whatever was not needed on the Bruderhof itself. The profits were handed over to the *Haushälter* and represented the major revenues of the entire closed economy. All the necessary regulations of the trades and crafts were discussed with these foremen,

4. The *Meier* and *Kellner*, finally, were responsible for farm, orchard, vineyard, fields, barns, and cellars. These men were particularly appreciated by the noble lords as stewards on their estates. No more expert or reliable men could be found among the peasants. It was a position of trust which these men filled in accordance with their Christian conscience. They had to have their eyes at many places, watching for any fire hazard, and be on the alert regarding the upkeep of buildings, fences, and roads.

In view of the great number and size of the Bruderhofs the number of stewards must have been quite considerable. Beck's *Geschichts–Bücher* (pp. 193–95) records that in 1548 four *Diener am Wort* were elected and fourteen *Diener der Notdurft*, two years later the text lists a total of seventeen ministers and thirty–one stewards (p. 195). Without doubt this number increased during the next generation, the "Golden Era" of the brotherhood. Around 1600 decline set in, due to persecution and wars, and the stewards carried much of the responsibility for salvaging whatever was possible. Plundering made a sound economy next to impossible, yet the Bruderhofs survived somehow, and were estimated at the moment of complete abandonment in 1622 to be worth more than 364,000 talers.

Naturally temptations were ever present, yet seemed to have become more noticeable in the later (seventeenth century) period. Hence the repetition in the *Gemeindeordnungen* of exhortations and admonitions to these stewards. "If a *Haushälter* does not comply with the orders of the ministers it is no small wonder that the Lord withholds His blessing." Or we read about dubious manipulations with material and money which are strongly reprimanded and cut short. Yet this was the failing of only a few, within a group which could exist only if strong Christian principles governed its entire life. The fact that this particular type of community life did survive is proof that these principles were more dominant than the human failings which could be more or less successfully kept in check.

Source: *Mennonite Encyclopedia*, II, pp. 54–55.

ECONOMIC ASPECTS OF EARLY HUTTERITE LIFE

A comprehensive study of the economic aspects of Hutterite life, in the main of their practice of community of goods, has never been undertaken, strange to say, even though material to this end is available in abundance.[1] The present paper attempts a first outline of this subject, admittedly leaving many questions open for further research both in archives and in the field itself. It must be emphasized, however, that a true understanding of the faith and life of the Hutterites is possible only as the economic aspect is considered in the context of their entire history and of their spiritual and social outlook, of what in brief might be called their basic motivations.[2] Although the history of the Hutterian Brethren reveals considerable change and variation in the details of their economic life, according to the degree of freedom experienced, the underlying principles and general patterns nevertheless were fairly uniformly held ever since the beginnings under Jakob Hutter in 1533.

The climax of Hutterite life and the most complete carrying out of their communal principles comes in the "good" and "golden" periods, about 1554–92, mainly during the reign of the tolerant Emperor Maximilian II (1564–76), who himself leaned toward a Protestant type of Christianity. We are fortunate to possess a fairly graphic picture of the communal life of the Brethren at that time, called *Beschreibung der Gemein Wohlstand*, inserted into the Great Chronicle of the brotherhood at the year 1569.[3] Here the details of their social organization are described at great length. We learn how Christian

---

1 The older works by Johann Loserth (1894) laid the groundwork, but it was Franticek Hruby, the late director of the Provincial Archives of Moravia in Brünn (Brno), Czechoslovakia, who for the first time concentrated upon the economic problem in Hutterite studies, using in the main hitherto unknown materials of these archives. Compare F. Hruby, *Die Wiedertäufer in Mähren* (Leipzig, 1935). For a general consideration of the economic consequences of "ascetic Protestantism" and the sectarian outlook compare Max Weber, *Protestant Ethics and the Spirit of Capitalism* (New York, 1930; first German edition, 1905) also Ernst Correll, *Das Schweizerische Täufermennonitentum* (Tübingen, 1925), especially chapter 2. As to the social background of the Hutterite group, see Paul Dedic, "Social Background of the Austrian Anabaptists," *MQR*, XIII (1939), 5–20. Helpful is also the similar study by Paul Peachey, "Social Background of the Swiss Anabaptists," *MQR*, XXVIII (1954), 102–27. The *Great Chronicle of the Hutterites*, published as *Die aelteste Chronik der Hutterischen Brüder*, ed. A. J. F. Zieglschmid (Philadelphia, 1943), remains the chief source for all Hutterite studies. These references apply naturally only to the past, up to about the middle of the seventeenth century. For recent conditions more will be said toward the end of this paper.
2 See Robert Friedmann, "The Christian Communism of the Hutterite Brethren," *Archiv für Reformationsgeschichte*, LII (December, 1955).
3 *Älteste Chronik*, 430–40, or *Geschicht–Buch*, 331–38.

community of goods was observed; how obedience and honor were given to the authorities of the world; how missions were established (*Aussendung*); also how *Diener des Wortes* (preachers) and *Diener der Notdurft* (stewards of the farm and economic affairs) were elected according to a prescribed procedure, and so on. In short, the chronicler assures us, they supported themselves with all manner of occupations (*man nähret sich mit allerlei Handwerk*), and in addition served also the manorial lords in many ways. No member of the community was allowed to be idle. "It was like a big clockwork where one wheel drives the other, promotes, helps, and makes the whole clock function." Still more graphic is another description offered by the Chronicle: "Such a Bruderhof is somewhat like a big beehive where all the busy bees work together to a common end, the one doing this and the other that, not for their own needs but for the good of all." This simile very characteristically hints at the essentially anti–individualistic attitude of the brotherhood. It was understood by all that hard physical labor for the common good (production) was expected of all, while at the same time consumption was restricted according to the principle of frugality as was befitting a life of discipline and Christian obedience.

Large–scale production and restrained consumption necessarily led to such a degree of economic success and wealth as almost inevitably to bring jealousy and slander on the part of the surrounding population.[4] The repute of the wealth of the Brethren (in their best time they numbered about 15,000 baptized members) spread as far as to the Emperor's court in Vienna; everyone knew, or claimed to know, that they buried "great treasures" to hide them from the authorities. Most likely this charge was true to a certain extent. It should be understood as an act of prudence, however, in the absence of a banking system in anticipation of times of hardship and persecution. During the period of the Turkish Wars (1605–6), and again during the early years of the Thirty Years' War (1618–22), almost all of the savings were confiscated by the government. Yet one generation later Grimmelshausen reports again of their considerable wealth in equipment, livestock, and all the rest in their new Bruderhofs in Slovakia.[5] We know from Max Weber's sociological analysis that this situation is typical of all "ascetic Protestantism" or "worldly asceticism,"[6] such as can also be observed in Puritanism or later Pietism. Grimmelshausen reports that he saw the craftsmen–brethren at work in their shops "as if they had hired themselves out for pay." Since no one could live in the group without contributing his share to the common weal, doing it with greatest conscience and discipline, the net result was a rational establishment of great efficiency, something otherwise completely unknown in Europe in

---

4   See the article, "Fischer, Ch. A.," in *ML*, I, 646–48, by Johann Loserth.
5   H. J. Christoph von Grimmelshausen, *Der abenteuerliche Simplicissimus* (*Neudruck deutscher Litteraturwerke des XVI. und XVII. Jahrhunderts*, Nos. 19–25) (Halle a. S., 1880). The section on the Anabaptists is found on pages 439–42 and 377. The first edition appeared in 1668.
6   See Weber, *op. cit.*

the sixteenth and early seventeenth centuries where the factory system had not yet been established. It might be helpful to stress here that there was absolutely no motivation for such organization from the profit angle, since the basic economic philosophy of the Brethren was that of stewardship of all earthly possessions,[7] requiring a dedicated care for and optimal organization of all work along certain previously laid out rational plans. In this regard Hutterite communism is truly unique in the entire history of Christian sectarianism.

As to the social status of the Hutterian Brethren, one cannot call them either peasants or craftsmen, and it would be misleading to derive their basic Christian convictions from their social background. Theirs was neither a peasant's Christianity nor a craftsman's Christianity.[8] Anyone who joined the brotherhood had to learn a craft or had to accept his particular assignment, often very different from his former background. This belongs to the pattern of "ascetic Protestantism" with its prevailing rational order and subsequent tendency toward saving (*asketischer Sparzwang*). All money earned was considered a part of the working capital (*Betriebskapital*), and not as wealth, and its management was entrusted to the bishop (*Vorsteher*), to the *Diener der Notdurft*, and sometimes to the buyers (*Einkäufer*). In many ways the entire economic organization and pattern was not unlike that of the medieval monastery, with the one difference that for the Hutterites married life was not only favored but almost required.

The education of the growing generation of the Bruderhof tended to make the young people fit into this accepted pattern. Industry, care, the utmost honesty, frugality, solidity of work, and reliability were the main virtues stressed in their economic pursuits; likewise unselfishness and concern were ever required. Luxury was out of the question; it was simply not valued, hence no longer desired. All crafts were strictly regulated, and these regulations, not unlike medieval guild regulations, were ever and again read before the assembled groups.[9]

The economic activities of the Brethren may best be divided into two distinct areas:

a. those within the Bruderhofs, including such activities as the pottery kilns and the bathhouses, and

b. those performed outside, on the estates of manorial lords or even in some cities, where occasionally Brethren barber–surgeons were found to be active.

On the Bruderhof we may again distinguish between farm activities proper, the care for food, shelter, and clothing (in this regard the Hutterites

---

[7] See Correll, *op. cit.*, ch. 2.

[8] See the studies of Dedic, *loc. cit.*, and Peachey, *loc. cit.*; also Robert Friedmann, "The Epistles of the Hutterites," *MQR*, XX (1946), 153ff.

[9] Compare the article "Crafts," in *Mennonite Encyclopedia*, I, as well as the article "Gewerbetätigkeit der Hutterischen Brüder," *ML*, II, 105–8, by Loserth. An article "Gemeindeordnungen" will appear in *ME*, II.

of today continue these practices as of old),[10] and the different crafts which brought in some needed cash for farm enlargement and the paying of taxes. As far as the farms were concerned, we meet here again the rationality of a large-scale enterprise. Nothing was wasted; everything was carefully used. For instance, hides came from the slaughterhouse to the tannery, and from there to the harness makers, cobblers, pouch makers, etc. Wool was sent to the women who spun it and then sent it on to the weavers or cloth makers and thence to the tailors. Since the cooking was done for an entire Bruderhof (200 to 300 adults plus all the children), utmost economy was possible and practiced. *Diener der Notdurft*, without ever having learned modern techniques of shop organization, soon developed an admirable tradition of efficiency on the farm level, supported also by the *Weinzierl*, the foreman or work clerk who supervised all agricultural labor.

As to the crafts, it is truly amazing how these Brethren developed skills otherwise nearly unknown in the early centuries of modern times. Their pottery ware (now called "*Habaner faience*")[11] reveals a taste for the shapely and aesthetically appealing which made them stand out in this craft, and was a competitor of the Italian (later also Dutch) *faience* or *majolica* ware. In the main this particular craft was developed primarily for cash sale and not so much for Bruderhof needs. The research of Hruby shows how much the nobles appreciated these products. Another cash product of high quality was the knives and cutlery ware of finest steel, again somewhat unique in the sixteenth century. Both crafts continued to be practiced among the "*Habaner*" (apostate descendants of the Hutterites) in Slovakia until after World War I, although among the Hutterian Brethren in Transylvania, Russia, and later America, this skill died out completely. Hruby tells of additional skills of the Hutterites otherwise little practiced in their day; thus we hear of an artistic clock sold for 170 talers to an Austrian archduke, and another one sold to the Cardinal Franz von Dietrichstein. Famous were also the Hutterite carriages, which were much in demand among the Moravian nobility. Likewise much appreciated were their new-fashioned iron bedsteads. In short, the nobles knew only too well why it was advantageous to protect these industrious Brethren and why they ignored as far as possible the repeated persecution order from the Viennese government or from the Counter-Reformatory clergy.

Unique features of Brethren life were also their bathhouses and their barber-surgeons and physicians.[12] These made for a high standard of hygiene and health among the Brethren, and likewise attracted many lords and their

---

10 See Bertha W. Clark, "The Hutterian Communities," in the *Journal of Political Economy*, XXXII (University of Chicago, 1924).

11 See article "Ceramics," in *ME*, I.

12 For an exhaustive discussion of this phase of Hutterite activity see the two articles: J. L. Sommer, "Hutterite Medicine and Physicians," *MQR*, XXVII (1953), 111–27, and Robert Friedmann, "Hutterite Physicians and Barber-Surgeons," in the same issue.

families from the surrounding areas. Christoph A. Fischer was most enraged about this fact. "Every Saturday their bathhouses are filled with Christians [Catholics]," he writes, "and not only the ordinary man but also the lords run to them if they need any drug, as if the Anabaptists were the only ones who understood this art." These facts explain why the Brethren thrived even after 1592, the end of the "Golden Age," when the Counter–Reformation set in with full force and wars raged over the country as a result of the Turkish invasion.

No less important were the economic activities of the Hutterites outside their Bruderhofs. There were two motives for this: the Brethren needed additional cash (all earnings of individual workers were pooled in a common purse), and even more the Brethren needed the favor of their noble manorial lords, whom they were willing to serve in many capacities, thus demonstrating their indispensability. The latter point was one of the strongest arguments for toleration in Moravia. Manifold were the services of the Brethren hired out; they were managers of the farms (*Meier*), vineyards (*Winzer*), wineries (*Kellner*), mills (*Müller*), sawmills, etc. There was hardly any noble estate in southern Moravia and adjacent Slovakia which did not have one or several Brethren in its service. By their excellent preparation and moral qualities these men quickly gained the utmost confidence of the lords and the respect of those who worked under them. This is incidentally also true after 1622, the fateful year of "complete" expulsion from Moravia. There was practically no one who could take their place, and in spite of increasingly sharp mandates we find Hutterites working on manorial estates in Moravia as late as 1630, and occasionally even in 1640.

No less significant was the service of the Brethren in the field of surgery and medical care; time and again we hear of Hutterite doctors employed by one or another lord (Cardinal Dietrichstein, the head of the Counter–Reformation in Moravia, always called a Hutterite for such service), or in resort places such as the mineral springs of Trencin in Slovakia. We do not know fully the inside story of these services to the "world" and their economic implications; but the motives of service and gaining favorable public opinion seem to have prevailed also in this field.

Very interesting are Hruby's studies concerning the financial situation of the Brethren, their cash reserves, and the way they were taxed and finally deprived of all their savings (capital). Around 1570 (the "Golden Age") the Brethren had to pay an annual tax of 2 percent on all house–assessed valuation for the needs of Moravia (about 10 guilders or florins per house). Besides this they also had to pay a poll tax (*Kopfsteuer*) and a tax on home–brewed beer. The house tax steadily increased; in 1600 it was already 100 guilders per house and in 1608–10 even as high as 160 guilders. The government was always in need of money for military purposes; since the Brethren refused to pay war taxes, the amounts were simply requisitioned in the form of cattle, horses, or casks of wine.[13] In 1602–5, during the Turkish invasion, which did much damage to the Bruderhofs, the need of the Hapsburgs for money grew immensely. In 1602 the government requisitioned 7,000 guilders, and in 1604 the Emperor asked for a "loan" of 20,000 guilders, which, however, was never obtained.

The request for money became more and more urgent as the catastrophe of the Thirty Years' War approached. Cardinal Dietrichstein and imperial messengers exerted unbelievable pressure upon the Brethren to extort all the money possible. In 1621 the authorities finally prevailed upon the *Vorsteher* Rudolf Hirzel to divulge the hiding place of the brotherhood money. A total of 30,000 guilders thus fell into the hands of the Cardinal and the Emperor Ferdinand II.[14] The story of this confiscation is one of the most exciting in the long history of the Brethren. The Chronicle admits, however, that some money remained (of which Hirzel did not know), buried somewhere in the fields. Hruby estimates that prior to 1619 the Brethren might have possessed around 60,000 guilders, but he calculates that this sum was by no means excessive as it represented the working capital of a community of about 15,000 Brethren, or about four guilders per member. Eventually, in 1622, the Brethren had to leave Moravia altogether, leaving behind practically everything, 24 Bruderhofs with their entire inventory of grain, wine, 200 head of cattle, 150 horses, 655 pigs and hogs, all furniture and kitchen utensils, woolen material, linen, tools, and all shop equipment. Not counting the value of the houses, gardens, fields, and meadows, the Brethren estimated the value thus lost at at least 364,000 talers.[15]

In spite of this very tangible loss and the ever–increasing fury of war (with plundering, etc.), the Brethren were able to begin rebuilding their communal life in nearby Slovakia, where about one generation later Grimmelshausen found them prosperous again and well organized under Andreas Ehrenpreis, the last great *Vorsteher*. The eighteenth century then saw a decline in both the religious and the communal life of the Brethren and the enforced conversion of most Brethren to Catholicism. These converted Hutterites, known as "*Habaner*," experienced a rapid decline after World War I in the new state of Czechoslovakia.

The Bruderhofs in Transylvania never were as flourishing as those in the Moravian and Slovakian areas. Then, around 1760, came the great exodus from the Hapsburg empire into Walachia and Russia, and now the Brethren became farmers exclusively. Although they were still sober and industrious, their previous well–being was gone, and thus also their remarkable skills and crafts. Beginning in 1874 the Hutterites settled in the United States and Canada, assisted in part by loans from the New Harmony community

---

13 *Geschicht–Buch*, 399 (the year 1579), and 428 (the year 1589).
14 Compare Hruby, *loc. cit.*, p. 91, note 1; also *Geschicht–Buch*, 576–88, or *Älteste Chronik*, 766–80.
15 *Geschicht–Buch*, 570 ff.

people, the Rappites. Bertha W. Clark, reporting on their colonies in 1924,[16] gave a description of their economy which reads as if she had been visiting the sixteenth-century Bruderhofs in Moravia. The only difference is that now the *Diener der Notdurft* or *Haushalter* was called "boss." He handled all the money, he had the keys to all storage rooms, and he organized the work of the entire community. Under him were found the foremen of the farm, mill, carpentry, forge, bootery, etc. Money was used exclusively in contacts with the "world." Needless to say, since there was no private possession, nothing could be bequeathed to one's children (save, perhaps, some handwritten old books). All savings were used to buy more land or machinery. (With respect to the use of modern machinery the Hutterites differ greatly from the Amish.) Every Bruderhof was supposed to be self-supporting, although loans between the colonies were not unknown. Crafts were no longer practiced except for the immediate needs of the colony. Since the Brethren have accepted farm machinery their economies have become fairly thriving again. Idleness is practically unknown, but so is also haste and rush. To avoid monotony, all work rotates among the Brethren within a certain time. In spite of their peaceful attitude even today their neighbors occasionally oppose their expansion and purchasing of land, as in Saskatchewan, Manitoba, and elsewhere. The old suspicions and jealousies which prevailed so long in Moravia have not yet completely died out.

Appendix

While crafts of all kinds were favored, trading was definitely forbidden. Since this theme is not discussed in this paper we simply include at this point a quotation from a section, "Concerning Traders," in Peter Riedemann's well-known *Account* (*Rechenschaft*) of 1540.[17]

> We allow none of our number to do the work of a trader or merchant, since this is a sinful business; as the wise man saith, "It is almost impossible for a merchant and trader to keep himself from sin."[18] And, "as a nail sticketh fast between door and hinge, so doth sin stick close between buying and selling."[19] Therefore do we allow no one to buy to sell again, as merchants and traders do. But to buy what is necessary for the needs of one's house or craft, to use it and then to sell what one by means of his craft hath made therefrom, we consider to be right and not wrong.

---

16 Clark, *loc. cit.* Quite valuable is also a more recent study by the Canadian Mental Health Association, *The Hutterites and Saskatchewan, A Study of Intergroup Relations* (Regina, 1953); and Joseph W. Eaton, *Culture and Mental Disorders: A Comparative Study of the Hutterites and Other Populations* (Glencoe, Ill., 1955).

17 Peter Riedemann, *Account of Our Religion, Doctrine and Faith...*, (written 1540; first printed 1565; English edition by the Plough Publishing House of the Society of Brothers, Bridgnorth, England, 1950), 126ff.

18 Ecclesiasticus 26:29.

19 *Ibid.*, 27:1–2.

This only we regard as wrong: When one buyeth a ware and selleth the same again even as he bought it, taking to himself profit, making the ware dearer thereby for the poor, taking bread from their very mouths and thus making the poor man nothing but the bondman of the rich.[20] Paul saith likewise, "Let him who defrauded, defraud no more."[21] They say, however, "But the poor also profit in that one bringeth goods from one hand to another." There they use poverty as a pretext, seeking all the time their own profit first, and thinking only of the poor as having an occasional penny in their purse. Therefore we permit this not amongst us, but say with Paul that they should labour, working with their hands what is honest, that they may have to give to him that needeth.[22]

The following section then prohibits the occupation of inn keeper, serving wine or beer, "since this goes with all that is unchaste, ungodly and decadent," etc. Although the Hutterites both in the past and at present do accept an occasional drink, the *Rechenschaft* still condemns expressly "standing drinks" (treating) as a cause of evil and transgression of the commandments of God.[23]

Source: *Mennonite Quarterly Review*, XXX (1956), pp. 259–66.

---

20 *Ibid.*, 26:29.
21 Eph. 4:28.
22 Eph. 4:28.
23 Riedemann, *op. cit.*, p. 128.

HUTTERITE MARRIAGE PRACTICES

In general the Hutterites had an ascetic outlook on life; in fact were it not for their acceptance of marriage their way of life could best be characterized as "monastic." Marriage, however, was to them a part of their principle of absolute obedience to the commandments of God. As God once had ordered His chosen people to multiply and be fruitful, all His children are to accept this "ordinance" of procreation and act accordingly. "God, however," wrote Ulrich Stadler in 1536, "will wink at our marital work...on behalf of the children, and will not reckon it upon those who act in fear and discipline." Naturally, emotional engagements of any kind in things connected with marriage were completely ruled out. Courtship and romance simply did not exist among the old Hutterites, and even among the Brethren of today are more or less frowned upon, although the general practice in selecting of the spouse was changed substantially about one hundred years ago. In former days the wife was called by the husband only "marital sister" (*eheliche Schwester*).

Peter Riedemann, in his *Rechenschaft unseres Glaubens* of 1540, has a special chapter "Concerning Marriage," in which he expressly declares that the two partners must not come together through their own action and choice but in accordance with the will of God. "One should not ask his flesh but the elders that God might show through them what He has appointed for him. This then one should take with gratitude as a gift from God...." One case is known, in 1541, where a young man had asked a girl to marry him without previously consulting the elders of the church. This was considered such a break with the rules of the church that this marriage was never realized.

The practice of choosing a spouse was indeed peculiar with the Brethren and extremely impersonal. Two reports of this practice have been given by outside observers. In 1578 Stefan Gerlach, a professor at the University of Tübingen, came to Moravia to visit his sisters, who had joined the brotherhood some years previously. He now wrote in his *Konstantinopolische Reisebeschreibung* what he saw and heard. "On a certain Sunday of the year the elders call all young people together and place the boys on one side and the girls on the other side such that they face each other. Two or three boys are then suggested to each girl, one of whom she has to accept. Of course they are not really compelled, but on the other hand there is not much chance to act against the counsel of the elders." According to Christoph Erhard such matching took place only once a year and was done exclusively by the elders.

In 1612 the Polish nobleman Andreas Rey de Naglovitz visited the colonies in Moravia and wrote about them to a friend in France in a letter in Latin, in which he also described the Hutterite marriage practices, only he reversed the procedure; namely, each young man was given a choice of three girls (whom he had possibly never seen before) and he had to accept one of them as the will of God, "whether young or old, poor or rich" (as Riedemann had written in his *Rechenschaft*). Should, however, one of the two absolutely refuse such a partner, then he or she had to wait for another six months. Apparently by 1612 this practice was performed twice a year.

The wedding itself was performed apparently right after this matching meeting so as to exclude any period of courtship. At the wedding meal the bridegroom used to sit with the men, and the bride with the women, and it was only after the meal that the couple was led to their own room (*Stube* or *Oertel*) in one of the big community houses.

During the seventeenth century these practices began to decline as in general the common life deteriorated. There had been some opposition to the former strict method of matching, and the young people asked to be told before the meeting with whom they were to be mated. Thereupon Andreas Ehrenpreis, the outstanding bishop of the brotherhood in Slovakia, assembled all the elders in Sobotiste in 1634, and gave them a *Gemeindeordnung* concerning matching, a sort of renewed regulation of this important brotherhood function. He first referred to Abraham who had sent his servants to Mesopotamia to get a wife for his son Isaac, and so forth. As in all other areas of life so also in this area of selecting a spouse all self-will should be subdued. Whatever is done in the brotherhood should be done in accordance with the will of God.

The Hutterites continued such strict practices, in part at least, until far into the nineteenth century. (As for an unpleasant disagreement in this matter which led to a three-year period of shunning, see *Klein–Geschichtsbuch*, p. 284.) But during their stay in South Russia things were radically changed, strangely enough, not by a decision of the elders but apparently by a fiat of the great sponsor of the Hutterites in the Molotschna district, Johann Cornies, the Mennonite trustee of the government. This change must have happened around 1845. D. H. Epp in his book on Johann Cornies (1909) reports in detail the event which eventually led to changes of great consequences. A young girl was about to be compelled to marry a man whom she did not want in any case. She then fled from her confinement and ran straight to Cornies begging him for help. Cornies quickly realized the precarious situation and at once put the girl on some distant farm and at the same time prevailed upon the

Hutterite Marriage Practices

Hutterian Brethren to abandon altogether the former practice. Apparently the brotherhood accepted this advice (as the practice had been most unpopular anyway by that time), and ever since young people may decide for themselves whom they want to marry. To be sure, much strictness remains, and the elders and parents have to approve any such choice before one can speak of engagement. Only a few days after their approval the wedding will take place. There is no room for courtship within the brotherhood, just as there is no room for divorce. But as a rule these marriages are very successful and the two partners share their life in mutual respect and love. Today the couple receives not only one room but usually a small house or a few rooms in a larger house in anticipation of a growing family.

SOURCE: *Mennonite Encyclopedia*, III, pp. 510–11.

MEDICINE AMONG THE HUTTERITES

There was a distinct difference between the medical experiences among sixteenth–century Anabaptists in general and the unique practices of the Hutterites. The settled and well–developed community life in Moravia and Slovakia almost necessitated attention to medical care and hygiene, and thus led to developments which singled them out among all the rest of the non–urban population of early modern times. Since the situation has been given careful historical study, a fairly correct picture can be offered in the following.

Hygiene

The Brethren were among the earliest to conduct what today would best be called boarding schools. Accordingly, much attention was directed to have these schools (from nursery age to about fourteen years of age) on their Bruderhofs well controlled and supervised. Peter Walpot issued his famous school discipline in 1568, in which almost modern principles of hygiene were set forth to be strictly obeyed. The Brethren were sensibly aware of contagion; particular care was directed to an early discovery of children's diseases, whereupon such children were separated, along with their clothing and linen, as well as food being kept completely apart from that of the rest. There were sicknesses like scurvy, eczema, even syphilis, and attention was needed to prevent epidemics. The enemies accused them of negligence and claimed a high child mortality, but the Brethren defended themselves effectively, and actually could point to their numerous strict regulations for such group living.

Bathing and Bathhouses

The sixteenth century in general experienced a decline in bathing. Bathing for cleanliness was deemed by the Hutterites not necessary more than once in four weeks. But for health's sake bathing found quite elaborate attention among the Brethren. To quote the archfoe of the Hutterites, Christoph A. Fischer, who involuntarily had to admit the fame of these Hutterite bathhouses: "Every Saturday their baths are packed full of Christians [i.e., Catholics]. And not alone the common people but also noble persons come running to them if they ever need treatment, as if Anabaptists were the only ones who possessed this art in the entire region." These bathhouses were administered by professional *"Bader"* (caretakers of the baths), who also functioned as barber–surgeons and generally replaced physicians, as these latter were a rather rare profession in the sixteenth century. These *Bader* must have been quite numerous among the Hutterites of the later sixteenth century, again a proof that the Anabaptist way had great attraction for all walks of life.

Bader–Ordnungen

Although generally highly respected the *Bader* nevertheless had to conform to the general pattern of communal life of the Hutterites. Apparently this posed a real problem for these rather independent people who quickly gained also a clientele outside the brotherhood. Thus, it is not surprising that strict regulations, called *"Bader–Ordnungen,"* were issued from time to time, particularly during the seventeenth century when a certain decline in discipline set in. The earliest regulation is no longer extant, but we hear of such documents of 1592, 1633, 1635, 1637, 1654, and 1657 (with the exception of the first named, they all come from the period of Bishop Andreas Ehrenpreis. The *Bader–Ordnung* of 1654 was published in an English translation, *MQR*, 1953, pp. 125–27). They insisted on cleanliness, asked the barber–surgeons to continue in the study of pharmacy and other medical knowledge, regulated the practice of blood–cupping, and so on. Special emphasis was laid upon the proper behavior of these important brethren: there should be no arrogance among them and no overbearing, in spite of the fact that they enjoyed certain privileges which differentiated them from the rest on the Bruderhof (e.g., horseback riding).

When traveling from Bruderhof to Bruderhof, these barber–surgeons often carried along a whole wagon load of extracts, pills, electuaries, ointments, etc. Needless to say, they were also much in demand outside the Hutterite communities, which made their exceptional position even more difficult. They received payment for their services, and these sums, too, presented a temptation. As the rest of the brotherhood was largely rural in character, the adjustment of these men posed a permanent problem.

Personnel

The Hutterite chronicle mentions at least three doctors or physicians among the Brethren: Georg Zobel (d. 1603) of Nikolsburg, who was called twice to the Imperial Court of Rudolph II at Prague (the first time, 1581, he stayed six months and is said to have cured the emperor; the second time, 1599, he was supposed to help to stop an epidemic in Prague); Balthasar Goller (d. 1619), likewise of Nikolsburg the personal physician of Cardinal Dietrichstein, who otherwise fought Anabaptism by all means at his disposal. In 1608–09 Goller was also the personal physician of the Imperial Ambassador, Count Herberstein, on his trip to Constantinople.

At the outbreak of the Thirty Years' War, Goller was slain in Nikolsburg and his pharmacy was destroyed. The third was Conrad Blössy, a former citizen of Zürich, Switzerland, who in 1612 went back to that city and rendered great assistance in fighting an epidemic there.

The number of barber–surgeons mentioned in the sources is quite considerable. One, Sebastian Dietrich, of Markgröningen in Württemberg, even became head bishop or *Vorsteher* of the entire brotherhood (1611–19). (For more names of such barbers see the next article.)

Training and Education

Very little is known about the training of the physicians. Most likely they got their training before joining the brotherhood, although the profession of barber–surgeon could also be learned at certain Bruderhofs, e.g., in Nikolsburg, or at the places of their bathhouses. It is also known that Paracelsus, the most famous physician of his century, lived in Moravia in 1537–38 on an estate where Hutterites also were admitted. But no sources about possible contacts have become known. It is, however, highly revealing that the Hutterian Brethren of today have preserved two very old medical books. The one, of 1575, was bought by Andreas Ehrenpreis in Sobotiste, Slovakia, in 1638 from a Hungarian book peddler. It is a manuscript book of 230 leaves octavo, entitled *Antidotarium, Composita oder Recepta der Schaden– und Wundarzney*, etc., by Lienhard Gargasser, 1575. The other, *Arzney Handbüchl, vieler Krankheiten Zustände Causam et Curam*, etc., is also handwritten, copied by the Hutterite barber–surgeon Johannes Spengler in 1635 while practicing his art at the mineral bath of Trenchin–Teplic, Slovakia. It comprises 470 octavo leaves, containing mostly prescriptions of remedies and good counsel as to how to cure ailments. The name of Paracelsus is mentioned in it at many places; unfortunately the original from which this book was carefully copied is no longer known. Both books are now in the possession of the Hutterites in Western Canada.

Later Period

The tradition of having doctors or barber–surgeons around on the Bruderhofs was never abandoned. The *Klein–Geschichtsbuch*, for instance, expressly mentions for the year 1780 (when the brotherhood had settled in the Ukraine) that the Brethren wished to have again a trained doctor with them, and accordingly dispatched the young and able brother Christian Wurz to study with the French house physician of Count Romanzov, the protector of the Brethren. At first Christian kept rigidly and faithfully to his Hutterite background, but after a while he got "to love the world," even put on a wig, and soon became fully secularized. He later went to Moscow. The Chronicle states sadly, "In a few years three members left our faith; they were among the most skilled and learned ones."

Again in 1792, the same Chronicle reports the death of a barber–surgeon. "Thus the brotherhood had no one any more who would understand blood–cupping and other medical practices. This fact became a real concern to the Brethren." In 1814, again, the death of another brother–medicus Zacharias Wipf is reported. He had served his brotherhood for sixteen years both in the pharmacy and in the art of medicine.

America

In America naturally the need for doctors has been more easily met than at any time before. Nevertheless the Brethren have had their own bonesetters, experts in medicinal herbs, and, of course, experienced midwives. Joseph Eaton reports that some of these bonesetters and masseurs are so much in demand that the Brethren set up a special office for one of them. It seems that they are not especially trained in their art but practice it rather out of a certain natural gift and intuition. All Bruderhofs have plenty of house remedies for all emergencies. As to physic disturbances, the friendly atmosphere of the community and the opportunity of talking confidentially to the preacher work strongly toward a high level of mental health.

SOURCE: *Mennonite Encyclopedia*, III, pp. 553–55.

HUTTERITE PHYSICIANS AND BARBER–SURGEONS

While the paper by John Sommer, published in the *Mennonite Quarterly Review* for April 1953, covers very comprehensively the subject of Hutterite medicine, the report concerning physicians and barber–surgeons (*Bader*) of that brotherhood still allows further supplementation. It is the intention of the following notes to discuss chronologically all the Hutterites in this field whose names appear in the available sources. Though their number is not too impressive, it is nevertheless astonishing to meet so frequently the mention of this noble profession in the Hutterite chronicles and other Anabaptist sources. In this regard the Hutterites present an almost unique feature among Anabaptist brotherhoods.

George Zobel

George Zobel has been ably treated in the above paper and only a few remarks need to be added to it. Zobel, a rather renowned physician of the Brethren, lived and died in Nikolsburg, Moravia, where a large Bruderhof existed. Nikolsburg, it should be remembered, was the seat of the noble house of Dietrichstein since 1575, and it was perhaps for that reason that we learn of two remarkable physicians living and working at this place. The Brethren, though oppressed, managed nevertheless to subsist in that area until Cardinal Franz von Dietrichstein began his Counter–Reformatory activities around 1599. The Hutterite Chronicle mentions Zobel for the first time in the year 1582 when he was called to Emperor Rudolph II, who then lived in Prague, for medical consultation. In 1593 this physician–brother was made officially *Diener der Notdurft* (steward).[1] The Chronicle then reports in 1597[2] that "a prince had asked for Zobel to come to Prague," but other records say that Zobel was called the second time in 1599.[3] We also learn that the abbot of the near–by Klosterbruck monastery in southern Moravia, otherwise an untiring foe of the Brethren, addressed Zobel as "dear friend" when he invited him to

---

1 *Älteste Chronik*, 567.
2 *Ibid.*, p. 594.
3 Paul Dedic, "Nikolsburg," *ML*, III, 259.

the abbey for medical consultation.[4] This should not surprise us, however, for we have the admission of another Hutterite–fighter, the ill–famed Moravian priest Christoph Andreas Fischer, that the bathhouses of the Brethren were always filled with "Christians" (meaning Catholics) and that the manorial lords came to the Brethren whenever they needed any remedy, "as if the Anabaptists were the only masters of that art."[5]

In 1603, Zobel died in Nikolsburg. He was "a fine old doctor," the Chronicle remarks on this occasion, "who had taken care of the entire barber business of the brotherhood and who had also been much in demand with many noble lords."[6]

Balthasar Goller

Balthasar Goller, the second physician named in the Chronicle, was a contemporary of Zobel, and, like him, lived and died in Nikolsburg. About him we read more in another Hutterite manuscript where he is mentioned as the personal physician of Count Herberstein, the imperial ambassador, on the latter's mission to the Sublime Porte (Constantinople) in 1607–8.[7] This fact seems to indicate a certain reputation of this brother in the medical field; apparently he was a physician rather than a barber, otherwise he would not have been selected for so responsible a function. We do not know how Goller got this particular job but the conjecture might be ventured that he had been an assistant of Zobel, who later recommended him as his successor to the imperial court. We should remember, however, that Zobel died in 1603, while the embassy did not start until 1607.

After his return from this mission, Goller continued his medical practice in Nikolsburg. A hitherto overlooked document tells us the surprising fact that he had become the personal physician of Cardinal Franz, the otherwise implacable adversary of the Hutterites. In his richly documented book, *Die Wiedertäufer in Mähren* (Leipzig, 1935), Frantiçek Hruby quotes a letter written by the Cardinal to a nobleman friend in Moravia, dated February 23, 1618, in which he announces the dispatch of "Balthaussern Kholert, the chief physician of the Brethren (*brüderischer Hauptarzt*)" to his friend, and then adds, somewhat apologetically, "even though I needed him myself because of my present physical frailty."[8]

One year later, this capable doctor was to meet a tragic fate in the Thirty Years' War as it swept across southern Moravia. We have two different reports about the violent death of Goller in Nikolsburg. The Chronicle[9] says that he was brutally slain by an "ungodly citizen" of that city (*in tyrannischer*

---
 4 *Ibid.*
 5 "Dietrich," *ML*, I, 442.
 6 *Älteste Chronik*, 611.
 7 *MQR*, XVII (1943), 80 ff.
 8 F. Hruby, *Die Wiedertäufer in Mähren* (Leipzig, 1935), 34.
 9 *Älteste Chronik*, 715.

Weise mit Schiessen, Stechen und Hauen entsetzlich ermördert worden) on September 5, 1619. On the other hand, the commander and defender of the castle of Nikolsburg, Johann von Denn, reports to the Cardinal in a letter of September 13, 1619, that his famous physician was murdered without any reason by a lord billeted in the castle.[10] And Hruby adds from the sources that the pharmacy (*Apotheke*) of the Brethren was also confiscated on the same occasion.[11] It was the time when the Brethren were completely expelled from their ancient location in Nikolsburg.

Sebastian Dietrich

Sebastian Dietrich (1553–1619), born in Markgröningen in Württemberg, joined the Hutterite brotherhood in Moravia in 1580. He became a preacher (*Diener des Wortes*) seven years later and was chosen *Vorsteher* or head bishop of the entire brotherhood in the difficult year of 1611. He died at sixty–six in Neumühl, Moravia.[12] The Württemberg records of the year 1600, dealing with Dietrichs claim of his parental inheritance, call him "an excellent and far–famed physician,"[13] a title, to be sure, not quite correct, since Dietrich was rather a barber–surgeon than a physician proper. But as such he enjoyed an extraordinary reputation indeed. From the records it is not quite clear where he got the knowledge of his profession. Bossert assumed that he learned his skills as a youth in Württemberg, but certain facts suggest also expert contacts with Zobel in Nikolsburg, and perhaps also with Goller. When Dietrich entered into a lawsuit with the authorities for his inheritance, he sent the physician Hans Jakob Knaub of Nikolsburg as his authorized representative and trustee to Markgröningen, "since he could not go there personally."[14] The suit was in vain anyway: after many years of correspondence the authorities finally refused to give him his rightful inheritance because of his joining the Anabaptists in Moravia.

Unfortunately, no more details about Dietrich's professional activities are known; the Chronicle simply acknowledges them in a general way as another proof of the brother's high standing.

Hans Zwinkelberger

Of the next physician of the brotherhood and his activities we learn from two sources: the Chronicle, which calls him Hanns Zwinckheberger,[15] and the great hymnal of the Brethren, the *Lieder der Hutterischen Brüder* (1914),

---

10 Dedic, "Nikolsburg," *loc. cit.*, written on the basis of new documents.
11 Hruby, *op. cit.*, p. 80.
12 *ML*, I, 442, and Gustav Bossert, *Quellen zur Geschichte der Wiedertäufer, I, Herzogtum Württemberg* (Leipzig, 1930), 754–847.
13 Bossert, *op. cit.*, p. 755.
14 *Ibid.*, p. 754.
15 *Älteste Chronik*, 630.

which calls the same man Hans Zwickelberger, a more likely family name.[16] In 1605 when the Turks, together with Hungarians and Transylvanians, invaded the borderland of Austria and Moravia, the Hutterite Bruderhofs suffered particularly severely at the hands of the Transylvanian army leader Stephen Bocskay and his "He iduks" (undisciplined militia). The tribulations of this memorable year 1605 are described in great detail in the Chronicle, which tells the story pertaining to our subject about as follows:

> It so happened that at that time our brother Hanns Zwinckheberger, a barber–surgeon, was present in the city of Tyrnau [now Trnava, Slovakia]. When he learned from one of the [captured] sisters where our people had been dragged away to, he turned to the magistrates of that city with the request to help him liberate his brethren and sisters. Thereupon the aldermen went with the barber into the camp of the colonel ... and solicited the freeing of these people without ransom. The colonel was willing to do this [for reasons not mentioned], and our people were returned and came safely back [to "unoccupied Slovakia"].[17]

The same story is told elaborately in a long hymn of 158 stanzas, called the *Botschkai Lied*. Here stanzas 104 and 105 run as follow:

Denn es war gleich in dem Trübsale
Hans Zwickelberger auch diesmale
In Ungarland zu dienen in diesem Falle

Der denselbigen Stadtherren
Dienstlich und tät viel ankehren
Mit Arznei und tät ihnen sehr geren.[18]

Freely translated the passage says about this:

> In these days of calamity Hans Zwickelberger was again on hand in Hungary to offer his good service. He was of much help to the magistrates of the city of Tyrnau and gladly helped them with his medical service.

From this we may gather that the brother had already been in the city when the hostilities broke out, doing some barber–surgeon work among the patricians of that city. Apparently, he did so well that he gained their gratitude and their willingness to return service for service. His reasons for going to this place are not indicated; we may, however, surmise that he was called there for

---

16 *Lieder der Hutterischen Brüder* (Scottdale, 1914), 809.
17 This story parallels the epic of the Brother Salomon Böger and his adventures in Turkey in his search for his wife, child, and other captives. Cf. Robert Friedmann, "Adventures of an Anabaptist in Turkey," *MQR*, XVII (1943), 80 ff.
18 *Lieder*, 809.

medical work, not unlike that of Zobel or Goller. It is well to remember that good doctors and good barbers were still exceedingly rare in the seventeenth century.

Burkhart Braitstainer

Burkhart Braitstainer was also a barber who was chosen as minister of the Word in Neumühl, Moravia, in 1608.[19] Later he became an elder of the Nikolsburg group and as such had to share all the sufferings of the years 1621–22, when Cardinal Franz von Dietrichstein extorted practically all the savings of the brotherhood and then expelled them from the country. Of his activities as a surgeon nothing particular is recorded in the Chronicle.

Conrad Blössy

Another name in the present context, also of the early seventeenth century, is that of the brother Conrad Blössy, according to all indications a physician proper. About him we read in the Chronicle for the year 1612 the following story:[20]

> At this time one of our physicians [Goller was then still alive] had been in Zürich for more than one year, as there was an epidemic rampant and more than eight thousand persons had died. The brother served many persons, also such in high places, very well with his drugs, thanks to divine blessing, and he received good pay for it. In recognition of such loyalty the magistrates and lords of Zürich allowed him to take with him to the brotherhood in Moravia a greater part of his inheritance than was usually granted. He was thus able to collect a very nice sum of money which, however, was stolen from him and from the entire brotherhood because of the betrayal of the apostate Klaus Bräuer.

From this report we may conclude that Blössy was a citizen of Zürich who had joined the brotherhood in Moravia and had now returned to negotiate his parental estate, somewhat as Sebastian Dietrich had tried to do. Thanks to his services on the spot he fared far better in this deal than his Swabian brother.

Johannes Spengler

Of the brother next to be mentioned nearly nothing was known until recently. The Chronicle[21] reports only that in 1647 Johannes Spengler, a barber, was made *Diener der Notdurft* (steward) and that he died in Slovakia in 1660. It is of some significance to remember that this was the period of

---

19 *Älteste Chronik*, 646.
20 *Ibid.*, p. 659.
21 *Ibid.*, p. 845.

the outstanding Hutterite *Vorsteher* Andreas Ehrenpreis, under whom the Slovakian Bruderhofs experienced their last great flowering. Fortunately the late Professor A. J. F. Zieglschmid discovered at one of the Hutterite Bruderhofs in South Dakota a bulky handwritten codex, dated 1635, which was written by Spengler, containing the most extensive Anabaptist medical tract ever known. Mr. Sommer had no knowledge of the existence of this unusual codex and therefore could say little about the medication and medical treatment of the Hutterite physicians. An expert analysis of this volume will be the future task of some historian of medicine, we are sure. At this place not much more can be presented than an external description of this strange volume, taken from notes left among the papers of Professor Zieglschmid.

The codex (3 3/4 in. x 6 in.) must be quite voluminous as Zieglschmid remarks: 3 inches thick. Its title runs as follows:

Arznei Handbüchl, Vieler Krankheiten Zustände, Causam et Curam, auch einfache nützliche Rezepte, Simplizien Gradibus der einfachen Gewächsen (aus den vier Elementen geboren), Leib– und Wundarzneiisch, samt anderen schönen Sachen, einem jeden Arzte not zu wissen, hierin beschrieben und aufs kürzest begriffen.

Samt einem ordentlichen Register, wie und wo ein jedes auf das ehest zu finden.

Der Herr hat die Arznei geschaffen, und
die Arznei kommt von dem Höchsten.

Geschrieben in Niederungarn, im Trentschiner Warmbad, vollendet den 15. Februar 1635. Johannes Spengler gehörig.

This title indicates that Spengler had a sort of medical and barber practice in the (still today) renowned mineral bath and warm spring of Trencin–Teplice (now Slovakia). How this fit into Hutterite community living is not indicated, but we may assume that Spengler's stay in the resort was temporary, perhaps for the purpose of serving (like Zwickelberger), and perhaps also to provide some needed cash for the brotherhood. As we know, such temporary outside services were by no means infrequent among the Hutterites.

From the few pages copied by Zieglschmid it is quite evident that the author (or compiler) proceeded in a scholarly fashion in his systematic work. The major source from which he seems to have taken most of his medical and pharmaceutical knowledge is the famous sixteenth–century physician Paracelsus. The work of this great doctor was widely known at that time and Spengler seems to have studied it extensively. On one of the very first pages of the codex we find for instance the following reference: "Look for it in *Tractatus Primus De Pestilitate, Opus Astronomia Mundis*, Paracelsus." The occasional use of Latin words indicates that Spengler must have had some better education in a "Latin School" prior to his joining the Hutterites.

Unfortunately, nothing more can be reported at present, and further investigations are certainly called for.

Hans Webel & Matthes Gauman

Strangely enough, of the two men next on our roster we learn nothing from Hutterite sources proper; what we know about them comes only from a very flattering letter which the well-known Moravian Protestant nobleman Karl von Zierotin sent to a friend. On November 3, 1635, this nobleman writes as follows: "I am sure that you have heard that I was rather sick last year until the Anabaptist barbers of your area [Levar or Gross–Schützen, Slovakia] cured me of the serious and dangerous illness which God sent upon me and from which he delivered me again, thanks to these men. Since I know that you, too, are seriously ill, it is my opinion that you would do wise to avail yourself of these barbers. For there are excellent masters among them, in particular the master Hans Webel and his assistant Matthes Gauman, who were also with me last year and served me so well."[22] The remarkable fact about this information is that the Hutterites had been expelled from Moravia in 1622, and that they nevertheless returned time and again to serve the nobility in many fields. Hruby, who prints this letter, adds the remark that "we could quote many more examples of this kind." The earlier quoted letter of Dietrichstein corroborates this contention.

Andreas Schmidt

The skill and fame of Anabaptist barbers did not die out in spite of unheard–of oppressions and exile. From Moravia these specialists moved with the entire brotherhood to Slovakia and further eastward, continuing their medical services both inside and outside their Bruderhofs.

The *Great Chronicle of the Hutterites* ends about the year 1665. A decline (*Verfliessen*) in the brotherhood set in and the sources become more and more scanty. Joseph von Beck, who ransacked all possible archives and even remotest sources for his *Geschichts–bücher*, mentions once more a physician of the year 1782. "Andreas Schmidt, brüderischer Wundarzt in Levar, Slovakia." It does not become quite clear whether at that time all Hutterites of this area had been converted by force to the Catholic faith (the so–called "Habaner") or not. In any case, the record reveals that a number of Anabaptist manuscripts and "heretical" books were confiscated in the house of the physician, thus indicating his Anabaptist background and learning.[23]

---

22 F. Hruby, *op. cit.*, p. 105, after a copy of the letter in the State Archive of Brno, Moravia.
23 *Geschichts–Bücher*, 635.

Joseph Müller & Lorenz Stahl

To learn more of the Hutterite physicians in this late period of their history, we must turn to the continuation of the Great Chronicle, namely the *Klein–Geschichtsbuch* or Small Chronicle. Here we read: "Anno 1792, Joseph Müller took Lorenz Stahl as his assistant [or apprentice] that he should learn with him bleeding and all the other medical treatments."[24] That was at a time when the Brethren had begun to settle at Vishenka, Ukraine. When by chance both these men died in rapid succession, the Small Chronicle remarks regretfully, "Thus the brotherhood had no one anymore who would understand bleeding and the other medical practices. This became a real concern to the Brethren."[25]

New men, however, appeared who could serve the brotherhood in this capacity, for once more we find a note in the Small Chronicle in this regard, the last note, to be sure, concerning our subject. On page 423 we read: "Anno 1814, May 16, the brother Zacharias Wipf passed away; he had served the brotherhood loyally for sixteen years, both in the pharmacy and in the art of medicine (*Arznei Kunst*). He was aged thirty–six."[26]

APPENDIX

Paracelsus and the Anabaptists

It is highly probable that Paracelsus, the famous sixteenth–century physician and philosopher, had personal contacts with the Anabaptists, in particular with the Hutterites. Dr. Kurt Goldammer in his recent book, *Paracelsus, sozialethische und sozialpolitische Schriften, herausgegeben von K. Goldammer* (Tübingen, 1952, 81 ff.), presents the main reasons for such a contention. First, a certain inner kinship is observable between the socio–ethical ideas of Paracelsus and the Brethren; proof is contained in the main bulk of this volume of source publications. Secondly, a number of external contacts can also be established as most probable: in Strasbourg in 1526, in eastern Switzerland and the Inn Valley of Tyrol during Paracelsus' years of wandering, 1532–34, and finally during his prolonged visit to Moravia in 1537.

Concerning this visit we learn that he had been invited to the estate of the manorial lord Johann von Leipnick (or in German: *Lipa*) at Moravian Kromau. It was there that Paracelsus wrote several of his great tracts, and most likely also that he met the Hutterites. About this Johann von Leipnick–Lipa, see the Chronicle (ed. Zieglschmid), pp. 146, 209, and 250; also the

---

24 *Klein–Geschichtsbuch*, 388.
25 *Ibid.*, p. 388.
26 It happened at the Bruderhof of Raditchev, Russia.

enlightening footnote on p. 250. From these passages we learn that this lord was much interested in all "Left–Wing" (sectarian) movements, protecting the Hutterites against the severe persecutions of 1535–40. The estate of Kromau saw Hussites first, then Picards, and finally Hutterites. Johann von Lipa knew Jakob Hutter personally but was unable to prevent the expulsion of the Brethren in 1535 (when Hutter wrote his famous letter to the governor in Moravia). But in 1540 he permitted the reestablishment of a Bruderhof in Kromau, and in 1545 its enlargement. Also Schäkovitz near by, a well–known Hutterite center, belonged to the same lord.

The invitation to Paracelsus, the homeless and restless wanderer, to come to Kromau and work in peace becomes thus more understandable, and the contact with Hutterites appears almost as a matter of fact. A more detailed study in this field, however, might be profitable.

SOURCE: *Mennonite Quarterly Review*, XXVII (1953), pp. 128–36.

HUTTERITE EDUCATION

Among the various Anabaptist groups of the sixteenth century, perhaps none had so much opportunity for a systematic Christian upbringing of the youth as the Hutterites, who on their large collective Bruderhofs in Moravia could organize and systematically take care of the entire education from the nursery school to kindergarten and through the grades. Education beyond that was expressly declined as non–conducive to the fear of God—the highest goal of all Anabaptist education. That Hutterite education had a very high standard can still be seen from all their handwritten books, done with excellent penmanship, good spelling, skillful style, and as for contents, with excellent Bible knowledge and often deft arguments—things not so commonly found among people of the sixteenth and seventeenth centuries.

The organization and spirit of Hutterite education is known through a number of preserved documents. The earliest perhaps is the *Handbüchel wider den Prozess* of 1558–59, which in its section XII contains an *Ordnung und Brauch wie man es in der Gemein mit den Kindern hält* (A Regulation Concerning the Upbringing of Children in the Brotherhood). Here we read for instance, "That our children are dear to our heart before God according to truth, and a precious concern, to this God would testify for us on the Day of Judgment." Most likely this document was written by Peter Walpot, later bishop of the brotherhood, from whom we also have an *Address to the Schoolmasters*, Nov. 5, 1568, and a School Discipline ("*Schulordnung*") of 1578. Also of 1578, we have further the report of a sympathetic observer, Stephan Gerlach, later professor at Tübingen. There exists also a catechism or *Kinderbericht*, used in Hutterite schools, of which two versions became known of 1586 and of 1620. It gives the impression that it was written by Peter Riedemann (d. 1556), the author of the great *Rechenschaft*, with which it shows much similarity. There is among the Hutterite manuscripts a third brief *Kinderbericht* which deals extensively with the ordinance of baptism and communion. The use of the *Kinderbericht* in child training accounts for the fact that the Hutterite prisoners always had a ready answer to the court questioner when on trial and also for the fact that they so often agreed word for word with each other.

Each Bruderhof had two types of schools within its organization: the "Little School," a nursery and "Kindergarten" (age two to six), in operation three centuries before the modern European kindergarten was developed, and the "Big School," i.e., the grades (age six to twelve). The latter was actually more than a mere school, and may be compared to a children's home where they lived and were taken care of practically throughout the year, in conformity with the Hutterite principle of community living. The two documents by Peter Walpot (above) laid down the principle which should guide the entire upbringing, and which were to be obeyed by the schoolmasters, the schoolmothers, and their assistants (*Kindsdirn*). "Let each schoolmaster," Walpot declared, "deal with the children by day and night as though they were his own, so that each one may be able to give an account before God…." The spirit which permeates the school regulation of 1578 is that of a free and cheerful discipline in love and the fear of God, peaceful in spirit. To be dutiful and peaceful is conducive to good discipline. One cannot take too much care of the children, and the adults should always be mindful of setting a good example, since the children watch them and learn from their behavior. Walpot takes great care to instruct the teachers how to handle difficult cases. The use of a rod may sometimes be necessary, but great discretion and discernment should be exercised therein, for often a child can be better trained and corrected by kind words whereas harshness would be altogether in vain. The exercise of discipline of children requires the fear of God on the part of the teachers and high sense of responsibility. Children should be trained to accept punishment willingly, and care should be taken that they do not become self–willed. But above all they should be trained to love the Lord and to be diligent in prayer.

Great care was also taken of cleanliness and healthful living—in an age when those hygienic principles were by no means generally accepted. Even small details are regulated and enjoined, about eating, washing, sleeping, the children's clothing, and then above all the separation of the sick and the special handling of their laundry. The major emphasis, however, is laid on the right spirit and the ever alert responsibility of those in whose care the children are entrusted, so that the honor of God may always be promoted.

Basically these principles have been preserved fairly unchanged among the Hutterites up to the 21st century, though documents of later times are lacking. Bertha W. Clark, who visited the Brethren in South Dakota in 1923, describes the Hutterite system of education in the Bon homme Bruderhof, showing that in spite of certain necessary adaptations to American ways the spirit of the upbringing of the youth is by and large the same as of old. It is true that in the grade schools the legally prescribed curriculums have to be taught (if possible by Hutterite teachers—though the teachers are usually non–Hutterite, since Hutterites do not meet the educational requirements of the state for teaching), but the nursery and kindergarten is still today "really Hutterian."

SOURCE: *Mennonite Encyclopedia*, II, pp. 149–50.

HUTTERIAN POTTERY OR HABAN FAYENCES

How do Christianity and art go together? Strictly speaking, not too well. Christ taught a new way of life not a style of art. Certainly there exists a vast amount of "religious art," simply because artistic urges are indigenous to human nature; man seeks expression of his devotion and dedication in the medium of art just as much as he does in the area of conduct and worship. But that type of religious orientation which Max Weber long ago called "ascetic Protestantism" has been, and still is, radically opposed to any kind of artistic expression whatever. Think of a Puritan or an Amish home to understand what is meant here: it is emphatically devoid of any form of decoration and embellishment, and that, of course, not by chance but by principle.

It goes without saying that evangelical Anabaptism of the sixteenth century, particularly in South Germany, Switzerland, and Austria, belonged to this "ascetic" puritanical type. Nothing would be further from normal expectation than that these people, being both solid and sober craftsmen and tillers of soil and vineyard, should indulge in artistic pursuits. And yet, at least in one instance, this is exactly what did happen. The Anabaptists of Moravia, the Hutterites, well-known for their unique way of living in Bruderhof communities, did produce one type of artful crafts which earned the deserved fame and admiration of connoisseurs, and, not the least, brought them also some highly needed material rewards. This was the craft of making beautifully shaped and decorated "enameled" pottery, named after its places of origin, usually fayences or majolica. Majolica ware is a particularly decorated and glazed (enameled) earthenware coming from Majorca (an island near Spain) and Valencia in Spain, where this art had flourished since the thirteenth century. Later it shifted to the Italian town of Faenca (then belonging to the papal state), hence its present name fayence. Many museums show most brilliant pieces of this art (for it is more art than craft), and we know very well that nobles everywhere were eager to decorate their tables and cupboards with such showpieces: plates, jars, bowls, jugs, pitchers, and a hundred and one other things. In the fourteenth and fifteenth centuries (the time of the Renaissance) Italy had a sort of monopoly of this art and craft. In the late sixteenth century the Netherlands took over the lead in this field. The seventeenth century then saw the production of lovely Delft wares, with its characteristic blue color, still appreciated today.

But in between the Italian and the Dutch phases, Moravia suddenly appears on the scene as the only place where these gorgeous house articles were produced, so appealingly that, as we know today from many inventories of castles or manor houses in Moravia or Bohemia, there was hardly any noble family that did not pride itself in possessing some of this novel *Täufergeschirr* (Anabaptist pottery). These pieces actually replaced more or less the older pewter wares, particularly for festive occasions (Hruby). We have not the slightest idea how the Hutterites ever came to learn this exquisite art in the sixteenth century. That it is by origin Italian cannot be doubted. Krisztinkovich claims that sectarians of Faenca were driven from the papal state and found their way to tolerant Moravia. We have no records of any such refugees. It is true that in the sixteenth century Moravia was a haven for people of all persuasions. But the only non–Catholic Italian group known were the antitrinitarian Socinians of the surrounding towns of Venice, Vicenza and Pavia, who later actually settled in Austerlitz, Moravia; in fact in the neighborhood of the Hutterites. But language and beliefs meant serious barriers which prevented any closer contacts. Had we no records of the Italian Inquisition we would not even know of this Austerlitz group. Moreover, the question arises whether they were potters. They certainly did not hail from Faenca.

To be sure, a few Italians did also join the Hutterite brotherhood around 1555–60, during the period when the antitrinitarian Socinians were driven out of Italy; but they all came from the area of Venice, Verona, Vicenza, in general from the area of the Republic of Venice. DeWind has told us their tragic story (*MQR*, 1954), when some of these men, returning to Italy as Anabaptist missionaries, were caught and subsequently drowned in the lagoon of Venice on the recommendation of the Inquisition. But no record tells us that they were potters, in fact in a few instances we even know their former or their new trade, learned in Moravia, which in no case was the *Hafner–Kunst* (potter's art). Thus we do not know how it happened that Hutterites learned the secret of this art and craft. We only know that toward the end of the sixteenth century *Täufergeschirr* appears in Moravia as a highly appreciated specialty.

Naturally, in a community in which the entire life is considered a service in the name of the Lord, and therefore subject to the discipline of the church, there exists no distinction between the sacred and the temporal. In a sense, all life is part of the sacred, also the production of artful earthenwares. Hence we are not surprised to find at a relatively early date, that is in 1612, the issuance of a regulation of this trade by the *Vorsteher* or bishop of the brotherhood, a *Hafnerordnung* (*Hafner* means potter). In an old Hutterite manuscript book, now at Esztergom–Gran, Hungary, we find such a regulation with the title as follows: *Was der Haffner und der köstlich tewern geschüers halben erkennt worden, Anno 1612 den 11 Decebris* (What Has Been Decided About the Potter's Trade and the Precious Expensive Earthenwares). In this regulation it is expressly declared that all these pieces of fancy quality have to be sold and must not be used on the Bruderhofs proper. The entire work of the potters is strictly regulated, good care has to be taken of everything, material, colors, kilns, etc. The document mentions in particular pieces in "bonewhite" (*Beinweiss*), something otherwise unknown prior to the coming of chinaware.

The craft of fayence pottery had started in Moravia, but soon moved over also into adjoining Slovakia, more secure from persecution than Moravia. Here in Sobotiste and Velky Levary (Sabatisch and Gross–Schützen), the trade was further developed among the newly established Bruderhofs. When in 1622 all Anabaptists were driven from Moravia without exception, the Brethren also took along with them the secret of this ceramic production, in particular the secret of producing colors for the glazing (enameling). The Moravian nobility, however, not wanting to be deprived of their lovely tableware, got all these pieces from Slovakia in spite of their otherwise hostile attitude. Hruby reports about coffee, tea and chocolate sets imported in this way and now mentioned in records or preserved in museums. I myself visited Velky Levary in 1925, and could see there the *Hafnerhaus* (potter's workshop), with the firm name high in the gable, that is a sign of the shop made in fayence technique, reading "J.H.1781" (i.e., Joseph Hörndl, whom the Chronicles call *Krüglmacher*—maker of jugs and jars).

As the brotherhood moved still further on into faraway Transylvania (1621), then a principality under Turkish suzerainty, the art of fayence ceramics moved with them, too. The princes of Rakocsi are said to have been particular patrons of these masters of ceramics. Toward the end of the seventeenth century the one or the other of them broke away from the brotherhood; the Chronicle of the Hutterites speaks of that period as the time of the *Verfliessen* (waning) of the brotherhood or church. It is reported that one of these now independent masters became a special favorite of Count Palffy, another of the Hungarian magnates, and in 1693 a member of a well–known Anabaptist potter family by the name of Imre Odler (apparently formerly Adler), who had adopted a Magyar name, was even knight—certainly a strange twist of fate for someone formerly belonging to an Anabaptist group of strictest discipline and separation from the "world."

The eighteenth century is a sad period in the story of the Hutterites: fewer and fewer members remained loyal to the old teachings and ways of life. The harsh and relentless activities of the Jesuits, under the regime of Empress Maria Theresa, meant the nearly total collapse of the brotherhood. The staunch and strongest ones joined the great trek into the Ukraine around 1770–90, while all those who remained behind could no longer resist the concerted aggression of the Jesuits. They turned Catholic, at least externally.

Wisely, the Catholic Church did not forbid communal institutions, and thus the Bruderhofs continued to function, after a fashion. Communal schools, bakeries, smithies, pastures, and so on, existed everywhere, also a communal treasury. Many of the former Anabaptists who had turned Catholic had also adopted the language of their country, that is Slovakian, and to a lesser degree Rumanian. Thus they were not molested when the German population was expelled after World War II and are most likely still living on Bruderhofs. These Catholic converts now are popularly called *Habaner* (or Slovakian *Habanski*), no one knows why. Joseph Beck (1883) conjectured that "hab" means in folk dialect dour, sullen, supposedly the external appearance of many of the Anabaptist "puritans" of later time. Be it as it may, all over Hungary (Slovakia belonged to Hungary up to 1918) one knows no Anabaptists, no Hutterites, but only "Habanski." That is the name accepted by Catholic writers as well as by the people at home. In the more recent science of folklore, their lovely ceramic products are called exclusively "Haban ceramics."

The secret of production was not completely lost, however, with the turn of the Brethren to Catholicism, and the art continued to flourish until far into the middle of the nineteenth century (1840 or later). Then, to be sure, competition with the still more delicate bone china from Meissen or Vienna was too strong; the nobles did not buy these earthenwares any longer and the craft declined and eventually stopped altogether.

A Hungarian collector and connoisseur in the art of Haban ceramics stimulatingly analyzed these products from the angle of artistic style. He found a three-step development, or shift. Of the oldest pieces, about 1590 to 1680, the style might be called Italian Renaissance (pointing back to the land of origin); prevailing is the tulip motif, not unlike the tulip of Pennsylvania–Dutch folk art; the colors are predominantly red, brown, and reddish brown, on clear white ground. Then, in the late 1600's, a change took place: from the Netherlands the color of blue was introduced, and the pattern of the workshops of Delft, the famous bulb, became preferred. Finally, in the nineteenth century, when they became increasingly assimilated to the civilization of the Hungarians (Magyars), the patterns of Haban ceramics also became magyarized, that is "folksy," indigenous. I myself find these latest pieces, though still artful, less attractive than the earlier work. Although the designs or decorations are less sophisticated and slightly rough (peasant style), the shape and appearance of these latest specimens are still worthy of any museum piece.

Is there any way of seeing such work, except by traveling to Budapest or Prague? Fortunately the answer is: yes. For by a strange coincidence, one of the curators of the excellent Brooklyn Museum (eastern Parkway, Brooklyn, New York) happened to travel through Hungary in the early 1920's. From this trip he brought with him a large collection of Haban pottery now on exhibit in this museum. It has to be said, however, that practically all the pieces of this collection belong to the craft of the nineteenth century. There are no pieces representing the very height of this art but rather its decline into a peasant craft. Still, there is an impressive wine jug of 1817, made for the carpenter's guild, and a lovely pitcher of 1835, showing a farmer plowing. This pitcher is particularly remarkable due to its bold, almost modernistic coloring: one of the two horses is blue while the other one is purple (violet); the remainder of the ornaments are yellow and green.

Museums in Budapest, Vienna, Prague, Berlin, Brno, and Bratislava are rich in such collections, many coming from former castles or manor houses. When, in 1937, Hutterite Brethren from America visited their former homesteads in Slovakia and Transylvania, they were shown old workshops of potters, still preserved, and results of excavations where potsherds were found. People in village and countryside still showed them pitchers and jars of their ancestors. But nothing was for sale. The folklorist, however, finds in these wares an unlimited field of research and study. Czech, Slovakian, and Hungarian scholars are, of course, foremost in this pursuit, unfortunately for all those who do not understand these languages. The Central European connoisseur everywhere appreciates these old and at one time rather expensive works, the true forerunner of later chinaware.

These works of dedicated craftsmanship are an unusual and unexpected legacy of Anabaptism. The creators of this legacy were people who had dedicated their lives to their Lord both in worship and in work and service.

Bibliography

Naturally, the literature about these people is rather remote and scarce. The articles in *Mennonite Encyclopedia* on "Crafts" and "Habaner" give a first orientation together with some literature. Karl Cernohorsky (Troppava) has written extensively about this subject. His book, *Die Anfänge der Habaner Fayence Produktion* (in Czech., 1931), has 35 halftone illustrations of masterpieces of 1598–1634, with an appendix in German (copy in Goshen College); of course, Johann Loserth, *Der Communismus der mährischen Wiedertäufer* (Vienna, 1894), contains some material, but still more is to be found in F. Hruby, *Die Wiedertäufer in Mähren* (Leipzig, 1935), based on a rich archival research in Moravia. My own travel report, "Die Habaner in der Slovakei," appeared in *Wiener Zeitschrift für Volkskunde*, 1927; the collection of the Brooklyn Museum is in part described by Julian Garner, "Haban Pottery in the Brooklyn Museum," in *International Studio* (New York), September 1927, pp. 20–25, with excellent illustrations; the most valuable contribution, however, is a study by Bela Krisztinkovich, "Beiträge zur Frage der Habaner Keramik," in *Kiss Janos*, 1956, with splendid illustrations. The Diary of the Hutterite Brethren who visited Europe after World War I (on microfilm in Bethel College Historical Library) contains information. Max

Udo Kasparek published two brief essays: "Die Habanerhöfe in Südmähren," *Südmährisches Jahrbuch*, 1957, pp. 92–94, with four good illustrations, and "Zur Tracht der Wiedertäufer in Mähren und der Slowakei," in *Südostdeutsche Heimatblätter*, München, 1956, pp. 91–95, with two illustrations. Karl Layer (former director of the Arts and Crafts Museum in Budapest), *Oberungarische Habaner Fayencen* (Vienna, 1927), with 70 halftone plates (text insignificant), perhaps the best group of illustrations in this area. *Mennonite Life* carried significant illustrations in July 1946, pp. 40–42, and January 1954, pp. 34–37.

More about Habaner Pottery

The October 1958 issue of *Mennonite Life* contained a report on the remarkable artistic achievements of the Moravian and Slovakian Hutterites, locally known as Habaner. Their ceramic masterpieces, called Habaner wares, are rightly considered worthy museum pieces which even be admired in this country (Brooklyn Museum, New York, and Art Institute of Chicago). It thus appears worthwhile to study the background and other details of this unusual production somewhat further, and report also about recent literature which might shed new light in this neglected and remote area.

The origin of this craft in Moravia is still an enigma even though all indications point to Italy; no document reveals the ties between Italy and Moravia. All that can definitely be said is the fact that around 1593–95 such majolica (or fayence) pieces suddenly appear in Moravia as products of the Anabaptists, showing from the beginning a remarkably high level of technical and artistic perfection. They represent distinctly the traditional Renaissance style of Italy both in shape and decoration. Workshops existed all over Southern Moravia and adjacent Slovakia at numerous Bruderhofs (a total of about forty such shops), producing the new type of majolica potteries, characterized by the use of finely sifted clay, the pure white glazing, and the four base colors of Italian majolica wares. The lords in castles and manor houses were only too eager to buy such fine pieces of tablewares (plates, jugs, pitchers, etc.), and there was scarcely any manorial inventory in Moravia and Hungary without such Habaner wares. To be sure, the Brethren produced them in the main for cash and not for their own use, and therefore allowed a certain amount of restrained artistic sophistication not usually appreciated at lower social strata.

But soon important changes came to pass: in 1622 all Anabaptists were expelled from Moravia, and from then on production was restricted to a few Slovakian and Hungarian places. Furthermore, competition was felt by the new Swiss (Winterthur) and Dutch (Delft) wares of a different design and coloring, which in due time also changed the pattern of Habaner production. Toward the end of the seventeenth century the remaining Moravian Hutterites went through a period of internal crisis and disintegration, and by 1685 their traditional way of communal living (both in consumption and production) was abandoned, at least in part. What formerly had been community workshops now passed into private hands, beginning a period of individual workshops of "Habaner" masters, in German also called *Krüglmacher*. Some of them even severed their connection with the brotherhood altogether while others remained faithful and continued the old ways until the late eighteenth century.

It is only natural that this brought many changes about: these independent masters had to adjust themselves more and more to their environment, Slovakian and Magyar, and we notice that quite a few even gave up their German tongue in favor of the local dialect. They also lost most of their noble customers, who now (in the eighteenth century) preferred the new bone china wares. Thus we see the Habaner potteries also changing noticeably, trying to please the new peasant customers and their taste, so different from that of the nobles. The sophisticated style of the 1600's gave way to one more suited to Czech, Slovakian, and Magyar folk tradition. In this form Habaner wares continued to be produced up to the 1830's and later, by now lacking, of course, all the remarkable graces of the beginning.

This brief resumé was in part stimulated by a recent book which certainly deserves our attention and interest. It is entitled *Painting on Folk Ceramics*, written by the Czech folklorist Josef Vydra and the curator of the Folklore Section of the Moravian Museum in Brünn (Brno), Ludvik Kunz (Artia Press, Prague, 1956, 78 pages text and 156 plates, partly in color; large folio size). The English edition was translated by Roberta Finlayson Samsour and published by Spring Books, London. The German edition has the title *Malerei auf Folksmajolika, Von der Wiedertäuferkeramik zur Volkskunst* (1685–1925).

It is a remarkable publication indeed, and in some ways exhaustive. The two authors, experts in the field of folklore, studied the numerous collections of folk-ceramics in Czechoslovakia (a total of nearly 15,000 items) and compared these Czech products with their forerunners, the Anabaptist Habaner wares. The subtitle of the German edition, "From Anabaptist Ceramics to Folk Art," indicates the very idea that the book tries to convey; it does not intend to investigate the story of the Anabaptist ceramic production as such but wants only to pursue the development of Czech and Slovakian folk art from 1685 to 1925, the date 1685 being, of course, the year when the Hutterites gave up their communal organization. Thus it considers the Habaner story only as a background, indispensable though it is.

The authors readily admit that the Czechoslovakian art of pottery-making begins with the high art of Habaner fayence or majolica, in fact it was these Habaner who first introduced the majolica technique into Moravia. They also established a special style for these wares. The authors analyze this

Habaner style in some detail, distinguishing in it three clear phases: the Italian Renaissance style, the Dutch naturalistic ornamentics and the Swiss preference for heraldic signs as decoration. While Renaissance decoration used mainly plant patterns such as tulips, acanthus, grape and grapevine motives, the seventeenth century introduced stylized animals (birds, deer, foxes, etc.) in a decorative way in opposition to the earlier Anabaptist principle of austerity.

It is regrettable that among the 156 halftone and color plates of the book only nine plates are devoted to Habaner wares (1654, 1686, 1713, 1745, and later), and even these pieces are by no means the best representatives of this art (illustrations in the October 1958 issue of Mennonite Life are by far more appealing). Thus, the book does not add too much factually to our understanding of the Anabaptist origins of this art, and yet it is also good to learn the new folkloristic aspect, all the more as literature on that subject outside Czechoslovakia is well–nigh nonexistent.

For this reason we also welcome the fine bibliography at the end of the text section of the book, listing about one hundred entries in the Czech and German languages, omitting, however, altogether the literature in Magyar language. The book was published in 1956; may I therefore be permitted to add a few more items of remote studies in this field of recent origin as they became known to me, in order to aid research in this worthwhile field:

Bela Krisztinkovich, "Beiträge zur Frage der Habaner Keramik," in *Mitteilungsblatt der Keramikfreunde der Schweiz*, Nr. 40, October 1957 (illustrated); Bela and Maria Krisztinkovich, "L'arte ungharese sic della maiolica detta habana," *Faenza, Bolletino del Museo Internazionale delle Ceramiche in Faenza* (Italy), XLIV (1958), pp. 58–63, with 13 illustrations; Paul Dedic, "Habaner Fayencen in Steyrischen Adelshaushalten," in *Blätter für Heimatskunde*, Graz (Styria), XXIV (1950).

SOURCE: *Mennonite Life*, XIII (1958), pp. 147–52; XIV (1959), pp. 129–30.

HUTTERITE CHRONICLES

Among the many groups of sixteenth century Anabaptists, not one was as history-minded as the Hutterites in Moravia. At the headquarters of their *Vorsteher* (bishops) they seem to have kept orderly archives where all material of significance was collected, incoming and outgoing epistles, official writings, doctrinal statements, records about martyrs, records about the affairs of the brotherhood itself, notes on weather, on prices of farm products, regulations (*Ordnungen*), speeches of elders, and all the rest. It was the fountain from which inspiration and strength could be gained and the assurance that their way was the right one. Wherever brethren were examined by the authorities they knew how to answer because they knew their history and the precious testimonies of their brethren. Numerous copies of this material were made, and often collected in well-bound books or codices. At these headquarters the Brethren must also have kept a small library, containing such books as Eusebius, *Church History*, Sebastian Franck's *Chronica*, and other works in church history, then all the printed books by Hubmaier, Denck, Hans Hut, and related men, and pamphlets like Michael Sattler's Epistles together with the story of his trial and end, the story of G. Wagner's or Leonhard Kaiser's martyrdom, and many more like them, then also various Bible concordances which were often carefully copied, and so on.

During the "Golden Age" of the brotherhood in Moravia, the time of the *Vorsteher* Peter Walpot, 1565–78, the idea must have arisen to collect all this material in an official chronicle to keep the memory of the great happenings alive, particularly the "heroic beginnings," and also to offer an object lesson to later generations. Perhaps they meant also to vindicate their peculiar way of life; and, not the least, the martyrdom of the many witnesses to truth should find a permanent record for posterity. Thus the work was begun, perhaps on suggestion of Peter Walpot, by the *Diener des Wortes* Kaspar Braitmichel. From the preface, where he apologizes that for reasons of poor eyesight and other frailties he could not carry on his work beyond the year 1542, we may assume that he wrote this book toward the end of his life. He died in 1573 in Austerlitz (Moravia), the seat of the *Vorsteher* and (probably) also of the archives. His original manuscript is no longer extant; it was copied, however, by Hauptrecht Zapff, the clerk of the next *Vorsteher* Kräl (1578–83) and the following *Vorsteher* Klaus Braidl (1583–1611). This Zapff manuscript is still extant, incidentally also a work of outstanding penmanship and artistic illumination. After Zapff, six more scribes or annalists continued this work in the given fashion, until the year 1665, when the manuscript abruptly ends with a letter of supplication to the brethren in Holland. Only one master copy of this chronicle exists, or, as it was called, the *Geschichts–Buch und kurzer Durchgang vom Anfang der Welt...*, also called *Unser Gemein Geschicht-Buch*. It is a bulky volume of 612 folio leaves, bound in leather and with the usual brass buckles. As their greatest treasure the Brethren kept it with utmost care, carrying it along on all their pilgrimages through the ages. Today it is with the Brethren in America. It is commonly called the *Great Chronicle* (*Gross Geschicht–Buch*).

For about 130 years no continuation of the Zapff manuscript was ever considered. It was the time of the decline of the brotherhood. But then, the revived brotherhood, then living in Russia, had the good fortune of having in their midst a man of outspoken gift in historiography: Johannes Waldner (1749–1824), bishop of the brotherhood from 1794 to his death. Waldner, a Carinthian by birth, studied all the old records, including the Great Chronicle, and decided to write a sequel to the first chronicle. He worked on this important enterprise from 1793 to 1802; we do not know why he stopped at this year. In this book, called by himself *Denkwürdigkeiten* (*Memorabilia*), he first briefly repeated the entire story of the former book, to be sure, with new and significant additions, then he carried the story forward from the year 1665 to the moment when the Carinthian transmigrants joined the nearly extinct brotherhood in Transylvania around 1755 (getting his material from written and oral sources otherwise unknown). And finally he told in broad details all the vicissitudes of the brotherhood which he had himself shared or, at least, had witnessed. While the older book, from now on called the *Great Chronicle*, was fairly unartistic in its form, more annals than history, the new book, now called the *Small Chronicle, Das Klein–Geschichtsbuch der Hutterischen Brüder*, is a real masterwork of historiography, a pragmatic account of great unity and dynamic. The manuscript consists of 370 folio leaves.

After Waldner's death very little was done to carry on this kind of work, and later notes are scanty and poor. This manuscript also exists in only one master copy in one of the Bruderhofs in Canada.

These Chronicles then are the two major source books of our knowledge of the Hutterites, whose story thus became better known and more easily accessible than that of any other Anabaptist group. However, they represent by no means the only historical material from this group. It is highly characteristic for the history–mindedness of the Hutterites that many a brother undertook similar literary enterprises, though on a smaller scale. These books were usually called *Denkbüchlein* or memorandum booklets, sometimes also simply "chronicle." To a certain extent they are but excerpts from the "larger" chronicle, omitting much of the non–annalistic material, but partly they are original works with their own (unknown, mostly oral) sources. They partly overlap and have the same contents, but partly they bring new data otherwise not available, enriching our knowledge in many a detail. Of these smaller chronicles we know about nineteen different specimens. Josef von Beck gives an account of them in the introduction of his remarkable edition of these chronicles, published under the title *Die Geschichts–Bücher* (note the plural) *der Wiedertäufer in Oesterreich–Ungarn,..., von 1526 bis 1785* (Vienna, 1883, in Fontes Rerum Austriacarum, XLIII). He enumerates them as codices *A* to *T*. The best known of them is perhaps the codex *A*, the "Resch–chronicle" (named after its writer who carried the work on until his death in 1592, while later Brethren continued it until 1639), entitled *Ein klein gründliches Denkbüchlein darin wird begriffen und angezeigt was sich seit dem 1524 Jahr mit den rechten christgläubigen und frommen Menschen hat zugetragen, und wie die Gemein Gottes wiederum hat angefangen* (meaning the restitution of the primitive church after 1400 years of decline) *und vermehrt hat*. Another remarkable book is codex *I*, *Beschreibung der Geschichten ... wie und was Gott mit seinen Gläubigen ... vom Anfang der Welt gehandelt und bis auf die jetzige Zeit sich kräftig in ihnen bewiesen ... durch Kaspar Braitmichel oder Schneider gestellt, und jetzt* (i.e., 1591) *wieder angefangen zu schreiben ... C.K.* Only part of the first hundred leaves seems to go back to Braitmichel, the rest (200 leaves) are a copy of the Resch codex. Whether Braitmichel himself made excerpts from his own "larger" chronicle or, what is more likely, whether this book represents a preliminary experiment in chronicling (and also in church history—as the title indicates), must remain a moot question.

These codices are usually octavo size, comprising between 200 and 300 leaves, produced in beautiful handwriting. Seven of them begin with a brief summary of the history of the church from the time of Constantine (when it was considered that the true church began its decline) up to about 1520. This part is an excerpt from Sebastian Franck's popular *Chronica*. In the Great Chronicle this introduction is more elaborate and takes up thirty–two (or forty–four) pages in print. Most of these chronicles continue their story almost to the end of the seventeenth century, several authors working successively on them similar to the way in which the Great Chronicle was composed. A complete comparison of both the Great Chronicle and these nineteen smaller ones has never been undertaken. Much material is identical but quite a bit is also new and different. In completeness and spiritual intent the Great Chronicle is certainly superior to the others.

More than one fifth of this Great Chronicle is made up of inserts of doctrinal statements and epistles (*Sendbriefe*) among the latter we find some of the finest ever written by Hutterites, such as those by Jakob Hutter, Riedemann, Peter Walpot, Paul Block, etc. From Hutterite epistle books extant it becomes apparent that also a great part of the remaining story was drawn from these unusual prime sources, a point to which particularly Wolkan called attention in his edition of 1923. Likewise hymns, so numerous among Hutterites, have served as a welcome source mainly for the stories of martyred brethren. The Great Chronicle contains also most welcome doctrinal material taken from proceedings of religious debates or from other documents in the archive. For instance, only the Great Chronicle has the *Five Articles of the Greatest Disagreement between Us and the World*, of 1547, written most likely around 1570 by Peter Walpot, or the *Brüderliche Vereinigung zwischen uns und etlichen Brüdern am Rheinstrom* of 1556, written by Hans Raiffer. At the year 1571, a lengthy insert describes in detail the organization and the work of the brotherhood (written perhaps by Peter Walpot), a major source for our knowledge of the life of the Hutterites.

For a long time the Great Chronicle was not known to European scholars, since it existed only in a faraway colony in Russia and was then taken to America. Only the chronicles which had been confiscated by Jesuits in the eighteenth century and kept in different libraries of Europe were known. Josef von Beck assiduously collected and copied most of them and then undertook the difficult task of combining all his material in mosaic fashion. He added whatever pertinent material he could get hold of otherwise and thus produced an admirable and still very usable work, the *Geschichts–Bücher* (1883), of about 700 pages.

In 1908 Rudolf Wolkan of Vienna, Austria, learned through John Horsch for the first time of the existence of the original chronicle and from a transcription received from the Brethren in America prepared an edition of this volume entitled *Geschicht–Buch* (note the singular over against Beck's plural) *der Hutterischen Brüder* (Vienna, 1923) in 750 pages. The language of this edition is adjusted to the present–day usage of High German. In footnotes much valuable material from epistles is added. It can be safely said that the Beck and Wolkan editions well supplement each other.

In 1943 another edition of the same book was published, this time in America, entitled *Die älteste Chronik der Hutterischen Brüder* (Carl Schurz Foundation, Philadelphia, 1943). It was prepared by A. J. F. Zieglschmid (then Professor of German Literature at Northwestern University, Evanston, Ill.) and was brought out in a letter–perfect edition of the original text (spelling, punctuation, etc.) It is a bulky volume of more than 1,100 pages and 20 plates (with samples of the handwriting). It contains many valuable helps—glossary, bibliography, and so on.

Four years later, in 1947, Zieglschmid published the sequel, the *Klein–Geschichtsbuch der Hutterischen Brüder* (again Carl Schurz Foundation). It is a first edition taken from the hitherto unknown *Denkwürdigkeiten* of Johannes Waldner, which was kept in custody on a Bruderhof in Canada. Though called "Small Chronicle," the volume is almost as bulky as the "Great

Chronicle," having 856 quarto pages. This edition is done in modernized language like the Wolkan book, and contains again an extensive apparatus. Its bibliography of more than 300 items is by far the most exhaustive one on the Hutterites in existence. As was mentioned above, Waldner's text goes only as far as 1802. From 1802 to 1947 very few notes are found in the manuscript, and the editor was compelled to supply supplementary material from even the remotest sources attainable (pp. 410–500). In an Appendix (500–686) a nearly complete collection of *Gemeinde-Ordnungen* (regulations or ordinances for the brotherhood) from 1651 to 1873 is published, further the revealing travel diary of Paul Tschetter (1873) while on a search for a place of settlement in America, then Canadian documents (since 1872), lists of colonies, preachers, etc.

Waldner's text of the Small Chronicle gives more than mere annals. Skillfully he emphasizes the dynamic evolution, condensing the earlier story to what is of true significance and adding material not known heretofore. Of great value are inserted selections of sermons which were to help revive the former spirit and strengthen the loyalty to the original institutions (pp. 204–14). They were taken from one of the remarkable sermon collections which have to this day been preserved in the colonies and are still in use at their worship services. An ordinance of 1633 by Ehrenpreis concerning nonresistance is another welcome insert into the text. Since Waldner's description of the sufferings in Transylvania and the exodus to Russia (1767 ff.) is based on his own experiences, the last part of his "memorabilia" is particularly dramatic and well written, proving that these Carinthian newcomers had certainly grasped something of the spirit of the Hutterite forefathers.

SOURCE: *Mennonite Encyclopedia*, I, pp. 589–91.

THE EPISTLES OF THE HUTTERIAN BRETHREN
A Study in Anabaptist Literature[1]

Introduction

The opportunities of studying the genius of the Anabaptist movement of the sixteenth century are limited. We know many facts, but the original products and representative expressions of this movement are comparatively little known and studied. Since Anabaptism was heavily persecuted in most of Europe, and further since it was not at all a literary affair (in contrast to the contemporary theological polemics of Catholics and Protestants) but an affair of living and testimony, writings of Anabaptists are scarce and widely scattered. All the historian can do is to put them together piece by piece in mosaic fashion, drawing from many sources, even the hostile ones. When, over twenty years ago, German scholars set out to collect all the available sources of Anabaptism in the great *Täuferakten* enterprise, it was therefore a great surprise to them to learn that at least in one respect the situation is much more favorable than expected. This one respect has to do with the literary remains of the Hutterian Brethren, whose descendants are still living as a small group in South Dakota and Western Canada. Once, in the sixteenth century, they were a most numerous group of South German and Austrian Anabaptists, renowned for their principle of community of goods, their peculiar understanding of the practice of Christian love and brotherhood.

In contrast to the Swiss Brethren, who did not cultivate the field of literary expression (the source materials of these Brethren are exceedingly scant), the Hutterites with their unusually strong sense of community developed the custom of written testimonies into a great passion, or better, into a great technique. It became their great legacy, one for which we should be most grateful. Their Chronicle is well known and appreciated; in fact, it is a unique source and as such has already found wide attention and use by historians. The Hutterite great hymnbook is no less noted. In 1914 the Mennonite Publishing House (Scottdale, Pa.) published a collection of these

---

[1] A translation and condensed revision of the author's study. "Die Briefe der österreichischen Täufer, ein Bericht," published in the *Archiv für Reformationsgeschichte*, XXVI (1929), 30–80, 161–87, with exhaustive bibliography. Christian Neff reviewed this paper in *MQR*, V (1931), 148–52, presenting also details concerning the sources.

hymns comprising more than eight hundred pages, which has found learned students on both sides of the Atlantic. A third and most significant group of such documents of genuine Anabaptist spirit, however, has remained almost unknown to the great majority of students of Anabaptist–Mennonite history. This is the rich epistolary literature of the Hutterites, collected in many old manuscript codices, preserved in part in America and Canada, and in part, in European libraries. Only a small fraction has been published so far, but even these few samples have aroused much interest.

Of course, letters were always highly esteemed in the world of faith, letters of saints and of divines, of mystics and of Reformers. And above all, one should not forget that a large part of our New Testament is made up of such letters, or epistles as they might more appropriately be called. Paul, John, Peter, James, and Jude, all put their testimony in this form, and it has remained to the present the liveliest form of conveying the spirit and the love of disciples and apostles of Christ. Letters, however, from plain people, simple folk from the countryside, unlettered believers—such letters are otherwise almost unknown, at least in large collections. The Hutterites, averse to publicity, had almost nothing printed. But their numerous epistles, together with all the other products of their religious writing, were collected in the above mentioned manuscript codices and handed down through the generations in manifold ways. Because of their unique importance in the history of Anabaptism, a report of these letters—or should it more correctly be called literature?—will be presented in the following pages. In truth, they do constitute a literature in a genuine sense, and not only a file of incidental letters. The Hutterites lived, and still continue to do so, separated from the "world." They read the Bible, but scarcely any books of the world, theological or otherwise. Their education and their edification came, one may safely say, in addition to the Scriptures, exclusively from their own *Büchlein*, their unique codices, of which several hundred, possibly three hundred or more, are still extant. They must once have numbered high in the hundreds, perhaps nearly one thousand.

To read these books is a delight also for "outsiders"; even unbelievers admit that they are gripped by the contents. Here we find the finest and most genuine representation of the Anabaptist genius. Today, as we try to reconstruct and appreciate this genius, we can find no better avenue to it than these books. Of course, they all are written in the antiquated German of the sixteenth century and for that reason are not easily translatable, but that has to be accepted, for it pays to read them in the original tongue.

Manifold are the contents of these books. Some are mere devotional tracts, but they are rather the exception. Certainly devotion is not the sole purpose of this literature; its aims were much more comprehensive. We will come nearer the truth if we formulate it in this way: these books were an introduction to the living out of faith, a kind of preparation or conditioning of the Brethren for their dangerous life of testimony in a pagan and most hostile world. Just as we today get our secular knowledge out of textbooks, the Hutterites got their wisdom out of their living experience, the oral teachings of their elders, and the reading of these codices. They contained a wide variety of content: chronicles, theological tracts, catechisms, creeds, many letters written to brethren active in the work of the Lord, or written by brethren in prison and facing death at the stake, admonitions and consolations, hymns, farewells of all kinds, tracts by such leaders as Denck, Hut, Hubmaier, Sattler, and others, and then again medical recipes and advice, regulations governing trades and crafts, pedagogical regulations, Bible concordances, even a bit of geography of the Holy Land, also highly cherished brief sketches of church history, excerpts from Eusebius or Josephus, the history of the deviations of the papal church, favorite stories of the Israelites from the Old Testament or the Apocrypha. Indeed, it was a great education that was carried by these books, an education to that austere life of Christian witness which did not shrink from the ultimate sacrifice, be it at the stake or in the rotting depth of a dungeon.

I am painfully aware that writing about epistles is somewhat like writing about music or painting for people unacquainted with these fields. Only a firsthand experience with these documents can satisfy, for all description can but faintly reflect the true value and power of these sources. Nevertheless, the following description will try to do more than merely register the facts; it will also evaluate and appreciate their special characteristics. As such, the study might be viewed as an interpretative introduction. A loving meditation upon these documents is necessary to discover their inner beauty, meaning, and spiritual value. Mennonitism of today (and not Mennonitism alone) could profit greatly from these testimonies.

The External Appearance of the Books

All the books I have ever handled were bound in leather, mostly provided with brass buckles, as was the general custom in olden days to preserve valuable volumes. They are still in an excellent state of preservation. The binding is usually nicely decorated with pressed leather ornamentation. The largest book I have seen was large folio size (about fourteen inches high), and contained a Bible concordance; the smallest book might be classified as 32mo (about two and one-half inches high); it is a hymnal with some additional tracts, most clearly and legibly written. The concordance has over a thousand leaves (in former centuries leaves, not pages, were counted). The next largest codex has about seven hundred leaves, the smallest, on the other hand, only about 150 leaves. The average is the octavo volume (seven inches high) with about three hundred leaves. The writing is done on good tough paper with ink, often with red headings, written in exceptionally good penmanship. Which proves that the Brethren must have been schooled well beyond the average of sixteenth-century common people. One author (Rochus v. Liliencron) has described one codex as "written carefully and by an educated hand." The title pages are usually beautifully adorned, yet never in the character of the Pennsylvania-Dutch designs, which originated at a much later time. Each volume always has one, often two registers.[2]

General Description of the Epistle and of the Character of the Whole Literature

The Brethren must have had an unusual eagerness for writing and recording. Apparently it was both their edification and consolation. There is only an isolated case of one brother confesses (like the imprisoned Veith Uhrmacher, 1570), "My dear brother Peter, I would have much to write to you, but I cannot write that much and never could."[3] The usual tone is much better represented by the following passage. "I must write you at once, dear brother, even though you might get sick of so many letters. I myself don't get tired of it, on the contrary, it makes me feel good since I feel bound to you in brotherly love. If I could, I would write you every week." This was written during a mission trip to Switzerland in 1584 (Benesh Köhler).[4] Or, "You beloved in the Lord, I wish I could write you more, but I am not skillful enough to do so with quill and ink. My heart, however, be your letter and your seal on it" (Ludwig Fest, 1533).[5]

This eagerness to write explains why letters from certain brothers are so numerous in our codices. For instance, from Hänsel Schmidt (or Raiffer) of the Tyrol, who was executed in Aachen while on a mission trip to the Rhineland in 1558, at least thirty-six letters are still extant. The same brother is also well known as one of the most prolific hymn writers, to whom we owe many "gracious and lovely" songs.[6] Peter Riedemann, well known in Hutterite history as the author of the great *Rechenschaft unseres Glaubens* (Account of Our Faith), produced at least thirty-four letters deemed worthy of permanent recording in our books. Next comes Paul Glock, who during a period of nineteen years in prison for the sake of his faith, wrote twenty long, beautiful epistles to the home church in Moravia.[7] From Hans Amon, the second elder (*Vorsteher*) of the church (1536–42), a man of extraordinary gifts, seventeen epistles are known, most of them letters of consolation and support sent to imprisoned brethren. And finally from Jakob Hutter, the

---

2   Neff reprints in his review of Friedmann's paper (see above note) the full text of two of these registers in order to show the richness of contents of these books.

3   *Geschicht-Buch*, 374 note, and Johann Loserth, "Zur Geschichte der Wiedertäufer in Salzburg," in *Mitteilungen der Gesellschaft für Salzburgische Landeskunde*, LII (1912).

4   Loserth, *Communismus*, 310.

5   A. J. F. Zieglschmid, "Unpublished Sixteenth Century Letters of the Hutterian Brethren, " in *MQR*, XV (1941), 24.

6   Rudolf Wolkan, *Die Hutterer* (Vienna, 1918), 134.

7   Published by G. Bossert in his *Quellen zur Geschichte der Wiedertäufer, Herzogtum Württemberg* (Leipzig, 1930).

founder of the entire Hutterian movement, ten unusually long and moving epistles are preserved. No doubt there once existed many more letters from these men, but these extant epistles were regarded as eminent enough to be preserved or rather to be presented to the community as edifying and helpful reading.

Some of the epistles were unbelievably long, particularly those by Jakob Hutter. Their length is understandable in view of Hutter's tremendous task of unifying and organizing the new movement in the right way, both spiritually and practically. To start colonies based on a sound system of community of goods, capable of enduring through four centuries and more, was surely no small undertaking. The letter, for instance, which relates the split of the brotherhood in 1533 (when Gabriel Ascherham broke away) comprises in print fifteen pages folio size.[8] Peter Walpot's beautiful letter to the apothecary Simon Ronemburg in Cracow (1571) covers nine large pages in print.[9] Another gem of this collection, the letter by the brother Franz Wälsch (Francesco di Robigo) from Venice, written originally in the Italian language and then translated, fills thirty–nine pages (octavo size) in one manuscript, in very small writing. Claus Felbinger's great epistle, reporting his arrest and trial (1560), was published by Johann Loserth on nineteen large pages in print. One might debate whether Andreas Ehrenpreis' great writing, *Ein Send–Brieff, brüderliche Gemeinschaft betreffend* (1652), can be considered as a genuine epistle or rather a treatise. It constitutes a book of 189 pages in print,[10] but in character it still preserved the features of an epistle "to whom it may concern."

In order to get a general survey of the entire compass of the Hutterite prose writings, I have prepared a catalogue (unpublished) the results of which will be reported in the following. It covers the period from 1527 to 1662, the year when Andreas Ehrenpreis, the last great elder of the brotherhood, passed away, and it comprises all codices which could be reached during my research in European libraries and archives. It is almost certain that the codices in possession of the Hutterites in this country contain many more items. In fact, the now deceased Elder Elias Walter of Standoff Colony, Canada, once sent me a long list of such writings available in the American colonies of the Hutterites, but unfortunately this list is no longer in my hands.

In my catalog I have listed about four hundred epistles and similar writings, composed by seventy–five to eighty writers. Of these writers, about half (that is, forty) were martyrs, having been executed by fire or sword. Most of them were ministers of the word (*Diener des Wortes*) or missionaries (*Sendboten*). This is easily understandable since they were the more educated ones, with greater intellectual and spiritual capacities. But it must be strongly

---

    8   *Geschicht–Buch*, 87–101.
    9   Robert Friedmann, "Reason and Obedience," *MQR*, XIX (1945), 27–40.
    10 Andreas Ehrenpreis, *Ein Sendbrief... brüderliche Gemeinschaft, das höchste Gebot der Liebe betreffend. Anno 1652. Aufs neue herausgegeben von den Hutterischen Brudern in Amerika* (Scottdale, 1920).

emphasized that the Hutterite epistles are by no means the product solely of such leaders. On the contrary, most simple and humble members of the brotherhood, without any outstanding function, often wrote exceedingly beautiful and valuable epistles in dungeon and tribulation. The Hutterites were a truly democratic group. Such a universal capacity to express one's deepest spiritual experiences was possible only in a movement completely separated from the world and characterized by a close spiritual intimacy without which no such group could ever have existed.

A great majority of the writers came from the Tyrol, where in the late 1520's the movement sprang up and where Jakob Hutter had worked the hardest. As to countries of origin, next comes Bavaria, then the Austrian provinces, and lastly the different principalities of Germany. In many cases the land of origin is unknown. Two writers came from Venetia. Concerning their social background I can be brief since Paul Dedic has thoroughly discussed this subject.[11] My catalogue shows the following data: only four writers came from the ranks of the Catholic priesthood: Leonhard Schiemer, who was a Franciscan friar and was beheaded for his faith's sake as early as 1528; Hans Schlaffer, "formerly a Roman parson" (*Pfaff*), who died in the same year in the same manner, one of the finest spirits of the early times, whose farewell letter is truly a pearl in our entire collection; Leonhard Lochmaier, who prior to 1526 had been priest for eight years and who, too, died by the sword in 1538; and finally Leonhard Dax, a priest and erstwhile foe of the Anabaptists until 1557, who died in Moravia in 1574, during the Golden Age. All four come from Tyrol.

It is worth noting that almost all the theological tracts of the Hutterites (and some of them have a truly great style) originate with lay members and not with the above-mentioned Brethren. Thus, for instance, Ulrich Stadler was an official in a salt mine, Peter Walpot was a wool-shearer, Peter Riedemann a shoemaker, Joseph Hauser a barber, and Andreas Ehrenpreis a miller. Strangely enough, there is only one school teacher among the authors of the epistles, Jeronymus Käls, executed in Vienna in 1536. It is but rarely that the Chronicle or the epistle names the trade of the writer; it was not important enough. In most cases we may assume that the writers were peasants skilled in many trades besides farming. I know of only the following cases where the special trade of the epistle writer is mentioned: five tailors, three blacksmiths, three millers, three cobblers, one watchmaker (Veith Uhrmacher), two wool-shearers, and one rope maker (Leonhard Lanzenstil or Seiler).[12] The Brethren had also some famous physicians, but to my knowledge they left no writings. One apothecary was in loose connection with the brotherhood (Melchior

---

11 Paul Dedic, "Social Background of the Austrian Anabaptists," *MQR*, XIII (1939), 5-20.

12 It is surprising that the two main trades of the Hutterites, those which made them famous all over the country, namely cutlery and pottery, are not represented in my list. Neither could I find barbers among the letter writers.

Platzer). No woman is ever quoted as a writer, although quite a few women accepted the ultimate sacrifice of martyrdom. Great is the number of epistles or epistle–like tracts of unnamed writers. After all, the contents were what mattered, not the author. This anonymity is most characteristic among the Hutterites, a feature of high symbolic significance.

The two hundred and eighty epistles (in the specific sense of a letter) of the collection under study may be classified as to type as follows: five official letters to the authorities on behalf of the entire brotherhood (as, for instance, the famous letter of 1535 by Jakob Hutter to the governor of Moravia, which has been published at least seven times); sixty letters written by Brethren to single individuals; and about 215 epistles with a collective addressee such as *An die Gemein in Mähren, An die lieben Brüder hier und dort wo sie zerstreut sind, An die Eifrigen im Oberland* (Tyrol), and so on. This collective trait is again most significant for this whole body of literature. Some letters are also signed in this way. For instance, "Signed by us, the ministers of the brotherhood at Schäkowitz together with the elders of the community. This letter has been read before more than one hundred brethren and is forwarded with the consent of the entire brotherhood." Thus, the individual disappears completely in the group as a whole. Someone once formulated this fact very fittingly by speaking of "the community in the unity of the Holy Spirit" (*Gemeinschaft der Geisteinheit*).

When we consider a classification of the letters according to their purpose or character, we find the letters from prison most prominent. The above-mentioned forty martyred brethren sent a total of one hundred thirty letters back to the church in Moravia. Of these, about eighty contain narratives about arrest, trial, and distress, interspersed with devotional meditations as usual. Twenty–eight letters are farewell letters to wives, among them some of the most striking ones of the whole collection, although very different from anything one would ordinarily expect. They are neither sentimental nor private, since the *eheliche Schwester* (marital sister) is but one particularly close member of the community. Finally, twenty epistles are letters of comfort or solace written by imprisoned brethren to other brethren in the same prison (*mitgefangene Brüder*), such as was the case, for instance, with Jeronymus Käls, Michel Behaim, and Hans Raiffer (fourteen letters). Of letters of comfort written by elders to imprisoned brethren there are twenty–two, the most important being those by Elder Hans Amon. Of confessions and "accounts" (*Rechenschaft, Verantwortung*) before judges, we know about eighteen. There are sixty–eight "general" epistles of miscellaneous content, namely *Bitt– und Vermahnbriefe* (letters of admonition and exhortation), letters of cheer, reports on mission trips, descriptions of extreme distress, and so on. Of letters of a specific missionary intention, "preaching the Gospel to every creature," my list contains eleven items. The above–mentioned five official letters could be added here as a last group of this survey.

At the time of writing, the letters cover a span of about 135 years. Four fifths belong to the sixteenth century; only one fifth were written during the sixty–two years of the seventeenth century, and written by only seven writers over against seventy of the earlier century. To be sure, this was already the period of weakening and gradual decline of the brotherhood; fresh blood from the outside was lacking, particularly from Tyrol, where prior to 1600 the movement had been completely crushed, mainly through the activities of the Jesuits. The richest literary period of all was the Golden Age under the Elder (*Vorsteher*) Peter Walpot, 1565 to 1578, a time of relative ease in Moravia, during which the most intensive missionary activities were carried on. At that time many epistles went to the "apostles" (*Sendboten*) and many were received from them. It was the time of their greatest success. They could point to Moravia as the "promised land" where earnest disciples of Christ could live in brotherhood comparatively unmolested. The strengthened Catholic Counter–Reformation finally also brought an end to all these hopes in Moravia. But the interest in letter writing has never died out and to a certain extent is still carried on today.

Concerning the Writing and Mailing of the Epistles

It seems at first surprising that the knowledge of reading and writing was so widely spread among the Brethren since it is known that formal education of the sixteenth century, particularly among the lower classes and peasants, was rather poorly developed. It is by no means a matter of course that simple tradesmen and peasants use their pen with so much skill and good taste. Of course the desire to read the Bible was a strong incentive for their basic education. One might guess that only those who could read later joined the Brethren. "Temptation makes one heed to the Word" (*Die Anfechtung macht auf das Wort merken*), writes Veit Grünberger. About the year 1500, all of Tyrol had not more than ten Latin grammar schools, but it is rather doubtful whether they were frequented by many of those who later turned Anabaptists. Much more is known about schooling within the colonies in Moravia. We read of one schoolmaster of the Brethren, Jeronymus Käls, who was arrested in Vienna in 1536 and burned at the stake. Copies of many beautiful letters from his pen are still preserved. In 1568, Peter Walpot called a great educational conference at Nembschitz in Moravia, where he presented his advanced pedagogical principles and his *Schulordnung* (rules for school management) which meant almost a revolution in that age.[13] In 1617 the well–known traveller Martin Zeiller reports in his *Topographia Bohemiae, Moraviae et Silesiae* (Franckfurt am Main, 1650) concerning the Hutterites:

---

13 See Harold S. Bender's translation of the "Hutterite School Discipline of 1578 and Peter Scherer's Address of 1568 to the Schoolmasters," MQR, V (1931), 231–44.

"As soon as the children come of age, the schoolmaster teaches them reading, writing and reckoning. They very seldom go beyond that."[14]

Of all the numerous brethren from whom we have some writings, only one single brother is mentioned who could not read nor write, Niklas Geyerspüchler, a miller from Tyrol, from whom a *Verantwortung vor dem Gericht zu Innsbruck* (Defense to the Court of Innsbruck in the Tyrol), of 1567 is known,[15] and which is praised for its modesty of expression.

How did this report come to Moravia? We may conjecture that it was accomplished as in a similar case of which the Chronicle reports for the year 1527. When in that year the well-known brother Jörg Wagner was tried in Munich (to be burned later at the stake), an unobtrusive brother listened to the trial and put down on paper the confession and defense of the martyr as he understood it (*ein gutherziger Mensch, der fast alle Worte gehört, hat es schriftlich verzeichnet*).[16] This was apparently a very common and efficient procedure. It was certainly in the highest interest of the brotherhood to collect the news and records of the martyrs and to have them circulate among the Brethren.

Otherwise, all letters were not only drawn up, but also written by the signing brother himself. This is expressly testified, for instance, by Jakob Hutter, in one letter of 1533: "I, Jakob, have written it myself with my own hand, but Claus had copied it for me, and the other epistle [the copy is meant] we will send to the Pustertal [Tyrol.]"[17] Or, in another instance, by Onofrius Griesinger (1538): "This letter I am writing to you with my own hand." Who is not reminded of similar passages in the Apostle Paul's correspondence, such as II Thess. 3:17, or Gal. 6:11? From the Jakob Hutter quotations we also learn that occasionally epistles were copied several times and sent to different places. One should keep in mind that these epistles were always letters "to all," written with a view to the greatest publicity inside the brotherhood. This is particularly true regarding all written enunciations from the *Vorsteher* living at the center of the settlement. There *Gemeindeschreiber* were employed, brothers functioning as clerks who not only recorded all the important facts and documents in the Great Chronicle but who also copied all the outgoing and incoming correspondence for their propagation or their collection in codices. The Chronicle mentions these clerks more than once. There was, for instance, Hänsl Summer, a furrier, or Hauptrecht Zapff, the recording clerk, writer and copyist of the Chronicle, a man of outstanding penmanship, at whose death the Chronicle reports, "He also was the writer of the elders for thirty years."[18]

---

14   J. H. Ottius, *Annales Anabaptistici* (Basel, 1672), 242.
15   *Geschichts-Bücher*, 249 note. Loserth, *Communismus*, 180, presents an excerpt of this account.
16   *Geschichts-Bücher*, 22.
17   *Geschicht-Buch*, 101.
18   *Geschicht-Buch*, 610. As for his penmanship see the fine plates in the appendix to *Älteste Chronik*, particularly plates II, IX, XI, and XIII.

The Brethren were eager to write not only at home but also while working abroad for the Lord. If a brother was caught and imprisoned, it was his duty as well as his favorite activity to record his experiences, internal and external, in letters and confessions of faith. We learn from the letters themselves how it was done. Leonhard Schiemer (executed in the Tyrol in 1527) reports that the judge himself had handed him ink, quill, and paper, for which the judge was later reprimanded by the government.[19] Johannes Bair, of Lichtenfels, a simple brother, who languished a full twenty-three years in a dungeon in Bamberg in Bavaria until he passed away in 1551, gratefully acknowledged in his letter of 1547 to the brotherhood in Moravia the receipt of a writing tablet, a confession of faith (by Riedemann, most likely), candles and quills. Then he asked for a Bible, "for he has been suffering great want of the Word for many years and has great thirst after the Word of the Lord."[20] And Claus Felbinger writes in his beautiful letter to Leonhard Lanzenstil, "I cannot desist from writing to you since God has presented to me paper and ink through a loyal wench [*durch ein treues Mensch*) and I still have some [sun–] light in the prison."[21]

Just as there were many opportunities to supply the imprisoned brethren with writing material; there were also numerous ways to send letters home to the brotherhood out of dungeon and prison. A lively postal service, if this expression be permitted, developed on such occasions. We have a welcome record of this situation again in Claus Felbinger's above-mentioned letter. "Since by good chance a messenger arrived at the prison I handed this letter to him that it might be brought to you. I know that you all are longing for a message from us." Such messengers, to be true, were always available; it was their business to keep the contact between the church at home and the Brethren in the world, so that their trail might not be lost. To give an example of this system of keeping in touch with all the Brethren on the road, a letter from Hans Amon will be quoted which this *Vorsteher* had sent to the imprisoned ones at Falckenstein Castle (Lower Austria) in 1540. "We delegated some Brethren to follow you on your way that they might see where God the Almighty will allow you to be led, and with the grace and help of God we will send still more to visit and comfort you."[22] In their fourth epistle these Falckenstein victims report of their deportation to the galleys of Trieste, then under the Doge of Venice: "About our condition the bearers of this letter will tell you more; They who have faithfully followed us and have heeded so little their own life on our behalf."[23] And then, when in the following year

---

19 J. Loserth, "Der Anabaptismus in Tirol von seinen ersten Anfängen bis zum Tode Huters (1536)," in *Archiv für österreichischen Geschichte*, LXXVIII (1892), 458.
20 *Geschichts–Bücher*, 28 note.
21 *Geschicht–Buch*, 306 note. The *treues Mensch* must be a girl, since in popular slang *"das" Mensch* indicates an unmarried woman, mostly a peasant girl. (In Austrian slang, a *Dirn* or *Dirndl*, corresponding to the English "wench.")
22 *Geschicht–Buch*, 157 note.
23 *Ibid*.

some of these poor galley slaves returned to Moravia while others remained of unknown whereabouts, Amon writes another epistle with the general address, *Den Ausbliebenen von den Hingeführten gen Triest* (To those among the Trieste exiles who did not return), and still another one, "To the Brethren in Genoa or on the Sea" (*Auf dem Mör*). It was the task of the messengers to deliver these epistles, however long it might take to find the addressees, and wherever they might be. How bitter, under certain circumstances, such a search could become, is revealed in the extant letters of the brother Salomon Böger, a miller, who from 1607 to 1610 wandered about in Hungary, Serbia, and Turkey proper, to find his wife and other sisters and brothers who had been carried away by the Turks. It was a moving epic until he, too, found his destiny, namely violent death.[24]

The General Form of the Epistles

In view of the wide use of the epistles it is little wonder that we find many formal elements in them which recur time and again. This observation was already made by von Liliencron, who comments as follows in his 1875 study of Anabaptist hymnology: "In their narratives certain features become typical in character. One is almost tempted to call the treatment 'stereotyped' were there not, on the other hand, so much genuine truth in it, so much lively and warm expression of inner experience. The reason for this phenomenon might possibly be found in the fact that the Brethren had developed a certain idea or picture as to how an earnest Christian ought to bear suffering, and it is this common pattern, so to say, which we meet in the writings both of the martyrs and of those who sing about them."[25] This gives us one explanation. Another is that the Brethren got their spiritual education mainly through reading these books, these epistles, knowing them often almost by heart, and discussing them in their assemblies and at work. They lived in such an atmosphere that a certain imitation of forms was almost inevitable, even though unconscious. Moreover, we know that there were even a few "formularies" for epistles (*Briefsteller*)[26] which in many cases might have provided the models for epistles of exhortation, consolation, and the like. They were certainly not used for letters out of the depth of a dungeon, which were spontaneous cries of distress and hope and trust in God Almighty.

In general organization these writings also reveal a certain uniformity. First comes a word of blessing which is sometimes extended to considerable length. An epistle by Jakob Hutter, for instance, contains blessings and greetings covering over thirty printed lines.[27] The subject proper is then often

---

24   See Friedmann, "Adventure of an Anabaptist in Turkey, 1607–1610," *MQR*, XVII (1943), 73–86.
25   Rochus v. Liliencron, "Zur Liederdichtung der Wiedertäufer," *Abhandlungen der historischen Klasse der kgl. bayrischen Akademie der Wissenschaften*, XIII (1875), 126.
26   Loserth, *Communismus*, 285.
27   *Geschicht–Buch*, 87.

introduced by an apologetic formula such as, "I cannot help writing you a little...," or the like. But even now the writer does not yet begin his topic proper but first elaborates (at least in many cases) upon devotional meditations intended to comfort and exhort the brother or sister to remain steadfast in the faith and to rely thoroughly upon God's loving kindness. Most effective is the frequent insertion of dialogues making the otherwise often monotonous letter more vivid and variegated. An examination by the judge, or a dispute with an "unbeliever," is thus reproduced word by word. I shall try to translate such a passage although the particular popular flavor can not be adequately rendered in such a version. The brother Veith Uhrmacher, who "for the sake of God's truth" had lain in the castle dungeon of Salzburg for many years when he wrote to the congregation in 1573,[28] describes in detail his conversation with Catholic priests who had come with the intention to convert him.

> I let him finish and then said to him, "Have you finished your speech?" To this he answered "Yes." Then I spoke, "Since you think of the teachings of Christ as a sect, I have nothing to answer, for I myself think of it as divine truth." Upon which the man uttered that he was not of such an opinion. Then I said, "Your Lord, the prince [Archbishop of Salzburg] has plenty of information (*Rechenschaft*) about us." The parson (*Pfaff*) answered that he had come for love's sake, otherwise they have plenty to do elsewhere. Then I said, "I have not asked for them, there was no need to come for my sake. If they thought this way why didn't they come long before."[29] Then they said again, "Saint Peter says, be willing to give an account." Upon which I said, "What shall I say? You are prosecutor and judge all in one person. What you cannot decide, constables (*Schörgen*) and hangmen have to carry out in your place. You tell it to the prince, the prince tells it to the judge, the judge tells it to the constable, and the constable tells it to the hangman. He then finishes up the case. He is your high priest, he helps you to win the field."

Another rather different example comes from the same year in a report of two brothers, Marx and Bernard Klampferer, about a discourse with some higher officials.

> Then did the marshal say, "I don't think that it is written this way in the Scriptures." They, however, answered, "Sir, if it is not written this way then you should be right and we wrong." Then the marshal spoke to his chamberlain, "Go, hurry up, and bring the Bible, we will see whether it is as he says." Thus he brought it and the marshal presented the book to the brothers and spoke, "Well, my man, now show me where it is written." Then the brother showed him the

---

28 *Geschicht–Buch*, 373–74 note.
29 Veith had been in prison for three years, 1570–73.

passage. Then the marshal read it overloud and then said, "Yes, my man, it is written this way." And thus he let it be settled.[30]

In this somewhat naive but always immediate manner the Brethren report their conversation often for many pages, thereby revealing what poor champions were sent against them by their adversaries. The letters give the impression that it was easy for the Brethren to win these debates. Certainly many of the counter arguments of the clergy were not too effective. This, by the way, also explains much of the captivating force of Anabaptist propaganda in the sixteenth century.

The letter of the aforementioned brother Veith Uhrmacher reveals still another feature which makes these descriptions so appealing. At first he reports the circumstances of his trip and his arrest by the men of the Archbishop of Salzburg. Then he continues:

> On Sunday we arrived in Salzburg ... and they brought us into the castle, each one in a separate cell. But they did not give us a hearing until the third year of our imprisonment. God be praised from the depth of our heart that we are still fresh and in good shape.[31]

Thus, a period of three years is briefly skipped over and the report of the later events is immediately tied to that of the first happenings without tiring the reader by details of the interval. The intention, to be sure, of such an epistle is never to complain about hardship or to arouse anger or hatred against the persecutors, but only to comfort and exhort the Brethren. For this reason those happenings alone are mentioned which seem to be essential, while all personal and subjective matters disappear.

The epistles are concluded with renewed formal blessings and farewell greetings. Occasionally such a conclusion becomes disproportionately long, as for instance in a letter by Jakob Hutter in which he says farewell to the congregation through two large folio pages in print.[32] Frequently there occur long farewell greetings to individually mentioned persons, such as in a writing of Klaus Felbinger to Leonhard Lanzenstil in which Klaus takes leave of each brother through thirteen lines in print.[33] However, we should be mindful that this type of greeting is no innovation either, since we find already in Paul's epistle to the Romans (16:3-16) a similar specified and extended farewell.

The Literary Style of the Epistles

As for the style of these letters, one must admit that the Brethren showed a surprising skill in the presentation of their experiences and thoughts. The narratives are simple and plain, unaffected and natural. A master of particular

---

30 *Geschichts–Bücher*, 262.
31 Loserth, "Zur Geschichte der Wiedertäufer in Salzburg," see note Ia, *supra*.
32 *Geschicht–Buch*, 100-1.
33 *Ibid.*, 306.

gift in this regard was Jakob Hutter, the great leader, whose warm, emotional tone and whose liveliness of expression make his letters true works of art. To convey a small idea of his style we shall present out of the fullness of examples one particularly appealing passage from a letter in which Hutter reports about the split of the church in 1533.

> Since there were so many unmarried brethren and sisters, I had set my mind to talk about married life, so that everybody would better know how to fit in and to behave (*auf dass sich ein jegliches dester bess wüsst zu schicken und zu halten*). However, I was greatly concerned that, in presenting the truth and the best foundation, I might not say too much for some people so that they would catch me in my own words or find fault with them and with myself, and so on. I was particularly apprehensive because of Philip [Plener] and Gabriel [Ascherham] and that not without good reason. Yet still more I feared God. Thus I intended and was minded to speak the truth with the right art and modesty (*die Wahrheit zu reden mit rechter Kunst und Bescheidenheit*), and wanted to hit the right and sacred medium so that I could stand before God and also that neither Philip nor Gabriel nor anybody else could get at me. For the great need, also the spirit and the fear of God, urged me so much that I felt constrained [to address the brethren this way]. And therefore I exhorted the people earnestly and faithfully with the utmost diligence and with many words to heed my talk so that they would know how to give testimony whenever it might be needed. And I gave such a talk out of still other and more motives as they were soon revealed to the people of God through me.[34]

If one notices the fine psychological strain in this whole report, one will easily understand that letters like this one rarely missed their purpose.

Passionate words and interjections are almost completely absent. On the contrary, one distinctly recognizes the prevailing endeavor "to speak the truth with the right art and modesty" in spite of a certain self-consciousness of belonging to a chosen people. It was this kind of modesty which in particular distinguished these *Stillen im Lande*. To illustrate also this feature by a quotation, another part of the account (*Verantwortung*) of Marx and Bernard Klampferer, already mentioned above, might be presented here. This *Verantwortung* was written in 1573 when the brothers were arrested in Vienna and put into prison. When Marshal von Rogendorf, a zealous Lutheran, in whose house or courtyard the brothers were caught, asked them what they had been doing here, one of the brothers answered:

> Then I said "I was not in your house but only in the courtyard to inquire after my brother and comrade who lives here with his

---

34 *Geschicht–Buch*, 91. Also Loserth in his article cited in note 19, pp. 526–27.

sister," and then I continued saying, "Sir, I hope you won't blame me for having asked a boy whether our comrade be yet ready or not. I don't doubt that you yourself would judge it as not very brotherly like if we had moved away and had left our brother here in a foreign place. If I had known, however, that you were so much against my entering your courtyard I'd have been sorry to go into your courtyard and would certainly have stayed outside. For we are not such people to offend or to do mischief to anybody. Sir, there is nobody who could witness against us in truth that we teach anybody anything evil; rather we witness everywhere against evil."[35]

This inner act and distinction stands in obvious contrast to the contemporary usage of crude and uncouth expressions or outright insults and filth by opponents. Anyone familiar with the writings of the Reformers in Germany will be acquainted with this feature. It is completely unknown in the literature of the Brethren, who purposely desisted from such practices. It is true that they too, now and then, drop a "slang" expression, particularly in speaking of the church of the country, which in view of their bitter experiences might be more excusable than the tone of the polemics of famous theologians. To give a few examples of this popular slang, I will again try to translate some passages as closely as possible, although just this more folkloristic trait is hardly translatable at all. There is, for instance, an extant paraphrase of the Lord's Prayer, entitled, "How the Pagans Pray," the oldest version of which is by Leonhard Schiemer, about 1528. It runs like this:

> That you understand me better, I shall indicate their blasphemous praying, that you might be better on your guard. They say, "Our Father" mockingly (*spottweis*), for they have never begun to become His children, they even don't want to be. "Hallowed be Thy name," and spit in His face for they are the first who dishallow (*verunheiligen*) His name. Ect.

Another example goes back to Klaus Felbinger, the brother who gave such a convincing account of his faith when examined by his persecutors in Landshut (Bavaria) in 1560. He calls the Roman church "a church of the godless, and an assembly of malice of all adulterers, liars, idolaters, misers, drunkards, gluttons, boozers, enemies of God, etc."[36]

It should, however, be born in mind that such passages are relatively very rare and that in particular in the epistles of the elders and ministers rough and

---

35 *Geschicht-Buch*, 365 note.
36 Loserth, *Communismus*, appendix. One must realize the very poor condition of the Roman church at that time. Also Lydia Müller, *Der Kommunismus der mährischen Wiedertäufer* (Leipzig, 1928), 79f, refers to similar examples. Particularly plentiful in such sharp terms is Antoni Erdfordter's *Urlaubsbrief* of 1538 (reprinted in Lydia Müller's *Glaubenszeugnisse oberdeutscher Taufgesinnter* (Leipzig, 1938), 258–62); but he wrote it as a farewell letter to the world before he actually joined the brotherhood in Moravia.

rude terms are almost completely absent. Also, the folkloristic element, the popular slang and immediacy of expression, which might easily be expected in source material like ours, is but sparsely encountered. Possibly the most striking example in this regard is a letter by one Kuntz Füchter, a simple brother, who was executed in 1532 in the Tyrol, "for the sake of the divine truth." Speaking of the Roman Church he writes:

> They think it is not possible that a man without sin will ever come into the Kingdom of God. And they believe that they will inherit the vineyard of the Lord with all their abominable works such as fornication, idolatry, gluttony, boozing, and murdering. It is to be deplored before the Highest that He should again be abused, reviled, and crucified by those in whom He is supposed to rest, but who rather listen to the hellish serpent to learn from the devil, yea, who are at one with the son of evil and perdition (II Thess. 2:3) in their fornication and vice and who make pleasant to him his damnable foul bath.[37] Those who are thus overcome (II Peter 2:19) then go and sing the devil a fine song of courtship. Satan with his children might well laugh and say, "Ay, this fellow has not been truly converted from sin and has not been rightly created yet until he goes thither and dishonors the sacred name of God." For in this name of Jesus every knee must bow, the heavenly as well as the hellish one (Phil. 2:10).[38]

It is good to bear in mind that this epistle among all the Hutterite letters thus far studied is perhaps the most extreme in the use of popular slang. Characteristically enough it comes from the earliest period of the Anabaptist movement (1532). To show also another side of the same letter, more appealing than the above quotation, we translate here a passage which obviously imitates the Pauline style—only natural with people who actually lived in the atmosphere of the Scriptures. Thus the brother Kuntz Füchter writes, "Since you know that the days are evil [*dass die Zeit gefährlich ist*] (Eph. 5:16), one brother should look after the other and you should lift up one another's heart in love. And be peaceful and brotherly among yourselves." Worth quoting is also the conclusion of this letter which in all its simplicity yet well reveals the natural tact and skill of the Brethren in their letter writing.

> My beloved brethren and sisters in the Lord, you know that I don't understand how to write since I am of too little wit for this. Yet love has urged me that I should write you a bit that you might the better know how to hold fast (*auf dass ihr wisst euch dester bass zu bewähren*). I want to ask you not to despise my simple mind. I have done it for you namely, the writing in hearty love. I would prefer to

---

37 The German expression is *Sudlbad*, whose exact meaning would be: bath of defilement. The writer of the epistle meant, of course, infant baptism.

38 A. J. F. Zieglschmid, "Unpublished Sixteenth Century Letters,...." *MQR*, XV (1941), 19. One must read the original itself to get an idea of the style. No translation can render the particular flavor of such popular slang.

write to you better and more clearly, yet I cannot. For just as I put down one word I forget the other one....[39]

To the folkloristic character of these letters belongs also a certain natural wittiness or witty rudeness, a trait which is occasionally found in our material, as for instance in the report of the former "Swiss" brother Hans Arbeiter who lately had joined the Hutterite group. In 1568 he was caught and imprisoned in the village of Kierweiler in the Palatinate where he had worked for the Lord. Now he describes in a long letter his experience in jail. One day a Jesuit comes to him to talk to him and, if possible, to convert him, quite as in the case of the aforementioned brother Veith Uhrmacher. Hans Arbeiter writes,

> I asked him for his name, and where he comes from, that I might know with whom I am talking.... I told him, "I have debated on infant baptism with a great many parsons (*Pfaffen*), Lutherans and popish, also with Zwinglian preachers, but never have I met a man as impudent as one who like you condemns the innocent children (of whom Christ says they are saved) if they are not baptized."

The priest tries now to prove the necessity of infant baptism from the third chapter of the Gospel of John.

> Upon which I said, "I think in this hamlet of Kierweiler there is not likely one old woman who by a habit of old standing would not know how to speak better and more reasonably about rebirth and infant baptism than you do."

The priest now points to circumcision of the Old Testament as an argument in his favor.

> There I spoke, "Since you want to derive infant baptism from circumcision which so obviously is straight against infant baptism, I must speak about it. Now, you tell me: did Abraham invent circumcision by himself?" Upon which he said, "It was ordered to him by God." Then I answered, "Then wait until infant baptism will be ordered to you by God." Then he said, "You are a rude straw–cutter and do not understand the Scriptures, and yet you want to teach me; you should rather believe me and follow me, I am a highly learned man and well versed in many languages." Upon which I said, "A long time ago there was not one sow–herd around Rome who would not have known Latin since it was a common language then, as ancient history clearly makes out. Nowadays it is a secular art and not at all divine piety or discipline (*nit göttliche frumbkeit oder zucht*)."

A further peculiarity of these epistles is the frequent use of similes and metaphors which, of course, fits well into the Biblical style so characteristic of

---

[39] *Ibid.*, p. 22. This and the following passages are very moving and full of tenderness.

these writings. By this method not only can essential ideas of religious life be easily conveyed even to the simplest mind, but also emotions and intangibles find most appropriate expression. It is another trait of the unsophisticated popular way of writing. For instance, Jakob Hutter, always the great master in letter writing, in one of his epistles of 1535 to the church in Moravia, says,

> Further I would like to tell you how things are going here with us. [He was at that time working for the church in the Tyrol.] The children of God, who are living here, flourish and grow in divine righteousness like the beautiful, lovely, fragrant flowers just as a fine flower garden gets green under a pleasant shower in May. Thus they flourish and grow before God…. Further I let you know that we no longer are hidden or concealed here in the land of Tyrol. Rather, the ungodly know about us in their hostile fashion. The godless Sodomite sea rages and boils (*tobt und wütet*). I am rather afraid there will be no rest until the pious Jonah will be thrown into it and until the cruel leviathan or whale has swallowed him down which is the cruel tyrant and enemy of the truth, Ferdinandus,[40] with all his associates.

On another occasion Hutter speaks of the green and lovely olive tree of the heart which should bring forth good fruit for the Lord.

Among other figures of speech taken from the Scriptures the one of the furnace is particularly popular with the Hutterites. "Just as gold is refined in fire, so also man must be purified and cleansed in the furnace of resignation."[41] All suffering and all martyrdom is viewed primarily from this angle. Other expressions of similar character, such as, "I extend to you the hand of my heart," or, "I am writing to you with a weeping heart," were apparently habitual figures of speech among the Brethren.

This predilection for similes and figures leads still further, namely, to an allegoristic and symbolistic manner of presentation. To be sure here, too, the Brethren are but followers and heirs of an ancient tradition of Bible study. For instance, Peter Riedemann, the leading theologian among the Hutterites, uses the well-known figure of Proverbs 9:1, "Wisdom has built her house, she has hewn out her seven pillars," as a theme for a fine tract entitled, "How to Build the House of God, and What the House of God is." There he describes the "seven pillars of this house," namely: the first pillar is the pure fear of God, the second pillar is God's wisdom, the third pillar is the mind of God, the fourth pillar is God's decree (*Ratschluss Gottes*), the fifth one is God's strength, the sixth God's art, and the seventh, finally God's grace (*Huld*) or friendship. An

---

40 Archduke Ferdinand of Austria (1503–64), brother of Emperor Charles V, later himself Emperor Ferdinand I.

41 Ecclesiasticus 2:5; Proverbs 17:3, "The fining pot is for silver, and the furnace for gold, but the Lord trieth the hearts." And I Peter 1:7, "Faith is tried with fire." Concerning translation from the Greek see below. Regarding the term "resignation" for the German *Gelassenheit*, cf. Friedmann, "Conception of the Anabaptists," *Church History*, IX (1940), 357. *Gelassenheit* means primarily "conquest of selfishness."

The Epistles of the Hutterian Brethren

earlier tract on the same idea was written by Jörg Hauck of Juchsen, a free-lance preacher of the early 1520's who had come into close contact with Hans Hut. His tract, *A Brief and Christian Order*, using the same symbolism, was widely circulated among the Anabaptists and might have served Riedemann as a model.[42] The comparison between building a house and founding the true church of God is indeed very popular. Thus, for instance, we find in a tract by Hans Hut, entitled *Christian Instruction*,[43] the following passage:

> In a forest there are many trees, all creatures of God, and well suited for the building up of a house. But of all of them together there would never be a house, it be yet that they first submit to the work of the builder, that is that they be felled, cut, planed, and prepared.... There are many people, but all of them would never become a house of God, for this will be built only of those who submit to God's work and discipline, are cut off from all vanity and evil will....

This passage was later used again by Peter Riedemann in his earlier, so-called *Gmundener Rechenschaft* (1530), where it is reproduced almost verbatim.[44]

Most profound is the symbolism of the Brethren in their interpretation of the words of the Lord's Supper. Here they follow an old Christian tradition going back to the earliest days of the church. The kernels of the grain as well as each single grape must first be pounded and crushed that they might become bread and wine. And the same holds true with a man who wants to become part of the Christian brotherhood. The old *Didache*, the "Teaching of the Twelve Apostles" (c. AD 120) as well as the sixty-third letter of Cyprian (AD 210–58) present this analogy. Martin Luther also knows it very well and uses it in his *Sermon von dem Hochwürdigen Sacrament des Heilig Wahren Leichnam Christi* (1519).[45] Its starting point might have been the text I Cor. 10:17. Now the Hutterite Brethren knew this passage very well, interpreting it in their own fashion as the truest expression of their institution of community of goods. Many Hutterite tract contain it.[46] Here we will quote one of the most appealing forms of this Bible interpretation, the one written by Andreas Ehrenpreis, the last great *Vorsteher* of the brotherhood, in his above mentioned *Sendbrief, brüderliche Gemeinschaft betreffend*, of 1652. He writes:

> Just as the kernel makes no bread unless it be first ground and broken, thus also must those who want to celebrate the Lord's Supper first be broken and ground by the millstone of God's word, and must

---

42 Ludwig Keller, *Die Reformation und die älteren Reformparteien* (Leipzig, 1885), 433 note, also Schwabe in *Zeitschrift für Kirchengeschichte* XII (1891), 470. It is found in many Hutterite manuscripts, and was reprinted by Lydia Müller in her *Glaubenszeugnisse* (see note 36 *supra*), 3.
43 Müller, *Glaubenszeugnisse*, 33.
44 Mährisches Landesarchiv, Brünn (Czechoslovakia), Beck's estate, file 42, p. 25.
45 Lydia Müller, *Der Kommunismus der mährischen Wiedertäufer* (Leipzig, 1928), 66.
46 *Ibid.*, pp. 4 and 66.

give up their own will and purpose. In the same way the kernels must merge together and contribute each one's strength to the one flour and the one bread, in which no one has anything of his own any longer. And whichever kernel remains whole and separated, not giving away its force and strength, that does not belong into the bread. It will be thrust out and deemed unworthy. Likewise with the wine, in which the grapes are crushed under the press, each single one giving all its juice and all its strength to one juice and one wine, in which one no longer can see and recognize anything individual. That is then the wine with which the Lord's Supper should be celebrated. That kernel and grape, however, which was not crushed, and kept its strength and power still by itself, that does not belong in the bread or in the wine. It is unworthy and unfit, it will be thrown out, it belongs to the swine or is poured away with the husks of grapes. And even if a whole grape should come into the cask, the cup, or even into the mouth, it yet will be spit out, and denied all community and dignity of the wine. That is what Christ the Lord wants to present to his guests at the Lord's table and to his companions at the Supper, as a model, that they too should live in such a communion.[47]

In the same Sendbrief Andreas Ehrenpreis produces still another daring and familiar metaphor, reminiscent of Matthew 13, worth mentioning.

Beloved Brethren, whenever the seed of the divine Word falls upon an egotistical, worldly goods–loving heart which cannot overcome itself because the field has not been worked upon and cultivated with the mattock of the Word of God, and yet this seed makes an impression upon such a heart, then the birds of worldly thoughts will come along and soon the good seed will be carried away and will bring forth no fruit.[48]

Another simile, although not all too frequently used in the letters, is taken from the language of the warrior, justified, so to say, by the example of the epistle to the Ephesians (6:11–17). Such a passage is, for instance, found in a letter of the Elder Hans Kräl to the apothecary Melchior Platzer who, in 1583, testified to his faith by the ultimate sacrifice.

Beloved brother. Since God has chosen and placed you at this very spot and has given into your hand the sword and spear of the Spirit to fight against world, sin, death, and devil, I want to ask you to stay loyal and steadfast under the flying banner of our supreme commander Jesus Christ, honestly, knightly, and manly.[49]

A few words should also be said concerning the attitude of the Brethren toward contemporary theological literature as far as they knew it. Basically

---

47 Reprint 1920 (see note 10 *supra*), pp. 43f.
48 *Ibid.*, p. 88.
49 Reprinted in *Mennonitischer Familien–Kalender 1928* (Scottdale), p. 20.

they were most suspicious of anything "humanistic." Scholarship, as taught in worldly universities, was looked upon as deceptive and misleading. Thus, for instance, Leonhard Schiemer, a former Franciscan friar who turned Anabaptist, not long before his great martyrdom in 1527, wrote a letter full of bitter scorn.

> The whole world talks and throws around in the mouth back and forth this little word 'grace." And in particular our scholars do so, and they do it much like the advanced students reciting from their Aristotle. They then call it *ens reale*, and distinguish between *genus, species, proprium, differentia, accidens, propositio, categorica*. They do not say it in German because they have such a high mind that the German tongue seems to them too low and too poor for it.[50]

Some of the Brethren were also much interested in the correct rendering of Scripture passages, a subject particularly acute in those early years of Bible translations. Of course, only very few had the background for such questions. The same Leonhard Schiemer, apparently a former university student himself, writes in his letter one full page concerning the pretended error of Martin Luther in his translation of the Johannine prologue, namely the "Word dwelt among us," instead of "in us." And in a similar way, Andreas Ehrenpreis argues in his *Sendbrief* of 1652 against Luther, "Just as gold is tried in the fire, so man in the furnace of resignation. Some translators have put affliction or tribulation instead of resignation (*sie haben für Gelassenheit Trübsal gesetzt*) as if the light would shine too close or too bright upon them."[51]

Finally, it should also be mentioned that at least one brother tried a new version of the Psalter. Wolf Sailer, by profession a joiner (died 1550), composed a rhymed Psalter translation which is praised by some scholars although others find it dry and unattractive. It is still preserved in two European manuscripts.

In reviewing the literary form of the epistles one must note that the Brethren understood well how to make these letters genuine mirrors of their spiritual experiences. They tried hard not to fall into the often insincere sermonic tone of theological instruction, although they did not always avoid it. Many a letter is rather dry because of its heaping of Bible texts and moralistic exhortations. Yet it might well be that the Brethren looked upon these letters with different eyes than we do. For instance, Leonhard Schiemer wrote a "letter of consolation to a weak brother,"[52] whose consolation consists almost exclusively of a long series of quotations from the prophets and apostles. Apparently he deemed it more consoling than any personal word which he could have added, being himself in prison facing the ultimate test. Also Peter Riedemann, the renowned writer of the *Rechenschaft*, should be mentioned

---

50 Loserth, "Der Anabaptismus in Tirol" (see note 19), 458.
51 Ehrenpreis, *Ein Sendbrief* (reprint 1920), 92.
52 A. J. F. Zieglschmid, "Unpublished Sixteenth Century Letters," 9f.

in this connection, because his stupendous knowledge of the Scriptures occasionally completely overshadows the liveliness of his numerous epistles. Yet, when he died, the Chronicle recorded, "He was rich in all divine secrets, and the gift of the divine Word poured forth from him like a spring of water which gushes over. All souls who ever heard him rejoiced."[53]

By and large, however, what the brother Hans Mändel wrote from his jail in Tyrol to the Brethren in Moravia shortly before his martyr death in 1561, remains true:

> For that reason, beloved brethren, accept my little writing in love and good spirit, not as a word of the pen or of the ink but as truth and living word (*nichts als Feder– oder Tinten–Wort, sondern als Wahrheit und lebendiges Wort*). All that I have taught you and shown to you I am set to seal with my blood through the grace of God.[54]

And in another letter the same brother writes:

> I do not write you all these things as if you would not have known them before. Nay, I am writing out of divine love which I have for you and the church, for my heart is full and open to you. With the help of God I will walk to death the more cheerfully, since I have revealed my heart to all of you.

He concludes, "My letter is not in pleasant words of human wisdom but in the testimony of the spirit and of power (*in der Beweisung des Geistes und der Kraft*)." That was the true genius of the whole literature and the secret of its captivating missionary force throughout the centuries.

What the Epistles Meant to the Brethren

The fact that such literature exists and that it had such a wide circulation can be correctly appreciated only if we answer the question placed at the head of this final chapter. What did these books, and each epistle in them, mean to the Brethren? With what mind were they read, and what effect did this reading have upon their life and behavior?

Fortunately our material contains many passages which aid in the answering of this central question. Our best witness perhaps is again the brother Veith Uhrmacher, who lay in prison in Salzburg from 1570 to 1573. From his dark dungeon he wrote a long, impressive letter back home to the community in Moravia, containing the following revealing passage:

> The bailiff (*Pfleger*) of Mittersill has told us that he had sent our books to the governor [*Landeshauptmann* of the archdiocese of Salzburg]. From them he might well learn our faith. For I could not give better account of this faith than did two of our teachers who had

---

53 *Geschicht–Buch*, 270.
54 Friedmann, "Die Briefe der österreichischen Täufer," *Archiv für Reformationsgeschichte*, XXVI (1929), 161f, where the epistle is reprinted in somewhat abbreviated form.

been executed some time before...."⁵⁵ He may do whatever he wants to do with us, we will with the help of God bear it with calmness for I have well read the account (*Rechenschaft*) which the aforenamed brethren Klaus Felbinger and Hänsel Mändel had given, so that I am now well aware that it [our way of life] is sufficiently justified (*verantwortet*) by divine Scripture.⁵⁶

Here we observe first hand both the purpose and the effect of the writings. The wealth of analogous material studied leads us to accept these remarks as typical and adapted to generalization. The Hutterites read hardly anything else besides the Bible and this home–produced literature.⁵⁷ At first the epistles might have circulated as such, but the need for more copies very soon led to the preparing of books, *Sammelbände*, epistle–books and books with miscellaneous contents. It was their world, their spiritual home, their education, their source of strength, and their ground of confidence of being on the right track. From these books, besides the Bible, they drew the conviction and the power to bear all that unbelievably hard suffering and martyrdom, suffered in innocence. Here they found the arguments and the strength for their defense and the justification of their faith, and that meant, at the same time, of their way of life. From the fact that the more important epistles and accounts (*Verantwortungen, Rechenschaften*) are found in so many codices, we can grasp the zeal with which these items were read and copied. It was truly a higher education in the discipleship of Christ.

Other proofs of the same sort are found in the numerous epistles of Hänsel Schmid or Raiffer, who worked as a missioner of the brotherhood in the Rhineland and who was finally arrested and later martyred in Aachen in 1558. Out of his dark dungeon he writes to his wife, that she should have the epistles by Jeronymus [Käls] copied for him and also the account of the same brother which she will find in a certain booklet [at home]. In another letter from his bonds he urges her again, "Send me my white hymnbook [also a handwritten codex] otherwise I need nothing." And he warns her, "Keep my books well until God will give me a place. And if you go down [to Moravia], have an eye upon these books and do not lend them around too much. I mean those handwritten ones."

Of course, the Brethren knew very well the function and effect of their epistles, particularly those sent out of prison and dungeon, and for that reason they valued them accordingly. Thus, for instance, we read in one of Hänsel Schmid's letters, "I am writing to you above all with the idea that you might be cheered by it, and might the more recognize the love which exists among us." The Italian brother Franciscus Wälsch (Francesco de Rovigo),⁵⁸

---

55 Whose accounts were written in these books.
56 Loserth, "Zur Geschichte der Wiedertäufer in Salzburg" (see note 1a *supra*), 58.
57 The *Vorsteher* (elders) most likely read some outside material also in order to know how to defend their faith.
58 *Geschichts–Bücher*, 239–43 and notes, also Benrath, "Wiedertäufer im Ventianischen," *Theologische*

whose letters from his mission work around Venice might rightly be called true masterpieces of religious literature,[59] writes in a similar manner. At one place he says,

> I do not want to abstain from writing to you, in particular about things which seem to me to be needed and of inner uplift so that everyone who has ears to hear may easily perceive them. For this is the strongest reason of my letter, that you may be comforted by it and edified.

The most striking example, however, and closest to the point in question, comes from the beautiful farewell epistle of Hans Mändel (1561) from which several excerpts have already been quoted. The last paragraph of this long letter, written almost on the eve of his execution, runs as follows:

> Beloved brethren, keep this epistle in great care, so that it will remain also for our posterity, and that they will also keep [my words] in memory after I have passed away from this world. For there is a divine solemnity and diligence in it (*denn es ist ein göttlicher Ernst und Fleiss darin begriffen*).[60]

The Brethren heeded this warning well, as the many copies still extant prove.

Each incoming letter was carefully preserved and often copied so that as many brethren as desired might have a copy. The Chronicle repeats time and again when recording the death of a brother, "There still exist among us epistles and letters from his hand." In a sense each single brother helped to increase the devotional literature of the community by his own suffering. That his memory and his letters then stood in high esteem, is only too natural.

When starting on one of their perilous missionary trips, the brethren usually carried some of these writings with them.[61] We learn, for instance, from a governmental record,[62] that when Jakob Hutter was eventually caught and arrested in the Tyrol in 1536, they found in his satchel the letters of Hans Amon. And when, in 1538, Onoffrius Griesinger likewise was arrested in the Tyrol, they found (thus the report runs) in his satchel also several letters from the brotherhood, loose leaves, apparently to be used for letters home, and a New Testament.[63] These epistles were true companions, both in days of success and in days of need. They gave strength, confidence, and uplift.

Studien und Kritiken (Leipzig, 1885), 38–53. Most recently this Anabaptist found attention in the book by E. M. Wilbur, *A History of Unitarianism; Socinianism and its Antecedents* (Cambridge, 1946), 83 and 87. His correct name was Francisco di Rovigo. He was not a Socinian. He joined the Hutterite brotherhood in Moravia, was later sent back to Venice and suffered here the ultimate sacrifice in 1562.

59   Their translations from the Italian circulated widely among the Brethren and were often copied. They have never been published.

60   See reference in note 54 *supra*. This epistle would deserve a full length translation and publication. It is one of the finest in the entire collection.

61   Departure and return of the missioners (*Sendboten*) was celebrated with great solemnity and full awareness of the extraordinary task and, in case of return, achievement. A vivid picture of such a celebration is presented by Loserth in his *Communismus*, 228–30, following a description in one of the Hutterite codices.

62   Loserth, "Der Anabaptismus in Tirol" (see note 19 *supra*), 557.

63   Loserth, "Der Anabaptismus in Tirol vom Jahre 1536 bis zu seinem Erlöschen," *Archiv für*

But letters, even such lively ones as most in our collection are, can never fully replace the personal contact and appeal, particularly not in things spiritual. Thus, many of these letters, in particular those written in Moravia, were intended to be nothing but a kind of introduction for the bearer. These bearers, *Sendboten*, missioners, apostles, were then the real propagators or rather disseminators of the Hutterite ideas of Christian living and suffering. Theirs it was to comfort, admonish and strengthen, while the epistles they carried, signed by the elders and often also by the entire community back home in Moravia, were more for the sake of confirmation, further support, and, if possible, inspiration. Often our letters state this frankly, saying that the missioner is "our living letter" (*unser lebendiger Brief*). Thus, for instance, Hans Amon, the successor of Jakob Hutter in the office of *Vorsteher*, writes to the church in Hesse, in 1540,

> In our great and ineffable love we are again sending to you our beloved brethren; they will be our living letter to you. From them you will be hearing the right and well-grounded truth (*die rechte und gründliche Wahrheit*). For to them we have manifested all our heart toward you that they will manifest all these things to you.[64]

It is good to be reminded at this point that here again the Brethren follow but an apostolic model of high standing. For we read in II Corinthians 3:2–3, "Ye are our epistle, written in our hearts, known and read of all men. Forasmuch as ye are manifestly declared to be the epistle of Christ, ministered by us, written not with ink but with the Spirit of the living God: not in tables of stone but in fleshy tables of the heart." In his great *Rechenschaft* Peter Riedemann repeats these words of the apostle at a conspicuous place.

And finally, if, on occasion, the Brethren should not be able to come into direct contact and to comfort each other, they still found ways and means to transmit their "living consolation," in spite of all guards, beyond and in addition to their epistles. The chief means for this was their singing. Of this we have a particularly fine and moving testimony in the letter which the schoolmaster Jeronymus Käls (arrested and later executed in Vienna in 1536) sent to his brethren Michel Seifensieder and Hans Oberecker, who were arrested with him although held in a separate prison. He concludes his letter as follows,

> I rejoice with all my heart whenever I hear you singing in the Lord, particularly you, my beloved brother Michael, when you sing at night time. Then I understand almost every word if I listen very sharply and if you sit near the window. I beg you, my gracious brother, awaken me, the sleepy one, oftener with your song in the Lord Christ Jesus. Often I am already waiting if I awake earlier because of our brother Hans, for, when I sang first then you both followed me with singing. And I want to listen to both of you. For it is a great joy to

---

österreichische Geschichte, LXXIX, 1893 (this is the second part of the paper cited in note 62), 157.
64 *Geschicht-Buch*, 165.

me whenever I hear you singing the hymn "Jerusalem." My beloved Brethren, since it hurts Satan so much, it is a good sign that it pleases God. As they [the jailors] think they have barred us from talking that we should not comfort each other, so let us cry until our throat cracks.[65]

With this we conclude our study. We have recognized the extraordinary vitality which permeated all the activities of the Hutterite brotherhood of the sixteenth century in spite of the strict discipline and all the regulations which such a community necessitates. It is the vitality of the spiritual life which becomes so strikingly manifest in these documents, and which led to a refinement of the inner life such as is seldom encountered elsewhere in the long history of the Christian church.

SOURCE: *Mennonite Quarterly Review*, XX (1946), pp. 147–77.

Bibliographical Note on Publications of Hutterite Epistles

A. J. F. Zieglschmid published five letters in the original orthography in *MQR*, XV (1941), 5–25, and 118–40, under the title, "Unpublished Sixteenth Century Letters of the Hutterian Brethren." These letters are: Leonhard Schiemer's "Trostbrief an einen schwachen Bruder," Kuntz Füchter's and Ludwig Fest's epistles, and two of Jacob Hutter's letters: "An die Gemeinde zu Hohenwart" and "An die Gemeinde zu Mähren."

Lydia Müller published a number of letters in her *Glaubenszeugnisse oberdeutscher Taufgesinnter* (Leipzig, 1938). This volume contains epistles by Leonhard Schiemer, Hans Schlaffer, W. Brandhuber, Jakob Hutter (two epistles), Ulrich Stadler and Anthoni Erfordter (*Urlaubsbrief*).

Johann Loserth published two important letters. The one by Klaus Felbinger was added to his *Communismus*. The one by Veith Uhrmacher or Grünberger was appended to "Zur Geschichte der Wiedertäufer in Salzburg," in *Mitteilungen der Gesellschaft für salzburgische Landeskunde*, v. 52 (1912).

The Hutterite Chronicle contains a great number of epistles, about one fifth of the entire text being made up of letters. The complete text was published by Rudolph Wolkan in modernized German under the title, *Geschicht–Buch der Hutterischen Brüder* (Vienna, 1923). In footnotes Wolkan added a great number of excerpts from other letters which greatly enhance the

---

65 *Geschicht-Buch*, 120 note. The last phrase is a direct quotation from Isaiah 58:1 in the rendering by Hans Denck and Ludwig Haetzer, *Alle Propheten nach Hebraischer sprach verteutscht* (Worms, 1527), which was very widely used by the Anabaptists prior to their use of the Froschower Bible, of which the part containing the translation of the prophets was published in 1529. The King James version of the passage reads very differently, as follows: "Cry aloud, spare not, lift up thy voice like a trumpet."

value of the edition. A. J. F. Zieglschmid's recent diplomatic edition of the same text, under the title, *Die älteste Chronik der Hutterischen Brüder* (Philadelphia, 1943), omits these footnotes. The older edition of *Die Geschichts-Bücher der Wiedertäufer in Österreich–Ungarn, 1526–1785* (Vienna, 1883) by Joseph von Beck contains a great number of excerpts from epistles in its footnotes, but no epistles in the text itself.

Gustav Bossert's great source publication, *Quellen zur Geschichte der Wiedertäufer,* I, *Herzogtum Württemberg* (Leipzig, 1930), contains an excellent edition of all the epistles by Paul Glock.

Robert Friedmann published one letter in English translation in his "Reason and Obedience, an old Anabaptist Letter of Peter Walpot (1571) and its Meaning," in *MQR*, XIX (1945), 27–40. It is the only Hutterite letter thus far translated into English. He also published an abbreviated edition of Hans Mändel's moving farewell letter (1561) in the *Archiv für Reformationsgeschichte*, XXVI (1929), 161–66.

Transcripts of a great number of epistles from the original manuscripts in European libraries, made by Robert Friedmann, are deposited in the Mennonite Historical Library at Goshen College, Goshen Indiana.

John Horsch, *The Hutterian Brethren, 1528–1928, A Story of Martyrdom and Loyalty* (Goshen, 1929), uses a great number of quotations from epistles in his text.

Wilhelm Wiswendel, *Bilder und Führergestalten aus dem Täufertum*, 2 vols. (Kassel, 1928, 1930) also prints long excerpts from these epistles in his very stimulating text. See the extensive review by Robert Friedmann, in *MQR*, XIV (1940).

HUTTERITE SERMONS

The existence of a large number of written sermons of Hutterite origin, mostly of the seventeenth century, was completely unknown until the publication of the *Klein–Geschichtsbuch der Hutterischen Brüder* in 1947. Even since the printing of excerpts in the *Klein–Geschichtsbuch*, no publication offers any reference or information concerning this material. When, around 1800, Johannes Waldner, then bishop of the Hutterites in Vishenka, Ukraine, decided to provide his brotherhood with another "Chronicle," summarizing the contents of the old Great Chronicle and continuing it up to his own day, he felt that some of the sermons found at Vishenka should also be included to give posterity an adequate picture of the spiritual life of the brotherhood in its best time, the era of Andreas Ehrenpreis. Thus shorter and longer excerpts of not less than twenty-six such sermons are given in the text of the *Klein–Geschichtsbuch* (pp. 204–14, and 218–21), all of them deriving from 1652–59. Most of these texts originated at a Bruderhof at Kesselsdorf in Slovakia, where apparently a kind of seminary for preachers existed. Even though Waldner does not mention names, at least six Hutterites are known who composed these sermons: H. F. Küentsche, who was the major contributor, Caspar Eglauch, Mathias Binder, Johannes Milder, Tobias Bertsch, and Benjamin Poley. But there were also other sermon writers, above all Ehrenpreis himself.

In 1954 the present writer visited a number of Hutterite colonies in Canada and the Northwest of the United States, and was shown the originals from which these sermon excerpts had been taken. Between 300 and 600 original sermon booklets exist, dating from the early seventeenth century to 1665 (not one later), modest notebooks written in pencil or poor ink, which have been reverently preserved by the brotherhood through the centuries.

In the eighteenth century Johannes Waldner and several co-workers decided to revive the time-honored custom of reading sermons during the worship hour, and thus they began collecting the contents of most of these booklets in carefully written sermon books, many of them of considerable size. The oldest of these volumes, still extant, is of 1786; then follows one of 1789 (the Mathias Müller book), and so on up to 1804 and slightly later. All this material, old and new, was brought to America. When a brother is elected preacher it is his first duty to make for himself as complete a copy as possible of the entire sermon material. Each of the hundred odd Bruderhofs today has a collection of thirty to sixty carefully handwritten and well-bound books of sermons for all occasions. Up to the 1960's, none has ever been printed, and it is the pride of each preacher to keep adding new sermon books to his bookshelves, written in excellent penmanship. All the long winter days are filled with this work. The selection changes slightly depending on whether he belongs to the Dariusleut, Schmiedeleut, or Lehrerleut; some of them have more, some less. All are written and read in High German, even though the Hutterites speak a sort of Tyrolean-Bavarian German dialect among themselves. Why are only old sermons read among the Hutterites today? The Brethren would answer that these sermons are so perfect that no one could improve upon them. More likely is the assumption that the tradition-minded Hutterites are simply continuing a custom which was widely accepted in all churches during the seventeenth and eighteenth centuries.

The oldest exegetical books of the Hutterites, as far as is known, date back to the later part of the sixteenth century: 1566 and 1579 (both codices in Budapest), 1593 (in Esztergom), 1598 (in Brno), and 1599 (Bratislava). Although these codices were known to European scholars they were never recognized as the prototype of the later (not known) Hutterite sermon books. There are about fifteen codices in European libraries containing such exegeses (*Erklärungen*) of different books of the Old and New Testaments (including the Book of Revelation), which are rather similar to the *Lehren* (homiletic instructions) as practiced by the Brethren at least since 1629 if not earlier. After that time the datable production increased tremendously up to 1665 and then suddenly stopped. Innumerable undated sermons which to all appearance belong to the same period—that of Ehrenpreis—are also extant. A rigid series of pericopes for the entire church year, including holidays, provided the texts for most of these sermons. To these must be added sermons for other church events, such as baptisms, weddings, or funerals, for which also standard texts were and are still being used. The sermon production then worked around this program, interpreting the texts from many angles, but always in a conservative biblicistic way, rarely indulging in the fashion of budding Pietism. Thus the sermons lack emotional elements and are distinctly more hortatory than edificatory. The style and ideas of these sermons would deserve a detailed analysis, but in the absence of this no final appreciation can be offered.

Hutterite sermons are basically of two types: *Lehren* and *Vorreden*. The *Lehr* is usually an exegetical sermon interpreting a certain chapter of the Scriptures verse by verse, often very long-windedly, and (at least today) rarely read in its totality. In former times, to be sure, sermons lasted two hours or more. This *Lehr* always occupies the second part of the worship program; the first part is filled (besides prayer and hymns) by a *Vorred*. This is a general expository sermon centered around a special verse. Also the traditional ceremonies of the church, such as baptism, have this dual type of homiletics.

The information as to the number of existing written sermons varies greatly: the late bishop Elias Walter of the Dariusleut counted 196 *Lehren* and 25 Psalm interpretations (a total of 221) besides 55 general *Vorreden* and 25 *Vorreden* for holidays, making a grand total of 301 sermons. The Lehrerleut, however, claim 250 *Vorreden* and 350 *Lehren*, while another preacher claimed 180 *Vorreden* and 230 *Lehren* (totaling 410). One of the preachers added the information that some of these sermons are said to have been copied from the Jacob Denner sermon collection (German editions since 1730), which most likely explains the difference in the counting of the existing written sermons.

The prevailing church tradition concerning sermons includes the following. Christmas being celebrated for three days requires three *Lehren*; New Year's Day needs one *Lehr*, and Epiphany (January 6), another. Palm Sunday, the usual day of the baptismal ceremony with its elaborate, prescribed ritual, requires one *Lehr*. On Good Friday another *Lehr* is read, while Easter, celebrated for three days, requires four *Lehren* (Sunday morning and afternoon; the Easter Sunday morning sermon deals with the Lamb of Exodus 12 as its traditional theme); Easter Monday is the day for the Lord's Supper with a lengthy sermon, usually lasting two hours; Tuesday is celebrated as resurrection day. Ascension Day requires one sermon, while Pentecost, celebrated for three days, has three *Lehren*. The Day of Annunciation (*Mariae Verkündigung*) is celebrated by the Schmiedeleut only, who use one *Lehr* for the morning worship; in the afternoon everyday work is resumed. There are also sermons for weddings (Eph. 5), funerals, election of ministers, confirmation of ministers, election of bishops, a total of at least twenty-one standard sermon assignments.

At this place no complete list of the Bible chapters and verses used can be offered. A scrutiny of the datable sermons shows, however, that the most-used Old Testament books were Isaiah (predominant), Ecclesiasticus (their favorite Old Testament book), Jeremiah, Psalms, Proverbs, and Tobit. In the New Testament preference is given to the Gospels, Acts, Romans, Corinthians, Ephesians, John, Peter, James, and Hebrews.

The entire worship of the Hutterites, as it developed during the Ehrenpreis era, is strongly ritualized and formalized. When the preacher reads the Scripture text of the sermon, the congregation rises; the reading itself is done in chanting fashion. Since the daily prayer hour comes after a long day of hard work, it should not be surprising that now and then a member of the congregation falls asleep. Actually some of the sermons which Johannes Waldner collected in the *Klein–Geschichtsbuch* contained a complaint about "the sleepy audience" (p. 206), and quoted the admonition "that one should not sleep even if the sermon should last for two hours" (p. 207). The reading of the sermon (at least today) sounds often more like a ritual than a living instruction or exhortation; certain passages are most likely no longer fully understood. Due to the uncompromising biblicism of all sermons they call their reading "sharp preaching" in contrast to the "soft preaching" in other churches. The Brethren are very fond of this "sharp" preaching, that is, of the outspokenness of the instruction concerning the meaning of the Scriptural text and its application in everyday life, realizing that it is this Biblical radicalism which distinguishes their piety and life from all their surroundings. Hence they like their worship period, with its sermons, prayers, and singing, both on weekdays (daily at 6 p.m.) and on Sundays. Needless to say, perfect attendance by all is taken for granted.

The minister, wearing a black frock coat almost down to the knees, enters the meeting room (usually, but not always, the schoolroom) first, then follow slowly the elders and those who have any office, taking their seats next to the preacher, facing the congregation. Next the congregation enters, men right (from the view of the preacher), women left, children in front, again boys separated from girls. At the conclusion of the worship, the exit takes place in the reverse, children first, and the minister last, who then locks the house. In 1957 the average Sunday service lasted one and a half hours, the Lord's Supper service lasted two and a half to three hours, and the ordination of a minister sometimes up to four hours.

The facts here described in no way exhaust the meaning and character of the Hutterite devotional life. Closer study of this subject would be needed, foremost by analyzing the sermon texts proper and comparing them with earlier and later texts from elsewhere. Therefore the material given above should not be taken as the final word.

SOURCE: *Mennonite Encyclopedia*, IV, pp. 504–6.

HUTTERITE *TAUFREDEN*

Hutterite baptismal instructions have, since ca. 1560–70, been standardized and strictly regulated. Baptism has for the Brethren always been a most solemn event, preparing the candidate for his life's pledge to the "narrow path," and thus the instructions preceding this event have always been given much attention. The procedure of instruction, baptismal examination, and the ritual itself has been preserved to the last detail almost unchanged. The standardized text of these instructions is also known from old codices and recent copies.

Ever since the "Golden Age" of the Hutterites (1560–90) books had been written containing the baptismal agenda and the instructional sermons or *Taufreden*, which afford a good insight into the doctrine and Bible exegesis of the Brethren. Very few of the baptismal candidates were newly won converts; most of them had grown up on the Bruderhofs, and were between twenty and twenty–three years of age, mature enough to weigh the obligation involved in their baptism.

The oldest known codex containing the famous *Taufreden* is of 1599 (in Bratislava); since its title page is missing, Beck called it *Codex Ritualis*. Two more or less identical codices containing these *Taufreden*, written in 1643 and 1652, are in the library of Esztergom, Hungary; an eighteenth–century copy was formerly found in the library of the Moravian Brethren, Herrnhut, Saxony. The text of the *Taufreden* probably goes back to the time of Peter Walpot, about 1570.

Up to recent times it was the custom among the Brethren to assemble the candidates on Friday and Saturday preceding the Sunday of the baptismal ritual, usually two hours before the regular evening prayer meeting for preparatory instruction. On Friday the First *Taufrede* (described below) was read, which treated Genesis 1–19. Then followed a lengthy prayer by the group, and a sermon (called *Lehr*) dealing with inner rebirth (John 3:3). On Saturday the Second *Taufrede* was read, followed by a penitential sermon and lengthy prayer, after which came the second *Lehr*, this time on Romans 6. On Sunday morning came the Third *Taufrede*, treating the church and its principles. After a prayer the meeting was concluded by the third *Lehr* on

Matt. 28:16–20 (baptism). This ended the worship hour. Then the candidates were examined before the congregation, answering the standardized questions with a simple yes, after which they were baptized. The Hutterites of today follow the same procedure, with the exception that the instruction is now spread over a week.

The text of the *Taufreden* is of a very high order. The First *Taufrede* is an exposition of the first book of the Bible, especially the first nineteen chapters: creation, fall, and man's very beginnings. The second *Rede* shows the difference between the Christian way of living and the secular way. The theological elements of this sermon are to a large extent borrowed from Riedemann's *Rechenschaft*, e.g., such topics as What Sin Is, Concerning Original Sin, and God Punishes Those Who Are Disobedient to His Word. Christians, we read, are not baptized to become poor sinners but to enter a new life (Rom. 6) . The third *Rede* makes it clear that Christ is and ever will be our Mediator, Redeemer, and Reconciliation. "True faith is nothing but an attachment of the heart to God and Christ. He who believes from the heart is assured and sealed by the Holy Spirit [here Ezekiel 36 is quoted as a reference!]. He receives strength from above to do the good which he could not do before, and to hate the evil he could not hate before." The candidate is to become aware of what is expected of him, namely, regret for his former sins, penitence, and readiness for a new, committed life, in which the old Adamic man has died away. All this leads to separation from the world, to Christian resignation (*Gelassenheit*), and to full communion of goods.

The text of these three *Taufreden*, together with the traditional agenda of the ritual, will be published in Vol. II of *Glaubenszeugnisse* as item No. 21. It is a very good illustration of the Hutterite sermon technique and gives an insight into the Anabaptist frame of mind as it reveals itself internally, that is, unobserved by the outside world.

SOURCE: *Mennonite Encyclopedia*, IV, pp. 686–87.

DIE LIEDER DER HUTTERISCHEN BRÜDER

Until the publication (Scottdale, 1914) of this large hymnal of 894 pages, the Hutterites had nothing that would compare with the *Ausbund*, the hymnal of the Swiss Brethren, in fact no printed hymnal of any sort. It is true that prior to the eighteenth century the Hutterites had a great number of manuscript hymnals in which their innumerable hymns were collected. Rudolf Wolkan describes twenty-one such codices in European libraries, to which he adds three more which he could not reach. In America the Brethren have a few such codices too, some of which have become extremely difficult to read with the passing of time. But no hymnal was ever declared "official" and nothing had ever been printed. It must be assumed that in former centuries most of the hymns sung at Hutterite services were learned by rote and handed on to the next generation by word of mouth. It was therefore almost a daring enterprise when Elder Elias Walter (1862–1938), then of South Dakota but later of Standoff Colony, near Macleod, Alberta, decided to prepare a printed hymnal. When he received the approval of the brotherhood the publication became a semiofficial undertaking.

In his preface Elias Walter reports briefly on the sources from which he compiled the book:

1. a codex with 165 hymns, written sometime before 1600 (275 leaves, well preserved, title page missing);
2. another codex with 140 hymns, written about 1650 in Slovakia (400 leaves, again title page missing);
3. a third codex of 390 leaves, of which the first 60 are missing, containing 80 hymns (the time is that of Ehrenpreis, 1650–60, the writing good but the paper slowly falling apart).

Many of these hymns are incomplete, although a century earlier they were said to have been known in full to the Brethren. Most likely even today many more codices are available than these three, but they are hidden in some of the 120 Bruderhofs in America and not easily found. Elias Walter arranged his book chronologically, though he did not always keep this plan, and the order is often quite confusing. The book begins with a hymn by Felix Manz (martyred in Zürich in 1527), *Mit Lust so will ich singen*, found in two of the sources named. Next follow hymns by Jörg Wagner (martyred in 1527), Michael Sattler (1527) (a hymn of 50 stanzas), Leonhard Schiemer (1528), Hans Schlaffer (1528), Balthasar Hubmaier (1528), of whom one hymn is printed—a supposed second was not available; two hymns go back to Jörg Blaurock (whom Walter reports as martyred in 1529, although the Geschicht-Buch gives 1527 as the date of his martyrdom); five hymns come from Ludwig Haetzer (d. 1529). Of special interest is the discovery that the hymn, *Sollst du bei Gott dein Wohnung han*, which was customarily ascribed to Haetzer, is here (pp. 28A) printed as deriving from Schiemer. It is this hymn whose fifth stanza was often quoted, *Ja, spricht die Welt, es ist ohn Not dass ich mit Christo leide*.... We may trust the manuscript and assume that the tradition was incorrect. Of Hans Hut's four known hymns two are printed here.

And so the volume proceeds through the hymn collections of the early times year by year. Elias Walter wrote a brief biographical sketch for each hymn writer, sometimes also listing his other works. Many of these hymns are extremely long (over 100 stanzas). Some of the Brethren were very productive, writing 30, 40, and even 50 hymns. Many of these hymns are anonymous; they could be identified only by reading the acrostic (where the initials of each stanza put in order reveal a name or message, a technique used mainly by brethren in prison). Walter points to this device whenever he decodes it. Three fourths of all hymns could thus be ascribed to individual authors; the rest may be assumed to have been composed collectively by groups of Brethren.

Rather famous among these hymns is the *Väterlied*, describing the work of the forefathers, the *Vorsteher* of the brotherhood. It was begun by Georg Pruckmaier (d. 1585), who wrote 75 stanzas, and then continued by others until 1639, with a total of 105 stanzas. On page 877 it is still later continued by other loyal writers up to the year 1734, with a total of 18 more stanzas. At the year 1605 the *Botschkai Lieder* attract our attention (author unknown), describing all the horror of the attack of Turks, Magyars, and Tartars on the South Moravian colonies (158 stanzas, pp. 840–12). The last part of the hymnal contains a number of hymns by the last great bishop of the brotherhood, Andreas Ehrenpreis (d. 1662); one hymn is about his death. Close to 100 hymns are versifications of Bible stories, which, however, are not quite as popular as the more personal hymns.

Not all these hymns are strictly of Hutterite origin. In fact A. J. F. Zieglschmid discovered that at least one is of Jesuit origin. But the Brethren are used to all of them, accept them, and are loath to change anything.

The *Lieder* has become "the" hymnal of the Brethren. It is used daily at the prayer hour, and at all services on Sundays, holidays, and other occasions. One is amazed that these stanzas, often quite unwieldy, can actually be sung.

Often they bear little connection with the worship service as such, and even their original meaning of three or four centuries ago is not always understood. But they are sung in many cases simply out of deference to tradition. The preacher "lines" the hymns, that is, he reads one line at a time, then the congregation sings it according to melodies familiar to all. (There is no notation.) Only the preacher has a hymnal at the service, but most Brethren know the texts by rote.

The singing of these hymns also deserves a few remarks. All hymns are sung in unison, not in parts, and they are overloud, almost shrill, with strained vocal chords. Zieglschmid, who discusses this kind of communal singing in a footnote in the *Klein–Geschichtsbuch* (p. 580, n. 3), points out that according to an old report the Mennonites in the Molotschna also used to sing "*über alle Massen grell und laut aus der Kehle gepresst.*" It is possible that this (not too appealing) method has its origin in sixteenth–century conditions when brethren imprisoned for their faith wanted to communicate with other brethren in the same place but in different rooms. At least some sources mention such overloud singing at a quite early date (1536). A reference is also made to Isa. 58:1, "Cry aloud, spare not, lift up thy voice like a trumpet" (*Lasst uns schreien, dass uns der Hals kracht*, in the Denck–Haetzer translation).

In recent years some brethren expressed dissatisfaction with some parts of the *Lieder* book, and a new edition was brought out in 1953, in which seventy–five hymns were omitted, mainly those which contained versifications of Bible stories. There is some grumbling, however, by others, since many liked the book as it was composed originally.

In the meantime, the late A. J. F. Zieglschmid began a thorough study and revision of this book. He found a great number of mistakes, inaccuracies, and false readings. Many hymns had been "*zersungen*," i.e., the words were changed and the meaning was lost, often even a whole line was omitted, and so forth. Moreover, he distinguished between genuine Anabaptist hymns and others which were adopted from outside, as was mentioned above (a Jesuit hymn). Thus he compiled a new, revised, purified and corrected edition, to which he added a number of Hutterite songs unknown at the time of Elias Walter, for instance, the versification of the entire Psalter by Wolf Seiler (d. 1550). The *Lieder* contains forty–eight of his hymns (see Wolkan's note in *Geschicht–Buch*, p. 257). The result of this scholarly work is a manuscript of nearly 4,500 sheets, still unpublished and deposited at the Mennonite Historical Library of Goshen College. It is yet uncertain whether the Hutterian Brethren will accept this "revision" or not, when a need for a new edition arises.

Elias Walter edited a smaller hymnal, the *Gesangbüchlein, besonders zum Auswendiglernen für die Jugend in der Schule geeignet, meistens aus alten Handschriften gesammelt und herausgegeben von Elias Walter* (n.p., 1919,

525 pp., octavo). In 1930 a second edition of this hymnal was produced, printed in Macleod, Alberta, with 480 pages. In 1940, after Elias Walter's death (1938), a third edition was brought out under the title, *Gesangbüchlein, Lieder für Schule und häuslichen Gebrauch, herausgegeben von den Hutterischen Brüdern in Kanada* (n.p., 1940, 591 pp., octavo). In neither of these editions is any reference made to sources, authors, or historic backgrounds. Thus the *Gesangbüchlein* has become more a popular hymnbook for school and family singing, and as such is a real favorite. Among other hymns it contains also the old (most likely not Hutterite) song, "Das goldene A–B–C." It contains Lutheran and pietistic hymns, but no old Hutterite hymns.

SOURCE: *Mennonite Encyclopedia*, III, pp. 339–40.

THE HUTTERITE ARTICLE BOOK

The Hutterite Article Book was a major doctrinal tract of the Hutterites, originating in Moravia around 1547, extant in about twenty manuscript copies of between 1547 and 1655, published in a condensed form only in the Great Chronicle of the Hutterites as *Die Fünf Artikel des grössten Streites zwischen uns und der Welt* (*Die aelteste Chronik der Hutterischen Brüder,* ed. Zieglschmid, pp. 269–316), and in Lydia Müller's *Glaubenszeugnisse oberdeutscher Taufgesinnter* (Leipzig, 1938, pp. 238–56) from a Hutterite manuscript which contains only a *Kurzer Auszug* (resumé) of the book as such. The term "Article Book" is not the official title though widely used, particularly among the American Hutterites of today. The original manuscript bears the title, *Ein schön lustig Buchlein etliche Hauptartikel unseres Glaubens betreffend*. The *Geistliches Blumengärtlein* (Amsterdam, 1680) contains still another edition of this tract under the title, *Schriftmässiger Bericht und Zeugnis betreffend die rechte christliche Taufe, Abendmahl, Gemeinschaft, Obrigkeit, und Ehestand*. There is no doubt that the Hutterites considered this book (about 300 leaves in ms.) of equal rank with Peter Riedemann's great *Rechenschaft unseres Glaubens* of 1545. It was one of their doctrinal statements, used both within the community and also as a source when dealing with the outside "world" in order to demonstrate the Biblical correctness of their particular teachings. The author of the great Article Book is not named, although one codex with a *Kurzer Auszug* names expressly the Hutterite elder Peter Walpot as the author, as does also Ottius, *Annales Anabaptistici* of 1672, p. 160. A careful investigation by Robert Friedmann (*Archiv für Reformationsgeschichte*, XXVIII [1931], 94–102) makes it highly plausible that Peter Walpot, *Vorsteher* (elder) of the Hutterite brotherhood 1565–78, was, if not its author, then at least its redactor, possibly together with Caspar Braitmichel and Hans Kräl. It is not unlikely that Peter Riedemann also gave some advice as to the first draft, for every Hutterite writing was in some sense the work of the entire community (this is what they call the "unity of the Spirit," *Einigkeit des Heiligen Geistes*). The occasion for the writing of such a succinct doctrinal statement of the Hutterite position (differing from Riedemann's larger and elaborate *Rechenschaft* of 1545) might be found in the discussion leading to the readmission of the remnant of the Gabrielite Brethren in 1545. The

Geschicht–Buch (ed. Zieglschmid, pp. 251–57) has a section, *Unterricht, die Hauptartikel betreffend* (Instruction Concerning the Main Articles), which was presented to these candidates. It appears to be the prototype of the Article Book, which is an elaboration of much the same material. The presentation of the Article Book is item by item, with arguments "*punkt– und argumentweis.*"

The book is in no way a theological tract, but rather like all Anabaptist doctrinal writings a collection of Biblical proof texts topically arranged to show the correctness of the position of the brotherhood with regard to certain selected problems. The title of the larger edition, *A Beautiful and Pleasant Little Book Concerning the Main Articles of Our Faith*, is quite colorless; more to the point is the title used in the Great Chronicle, *The Five Articles of the Greatest Conflict Between Us and the World*. It does not pretend to contain a complete system of Anabaptist thought but only a collection of those points and their arguments which distinguish the Brethren from the "world" and justify their particular stand. (The Schleitheim articles were of the same kind of Anabaptist doctrinal writings.) The large Article Book comprises in one codex 286 quarto leaves; this size explains the later appearance of a condensed edition, which in print comprises only eighteen pages.

The book deals with the following five articles:

1. Concerning true baptism (and how infant baptism contradicts it);
2. Concerning the Lord's Supper (and how the sacrament of the parsons is against it);
3. Concerning the true inner surrender (*Gelassenheit*) and Christian community of goods;
4. That Christians should not go to war nor should they use sword or violence nor secular litigation. Those functioning in such offices (authorities) cannot be considered (true) Christians;
5. Concerning divorce between believers and unbelievers. (One codex has as a fifth article, Concerning taking the oath.)

The most stimulating article is, of course, the third where community of goods (*Gütergemeinschaft*) is interpreted as the supreme expression of brotherly love and of true *Gelassenheit*. It closes with the rhyme,

> *Gottes Wort wär nit so schwer*
> *Wenn nur der Eigennutz nit wär.*

Gelassenheit means nothing but self–conquest and sharing all earthly goods with one's brother. It is a top concept among the Hutterites.

The text is presented almost like a catechism: statement, proof text, etc. The tension between spirit and letter is resolved in favor of the latter; that is, the Article Book represents a literalistic type of Christianity in simple obedience to God's Word. Remarkable is the documentation of each article by extensive quotation from the Church Fathers and other ancient authorities. The knowledge of the history of Christian thought and church history thus revealed is quite amazing, a fact which can be noticed in the study of any Hutterite tract. A major source for this knowledge must have been Sebastian Franck, whose various books were certainly well known to the Brethren; it was he who supplied the contact between Anabaptism and humanistic studies. Besides Franck the *Ecclesiastical History* of Eusebius was rather popular among all Anabaptist groups, likewise Flavius Josephus. That Balthasar Hubmaier too, a scholastic doctor of theology, was of great assistance (through his writings) in this endeavor of proving arguments by old authorities, is quite certain.

The Article Book must have been widely known in its time. Catholic as well as Lutheran polemics against it are known. The Brethren continued to use and to copy the book at all times. The new Carinthian transmigrants of the eighteenth century who joined the Hutterites in Transylvania soon became familiar with this book, too, as late codices, now in Canada, prove.

SOURCE: *Mennonite Encyclopedia*, I, pp. 173–74.

JAKOB HUTTER'S LAST EPISTLE TO THE CHURCH IN MORAVIA, 1535

If one wants to know Anabaptism at its very best, its spirit and its testimony in the days of harshest persecution and at the same time the most emphatic affirmation of this new (actually oldest) way of Christian life and witnessing, then few documents would match Jakob Hutter's numerous epistles to his beloved church and brotherhood in Moravia. The one here published for the first time in an English translation[1] is certainly one of the finest of the eight extant letters of this outstanding leader of the first generation of Anabaptists.

Jakob Hutter, born about 1500 in the small village of Moos near Bruneck in the Puster Valley, Tyrol, did not invent the community type of brotherhood living characteristic of the "Hutterites" in Moravia (Wideman, Zaunring, and Schützinger preceded him), but he is called "the second founder" of his brotherhood, inasmuch as he established it (1533) on such solid spiritual foundations that it has survived all the vicissitudes of nearly 450 years of history and is still vitally alive both in the old Hutterite colonies and in the more recent Society of Brothers. When after only two years of Hutter's work in Moravia (1533–35) the situation there became too dangerous, the brotherhood prevailed upon Hutter to return to Tyrol for greater safety, unaware that thus his situation only became worse.

From Tyrol Hutter sent back to Moravia four epistles (entrusted to loyal brothers who functioned as carriers under most precarious conditions) filled with expressions of pastoral care and concern, full of love and comfort, strengthening the faith of the faithful and admonishing them to continue on their narrow pathway in full awareness of the "raging dragon" of worldly authorities. Hutter was indeed a charismatic leader of unique spiritual qualities, and absolutely certain that he was called to be the bishop or shepherd of his flock and that it was his task to imbue the brotherhood with his unshakable eschatological vision of the Kingdom of God which was to be promoted among the children of a world which had not yet grasped the true light.

---

1 This translation was made by Maureen Burns of the Wheathill Bruderhof in England, one of the communities of the Society of Brothers. We acknowledge the kind permission of the Society to publish this translation.

All Hutter's epistles, especially the one published here, breathe strongly the spirit of early Anabaptism, in particular the conviction that conflict of the two "kingdoms" leads unavoidably to suffering, tribulation, and finally to martyrdom.

In fact, it cannot be otherwise, and all this suffering is not only no argument against God's immeasurable grace bestowed upon His faithful children, but is actually proof that the true believer and disciple is on the right path, since the path will and must always be contradicted by the "world."

This letter, sometimes called Hutter's fourth epistle, but actually his eighth and last, is typical of this mood and of his pastoral concern. It conveys a particularly pathetic quality if we realize that it was unknowingly Hutter's last word and testament, written shortly before he, too, was caught by Anabaptist hunters in Klausen, Tyrol, brought to trial in Innsbruck, brutally tortured, and finally burned at the stake in Innsbruck on February 25, 1536, under unbelievably cruel and repulsive circumstances. Thus he proved to his brotherhood the genuineness of his writings, remaining faithful even at the moment of excruciating torment. The letter is in no way theological; in doctrinal beliefs Hutter is as orthodox as any Christian could be, and the words of Holy Scripture are to him unquestioned reality, to be lived, not speculated about. What characterizes all his letters and especially this one is the unusual warmth and liveliness of his words. The term "heart" appears more often in the text than any other word, and "heart" means to him the inwardness of his faith, its existential character and spiritual concreteness in obedience to God and in discipleship to Christ.

The letter, like the others, is exceedingly well written. In fact one may safely say that Hutter ranks highest among the many Hutterite epistle writers. We can easily imagine the effect of the reading of such missives aloud before the assembled brotherhood, at that time most likely hiding in the forests or remote valleys of Moravia. It brought about a renewed commitment or pledge by those already in the fold but now perhaps weakened by the terrible persecutions and dangers. In this way a "primitive" or apostolic form of Christianity was carried on in full awareness of lurking dangers and martyrdom, and yet also in great rejoicing that one was privileged to witness to such glorious faith and was enabled to practice the greatest of all Christian virtues, namely brotherly love, in actual sharing and togetherness.

A realization of the setting of this letter, as partly indicated in its last section, will reveal the tremendous spiritual power behind its words. Hutter was separated from his "children" in Moravia whom he had "borne and planted through the word of God," but he felt his continuing responsibility for their spiritual well-being and steadfastness. The imagery of the Pauline epistles breaks through time and again. He who fights (he writes) like a knight (Ephesians) will receive the crown. But of course, such a fight does not mean any form of external resistance, but rather resistance to sin and temptation, however overwhelming they may be, because only by such resistance does one become a true follower of Christ. It is not his person, he claims, but God's grace and mercy which have enabled him to serve and to comfort his "children," inasmuch as it is God's compassion which has made him their shepherd "without any merit" of his own. He warns his brothers and sisters not to get drowsy while "the dragon rages" (in his famous epistle to the government of Moravia, of the same year, he identifies this "dragon" with King Ferdinand) lest they fall victims to sin and the flesh; only in alertness can the spirit become victorious and lead the faithful to the perfection of God's Kingdom.

This is roughly the contents of the epistle. It contains very little of concrete news, and nothing at all of a speculative nature. It is a cry of a heart in tribulation and sorrow, and yet at the same time also a heart full of joy; it is a unique apostolic document. From the conclusion we learn that it was taken to Moravia by the brother Jeronimus Käls, the schoolmaster of Kufstein, Tyrol. It reached the brotherhood as did all the other epistles of Hutter. But Jeronimus was not to see his homeland again. On his way back he was caught by the authorities, this time in Vienna, and soon thereafter forced to pay the supreme penalty for his faith. After months in prison, where he also wrote several epistles, he was martyred at the stake in the same year as Hutter, on March 31, 1536.

The German text of the epistle has been preserved in numerous Hutterite codices, and has been published twice. Lydia Müller presented it in her *Glaubenszeugnisse*[2] in its original sixteenth-century language, calling it "the fourth epistle of Jakob Hutter" according to the heading in the codex of Bratislava which she used. Hans Fischer published the letter correctly as number eight in his *Jakob Huter*,[3] using a copy in the Beck collection in Brno, but presented it in a modernized German version, omitting also all Bible references.

We are much indebted to the Society of Brothers for producing a fine English translation. Of course, the real flavor of the German cannot be rendered in another tongue, as the refinement of verbal expression and the overtones are beyond reproduction.

We conclude these brief introductory remarks by presenting a map of the area mentioned in the letter, the area of Hutter's home town and missionary activities. It was the area of the Bishopric of Brixen south of the Brenner Pass. Even though the bishop was not under the jurisdiction of King Ferdinand, he nevertheless rivaled him in the hunting of the Anabaptists. When Hutter was caught he was immediately sent to the provincial government in Innsbruck.

---

2 Lydia Müller, *Glaubenszeugnisse oberdeutscher Taufgesinnter*, (Leipzig, 1928), 150–59.
3 Hans Fischer, *Jakob Huter, Leben, Frömmigkeit, Briefe* (Newton, 1956; *Mennonite Historical Series*, No. 4), 62–72.

The Brixen bishopric has its own Anabaptist history. It was here that the first apostle of the Anabaptists in Tyrol, Jörg Blaurock of Chur, was to suffer his martyrdom in 1529. Here Ulrich Stadler, Hans Mändl, and Peter Walpot, outstanding leaders of the movement, were born. Here Offrus Griesinger was active as a missionary around 1535, and here a noblewoman, Agnes von Waldenhofen, turned Anabaptist. Thus this area can be rightfully designated as one of the major cradles of Austrian Anabaptism.[4]

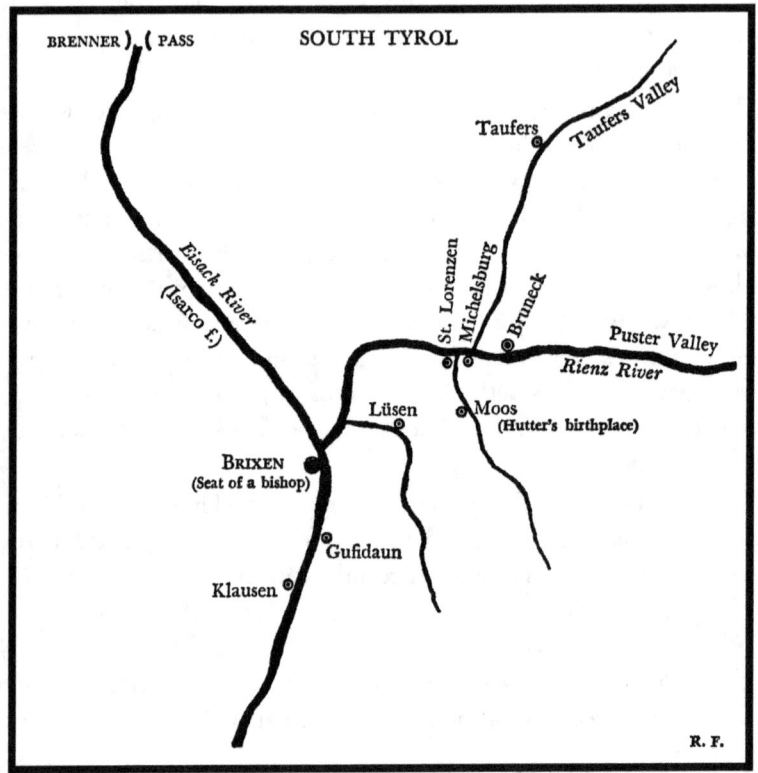

Section of South Tyrol with places mentioned by Hutter

---

4 For all further details see the articles in *ME* on Bruneck, Brixen, Gufidaun, Klausen, Lüsen, Puster Valley, Tyrol, and all articles pertaining to persons of this area.

A Holy, Beautiful and Comforting Admonition of Our Dear Brother and Servant of God, Jakob Hutter, Who for the Sake of Holy Truth Was Executed at Innsbruck on Friday Before Lent Anno 1536.

(This epistle was sent to the Church in Moravia from Tyrol through the brother Jeronimus Käls anno 1535.)

Jakob, a servant and apostle of Jesus Christ and a servant of His chosen saints here and there in all lands through the great and unspeakable grace and mercy of God who has called and chosen and fitted me for this in His fathomless mercy; in no wise had I deserved this but only His overflowing goodness and faithfulness perceived my faithfulness and has made me good and worthy with Abraham and his seed forever, and has trusted me and given His godly and eternal word into my heart and mouth, and the heavenly treasure and goodness of His divinity and His Holy Spirit, which are hidden and remain in the tabernacle and the ark of the eternal invisible God in heaven above, who is lord and king over all kings. He has blessed me with His heavenly blessing and has made His divine word living and active in me and in many others (to whom He let it be preached through me). And He has given testimony to the same through the pouring out and working of the Holy Spirit with all evidence of power, miracles, and signs. And He has appointed me to be a watchman, shepherd, and guardian of His holy people, of His elect, holy Christian Church (Rev. 21), which is the bride and spouse, yes, the dear and blessed consort of our dear Lord Jesus Christ, which He has bought, purified, and washed through His precious and holy blood, and has given me many devout, holy and Christian hearts forevermore. In this and for all this together let God the Father in heaven's kingdom, the King and Creator of all things, be honored and praised; let Him alone be glorified, blessed, and magnified. And from the very bottom of my heart be said praise and thanks to Him in His royal and eternal majesty, from me and from all saints and from all heavenly hosts through Jesus Christ for ever and evermore. Amen.

You saints, chosen and elect, fighters and witnesses of God and of our dear Lord Jesus Christ, my most beloved brothers and sisters, and my longed for chosen children, whom I have borne and planted through God's word, grace and gifts from heaven above; yes with much pain and work and in many great tribulations, wherever they may be, in Moravia and here and there in all parts, hunted and dispersed in distress, in poverty, in tribulation, in anxiety, in need, in much pain and great persecution, and in manifold temptations that you suffer for our Lord's sake; I wish you all from the depth of my heart grace, peace, and eternal mercy from the almighty God, and much love and faith, victory, strength, and self–conquest. And may God in heaven comfort and strengthen you, may He feed and give you to drink, and care for you, both in body and in spirit with heavenly and temporal gifts. May He help and support you, and may you be committed to Him in all eternity through His dear son Jesus Christ. Amen.

Beloved and chosen children of the living God, we have heard and know about your tribulations and persecutions, your distress and trial that you suffer for the Lord's sake. We know this for the greater part, although what has happened and taken place in the meantime we do not know. We consider and reflect on this diligently in our heart without ceasing. Your tribulation and suffering strike at our heart; oh, we hear and suffer faithfully with you together, apart from what else we suffer and endure here for the Lord's sake. And we think of you constantly towards God and all the saints, calling earnestly in prayer, for you are grown and planted in our heart, and are for us a living letter written in our heart through God's love and spirit which is read constantly at all times.

Beloved ones and elect, sometime ago I sent brother Christle to you and wrote and told you how matters stand with us here, and comforted you as much as God gave me to do. And now I hope and trust to God that you received that message. Now I would gladly have sent the brother Hänsel to you soon and with all speed, as you have asked and required, and he would gladly have come, too, with all his heart in godly love that he and we have towards you. But now it cannot be, for he is ill. I can and may also not use him here, in spite of needing him and others too so badly, for the need is great here, too, as you have probably heard.

But now I cannot and may not refrain (because of the godly holy love that I have toward you) to send you in this distress our dear brother Jeronimus, and will rather suffer a still greater privation in order that your need might be lightened. Oh, would to God in heaven that we might make good your need according to your heart's wish and desire, and that we might do enough to suit our heart. Oh, that God in His heavenly kingdom would grant that we might offer you the joy and delight we have in you, and that the desire of our heart might be fulfilled, that we might take you and serve and help you in your need, that we might house and shelter you, yes, feed and give you to drink, and show and bring you love and faithfulness and honor, and that we could and might serve you with heavenly and temporal gifts. What great and heartfelt joy in the Holy Spirit that would be; we wish for no greater joy. Here then is our greatest sorrow, that we are robbed of your presence, and we can and may not do all this for you. How gladly we should suffer poverty, yes, need, tribulation and pain of our flesh, yes, torture, suffering and even death itself, that we might have now fellowship together, and that we might show and bring service, love, faithfulness, and honor to you, for our soul and heart is completely open toward you.

Oh, devout children of the living God, how greatly your need distresses me, my heart is full of compassion for your tribulation and persecution that you suffer for the Lord's sake. But be comforted, you devout Christian hearts, reflect and consider well that all prophets, Christ the Lord, His apostles, and in short all saints from the beginning of the world have suffered the same, yes, all those who loved the Lord. This has been often and unceasingly proclaimed to you, that is that this will be done to all the saints and elect, to all lovers of the divine truth, until the Day of Judgment, as the Holy Scriptures testify enough and in many passages. Reflect and consider also that I have often and many times told and showed you this, when I was still with you, before ever this happened to us. For some did not want to recognize His goodness, love and mercy; so God had to give this recognition to them through tribulation and suffering. Some wanted to be thankless toward the Lord, many of whom have perished and have been confounded. But to us and to all those who love and fear Him, God will reveal and give to know the riches of His mercy and of His fatherly will through such affliction and tribulation, in order that we do not forget Him or become thankless toward Him, also that we do not become drowsy or careless in God's service, so that sin or our flesh does not rule or get the upper hand in us, and that we may not defile ourselves with the world and with earthly creatures or take pleasure and lose ourselves in these things, but that our flesh should be crucified and killed with all its lusts and desires, and that our inward man might grow and increase, so that God and His Holy Spirit might rule, lead, guide, and point us in all truth and righteousness. Also that we might know God and His mercy more fully, and glorify, honor and praise Him, and serve Him with fear and trembling, that we might grow and flourish in love and faith, in all godliness, in all truth and righteousness to the perfection that God gives and has promised to His own. So that we might not be dry and fruitless trees, and not be burned with the fire of hell, but that we might be a good, green olive tree of the Lord, to bring Him good fruits, that we might not waste unprofitably the time that we still have to live, but that we might serve God and be obedient to His saints our life–long, and no more do that which our flesh wills and has a liking for.

Therefore the Lord chastises us as His dear children, for Peter writes that he who suffers in the flesh shall cease from sinning, so that for the time that he still has to live in the flesh he shall no longer serve the world and his own flesh, and no longer live in sin, and so forth. But that he should live for God and use his life here on this pilgrimage to God's honor and praise. Therefore God makes us free and purifies us from the world and from all creatures through tribulation, that we might turn away our heart from this, and that with our whole heart we might set our trust and hope in the Lord alone, that we might confide and commit ourselves to Him altogether, and that our delight and joy should be only in the Lord, and in His word, in His eternal law, and that we might walk in all this day and night, loving God the Almighty and His children from the very depth of our heart, with all our strength and all our being, and that we might have our treasure only in heaven.

For this reason then all this happens to us out of love and great mercy of the almighty God, that we may not be damned (I Cor. 11) with the world, but may have joy indescribable in the future eternal life. Otherwise our flesh would rule us, gain the upper hand, and break forth so that we would sin. Now the wages of sin is eternal death (Rom. 6). For those that are carnal cannot please God; those that are carnal and sinful shall not inherit God's kingdom as the Holy Scripture says (Gal. 5). Wounds and blows for the body drive away evil (Prov. 20), that is, all that is sin and unrighteousness. This is driven off through the cross of Jesus Christ, which is the rod of the Lord. Therefore, be comforted, you beloved and elect, for all this is a sure sign and proof that you are dear and well-pleasing to God, and that God will also give eternal life, eternal rest, peace, joy, and eternal glory with all the elect saints and with the heavenly hosts. May God the Father help you and us to this through His most beloved Son, to whom be praise and honor for ever and eternally. Amen.

Oh, beloved and chosen children of the living God, how terribly and mightily enough this tribulation and anxiety was mirrored and shown for a long time in my heart through God's grace and Spirit. Therefore have I unceasingly shown it to you day and night, pointed out to you and taught you to bring your hearts to this, to prepare yourselves and surrender yourselves, and resign yourselves to tribulation and trial. Also how you should stand in all this, how you should believe and trust in God the Lord, and not let yourselves be frightened away from God, from His truth and from His holy church. But you shall remain constant in all manner of tribulation unto your end. For whoever endures to the end shall be saved, says the Lord (Matt. 24). Also as you strive in knightly fashion for the truth, so shall God the Lord strive for you; and I have shown how you shall be devout, righteous, patient and faithful to God and to all His saints in all things. I have also told you and shown you enough that you should hear and grasp the divine Word with the utmost diligence, and write it into your hearts. For it is probable that we shall not be with you at all times and able to speak with you, for God will perhaps take us from you whether it will be through prison, tribulation or death, whatever God ordains. May you have something to draw upon in the time of need.

You should gather in when it is summer, so that in the extremely cold and dangerous time of winter you will have something to draw upon, yes, that you are clad and prepared and can draw out the treasure of your hearts, that which you have heard and gathered in and received of God. O how often and at great length have I told and shown you this. Would to God that you have richly understood and grasped it. For you have heard often and enough the word of divine truth, many fine and mighty examples of saints, of what

God has worked and done with them. Well for him who has heard it and has written it in his heart.

You have also heard and understood that the Lord has for a long time led you during the day as a [pillar of] cloud, that is through His ministers and preachers. But now the night shall come, when one cannot and may not see the cloud any more, and the Lord will no longer go before us in the cloud. But God shall go before those who are His in a pillar of fire. That is through the light and glow of His Holy Spirit and through God's word, which word and Spirit are in all devout Christian hearts, that through this and through a true Christian, well-founded faith [His children] be ruled, instructed, taught and led in all truth. That is the pillar of fire in our hearts. Well for him whose light lightens and shines, he shall neither fall by night nor be confounded, as the Scripture testifies. The righteous man shall live his faith and shall never more be confounded.

So think now, dear brothers, and sisters, consider well and take to heart, reflect and weigh up all this in your hearts. For the time and everything that has been proclaimed to you in the name of the Lord has already come. Oh well for the man who has heard the word of God and has taken it into his heart, and whose heart is full of love and faith, of great patience, righteousness, truth, fear of God, and of His Holy Spirit; he shall stay steadfast indeed in this need. So see to it now, dear brothers and sisters, that although I or other devout servants of God may no longer speak with you by word of mouth in this world, and may no more see you with our eyes in this time, that you nevertheless remain steadfast and believe and trust firmly in your hearts in God the Lord.

Be diligent to do His will and keep His commandments. Confess the Lord with words, with works, and by a Christian holy life. Let your light so lighten and shine among men, and let your good works be seen and revealed, that God the Father might be glorified through you. In the same way shall Christ the Lord also confess you before God, His heavenly Father, and before the angels in heaven, yes, as His sons and daughters, as His brothers and sisters, and as coheirs in His glory. Love God and His holy word and people—so shall you also be loved by God the Lord and by His dear Son and by all saints. Serve God the Lord and His children with all your heart faithfully and diligently in all things; so shall the angels in heaven serve you. Nevermore forget the Lord and His divine word and His holy people—so shall God the Lord nevermore forget you. Remain in God and in His word, in His truth and in the holy fellowship of His elect—so shall God the Lord remain with and in you eternally and will not forget you. Bear in mind and consider what we have taught you through God's gift and grace with His word and through His Holy Spirit. Act all of you diligently in accordance with it. For we have not presented and preached fables and tales and human inventions to you, but the divine eternal truth, that which is pure, clear, and well-founded, that which is yea and amen before God and before all saints, and what we in the truth know and have heard and received from the living God; which also is sealed and testified enough with Holy Scripture and with much holy blood, and which also we desire to testify with our blood and with godly truth through the help, strength, and grace of God. This is the right way and the door into the sheepfold, the true and unfeigned foundation and truth, upon which all the prophets and apostles have built as we have pointed out and shown to you. Let yourselves not be taught or counselled otherwise. For a thief comes for nothing but to steal, rob, and destroy. So they are all thieves and murderers before God, as Christ says. And let him that will instruct and teach otherwise be cursed and damned, as Paul says in his teachings. For we have neither lived in error nor wavered, and do not waver here and there like a reed that is moved in the wind; and through the help of God we shall not be moved, neither by tribulation nor temptation nor trial. And no man, no torture or pain, no power, no hunger or thirst, no tribulation or temptation, no creature or anything that one can speak or name, shall confuse or injure us to turn away from God and from His divine truth, in which we walk and which we preach. For the word we speak and preach is well-founded and sealed by God and by all His saints with miracles and with powerful signs, as is written above. Neither do we bring something new to your years, for we are not fickle, inconstant, or light-minded, that today we speak one thing and tomorrow something else, as light-minded and false teachers do. But we are firm and immovable in the divine truth for evermore, let it cost us what it may, and however cruel the consequences may seem. And what we have spoken from the beginning and preached, we preach still untiringly and unashamedly. This should rightly make you certain and brave, manly, and well-secured in the Lord. Oh, would to God, you devout Christian hearts, that I could be only one day or a few hours with you, that I could let my voice be heard among you and might rejoice, quicken, and satisfy myself in the Lord with you. But God has not appointed things thus, which we shall bear and accept with sorrow and with great patience.

But be comforted, ye elect of the Lord, for the time of your redemption is at hand. Lift up your heads to God the Lord in heaven, and wait in meekness, in great long-suffering, in righteousness and truth, in godly love, and in strong faith and trust, for your Shepherd and King to come from heaven. For He will soon come, He that is to come in the clouds of heaven with great power and glory, the King and Comforter of Israel, and He shall save, redeem and liberate those that are His, and shall set upon their heads a glorious crown that shall never more fade. But before this there shall be struggle and strife.

Whoever fights as a true knight and overcomes, yes, conquers through God's Spirit, shall be crowned and shall gain the victory and the prize, and shall receive peace and joy, eternal rest and glory with all the elect and all the heavenly hosts. He shall be with God the Father and with His dear Son,

Jakob Hutter's Last Epistle to the Church in Moravia, 1535

and with the saints forevermore in the covenant of eternal life. May God the Father help us to that through Jesus Christ, to whom be praise and honor forever and eternally. Amen.

Oh, beloved and elect children of the living God, I rejoice and comfort myself with the assurance of God which He has promised and given to us that we shall see and behold Him in His holy temple, that our suffering and misery shall one time come completely to an end, that our weeping and wailing shall cease, and that we shall behold and embrace one another with great and unspeakable joy, etc. And no one shall hurt or injure us anymore, for all tribulations and suffering shall pass away. For the veil of the temple shall be rent through the power of the Lord, that is, all earthly and carnal pomp and power. But the devout shall reign and rule, and their mouth shall be full of laughter, as the Lord says, and they shall rejoice in the Lord, and they shall sing songs of praise together for evermore. May God grant you through His mercy that we might await His grace and His eternal perfect compassion. So for our sorrow and distress joy shall be given to us a thousandfold.

Here in this world we have no rest and no continuing city but tribulation, anxiety, distress, and pain. But be comforted, for Christ has overcome the world, and will give both you and us grace and victory, that we also may courageously overcome it. For our sakes He has overcome, that the same victory might be given to you, to us, and to all who fear God and love Him with all their heart and keep His commandments. For the right, true Christian faith is the victory that overcomes the world. Would to God in heaven that you might be well comforted and endowed by God the heavenly Father in all your tribulations. Oh, that it were God's will that I might be with you and you with me. How greatly and deeply my heart longs for you; it burns with great desire to be with you in the tribulation, yes, in great torture and pain; I would a thousand times rather be with you than be with the ungodly in their pleasure and luxury, etc. Now I comfort myself in the Lord that if it cannot and may not be now, we shall truly be together in the future and everlasting life.

Oh beloved and elect children of God, my heart, soul, and spirit shall be with you at all times, and you with me, and God with all of us, and we all with God, for evermore. Be therewith faithfully commended to God the Lord in heaven, and to the faithful shepherd Jesus Christ, beneath His powerful care and protection. May He comfort and strengthen you, may He feed and give you to drink in body and in soul with heavenly and temporal gifts according to His will and pleasure, and the richness of His great mercy, and be commended to Him in all things for evermore. Amen.

Further, beloved and elect brothers and sisters, my dear children, I let you know again how things are here with us, namely as follows: we live and walk in love and faith, in peace and unity of the Holy Spirit. We have also great tribulation inwardly in our hearts for your sake, and also otherwise great and heavy persecution outwardly from the ungodly tyrants. The cruel, raging dragon has opened wide its jaws and throat and wills to swallow up the woman that is clad with the sun, which is the bride and the church of our Lord Jesus Christ.

Soon after the meeting of the church, the first day, one of our dear brothers was imprisoned in Taufers. Soon after he had got home from the meeting of the church, the judge of Brixen rode into Lüsen and called together men, women, and children, everyone that could possibly walk, and read to them a cruel mandate and commanded them that no one should house or shelter us. Whoever should do so would be more cruelly punished than ever before and his house would be burned to the ground. For our cause was taking root and gaining ground. And the devilish lord of Brixen would not suffer this but wanted to exterminate it. This lord came home recently and offended the people with many words and forbade them to do what was good and right, and commanded them to do what was evil and wrong, etc. The devout were well comforted in heart though, and heeded not his offense and threats, but served God and were diligent to do His will. The judge wanted to wait awhile to see whether they would be frightened and go into their accursed idolatrous temple, and he would gladly have ignored them. But our betrayers gave him no rest; for the dear brothers and sisters were known to all men in the whole valley and to many others besides in the neighborhood. When the judge saw that his commandment counted for nothing among the devout, he came up and took of us five or six brothers and sisters and led them captive to Brixen. The Lord shielded the others this time, but just now at his house another message has reached us through an ungodly man. He has again taken five captives from Lüsen to Brixen, but we know nothing more definite yet. It is to be feared though. What they will do with them and how they are, here and there, where they are imprisoned we do not know this time, but God knows. I have hurriedly sent brothers into Lüsen and all around to visit the beloved brothers and sisters, and to see how things are in all respects. They have not yet returned so that I do not know definitely how matters stand everywhere. But one can well imagine and think that they are all hunted and driven out, and are everywhere in great danger.

We have heard nothing more about the captives than all uprightness and devoutness. May God comfort them and strengthen them from heaven above with His word and His Holy Spirit, and keep them in His name and His divine truth right to their end, and support them through Jesus Christ. May He help and aid them through His great mercy. Amen.

What else there is to say and what is going on everywhere among us our dear brother Jeronimus will tell and inform you by word of mouth, for he knows everything just as well as I at present; he knows what there is to be told and said concerning this. He will be our living letter to you whom you may ask and hear. Above all, we all wait for the Lord with great patience.

Last of all and in conclusion, we ask you for the sake of God's mercy to pray unceasingly to God for us with earnestness and diligence as we do for you, and as we know also that you are doing for us. But be not negligent in this but fuller, and the longer the more zealous, for there is truly need for it. But I know that God will provide ways and means for His own people according to His promise and great mercy. God be with us and with you, and comfort all grieved Christian devout hearts with the comfort of His Holy Spirit through Jesus Christ, here and there for ever and evermore. Amen.

All children of God with us here, the holy Christian Church, greet you most faithfully from the very depth of their hearts, in godly love and peace, each and everyone, many thousand times. And I, Jakob Hutter, your minister and servant, your brother and companion in the suffering of Christ, I greet you all together, each and every one, all devout Christian ministers together with all saints, many thousand times, in godly, burning, brotherly love, with a peaceful heart and with the holy kiss of our Lord Jesus Christ. God in heaven, the Father of all grace and mercy, greet and bless you from heaven above with His gracious comfort and Spirit through Jesus Christ, ever and eternally. Amen.

Beloved and elect in the Lord, our body, soul and spirit is all the Lord's; so give yourselves wholly, and be comforted in the Lord. God keep us in His love and in the covenant of His peace for evermore.

Sent from the county of Tyrol through the brother Jeronimus. By me, Jakob, your brother and companion in the kingdom, suffering and the patience of Christ.

SOURCE: *Mennonite Quarterly Review*, XXXIV (1960), pp. 37–47.

THE OLDEST CHURCH DISCIPLINE OF THE ANABAPTISTS

The Anabaptist Church has been correctly called a church of order,[1] that is, a disciplined and regulated church whereby this order is accepted by all on a voluntary basis. This fundamental orientation distinguishes Anabaptism from many related movements of a more individualistic and loose organization. From its very inception the Brethren realized that a church cannot exist unless some basic rules and regulations are laid down whereby the brethren express their willingness to live accordingly or to suffer the penalty of the ban and exclusion. Such a "church order" (*Gemeinde–Ordnung*) or "discipline" then is a set of rules "how a Christian should live in the brotherhood," if he wants to be a disciple of Christ, and likewise how a fellowship of such committed disciples should be "organized," if the precepts of the Sermon on the Mount are to be translated into practical terms here and now, applicable for the entire brotherhood.

The oldest church discipline of this kind seems to be that famous document called *Brotherly Union of Several Children of God*, commonly called briefly the *Seven Articles*, adopted at Schleitheim, Germany, on February 24, 1527.[2] Usually these articles are described as a confession of faith, which to a certain extent they actually are. But they also lay down some of the more practical rules, thus representing in a rudimentary form a real church regulation or discipline.

It has not been known until now that the early Anabaptists of Tyrol likewise possessed a church discipline (so entitled) of about the same period as the Schleitheim Articles. It has been available ever since the original text of the Hutterite chronicle was published in 1923 (Wolkan, *Geschicht–Buch*) but has never been recognized in its true meaning. Recent research in Hutterite manuscript literature has convinced the present writer that this section in the Chronicle is of prime significance, all the more since in numerous Hutterite codices a certain document is found which, if not completely identical with

---

1 See Harold S. Bender, article "Church," *ME*, I, p. 595; Friedmann, "Anabaptism and Protestantism," *MQR*, XXIV (1950), 21.

2 John C. Wenger, "The Schleitheim Confession of Faith, translated and edited with an Introduction," *MQR*, XIX (1945), 243–53.

the above–mentioned passage, is yet so clearly related to it that it must be considered the original from which the chronicler took his text, slightly adjusting it to the need of his work.

I refer to the passage in the *Geschicht–Buch der Hutterischen Brüder*, pages 60–61, called *Ordnung der Gemein, wie ein Christ leben soll* (Discipline of the Church, How a Christian Ought to Live), in twelve brief articles, inserted at the year 1529. It gives the impression that the chronicle writer (Caspar Braitmichel) had our document at hand, liked it, and thought it worthy of inclusion in his Chronicle, although he did not know either who wrote it and when, nor where it had been in use.

The manuscript codices present our document, anonymously to be sure, consistently in the context of writings of Hans Schlaffer[3] (who was martyred in Tyrol on February 3, 1528) so that his authorship may be assumed with probability.[4] It is certainly a church discipline of the pre–Hutterite period (say before 1529–30), since community of goods is not yet taught but only a "community of charity," that is, the care of needy Brethren. Schlaffer comes from Upper Austria near Freistadt, but became active in the Inn Valley in northern Tyrol, beginning about the middle of 1527.[5] From his several epistles to the church (*Gemein*) at Rattenberg on the Inn, which are full of love, concern, and words of fatherly admonition, we get the impression that he was the very *Vorsteher* or bishop of the Anabaptist group of that place, even though it was but for a short time. No document has survived the brutal persecutions which would tell us much about the life of this group. We know, however, of much martyrdom here and all along the Inn River in these early years of the Anabaptist movement. Hans Schlaffer was arrested and put into prison at Schwaz on the Inn in December 1527. If our conjecture as to authorship is right, then his leadership was truly short–lived. But it must have been in these few months of 1527 that this outstanding (and too little studied) brother drew up his discipline for the apparently very live congregation at Rattenberg.[6] Whether he knew of the Schleitheim Articles, or even used them as a model, cannot be determined, but his *Ordnung* gives the impression of an original work by an Anabaptist leader.

The document is very brief, almost too brief (*ca.* 500 words only); hence it gives the impression of a first or preliminary draft of what a church discipline should be. The quick interference of the Tyrolean government in all Anabaptist activities destroyed this incipient congregation of Rattenberg

---

3 W. Wiswedel, "Hans Schlaffer, ein ernster Beter und eifriger Verteidiger der göttlichen Wahrheit," in his *Bilder und Führergestalten aus dem Täufertum*, II (Kassel, 1930), 191–200.

4 ERRATA: In this essay, written in 1955, Friedmann attributes authorship to Hans Schlaffer. In 1958 he concluded that the authorship should be attributed to Leonhard Schiemer, and reported this in "A Correction," which appeared in *MQR* 32, 236–238 (Jl '58). Consequently his essay "Leonhard Schiemer and Hans Schlaffer" (*Hutterite Studies*, pp. 259), written in 1959, gives the correct identification of authorship as Schiemer.

5 Loserth, article "Inntal," *ML*, II, 421 ff.

6 Called Rothenburg in all Anabaptist documents. Incidentally, it is the same place where *ca.* 1490–95 Pilgram Marpeck was born.

also, and gave it no chance to develop its organization. Soon Moravia was beckoning and those who could possibly do so left the Inn Valley, where, according to a chronicler,[7] the martyr pyres burned all along the river, costing the lives of close to a thousand Brethren in the first decade.

Little needs to be said about the contents proper. It is genuinely and typically Anabaptist in spirit. Schlaffer belonged to the first generation when Biblicism and spiritualism fused into one primitive Christian attitude of vigor and strength. Every Anabaptist, although building his own church, well knew that his time would be short. Article ten expressly states that a Christian must always be prepared for the cross, in fact he should anticipate it. The entire tone of the document is practical—"how a Christian should live" within the brotherhood, and very little "technical" or legal. One might call it a "prophetic church discipline."

If the conjecture as to authorship is correct, then the document belongs to 1527, and not, as Braitmichel guessed, to 1529 when the Rattenberg group probably no longer existed. The text presented is not the one of the Chronicle but is taken from one of the numerous Hutterite codices still extant among the Brethren in Canada and the United States. The translation was made by Elizabeth Horsch Bender. In brackets are added those passages which are missing in the document in the codex but present in the Chronicle (*Geschicht–Buch*). The brackets also contain completions by the writer necessary to give full meaning to the statements. The text of the Chronicle has almost no Bible references, while the codex document abounds in them. The text follows.

DISCIPLINE OF THE BELIEVERS: HOW A CHRISTIAN IS TO LIVE

Introduction (missing in the *Geschicht–Buch*)

Since the almighty God and heavenly Father is permitting His eternal and all–powerful Word to be proclaimed to all creatures in these most perilous times (Col. 1) and has called us at this time out of pure grace into His marvelous light (I Pet. 3) to one body, one spirit, and one faith, united in the bonds of love (Eph. 4; I Cor. 1), to which we have all agreed, in order that our calling be found worthy, not only with the word of the mouth but in the truth and power (II Thess. 1;1 Thess. 1; I Cor. 4; James 1), we have all in one another's presence openly agreed to regulate everything in the best possible way. For the improvement of our brotherhood [*Gemein*, so translated throughout], for the praise and honor of the Lord, and for the service of all the needy, we have unanimously agreed that this *Ordnung* shall be kept among us by all the brethren and sisters. When, however, a brother or sister is able to produce a better *Ordnung* it shall be accepted from him at any time (I Cor. 14).

---

7 See Kirchmaier, *Chronik der Stiftes Neustift bei Brixen* (*Fontes Rerum Austriacarum*, I), p. 487.

First Article

And beginning when the brethren are together they shall sincerely ask God for grace that He might reveal His divine will and help us to note it (Psalm 86, 118) and when the brethren part they shall thank God and pray for all the brethren and sisters of the entire brotherhood (I Thess. 1 and 5; II Thess. 1 and 2; II Cor. 1; Col. 1, 3, 4).

Second Article

In the second place: we shall sincerely and in a Christian spirit admonish one another in the Lord to remain constant (Heb. 10:1; Acts 14, 15, 18; Col. 2). To meet often, at least four or five times, and if possible…even at midweek (I Cor. 11, 14; Acts 1, 2, 9, 11, 20; Heb. 10; II Cor. 6; Matt. 18).

Third Article

In the third place: when a brother or sister leads a disorderly life it shall be punished: if he does so publicly [he] shall be kindly admonished before all the brethren (Gal. 2, 6; I Cor. 5; II Thess. 3); if it is secret it shall be punished in secret, according to the command of Christ (Matt. 18).

Fourth Article

In the fourth place: every brother or sister shall yield himself in God to the brotherhood completely with body and life, and hold in common all gifts received of God (Acts 2 and 4; I Cor. 11, 12; II Cor. 8 and 9), [and] contribute to the common need so that brethren and sisters will always be helped (Rom. 12); needy members shall receive from the brotherhood as among the Christians at the time of the apostles (Acts 2, 4, 5; I Cor. 11, 12; Eph. 4; Prov. 5; Matt. 8, 15, 16, 17, 19; Luke 3, 6, 8, 9, 10, 12, 14, 18; I John 1, 2, 3, 4; Mark 3, 10, 12; Gal. 6; Heb. 13; Dan. 4, 8; Luke 6, 8; I Tim. 1; I Cor. 14, 16; Rom. 6, 18; James 1; Phil. 2).

Fifth Article

The elders [*Vorsteher*] and preachers chosen for the brotherhood shall look after the needs of the poor with zeal, and with zeal in the Lord, according to the command of the Lord, extend what is needed for the sake of, and instead of, the brotherhood (Gal. 2; II Cor. 8, 9; Rom. 15; Acts 6).

Sixth Article

In the sixth place: decent conduct (*ehrbarer Wandel*) shall be kept among them (Rom. 12, 13; Phil. 1, 2; I Pet. 2, 3; I Cor. 1, 3; Gal. 5; Eph. 5) before everyone (Titus 3; Matt. 5; I Pet. 3) and no one shall carelessly conduct himself before the brotherhood either in words or deeds (Rom. 1, 6; II Tim. 2), nor before those who are "outside" (I Thess. 5; I Pet. 3).

Seventh Article

In the seventh place: in the meeting one is to speak and the others listen and judge what is spoken, and not two or three stand together (I Cor. 14). No one shall curse or swear (Matt. 5; Rom. 3; James 5) nor shall idle gossip be carried on, so that the weak may be spared (I Cor. 15; Eph. 5; Col. 3; II Tim. 2; Psalm 118). [*Geschichtsbuch* here cites only Ecclesiasticus 23].

Eighth Article

In the eighth place: when the brethren assemble they shall not fill up with eating and drinking, but avoid expenses [reduce expenditures] to the least, [eat] a soup and vegetable or whatever God gives (I Cor. 11; I Pet. 4; Gal. 5; Rom. 13; Eph. 5; Eccles. 37; Luke 21), and when they have eaten, all the food and drink shall again be removed [*Geschichtbuch*: "from the table"] (John 6; Matt. 4; Luke 9; Mark 6), for one should use with thanksgiving and moderation the creatures which God has created, pure and good, for our subsistence.

Ninth Article

In the ninth place: what is officially done among the brethren and sisters in the brotherhood [*Geschichtbuch*: "or is judged"] shall not be made public before the world. The good-hearted [an interested but not yet converted or committed] person, before he comes to the brethren in the brotherhood shall be taught [*Geschichtbuch*: "the Gospel"] (Mark 16; Rom. 1; Col. 1). When he has learned [*Geschichtbuch*: "understood"] and bears a sincere desire for it, and if he agrees to the content of the Gospel, he shall be received by the Christian brotherhood as a brother or a sister, that is, as a fellow member of Christ (Matt. 7; Prov. 19, 29; Col. 4; Rom. 14; II Cor. 6; I Cor. 10; I Tim. 6; Matt. 10). But this shall not be made public before the world to spare the conscience and for the sake of the spouse (I Cor. 9, 10; Matt. 15).

Tenth Article

In the tenth place: all the brethren and sisters after they have committed themselves, shall accept and bear with patience all that He sends us [*Geschichtbuch*: "accept with gratitude and bear with patience"] (Rom. 6; John 13; Matt. 16; Luke 9; I Pet. 4; II Cor. 12), and [shall] not let themselves be easily frightened by every wind and cry.[8]

---

8   The *Geschicht-Buch* adds as a marginal note: "to be ready for cross and suffering."

Eleventh Article

When brethren and sisters are together, being one body and one bread in the Lord and of one mind, then they shall keep the Lord's Supper as a memorial of the Lord's death (Matt. 26; Mark 14; Luke 22; I Cor. 11), whereby each one shall be admonished to become conformed to the Lord in the obedience of the Father (Phil. 2, 3; I Pet. 2, 4; Rom. 8; I John 2.) (Obedience: Rom. 2; Phil. 2; II Cor. 2, 10; II Thess. 1; I Pet. 1).

Twelfth Article

In the twelfth place: as we have taught and admonished the brethren and sisters we shall always watch and wait for the Lord that we may be worthy to enter the kingdom with Him when He comes, and to escape or flee from the evil that will come to the world. Amen. (Matt. 25; Luke 21; I Thes. 5; I Pet. 5; II Pet. 3; Rom. 2).

God be merciful to me. I commend my spirit and your spirit with our brother in Christ into the hand of the eternal Father. Amen.

Here follows Hans Schlaffer's *Prayer and Thanksgiving at Mealtime.*

SOURCE: *Mennonite Quarterly Review,* XXIX (1955), pp. 162–66.

THE *BRÜDERLICHE VEREINIGUNG* OF 1556–57

Brüderliche Vereinigung zwischen uns und etlichen Brüdern am Rheinstrom was a Hutterite tract of 1556–57, written by the Hutterite missionary brother Hänsel Schmidt or Raiffer who was then working in the area of Kreuznach (Palatinate) and Aachen (Lower Rhine province). It exists in two handwritten books, now in the Primatial library of Esztergom, Hungary, in the form of an appendix to the otherwise well–known *Sendbrief* by Andreas Ehrenpreis of 1652. Its significance lies in its statement of the fundamental doctrinal and practical points in which the Hutterites were distinguished from the Swiss Brethren who lived in that area. The tract consists of two parts,

1. the negotiations in Kreuznach with a brother Lorenz Huef and his fellow Swiss Brethren, in 1556, with whom seven points were discussed, and
2. similar negotiations in Aachen in 1557 with the Swiss brother Hans Arbeiter discussing not less than seventeen points of doctrine and practical distinctions.

Hänsel Schmidt, always an effective missionary worker of the Hutterites, could win both groups for his brotherhood, only to be caught himself finally by the authorities of Aachen and to suffer martyrdom for his faith's sake in 1558. The tract says expressly that the brethren in Kreuznach demanded a written statement concerning the seven points with all Scriptural references, which was also done, whereupon the statement was read before the entire congregation of the Swiss Brethren. This is apparently the document which forms the major part of the pamphlet at hand. Schmidt drew it up himself out of his intimate knowledge of Hutterite teaching. The seven points discussed concern: marriage, taxes for war (*Blutgeld*), separation from other groups who claim to be brethren, support of the ministers and deacons for their secular needs, "idol worship" (meaning the Catholic Mass), the buying of houses in Moravia, and finally, who should move to Moravia. The seventeen points of the *Aachen Gespräch* (for which no Scriptural references are presented—perhaps because no written statement was asked for) deal with much more central issues, such as original sin, incarnation of Christ, community of goods, ban, etc.

The text is preserved in full in the two codices, IX and XI of Beck's description (*Geschichts–Bücher*), from which Beck prints only the main parts without the doctrinal details (225–29). The *Great Chronicle* (ed. Zieglschmid) contains the full text (pp. 359–67, and 384) including the Scripture references. It presents a complete copy of the original tract. The Ehrenpreis epistle, finally, our prime source, was published by the Hutterian Brethren in 1920 (Scottdale, Pa.) from a manuscript preserved by the Hutterites in South Dakota, and here again one finds the complete text of the tract on pages 155–83. In this *Sendbrief*, to which Ehrenpreis himself had apparently appended this doctrinal statement from a now lost original, this otherwise unnamed tract is given the heading (in Beck, p. 225) *Brüderliche Vereinigung...*, reminiscent of the similar title of the oldest doctrinal statement of the Anabaptists, the *Brüderlich Vereinigung etlicher Kinder Gottes* of Schleitheim, 1527.

The document is very significant for its discussion of relations between the various Anabaptist groups.

SOURCE: *Mennonite Encyclopedia*, I, p. 448.

THE ANABAPTISTS ANSWER MELANCHTHON: *HANDBÜCHLEIN WIDER DEN PROZESS*

One of the most important Hutterite writings of the sixteenth century was the *Handbüchlein wider den Prozess, der zu Worms am Rhein wider die Brüder so man die Hutterischen nennt ausgangen ist im 1557 Jahr*. It was a polemical writing, considered with the *Rechenschaft* by Peter Riedemann and the *Article Book* as one of the most significant doctrinal books of the early Hutterites. It was an official pronouncement of the brotherhood, prompted by a document which some Lutheran theologians (Melanchthon, Brenz, Andreae, etc.) had issued at Worms in 1557. In this document, named *Prozess wie es soll gehalten werden mit den Wiedertäufern* (in Württemberg also called *Bedenken...*, published by Bossert in the *TA Württemberg* in 1930), the Anabaptists are accused of a number of damnable doctrines and practices (see John Oyer's analysis); their teachings are declared blasphemous; hence Levit. 24:16 (death penalty) should be applied. Toward the end of this document also the upbringing of children in the communistic colonies in Moravia is briefly but violently attacked as a devilish institution (*teuflische Communion... wider die Natur und alle Rechte*, Bossert, p. 166, lines 14–19).

The Anabaptists in Germany felt the need of defending themselves against these accusations, which were much more severe than Melanchthon's attack of 1536 (*Several Unchristian Points Which the Anabaptists Advance*), although by 1557 Anabaptism had already lost some of its prime vigor. At a conference in Strasbourg the Swiss Brethren decided to produce an answer (see letter to Menno Simons, 1557), but apparently this plan was never carried out. At the Frankenthal Disputation of 1571 the *Prozess* was mentioned but no reply was given.

The Hutterites, on the other hand, although less involved (as they lived in faraway Moravia, where the Lutheran theologians had but a minor influence), nevertheless produced an elaborate answer in which they developed at some length their own doctrine and position. This answer was then called *Handbüchlein wider den Prozess*, but neither author nor year is mentioned in it. One would not err too much in assuming that this book was written between 1558 and 1560, and although it was a document issued by the entire brotherhood in Moravia, it seems to have been drafted by Peter Walpot, then by far the most outstanding spiritual leader of the Hutterites. As far as Anabaptist manuscript literature is known, this book is the strongest polemical writing of the Brethren against the Lutherans, and has always been understood by the Brethren in this spirit.

The *Handbüchlein* is subdivided into twelve sections called "books" which answer point by point the specific accusations of the Worms theologians; viz.,

1. concerning worldly authority and whether such an authority can be a Christian;
2. concerning the use of law courts and lawsuits;
3. concerning the taking of an oath;
4. concerning the Anabaptist claim that whoever does not belong to their church (*Gemeinschaft*) is condemned and not saved;
5. concerning infant baptism;
6. concerning the Lord's Supper;
7. concerning original sin and whether children have it;
8. concerning the necessity to preach and to hear the Word of God;
9. concerning the Holy Trinity, whether Christ was the Son of God;
10. concerning whether rebirth prevents any backsliding hereafter;
11. concerning justification, whether man is justified through Christ or by his own endeavor;
12. concerning the upbringing of children in communal establishments.

A comparison of these "books" with the *Prozess* shows that the latter condemns the Anabaptists only on seven points while the *Handbüchlein* answers in twelve points. Some of the additional five items were taken from the 1536 accusations of Melanchthon. Item twelve, concerning children, is mentioned in the *Prozess* only casually (in Bossert's print only five lines, though sharp in tone), yet the Hutterites felt particularly sensitive in this area, since they were very conscientious with regard to the upbringing of children, and wanted to make it clear to everybody that children were to them the most precious things in the world, and their proper upbringing was one of their most important tasks. We might here remember that it was Peter Walpot who in 1568 wrote a very thoughtful and much advanced *School Discipline* for the Hutterite schools.

The *Handbüchlein* answer to the Worms theologians is a rather skillful, effective work. The arguments are thoroughly but soundly Biblical as was the Anabaptist way of thinking; the words are straightforward, yet never acid (as most polemics of the sixteenth century were). The author (Walpot?) also quotes amply from old authorities such as Origen, Jerome, Augustine, the Councils, and recent authorities such as Luther (*Deutsche Messe*, 1526), Zwingli (*Contra Fabrum*), and Cellarius. It is most likely that the learned book by Christoph Eleutherobios, *Vom wahrhaftigen Tauff Joannis, Christi und der Aposteln. Wann und wie der Kindertauff angefangen und eingerissen hat* (*How Infant Baptism Originated*) (1528, sec. ed. 1550) was much used, mainly for "book" five. It is found in many Hutterite manuscripts.

The chapter "Concerning Original Sin" is one of the most decisive sections of the *Handbüchlein* and expresses a viewpoint accepted by practically all Anabaptists. The Brethren declare: man as a child of Adam stands under the general curse of original sin; hence physical death. But Christ *is* the reconciliation of this world including small children. The mere "inclination" to sin (which is inborn in all of us) does not yet condemn man. Only the doing of sin will cause eternal death. Moreover, the Scriptures declare that the children will not bear the consequences of the bad deeds of their fathers, rather everyone dies for the deeds that he has perpetrated himself (Ezek. 18:17, 20). This argument, incidentally, is the main argument suggested by Peter Riedemann in his *Rechenschaft* of 1540. The *Handbüchlein* closes this chapter by declaring that if the inclination to sin is not carried out into works of sin, it does not harm man and does not cause eternal death. "Whosoever is born of God does not sin" (I John 3:9).

Strange to say, the *Handbüchlein* is nowhere mentioned in other Hutterite writings, not even in their Large *Geschichts–buch*. But from the *Klein–Geschichtsbuch* we learn that the knowledge of it was kept very much alive in Hutterite tradition. Johannes Waldner, the author of the *Klein–Geschichtsbuch*, tells us that in 1756, when the Lutheran transmigrants from Carinthia came to Transylvania and there showed the greatest interest in both Hutterite life and doctrines, the Brethren gave them Riedemann's *Rechenschaft* and the *Handbüchlein* to read. "In this little book the Lutheran Church is sharply attacked and its false teachings and errors are clearly brought to light" (*Klein–Geschichtsbuch*, p. 274). It appears that the arguments of the *Handbüchlein* as well as those of the *Rechenschaft* impressed the newcomers so profoundly that they decided to join the Hutterites and to embrace completely their teachings.

The original of the *Handbüchlein* is no longer extant. That no Hutterite codex in European libraries contains it accounts for the fact that it was completely unknown to scholars like Beck, Loserth, and Wolkan. The oldest copy is one made in Velke–Levary in 1637 and now in Paraguay. Several copies of this manuscript were made, of which one is in Canada, and one in the Goshen College Library (produced by the late Elder Elias Walter, and given to Christian Hege).

SOURCE: *Mennonite Encyclopedia*, II, pp. 645–46.

PETER RIEDEMANN'S *RECHENSCHAFT*

This very important Hutterite confession of faith was written in 1540–44 by Peter Riedemann. Its full title is *Rechenschaft unserer Religion, Leer und Glaubens Von den Brüdern so man die Hutterischen nennt ausgangen*. Among the not too numerous doctrinal tracts of the sixteenth-century Anabaptists, Riedemann's *Rechenschaft* (*Account of our Religion, Doctrine and Faith*, the title according to I Peter 3:15, "Be ready to give an answer to every man that asks you a reason of the hope that is in you.") is one of the most important and significant documents, a basic source for the knowledge of Anabaptist doctrine and theology, a true spiritual foundation for the Hutterite branch of Anabaptists, but beyond that, characteristic of this great movement at large, save for the one specific doctrine concerning community of goods. It is a book of much inner beauty and spirituality which did much to enable the Hutterites to survive through the centuries more or less loyal to their beginnings. Together with the great *Article Book* of 1547 (and 1577) and the *Handbüchlein wider den Prozess*...of 1558, it represents the official position of the Hutterites in matters both of doctrine and practice. That the *Rechenschaft* was better known to the outside world than the other two statements was mainly due to the fact that it is one of the few Hutterite books ever to have been published in print (1565).

The history and theology of this unique work has not yet been given a thorough study, although there have been some recent attempts in this direction. Thus it was not known until the present that Riedemann (who began this *Rechenschaft* during his imprisonment in Hesse, 1540–41, at the castle of Wolkersdorf) got the idea for this work when he wished to inform Landgrave Philip of Hesse about the true Anabaptist doctrine. "Since he has never interrogated us personally...since, perhaps, others slander us, he should at least know why he is keeping us imprisoned" (Epistle 21, of 1540–41, sent to Hans Amon and Leonhard Lanzenstiel).

The original manuscript is very likely lost; yet two old manuscript codices are still extant: one in the primatial library in Esztergom, signature IV, 1, dated 1614, having 364 leaves in 16⁰, very carefully written, apparently intended as a pocket "companion"; and a second in private possession in Freeman, S.D.

(of which no description is available). In 1565 the book came out in print; its last page says: "This year the Confession was reprinted by Philips Vollanndt." Nothing is known about this printer, and it may be assumed that he was an itinerant printer who chanced to pass by the Hutterite settlements in Moravia, offering his services to everyone, and there (perhaps at Neumühl, the seat of Bishop Peter Walpot) accomplished this work. It was the Golden Age of the brotherhood and the Brethren probably felt that each of the many Bruderhofs in Moravia and Slovakia should have a copy of this basic work. Nevertheless, the edition must have been small since only a very few copies have come down to our time (list at end of this article). The expression "reprinted" has puzzled scholars regarding the possibility of an earlier print, but it can hardly mean this since no such print has ever been discovered. Apparently it means: first written by hand but now also printed. In modern times the book has been republished three times (1870, 1902, 1938) and also translated into English (1950), thus making the text easily available to anyone interested (list of editions at end of article).

Although the *Rechenschaft* is the work of but one man, it must be assumed that the brotherhood, after careful study, promptly approved of it as an official church document. When the Brethren in their dire predicament in 1545 sent a collective letter to the Lords of Moravia, they enclosed a copy (apparently in manuscript) of this *Rechenschaft* to inform the authorities about their stand both as to doctrine and practice. The work has kept its place of pre-eminence throughout Hutterite history because of its excellence and clarity.

The *Rechenschaft* is divided into two unequal parts (in the English edition of 1950 of 127 and 86 pages respectively), the first part being the more important while the second is made up of seven lengthy meditations on various topics, not considered as part of the official "Account." The first part is made up of ninety articles, most of them brief. The initial group of twenty-nine articles represents an interpretation of the Apostles' Creed, followed by the articles "What faith is," "Why God created man," "What sin is," "Concerning original sin," "Concerning remorse—repentance," "Concerning the baptism of children," and the refutation of the arguments for infant baptism. Then follow articles about the Lord's Supper, community of goods (less than four pages), separation from the world, etc. The first part is concluded by a set of articles concerning practical matters: government, warfare, taxation, manufacture of swords (forbidden), litigation and swearing (both forbidden), traders, innkeepers, standing drinks (all forbidden), education of the young, ban and readmission, and finally an article concerning the whole life: conduct, dress, adornment, etc.

It is impossible to give here an adequate presentation of the ideas of this comprehensive document; reference to literature at the end of this article will be of some help as well as the pertinent articles in the *Mennonite Encyclopedia*. That the theological emphasis is thoroughly different from that of Luther, Zwingli, and Calvin, is worth mentioning. The great issue of original sin (in many Anabaptist documents completely missing) is here dealt with on not more than three pages. Justification "by faith alone" is not mentioned at all, and the classical *loci* used by Luther for his basic doctrines are conspicuously absent. In short, Riedemann was not familiar with the Lutheran theological tradition. Rather, his sources are various texts from the Scriptures. Thus, for instance, baptism is called, after Titus 3:5, "the bath of rebirth"; and as for "the harm wrought by original sin" Riedemann refers back to the Old Testament *locus* in Ezekiel 18:20, where it is said that children shall not bear the iniquities of their fathers. "The mother of sin," however, Riedemann emphatically declares (English text, p. 56), "is disobedience" to the commandments of God, alluding to Romans 5:16–19. There is but one reference to Luther (English text, p. 35), followed by a passionate denial that the Brethren taught "work righteousness." "To this we say 'no,' for we know that all our work, in so far as it is our work, is naught but sin, but in so far as it is of Christ and *done by Christ in us*, so far it is truth, just and good" (English text, p. 36). There is nowhere an explicit theology of atonement but there is the emphasis that redemption follows repentance and inner rebirth: "fleeing from sin as from a serpent" (English text, p. 59). Thus "man is grafted into Christ." "We, redeemed from death through Him, might thus be the children of His covenant" (English text, p. 63) (Acts 3:17–26); indeed a "covenant of childlike freedom" (English text, p. 68) (Gal. 4:4). The emphasis is thus laid not so much upon justification from sin but upon sanctification of life, which is the very proof of inner rebirth and obedience, i.e. discipleship.

The church, however, of these reborn children of the "new covenant" (67) is basically a spiritual thing. "It is a lantern of righteousness (39) in which "the light of grace is borne and held before the whole world." "Whosoever endures and suffers the work of the Spirit of Christ is a member of this church." It is the Spirit and not man who leads men to this church (pp. 39–41). This church, then, in the concrete here and now, is defined as "the fellowship of the Lord's Table" (*Abendmahls–gemeinde*), the assembly of the reborn ones. Such a fellowship to be sure, is not established by the Lord's Supper, but the latter is rather an expression of this fellowship previously entered into. It is a church, as far as humanly possible, "without spot and wrinkle," and in order to achieve this end separation from the world and inner discipline are needed. This leads to all the ensuing statements concerning conduct of life and the practice of the ban ("exclusion," pp. 131 f.). For the world "which is without" (I Cor. 5:12) no further concern is expressed, for this world will eventually be judged by God Himself.

It is obvious that a document of such inner richness could not be drawn up without some forerunners who prepared the spiritual framework in which Riedemann developed the ideas which are specifically Hutterite in character. In 1894 Johann Loserth presented the thesis that the theological framework of this *Rechenschaft* was taken in its entirety from the work of Balthasar Hubmaier and that therefore the *Rechenschaft* is not so much an original work as an adaptation of ideas developed by Hubmaier in 1525–27 and assiduously studied later by the Hutterites in Moravia. Loserth's claim was challenged by Franz Heimann in a doctoral dissertation (Vienna, 1927), in which he concludes that Riedemann borrowed from Hubmaier only in those parts which deal with the doctrines of baptism and the Lord's Supper, doctrines which are common to all Anabaptists. The assimilation of these ideas from Hubmaier does not detract from the originality and genuine spiritual eminence of Riedemann' s comprehensive work. Hubmaier's most outstanding contribution to the Anabaptist vision is his very convincing discussion and refutation of the several arguments in favor of infant baptism. This discussion Riedemann takes over point by point into his *Rechenschaft* (English text, pp. 70–77), according to Heimann.

Otherwise, Heimann emphasizes, in all practical and ethical items Riedemann is by and large independent of Hubmaier, rendering Loserth's theory invalid. It must not be forgotten, for instance, that Hubmaier approved the "sword," i.e., the right of the government to use force in the execution of its laws, while the Hutterites, like all evangelical Anabaptists, stood passionately for nonresistance and non–participation in any government or military operations.

Finally, Riedemann was not solely dependent upon Hubmaier in the shaping of his Anabaptist doctrines. He must certainly also have known the ideas of his earliest teachers such as Hans Hut, Hans Schlaffer, and Leonhard Schiemer. But no such research has as yet been undertaken. It is also possible that Riedemann was influenced in part by Ulrich Stadler, the most important doctrinal thinker of the 1530's in Moravia, but again this question has never been studied. Since Riedemann's Biblical spiritualism was shaped in the second half of the 1520's, one might think of Hans Denck as a strong influence; but this was again the general Anabaptist vision of that time. The value and genuine contribution of the author himself should not be diminished by pointing to some forerunners. Since the work was written in prison in Hesse, it is very likely that Riedemann had no reading material on hand, and his formulations must be considered as his original personal viewpoints and conceptions arising out of his own spiritual pilgrimage.

Of the original *Rechenschaft* edition in 1565 only a few copies are known to exist: one at the British Museum in London (sign. 3908 a8), one in the University of Chicago Library, one in the National Museum of Brno, Moravia, one at a Bruderhof in the United States (formerly at Rockport, S.D., but now of unknown location), one used in 1870 by Calvary but supposedly acquired by the Prussian State Library, one reported by Beck to be in the University of Breslau Library, and one at the National Library of Vienna, Austria.

Peter Riedemann's Rechenschaft

The following are known modern reprints:
1. *Mittheilungen aus dem Antiquariat S. Calvary* (Berlin, 1870) 254–417, reprinted from a 1565 copy;
2. A reprint from the Chicago copy as *Rechenschaft unseres Glaubens..., neu herausgegeben von den Brüdern in Amerika* (Berne, 1902). This edition was probably edited by John Horsch, who lived in Berne at that time, and who had been in close contact with Elias Walter, the leading Hutterite elder of that period.
3. A reprint in 1938 from the copy in the British Museum by the Society of Brothers (Plough Publishing House in England);
4. An English translation, *Account of our Religion, Doctrine and Faith...*, published by Hodder and Stoughton (London) in conjunction with the Plough Publishing House in 1950, 283 pages. The English translation is by Kathleen E. Hasenberg. In this edition the nearly 1,800 Bible references are all collected in a special appendix of nearly thirty-eight pages (229–66).

SOURCE: *Mennonite Encyclopedia,* IV, pp. 259–61.

AN ANABAPTIST ORDINANCE OF 1633 ON NONRESISTANCE

All evangelical Anabaptists of the sixteenth and seventeenth centuries believed very strictly in the practice of nonresistance. In fact, it is their distinguishing mark. Its roots are the commandments of the Sermon on the Mount and the entire spirit of true discipleship. In this regard there was no digression among the different groups, Swiss Brethren, Dutch and North German Mennonites, and Austrian Hutterites. As early as 1524, Conrad Grebel, the founder of the Swiss Brethren, emphasized this principle in his well-known letter to Thomas Müntzer.[1] Time and again we meet the same emphasis in our sources, be they epistles, confessions before a court (*Verantwortungen*), debates, admonitions to the brotherhood, and so forth. For instance, in the famous epistle to the governor of Moravia of 1535, Jakob Hutter writes thus:

> All our doings, word and work, life and conduct, are open to everyone and in no way hidden.... Ere we would knowingly do injustice to anybody for a penny's worth, we would rather suffer to be deprived of a hundred florins, and to be wronged. And ere we would strike our worst enemy with our hand, let alone with pike, sword, or halberd, as the world does, we would rather die and have our lives taken from us. Moreover, we do not possess material arms, neither pike nor gun, as anybody may well see and which is known everywhere. In summa, our message, our speaking, our life and conduct, is this that one ought to live in peace and unity in God's truth and righteousness, as true Christian disciples of Christ.[2]

There is no doubt that the Brethren accepted this basic principle with never-swerving loyalty; the long list of martyrs is a speaking proof of it. But individual martyrdom in days of great dedication is one thing, and the conduct of an entire group (brotherhood, *Gemein*) under more settled conditions is another thing. How are the Brethren to behave in externally difficult situations when dangers arise, such as foreign invasions (e.g., the Turks in Austria around 1600) or high-handed acts of the lords who try to

---

1 H. S. Bender, *Conrad Grebel, the Founder of the Swiss Brethren* (Goshen, 1950), 284–85.
2 *Älteste Chronik*, 151 f.

extort money or services according to the usage of the time? What should be the right conduct if loss of goods or even lives are at stake, and this all not so much for the sake of one's faith, but rather in the course of violent incidents of some sort? Might then "self–defense," *Selbstschutz*, not seem to be justifiable?[3] Anabaptists lived a disciplined life, and the principle of regulated "order" within their group was paramount to their brotherhood idea. Discipleship to them did not mean that every brother should decide for himself individually how to follow the Lord, and the idea of the "ban" was but another expression of this principle of order in the brotherhood to which each gladly submitted.

Hence, written rules or "ordinances," *Ordnungen*, issued by true leaders with an inner calling for their work, are very characteristic for Anabaptist life.[4] They are particularly characteristic for the Hutterites, the most closely organized brotherhood in Anabaptist history. A great number of such *Ordnungen* have been found in Hutterite manuscripts, dealing with almost any and every possible subject of their common life: rules concerning the particular activities in the colonies (*Bruderhöfe*), such as work in the fields, stables, vineyards, shops, kitchen, nursery, laundry rooms, and so on, the way of marriage and weddings, the way of assembling, praying, and acting in common affairs. Likewise orders concerning dress, speech, demeanor, and so on. In short, the spiritual as well as the social and economic functions were regulated, directed, and put under discipline which all the Brethren voluntarily accepted. In this regard we might discover a certain external similarity with medieval monasticism. The recent publication of the so–called Small Chronicle of the Hutterites[5] is particularly valuable in this regard since it reproduces in an "Appendix" of nearly fifty pages a good number of these Hutterite ordinances dating from 1651 to 1873,[6] some known and discussed before,[7] and some new.

But one topic seems to be completely absent in these rules: the practice of nonresistance.[8] We read, to be sure, that in 1595 such a rule had been issued,

---

3 The "Selbstschutz" among the Mennonites in Southern Russia during the Bolshevik revolution, 1918–20, is well discussed by C. Henry Smith, *The Story of the Mennonites* (Berne, 1941), 487 f. It was later strongly condemned by the elders, and even some of the young men confessed their mistake. It had tragic consequences.

4 The term "church discipline," though somewhat approximating this type of regulation, reflects a different spirit, hence it had better not be used in our present historic interpretation. The monastic term "regula" (rule) comes still nearer to what we face here.

5 *Klein–Geschichtsbuch*. The original manuscript was written by Johannes Waldner (*Vorsteher* of the brotherhood from 1794 to his death in 1824) most likely between 1793 and 1802. It consists of two parts: in the first one, Waldner retells the story of the Great Chronicle, 1525–1665, while in the second part he continues the story, up to 1752 from other sources, and from 1752 to 1802 from his own memory.

6 The *Klein–Geschichtsbuch*, 519–65. The first *Ordnungen*, pp. 519–32, are dated 1651, and have Andreas Ehrenpreis as their author. The volume has some more such *Ordnungen*, namely: the earliest one of 1529 (p. 16); another one by Ehrenpreis, concerning marriage, of 1643 (pp. 214–18); and the general description of the organization of the *Gemein* during its golden days 1570–1590 (pp. 95–97). An original manuscript by Ehrenpreis with a complete collection of such orders is kept in the library of the Catholic primate of Hungary at Gran (Esztergom); a copy of it is in the Beck collection in Brno, Moravia, file No. 87. See *MQR*, XXIII (1949), 106.

7 Loserth, *Communismus*, where these *Ordnungen* are discussed at great length. Also Wolkan, *Die Hutterer* (Vienna, 1918), prints some of these documents and discusses them.

8 The principle of "Nonresistance" is most exhaustively discussed by Guy F. Herschberger, *War, Peace and Nonresistance* (Goshen, 1944).

An Anabaptist Ordinance of 1633 on Nonresistance

most likely by the *Vorsteher* Klaus Braidl, in the face of terrible pressure by the rising Catholic Counter-Reformation, but its contents are not known, hence the arguments, the spirit, and the extent of this most central principle remain somewhat vague. It was therefore a real surprise to discover that in the text of the Small Chronicle a lengthy insert to the year 1633 represents actually just such a Hutterite ordinance concerning the practice of radical nonresistance as it had been in use since the days of Jakob Hutter. A detailed study of this document is therefore well justified and may help in clarifying the spirit of the Anabaptist forefathers. The incident which led to this elaborate discussion has long been known from the Great Chronicle of the Hutterites.[9] But this older book does not mention at all the ensuing ordinance or, as our text says, "the assembly speech by the chosen Elders." It was Johannes Waldner (d. 1824), the author of the *Klein-Geschichtsbuch*, who inserted this document in his narrative[10] obviously with the intention to strengthen the spirit of his group in its heroic struggle of maintaining the nonresistance behavior. He tells us in his introduction to the new document that he took it from another book of Hutterite origin otherwise unknown. In so doing Waldner performed a real service to his group as well as to all those who are concerned with this idea of nonresistance, for it not only elaborates the details of practical behavior in an actual situation, but also deals with the Scriptural arguments for the principle.

Yet, before discussing these more fundamental points, it will be necessary to summarize briefly the background (the "incident"), which prompted the enunciation of these commandments. To begin with, we should keep in mind that the seventeenth century was still a period of feudalism, or, to be more specific, of the time-honored manorial system. Lords, great and small, owned the land which was tilled by peasants. They were partly free—such as, for instance, the Hutterites—and partly villeins or even serfs who enjoyed but a very small amount of freedom. But even the free peasants possessed only very restricted rights, since the lord of the manor (*Gutsherr, Grundherr*) had full jurisdiction over all his tenants. Naturally, arbitrariness and high-handed conduct were common events, and the lower classes had no ways and means effectively to defend themselves. As a rule, the lords had the right to ask from all their tenants, including the free ones, certain services in the field or vineyard or with "cart and horses," as the saying goes. The technical term for these services in England and France is *corvée*, and in German lands *Robot* or *Frohndienst*. It always meant a heavy burden to the peasants, particularly since its interpretation was at the mercy of the superiors.

The Hutterites were excellent tillers of the soil, and for this reason welcomed by the lords, who were more interested in thriving estates than in carrying out the orders of the Catholic Counter-Reformation. This was

---

9 *Älteste Chronik*, 817–25.
10 *Klein–Geschichtsbuch*, 168–72.

especially true in Slovakia, then a part of Hungary. Around the village of Sobotiste the land given to the Brethren belonged to not less than thirteen lords of the manor, and it was quite obvious that the Brethren could not serve all these thirteen lords "with cart and horse." Thus in their contract or *Hausbrief* [11]—they were a free party in this contract—they agreed to pay a certain sum of money instead of any service. Thus the Brethren became legally exempt from any claim to a *corvée*. Furthermore, they also stipulated in this *Hausbrief* that, as Christians, they would and could not appeal to any court, manorial or otherwise, in case of conflicts. This, too, was granted, most likely with little understanding on the side of the lords.

Now then, in the year 1633, a small incident occurred at the Sobotiste Bruderhof which at first looked quite serious. One of the thirteen lords, a certain nobleman Francis Nagy–Michaly, was in need of some horses. Disregarding the contract, he came down to the Bruderhof and demanded horses. Unfortunately, the manager of the colony (*Diener der Notdurft*) had died a few nights previously, and the bishop (*Vorsteher*), Heinrich Hartmann (1631–39), was sick in bed. No one was around who carried a particular responsibility. The impatient lord tried to get the horses from the stables right away, and ordered his servants to go ahead. The Brethren, who had not known the lord personally, took his servants for marauding hussars, and got excited. On the spur of the moment (with no leader present) they grasped whatever they could take hold of, sticks, flails, pitchforks, axes, and so on, and thus prevented the removal of their good horses. According to the narrative, no harm was done to the lord.

This was the incident, a case of *Selbstschutz*, somewhat reminiscent of similar events among South Russian Mennonites during the revolutionary days of 1919. There is no need to discuss here the moral principle involved. From a consistent Anabaptist viewpoint no such *Selbstschutz* can ever be justified, even if the situation is difficult, involving loss of goods or lives. In the long run, the nonresistant attitude is more conducive to the well-being of the brotherhood (and to their basic Christian witness, too) than the temporary advantage reached by abandoning it.

Soon the results of this inconsiderate and irresponsible act became evident. To resist the lord of the manor with violence—even in a case of arbitrariness on the lord's part—was regarded as a major crime, and the *Vorsteher* Heinrich Hartmann together with four brethren were arrested and dragged before a court of noblemen. All his excuses, apologies, references to the contract, and so on, were of no avail. The brethren had to suffer many months of jail, with irons on their legs, not to mention their continuous fear of finally being sent to a frontier fort against the Turks. It was only after a long time, when some of the more sober lords grew concerned about their estates and the

---

11 *Geschichts–Bücher*, 364. The renewal of the *Hausbrief* in 1640 is published in the *Klein–Geschichtsbuch*, 128 n. The first contract was signed in 1613.

work thereon, that they asked a supreme mediation by the Lord Palatine, the representative of the King of Hungary[12] and head of the entire Hungarian nobility. Eventually, in October 1633, a compromise was worked out and accepted, and with the payment of some money to Mr. Nagy–Michaly the case was legally closed.

Yet it was not closed morally and spiritually. Something had happened in the brotherhood which spoiled their record, and which, a generation earlier, would have been thought impossible. The Brethren, in their Christian conscience and their earnest endeavor to live up to the principle of absolute discipleship, had never before committed such an act of "self–defense" with arms, not even in the worst days of the Turkish invasion (1605)[13] nor during their painful expulsion from Moravia (prior to 1622). It was a serious breach, or rather backsliding, a defection from their old ways of witnessing to Christ's commandments. If true Christian discipline was to be kept alive something had to be done. Thus the elders called a meeting of the brotherhood in Slovakia to amend its ways which had become faulty and uncertain, and at the same time to exhort the Brethren to remain staunchly on the one way that they had accepted with their baptism, the way marked out by Jakob Hutter and the many loyal followers afterwards. This, then, is the background of the "ordinance" of 1633, a translation of which will be published on the following pages.

The text says simply this: "On November 28, 1633, the great assembly at Levar resolved to profess the following points before the entire brotherhood." Obviously this does not quite sound as an ordinance in the strict sense of the word, and for that reason it is not easily recognized as such. Yet in the run of the speech (and our text is essentially just this), delivered by one of the elders (or *Diener des Wortes*), we read this passage: "We therefore command you by the power which the Lord has given us, that henceforth no brother should protect himself with violence." Any disobedience in this regard would be punished with the ban. It is quite clear that such a proclamation represents nothing less than an "ordinance," an *Ordnung*.—Who is its author? It does not seem likely that the *Vorsteher* Heinrich Hartmann, an elderly man of good standing, but apparently mediocre leadership qualities, could have produced this forceful speech. John Horsch, who published part of the German text of this speech in 1929,[14] surmised that no one but Andreas Ehrenpreis could have been the originator of this document. We know that during his long years of service he had tried hard to revive the old spirit and all the time–tested Hutterite principles. Thus it seems almost certain that this conjecture of Horsch is correct. The brotherhood had no greater leader during its seventeenth–century history than this simple miller from

---

12 The Emperor Ferdinand II, a Hapsburg, who was at the same time also the King of Hungary.
13 Compare *Älteste Chronik*, 628–41, and Friedmann, "Adventures of an Hutterian Brother in Turkey, 1607–10," in *MQR*, XVII (1943), 73–86.
14 John Horsch, in *Mennonitischer Familien–Kalender für das Jahr 1929* (Scottdale), 34–36.

Sobotiste. Born about 1590 in a Hutterite colony in Moravia,[15] he became a minister of the Word of God in 1623 (or 1621?), and after the death of the *Vorsteher* Hartmann, in 1639, was unanimously elected *Vorsteher* or bishop of the entire Hutterite brotherhood. In this function he served until his death in 1662. Considering the trying times, it was a glorious period of leadership and witnessing. His writings breathe the spirit of an outstanding man, a true "evangelical Anabaptist" of the great tradition. The reading of his tracts, epistles, and so on, means still today an enrichment to the sensitive mind. He was a man of great brotherly love, spiritual vision, and stern principles concerning the practice of discipleship. We know that he was the author of a great number of ordinances, to be sure in the main of a more practical nature. It was he who stopped the threatening decline (the *Verfliessen*—as the text says) of the brotherhood for at least half a century. The ordinance is just one step in this direction.

What he actually wanted to convey to his brethren in his address of 1633, he said almost at the end of it:[16] "Take off your spotted garments of sin, and make them white in the blood of the Lamb" (Rev. 7:14). The argument of the evangelical advice in the Sermon on the Mount not to resist evil is the main theme of the speech. It is not only unwise to attempt "self–defense," it is actually "a defection from faith that a brother should dare to knock down the one who did violence to him, to run after him who is already fleeing, and still to beat him when down on the ground." It means "spot and wrinkle" on the *Gemein*, the true church of Christ.

But how? Might not somebody object, and out of an economic concern (or mentality) talk back somewhat in the following fashion: "Are we then to permit any violent taking away of possessions of our brotherhood?" To this, Andreas Ehrenpreis answers unequivocally, "According to the teachings of Christ: yes. It is more blessed to us, and in the long run also of greater profit than if we would resist with violence…. It would be a pity if anyone among us who had shared all the suffering with the Brethren, would then forfeit his salvation just for such reasons."

This is obviously not a theological tract but an ordinance. Though filled with quotations from the Holy Scriptures, it is yet nowhere theoretical. It is a simple confession, or should we rather say profession, a renewed and authoritative statement concerning the basic way of Christian discipleship. In this sense it has its great value, providing an object lesson in the handling of such a situation, loyally continuing the tradition of true evangelical Anabaptism.

The text, taken from the *Klein–Geschichtsbuch der Hutterischen Brüder*, pages 168–72, follows.

---

15   See the article on "Ehrenpreis" by Loserth in *ML*, I, 530–32. There is no newer literature on this outstanding man though he would deserve an extensive biography.
16   *Klein–Geschichtsbuch*, 172.

To the reader[17]

One should not think that the brotherhood (*Gemein*) approved of such resistance and upheaval which men without the fear of God in their hearts had aroused against their lord of the manor, even though in the above description[18] these brethren were declared innocent. This might well be true when seen with the eyes of the world and judged according to secular law. It is true that the brethren did not know their lord by face, and they had certainly no intention of slaying him as they had been accused at the court. In this regard they really were innocent. Yet, their deed and violent self–defense was nevertheless contrary to the Gospel and also against their faith and conscience. For this reason the elders discussed this matter before the entire *Gemein*, and faithfully admonished everybody to be on one's guard that henceforth no such events would ever happen again. Although the Great Chronicle does not record this meeting, it still can be found in another book, and I think it is fitting to insert here the main points of these talks in order to fully recognize the disapproval of the elders and the entire *Gemein* of the afore–mentioned acts.

On November 28, in the year of our Lord 1633, the great Assembly at Levar (Slovakia) resolved to profess the following points before the entire Gemein.

Beloved Brethren, For many and great reasons we feel prompted not only to profess earnestly the following points before the entire *Gemein* but also to insist upon their observation henceforth.

Recently it came to pass in our *Gemein* that the brethren, very much against our calling and the Word of God, yea, against the Spirit of Christ, made themselves conspicuous by rioting, beating, violently resisting against a sword–minded magistrate, his servants, and other people of that kind. By that, we not only sinned in our conscience against God, but we also have become gravely punishable in the eyes of the authorities and are labeled as impudent and refractory people, even proud scoundrels, by the big lords of the country. Besides and for that reason, we are afraid lest this would bring tribulation and ruin to the *Gemein*, even to our widows and orphans.

And if it should happen (as it has been strongly hinted at by the high powers of the country) that we bring tribulation to the *Gemein*, then we would have a poor consolation in our Christian conscience that we suffer for the sake of truth and faith, particularly those (of us) who stained themselves with such deeds.

---

17 This "To the reader" is written by Johannes Waldner, the author of the Small Chronicle, as an introduction to his insertion of the document which he wanted to be included in the story but which was missing in the Great Chronicle. The document itself was taken from another manuscript book, and has as its author Andreas Ehrenpreis, then minister of God's Word at Sabatisch, Slovakia.

18 *Klein–Geschichtsbuch*, 160–68; *Älteste Chronik*, 817–25.

For Christ the Lord teaches us: it has been said an eye for an eye and a tooth for a tooth, but I say unto you that ye resist not evil, but whosoever shall smite thee on the right cheek, turn to him the other also. And again: give to him that asketh thee and from him that would borrow of thee turn not thou away. Do good to them that hate you and pray for them which persecute you.

And this we must understand above all with regard to the authorities (much more than with regard to soldiers and robbers), and there is not the slightest excuse, argument, or comfort in taking the liberty of standing up against the authorities and defending ourselves.

Paul says: Whosoever, therefore, resisteth the power resisteth the ordinance of God. And they that resist shall receive to themselves damnation (Rom. 13:2).

Peter, the Apostle, commands: Submit yourselves to every ordinance of man for the Lord's sake whether it be to the king as supreme or unto governors as unto them that are sent by him (and that not only to the kind and friendly ones, but also to the uncouth). For so is the will of God that with well–doing ye may put to silence the ignorance of foolish men. As free, and not using your liberty as a cloak of maliciousness. For this is thankworthy if a man for conscience toward God endures grief and suffering wrongfully. For what glory is it if when ye be buffeted for your faults ye shall take it patiently? But if when ye do well and suffer for it ye take it patiently, this is acceptable with God (I Pet. 2:13f.).

In the year of our Lord 1595, the elders declared before the *Gemein* and also earnestly commanded that if something is taken away from us by force, for instance, taxation by the authorities, one should not resist them with improper words. Or if the soldiers take something away from us or press hard upon us with wicked words then nobody should be caught in talking back to them which might cause them to do harm to the *Gemein*. In this every earnest Christian should be very careful. Our forefathers also recognized and warned that if ever so little was taken from someone or he otherwise went through a bad experience he should not at once, without being advised, run to the judge to accuse or incriminate. This brings often nothing but evil consequences along with it and only complicates the issue. And even though we should suffer some robbery and harm in our worldly goods, yet it is more comforting and blessed that we keep our conscience clean and pure. For it is written: Ye took joyfully the spoiling of your goods, knowing in yourselves that ye have in heaven a better and enduring substance (Heb. 10:34).

Thus we clearly see that to riot, to resist, to push, to run around and to beat the lord's bondsmen (and as actually happened at Sobotiste even against one lord of the manor himself) cannot be done without hurting the conscience. Also it does not do any good with the authorities.

As we all still remember so clearly that one elder of the *Gemein* together with four brethren by such acts got into danger of life. They were led around the country as in a spectacle in a most disgraceful and shameful fashion; it almost looked as if he and some of the brethren would be taken to a frontier fort against the Turks. Neither the elder nor the brethren taken with him had had any part nor guilt in these upheavals and doings, yet had to suffer innocently such shame, fear and danger of life, even jail, beatings and fetters because of those who had shown no concern.

And if God the Lord, whose help we felt so strongly, would not have taken our part through the supreme lords of the country, our *Gemein* would not have escaped without great harm, loss of goods, or even hurt and ruin of some brethren, being driven out to forests and highways, or maybe even the destruction of our entire colony (*Bruderhof*) at Sobotiste. And even though the great lords took our part they could not achieve any real compromise. Rather it became necessary that the prince of the country, the Palatine, through one of his aides, gave order to such a settlement.

To prevent greater danger and harm, and to preserve the house in Sobotiste, and to protect the *Gemein* from greater perils, the *Gemein* was forced to accept the counsel and mediation of these lords (though it was not done too gladly). We were also warned and advised by some lords to compromise, that we might not be looked at as disobedient or as people who resist the authorities or even as Münsterites, and then would be driven out of the country. Since there was no other way out, such a settlement was eventually accepted.

Since the Lord, through the election by the faithful ones, has placed us as shepherds and watchmen over His *Gemein*, and by special means of grace appointed us to these functions, [we are mindful that] the Lord (through His prophet) speaks thus to the watchmen of Israel: Son of man, speak to the children of thy people and say unto them, When I bring the sword upon a land, if the people of the land take a man of their coasts, and set him for their watchman: if when he seeth the sword come upon the land, he blow the trumpet and warn the people; then, whosoever heareth the sound of the trumpet, and taketh not warning; if the sword come, and take him away, his blood shall be upon his own head. He heard the sound of the trumpet and took not warning; his blood shall be upon him (Ezekiel 33:2–5).

So, beloved brethren, we ask for the sake of Christ that you would desist from rioting, beating, pushing around, scrambling for work, and like acts of violence. They all are nothing but sin. And if someone should object to this (so to speak in an economic spirit): are we then to permit any violent taking away of the possessions of our *Gemein*? To this we answer according to the teachings of Christ: yes. For it is more blessed to us and also of greater profit than if we would resist with violence, and thus would spoil our conscience.

We would bring ourselves into such danger with the authorities, and besides would have to pay so much hush–money, that it hardly can be imagined. For as you well know: if someone of us just once said a word, even in the best intention, we never could pay them enough. If, however, we hold back whenever violence is done to us, be it by the lords, servants or subjects, then we can ask help and counsel from the authorities, in the hope to receive more than if we would protect and avenge ourselves with such danger in view (I mean the penalties of the authorities), not to speak of the hurting of our conscience. For it is very shameful and not at all in accordance with the faith in Jesus Christ, that a Christian be condemned by the world for his evil deeds.

We therefore command you by the power which the Lord has given us through His word, to better the *Gemein* of God that henceforth no brother shall protect himself with violence from such robbery, iniquity, and pressure. And if someone should be disobedient to our word and command (which is not ours, but God's word and command), to him will be meted out ban and penalty according to the Scriptures and the example of our forebears as we have learned it in our *Gemein*. Such a one we will leave to his own defense before the authorities, since he has trespassed against God, the *Gemein*, and the authorities. Once his case has been cleared by the authorities, and he is willing to do penance for his offense and foolishness, then we shall readily pardon him and take him back.

Also we will not suffer it any longer that people go their way with hoes, pick–irons and such abominable big sticks. If someone wants to go out then he should do it as a brother does according to old custom. Nowadays nobody wants to guard the cattle without having an ax with him. Long ago such practices were not allowed in the *Gemein*, for a cowherd has a better control of the cattle with a stick than with an ax. And if someone carried an ax with him for self–protection, then it will avail him to detriment as much as to profit. There is also some rumor that some brethren (mainly those on lonely farms) own and use guns. This should not be, for what profit is a gun to the brother ? It has never been permitted in the *Gemein* (in the past), and shall also not be permitted in the future.

We, the elders, are no longer willing to stand up with goods, chattels and life for such rowdies as it was done this time at Sobotiste. Rather the one who sins should suffer penalty and make amends, so that the innocent may not suffer for him. This we have proved to you with writ and example of our forebears.

For it is a defection from faith that a brother should dare to knock down the one who did violence to him, to run after him when he is already fleeing, and still to beat him when down on the ground. Such brethren do not walk in the light but they walk in darkness, and the darkness has blinded their eyes. We do not want to have communion with them.

We hope and trust, however, that the faithful and good hearted ones, who forgot themselves and acted rashly out of human weakness and in eagerness to preserve the property of the *Gemein*, that they will be willing now to listen to the warning sound of the trumpet of the Gospel and (henceforth) be deterred from endangering their salvation. Have they not left everything they possessed out of faith in the One who will judge all men on the Day of Judgment, namely Jesus Christ? However, remember well that He has said: I shall not judge you but the word that I have spoken, the same shall judge you on the Last Day (John 12:48).

We also admonish you, beloved brethren, that you would shun not only rioting and beating, but also cursing and slandering and everything which could provoke anger with the authorities, their servants and all other men. Christ, our Way, Example, and Savior, never chided when reviled, never threatened when suffering but left it to the One who judges righteously. Christ also teaches us: I say unto you that every idle word that men shall speak they shall give account thereof in the day of judgment (Matt. 12:36); also: For by thy word thou shalt be justified and by the words thou shalt be condemned (Matt. 12:37).

Beware also of slandering the authorities, highest and lowest, whoever they may be, for it will not remain hidden among us anyway. You know that we are a poor and wretched people. It is true that we pride ourselves and declare at the Lord's table to be one bread and one body, in fact members of one body, and what is more, of the most noble body of which Christ is the head. And yet it must be admitted with sorrow that nothing is kept strictly among us. Rather that which has been spoken in confidence in the house soon leaks out and is even brought before the authorities. This means spot and wrinkle to us, a people of God. (The Jews, by contrast, are much more close than we.) Whether those who act in this way may still be considered members of the body of Christ, that we leave to the judgment of every faithful one.

Be it as it may; even if we would keep it secret that we are slandering the authorities, calling them names and cursing them, it is yet not fitting the faith in Christ. As Job says in his book: Is it fit to say to a king, "Thou art wicked?" And to the prince, "Ye are ungodly?" (Job 34:18).

Everything will come to the fore at its time, as the proverb says: no thread is spun so fine, it yet will come to light.[19] They also say, "the fields have eyes and the forests have ears." Look only at the word and teachings of Christ, who says, There is nothing covered that shall not be revealed, and hid that shall not be known (Matt. 10:26). "Therefore," says the Scripture, "curse not the king, no not in thy thought; and curse not the rich in thy bedchamber: for a

---

19 In German the proverb runs like this:
 Es ist kein Faden so fein gesponnen
 Er kommt doch an die Sonnen.
Waldner (or Ehrenpreis) writes "klein" instead of "fein" which is less correct to tradition.

bird of the air shall carry the voice, and that which hath wings shall tell the matter" (Eccl. 10:20).

Thus, we pray you for you and your salvation's sake that every earnest Christian should fear God in these things as much as in other sins, and likewise should keep the commandments of God and Christ. Too, they should take off their spotted garments of sin, and make them white in the blood of the Lamb (Rev. 7:14), so that nobody may be found naked on the Day of Judgment. It would be surely pitiful if one had shared in suffering with the brethren, and then would forfeit his salvation for such reasons.

To forestall such happening we pray you and warn you from the depth of our heart. For the glory of God, also for the sake of the well–being of the *Gemein*, and for your own hoped–for salvation, [we trust] that every earnest Christian will suffer this [ordinance], and will diligently seek to live up to it. For this will serve his salvation and the weal of the entire brotherhood. Amen.

SOURCE: *Mennonite Quarterly Review*, XXV (1951), pp. 116–27.

CONCERNING THE TRUE SOLDIER OF CHRIST
A Hitherto Unknown Tract of the Philippite Brethren in Moravia

In the history of the Anabaptist movement, Moravia plays an outstanding role, as is well known. Here the Brethren found generous tolerance at the hands of the nobility and were permitted to establish their congregations in peace and quiet—a peace which was, it is true, frequently disturbed by an imperial mandate—and to begin a primitive Christian life. After Balthasar Hubmaier left Nikolsburg there were three groups which attempted to develop the real essence of Anabaptism: the well-known churches of the Hutterites on the one hand, then the church of the Philippites (so named after Philip Plener or Blauärmel), which had settled in Auspitz on the lands of the Abbess of Maria Saal, and finally the church of the Gabrielites at Rossitz, led by Gabriel Ascherham or Kürschner. Originally these three groups formed a unit although each possessed its own independent leaders. Soon however an unfortunate and unavoidable division arose, since each of these three leaders wished to establish a variant form of the new Anabaptist life. A comprehensive survey of all this is given in the *Great Chronicle* (*Geschicht-Buch*) of the Hutterian Brethren (pp. 76–101), so that it is not necessary to discuss this further here. The Hutterian Brethren, as is well known, have been able to maintain themselves through all the storms of history to the present day. The Gabrielites left Moravia soon after the split of 1533 and lived in Silesia until they were gradually reunited with the Hutterites (1545). Concerning the Philippites, however, it is necessary to give a more detailed discussion, since their history is to the present time not well known.

At first the Philippites lived not far from the Hutterites and occasionally came in contact with them at Auspitz, 1533–35. Up to the present time nothing at all had been known about any of their writings, so that it has been impossible to form a sound judgment of the inner character of the personality of Philip Plener. We know only that he came from Strasbourg and that later, after he was driven out of Moravia, he returned by way of Württemberg and Strasbourg to the Palatinate.[1] Naturally what the *Geschicht–Buch* reports

---

1 Literature: The two editions of the Hutterite Chronicle by Beck and Wolkan, further the works on the Hutterian Brethren by Loserth, Wolkan, and Lydia Müller, and in particular Hege's important book on the *Täufer in the Kurpfalz* (Frankfurt, 1908), 60, 74–78. W. Wiswedel plans to give a detailed biography of Plener in his third volume of *Bilder und Führergestalten aus dem Täufertum*. Unfortunately the *Täuferakten* for Württemberg contain nothing about this group.

about him is partial and is not verified as yet by other sources. Little has become known about the teachings which his group upheld, except that they rejected communism in the form which the Hutterites adopted. The group was not permitted to continue its life in peace very long, for soon came critical days in which the new faith was to be put to the test. Following the tragedy of Münster in 1535, the Brethren in Moravia soon felt the reaction, although they had absolutely no connection with Münster. Strict mandates of Ferdinand I compelled the nobles who had been tolerant toward the Anabaptists to drive the Brethren from their lands. It is from this period for instance that the moving letter of Jakob Hutter comes, which begins *"Nun ligen wir hier auf der heiden unter freiem Himmel,"* which has often been reprinted (cf. *Geschicht–Buch*, p. 110 f.). The Philippites were driven away just like the Hutterites. Indeed the Abbess of Maria Saal was one of the first to apply radical and merciless methods in driving the brotherhood away. In contrast with the Hutterites, who suffered their hard lot as a united group and consequently soon were able to return to their former places of abode, Philip Plener soon left his people, according to the report in the *Geschicht–Buch*, so that the group now became leaderless.[2] Some of them thereupon united with the Hutterites, while others remained hidden somewhere, for we know that Riedemann visited a small group of them in Moravia in 1537. Most of them, however, attempted to emigrate in small groups to South Germany, as Plener himself did, reaching Württemberg, an apparently more tolerant country. The route led upwards along the Danube by way of Passau and through Bavaria. The authorities, however, had expected such a "flight" and had issued strict orders to guard this route along the Danube. Consequently in the same year, 1535, a large number of Philippite Brethren were captured at Passau. A period of suffering and misery had begun. Many were to die in the dungeons of the castle of Passau. Many recanted sooner or later in order to finally have freedom, and most of them were pitifully tortured and persecuted. There are documentary reports of these severe persecutions and Wolkan (*Die Lieder der Wiedertäufer*, 1903), as well as Wiswedel (*Bilder und Führergestalten*, Vol. III, 1930), have given us touching examples, extracts from the archives which testify again and again to the living convictions and faith which characterized all the groups of Anabaptists. In these dungeons at Passau the first form of the well–known hymnal, the *Ausbund*, was composed, as Rudolph Wolkan proved for the first time. We hardly know what happened after this to the rest of the Philippite Brethren. Most of them were no doubt scattered far and wide and were gradually absorbed in the more quiet stream of the official Reformation movement, in spite of their original enthusiasm. A number of those with stronger faith united with the "Swiss Brethren" in South Germany.

---

2 Apparently this report is partial, since it is probable that Plener moved to Germany with a small group. Nowhere in the later court records of trials do we meet any real complaint about Plener's conduct. It is certain, however, that in any case a large group remained alone.

Concerning the true Soldier of Christ

Among the Philippite Brethren in prison in Passau there was a man called Hans Haffner of Riblingen, near Schwäbisch Hall (Grafschaft Hohenlohe, Württemberg). In the report of his trial we learn that he had been an Anabaptist for two years, that is since 1533, had been baptized at Auspitz, and had been driven from that place six weeks earlier by the King. Haffner was forced to testify by means of torture, and admitted that a "Bishop" (*Vorsteher*) by the name of Michael Schneider had fled with them.[3] In the second part of the *Ausbund*, p. 98, there is a hymn which was the joint production of fourteen prisoners. The eleventh stanza of this hymn is signed H. H., which Wolkan quite rightly assigns to Hans Haffner. He lay in prison in Passau until about 1540–41, yet he finally recanted, together with his wife Angella, or Agnes, whereupon both were released. According to the archives he had supposedly been married to Agnes for forty years (?) and would likely have been an elderly man.[4] We later hear very little more about him.

But now an extraordinarily interesting tract by this scarcely known brother Hans Haffner has been found in a Hutterite manuscript of the year 1570. The tract is entitled *Von einem wahrhaften Ritter Christi*. This discovery is remarkable since the Hutterites and Philippites supposedly had no fellowship after 1533 and since the *Geschicht–Buch*, as well as all the other manuscripts, scarcely has a word to say about this "foreign" group. Furthermore, the tract is quite foreign to the Hutterite viewpoint and in its basic teaching frequently quite different, so that it cannot possibly be Hutterite in its thought and faith. Nevertheless it is to be found in the codex[5] and is even written with special care (fol. 59–72), wherefore it must have been in some way handed down in the Hutterite brotherhood from about the period 1533–35. This is quite remarkable in view of the great differences in teaching between it and the Hutterite writings.

What makes the writing especially valuable and interesting is the fact that it is really the only dogmatic writing which we have out of the circle of the Philippite Brethren which has yet come to light.[6] It is true that the hymns of the Passau prisoners, the *Ausbund*, on the whole are likewise of doctrinal character, especially those which later became authoritative for the Swiss Brethren. The archives at Passau also contain valuable documents of a doctrinal character, but such an independent treatise as the Haffner booklet is invaluable. It is a document of the first rank all the more since it apparently

---

3 On him cf. Wolkan, *Die Lieder der Wiedertäufer* (Berlin, 1903), p. 36. He is not named in the Chronicles, very likely because he was a *Vorsteher* of the Phillippites.

4 I doubt these reports. Very likely what was meant was that he had married his wife at the age of forty years.

5 This codex which was previously in the library of the Cathedral Chapter at Pressburg as number 235 is now in private hands in Austria. Beck described it as *Codex I* in his work. In many respects it agrees with *Codex Artloff* in Gran, III, 128. It is very well preserved and beautifully written.

6 Probably the reason why it was not noticed earlier was that the manuscripts in Pressburg were very difficult to reach and that the name Haffner appears nowhere else except in the hitherto scarcely used Passau archives. Beck possibly was aware of the connection, but Wolkan and Wiswendel were not acquainted with the Pressburg manuscript and its rare contents.

goes back to the more peaceful time before the persecution. Finally it should be noted that this writing furnishes us with a testimony of great religious power and depth, a treatise which would have been worthy of any one of the better known leaders. For this reason a more thorough-going presentation and evaluation is quite in order. Our historic understanding of the age and its tendencies may thereby be advanced. At any rate doctrinal treatises of the Anabaptists do not fill our archives, and up to the present those that do exist have scarcely been examined.

The title of the booklet is: *Von einem wahrhaften Ritter Christi, und womit er gewappnet muss sein, damit er überwinden möge die Welt, das Fleisch und den Teufel.* The title refers to the metaphor in Ephesians 6:10 f.; this metaphor runs throughout the entire book. The four weapons are nothing else than faith, love, hope, and in the fourth place and in particular, resignation (*Gelassenheit*). The motive which led the author to write is stated in the preface to the reader in the following words:

> Since there is so much hypocrisy in the world and each one desires to be the most pious and the most holy and since therefrom arise envy, jealousy, dispute, division [think of 1533!], therefore I desire to show how the true disciples of Christ should be. Let us therefore hear what belongs to a genuine soldier of Christ and of what character he ought to be, or wherewith he must fight.

"A genuine soldier of Christ must have true resignation, and must mortify his own life" (Luke 9:23 & 57). In this expression the basic conception of the booklet is expressed, for almost the entire content concentrates itself about this thought of true "resignation," which is a conception taken from the old German mystics, a conception of inner clarity and peace (*Abgeklärtheit*) and victory over "the world, flesh, and the devil." Everything else is only further explanation and exposition of this concept of resignation, or as it is once called, this "holy, reasonable, living sacrifice." A new birth which changes the sense of the entire man is necessary (Rom. 2), but to this new humanity belong the four things already mentioned—faith, love, hope and resignation—whereby these things condition each other and no one of them can exist without the other. We observe thereby that it is the old Pauline conception which is here enlarged by means of the concept of resignation. We note also that this "resignation," which seems to have been the primary experience of the Anabaptist brotherhood, further explains and clarifies the three other fundamental pillars of all faith. Resignation is "the true discipline and test" (of faith), namely "that we must let ourselves be despised, persecuted and killed." Even love is viewed from this point of view as in the last analysis only a sort of resignation, and there is no question but that all the Anabaptist circles take this position which emphasizes so strongly the ascetic attitude. Truly, sufferings are unavoidable and have a deep meaning, they are the ultimate touchstone of faith, but they are nevertheless not the real and ultimate meaning of life, are not its characteristic mark or positive essence. Anabaptism also possesses the great teaching "of true love" (*Von der wahren Liebe*) as Hans Denck, for instance, expressed it and as it has remained in living form down to the present time.

Another very fine and thorough Anabaptist conception which is common to all Anabaptist groups is the constantly recurring thought: "The world gladly accepts Christ as a gift, but does not know Him as a suffering Christ." ("*Es nimmt die Welt Christum wohl gerne an als ein Geschenk, aber leidender Weise kennt sie ihn nicht.*") This thought expresses briefly and succinctly what Thomas Müntzer had already expressed in his polemic against Luther, namely that "the bitter Christ must precede the sweet Christ" ("*der bittere Christus dem süssen Christus*"), or what Pilgram Marpeck later formulated against Schwenckfeld: "The crown of thorns precedes the halo of glory" ("*die Dornenkrone steht vor dem Glorien-schein*").[7] And is not the well-known hymn by Ludwig Haetzer,[8] "*Ei spricht die Welt, es ist nicht not, dass ich mit Christo leide...*" filled with the same thought, this rejection of a justification by faith alone which too often has made Lutheranism a very convenient escape from reality? Furthermore, this easy-going conception was to be found not only with Luther, but also with many of the most pious Christians, especially with all those for whom the mystical phase of faith, what one might call the rapturous experience, was more prominent than the will to follow Christ in what were often burdensome and difficult steps in life. Following Christ "always requires in contrast to such a rapture, the already mentioned resignation: when we truly realize the love of God we will be ready to give up for love's sake even what God has given us" (Haffner). The mystics of the Middle Ages, it is true, did not understand resignation exactly in this sense, but it seemed as though this very concept—that of conscious surrender and giving up what was really dear and valuable to one—formed the center of Haffner's teaching, or in other words, that of the Philippite Brethren.

And now the author proceeds to discuss the four weapons in detail. First he deals with faith. What the brother has to say to us on this point is indeed not very deep; in Hutterite writings one frequently finds much more thoroughgoing discussions. Notice here also how important the true Anabaptist's activism is in the concept of faith. According to Haffner, as little as living water remains hidden in the earth, so little will faith remain without works. Where there are no works there is no faith, but rather a fancy (*Wahn*). Neither singing nor talking will help, but only true faith, faith which is true "only when it works through love." Here it is necessary to emphasize that the

---

7 Loserth's edition of Marpeck's *Verantwortung*, p. 160, and passim.
8 The hymn according to the Hutterite *Lieder*, p. 29, and the manuscripts, is ascribed to Leonard Schiemer instead of Haetzer.

section of faith contains many citations from the Gospel of John. "He that believes on Christ will also do the works which He did and greater (John 14:12), for Christ is the natural Son of God…but we are only adopted and chosen children, wherefore we also will constantly have to contend with the flesh as long as we live here." (It is this therefore which in this connection means "Do greater works.")

Now such faith comes through love "for it is impossible that those who truly have faith, which is given to them through Christ, should not love God in return, yea, not only God, but also their neighbor because of the commandment of God." He who desires to have fellowship with Christ must therefore walk in light, that is, he must love his neighbor, and not with words, but in deed. But this deed—love—is however rather that of the epistle to the Ephesians than that of the epistles of John. Eph. 4:28: "Work with his hands, that he may give to him that needeth." This characteristically anticapitalistic, craftsman's and common man's conception is emphasized very strongly. The author attacks "deception, profiteering and finance" (*Trug, Wucher, und Finanz*), fine living and luxury.

> Yea, before the rich man will help his brother and his children he will spend his wealth in luxurious living which would be sufficient to support three or four households, and ye say the love of God is in you? Christ says, invite the poor (Luke 6), lend to the poor, and give to those who cannot give it back again.

Love is therefore chiefly the giving of alms, not the ultimate sharing with the brother of everything material as well as spiritual. Love is primarily a "command" of God, of course a command which is based upon freedom and not compulsion, "for perfect love casts out all fear" (I Cor. 13). In spite of everything, the impression one receives from this section still is: love is not the basic primary conception in this booklet, but it also is only a phase of "resignation," or the true following of a command, in short, an ascetic attitude.

In the third section, "hope" is interpreted as follows: hope means much the same as patience and long-suffering in the bearing of the cross. When we suffer the cross and persecution and can take up the cross by patience, then first may we glory in the Lord. "So true resignation consists of these three things, faith, hope, and love."

Here follows the fourth section, namely resignation, by which the Christian is first recognized, as the tree is recognized by its fruit. Therefore the blind world will here look up and come to know itself and learn and recognize the true disciples of Christ, for the hypocrite cannot long stand…. Peter says (I Peter 4), "When we suffer we cease to sin." Therefore the cross alone is the true touchstone of the

Concerning the true Soldier of Christ

Christian. But he dare not carry the cross because of his own guilt, but for the sake of mercy toward others, just as Christ bore it, and we do not want to be hypocrites like the world, but do away with the world's works. As the Lord says: "The world hates me because I show them that their works are evil."

It should be noticed in this passage that there is a hidden theodicy, namely one which is designed to free the concept of cross-bearing (quite otherwise than with Paul) of all sense of inherited sin and guilt. "Now let us hear what resignation is...." Unfortunately the manuscript is damaged just at this point and the meaning is difficult to decipher. It is something as follows. Resignation is nothing but forsaking for God's name's sake everything which is of the creature, and to let oneself be led by the hand of God. "Such resignation is called by Christ in Luke a hate, where he says: 'He who does not hate his father and mother and renounce everything which he has is not worthy of me.'"

But resignation is nothing else than a true mortification of our flesh and a true new birth. But since the whole world wants to have Christ but misses in its desire the true goal, in this that it only wants to have Christ as a gift, that is it wants to have Him as its gracious and only Mediator, which is of course right,... but errs nevertheless in this, that it accepts Him only as a gift and not also as a suffering Christ (*nicht auch in leidender Weis*), for a Christian must not accept Christ in one thing and reject Him in another, for the very one who says: "All those who are heavy laden come to me and I will refresh you"; the same one says also: "Whoever will not forsake father and mother the same cannot be my disciple." Therefore whoever loves truth must have Christ as sincerely in one way as in the other. For whoever wishes to follow Christ must follow Him "in the suffering manner." For this reason it is only a fancy and a matter of delusion when one says [like Luther or Schwenckfeld]: "We believe that Christ has redeemed us, but do not wish to live like He lived."

Therefore, we now wish to let this be enough of the first part, in which we have pictured Christ as a gift, and now want to present the other part, namely resignation, which consists of two sections, the first the overcoming of ourselves, and the second of the enduring of persecution by others.

Now the author presents a more detailed description of this sort of resignation. For instance, right at the beginning he refers to the saying of Christ about the right and the left cheek, but states that this does not mean "that we should admit that the ungodly tyrants are right in their wickedness," but it only means "that we should not strive with them in pride and accuse them, but that we should come to them in the most simple and humble manner, as becomes a Christian." Therefore a new birth must first be experienced, and the Christian must be weaned from his mother's breast (Isaiah 28), that is from the characteristic of human nature. In the second place we must be able to forsake wife and children, father and mother, lands and property, yea, our own life and everything which God has given us, as has been stated above.

Here observe, thou blind world, thou who desirest to serve God *and* the world, that thou canst not serve two masters, yea, so great a blindness does God permit to fall upon this godless world that all those who kill the devout will think that they do God a service thereby. Oh, woe, for such a great blindness which God sends upon the world.

Therefore, dear Christian, do not be disappointed that the world hates you, but only continue, be patient, wait on the great God with joy, for blessed are those who weep here, for it is only for a short time. When He comes who will not excuse, the time will be full of joy which will be nevermore taken from you. The Lord grant us His spirit to fight unto the end. Amen.

It is an unusually strong appeal to suffering that we meet here in this booklet, at the same time a remarkable and not usual change in concept: love, resignation; but resignation is mortification of the flesh, that is, the surrender of everything that is dear to one. These are thoughts which I have never met in any dogmatic writing of the Anabaptists and which without doubt represent the individuality, the difference, and at the same time also no doubt the shortcomings of this tract, for there is apparently lacking in it an ultimate meaning to be put into such a way of life, at least in so far as suffering is viewed only as the negative, the inevitable phase of following Christ, but not as the positive, the power which transforms. Concerning this power really very little is said, although it is just such power which the "four weapons of the soldier of Christ" should of necessity furnish. This becomes particularly clear when one attempts a comparison with similar passages in the writings of the Hutterian Brethren, especially with what they say about love and resignation. It is true that in the Hutterian writings these two conceptions are frequently brought together in very close connection, but they lead consequently to altogether different demands and admonitions. Ulrich Stadler (*ca.* 1537–40), for example, discusses this point in detail in his excellent writing, *Concerning Fellowship Between the Saints Here and Yonder*.[9]

---

9 *Von der Gemeinschaft der Heiligen heir und dort*, printed by Wolkan in his book, *Die Hutterer* (1918), 153–61, who takes it from a manuscript in Vienna. In Stadler's writing, which was much read, both resignation and love find their fruition not in asceticism but in the true fellowship (*Gemeinschaft*), which as is well known was a communism of goods (*Gütergemeinschaft*); that is, it was more than a simple communism of love (*Liebeskommunismus*).

All gifts and goods which God gives to His own are to be had in common with all the children of God, and for this too, sincere, resigned, willing hearts in Christ are necessary who truly believe and trust God and are completely surrendered in Christ.... Also, we are criticized and told that nowhere can one read that it is a command of the Lord to have goods in common and to appoint ministers and stewards over everything. The answer is, "It is true resignation to consecrate oneself with his lands and goods to the service of the saints, and it is the manifestation of love; yea, we learn in Christ to lose ourselves in the service of the saints, to be and become poor if only others may be served." Further, "to hand over all lands and goods and cast them away from oneself, that is a high degree of resignation and voluntary consecration to the Lord and His people through the Lord." In conclusion, "each brother shall serve another, shall live and work, but not to himself...."

Riedemann already sings in his first and little-known *Gmunden Rechenschaft* (1529–32) the praise of the love (*Das Hohe Lied der Liebe*) which leads to this fellowship (*Gemeinschaft*).

The love of Christ and our love are manifested in bread and wine. For like as many kernels are ground together by the mill stone and formed into a meal and finally made into bread, so that no one recognizes in the bread which part of the meal composes this or that kernel, so also we many men, if we are truly ground together by the noble millstone of Divine power, believe His word and yield ourselves to the cross of Christ, we also shall be formed together through the bond of love to one body of which Christ is the head.... Those, therefore, who have truly surrendered themselves to the Lord shall become one in heart and spirit, just as the kernels are made one in the bread....

That not only Riedemann, but also Walpot[10] and all other Brethren who composed dogmatic writings, viewed love in the manner of I Cor. 13 and not in that of Eph. 4:28, need only be mentioned here in passing. Finally, Andreas Ehrenpreis in 1652 repeats once more all the arguments of Hutterianism for the union of resignation, love and fellowship (*Gelassenheit, Liebe, Gemeinschaft*) in his famous printed epistle (*Sendbrief...brüderliche Gemeinschaft, das höchste Gebot der Liebe betreffend*).

Where the love of Christ is not able to accomplish as much toward one's neighbor as to have fellowship in temporal needs, there the blood of Christ cannot cleanse from sin.... Whoever does not have this service-love, and loves temporal goods more than his

---

10 Peter Walpot writes in 1547 (*Geschicht-Buch*, p. 225): "Love does not seek her own—therefore she seeks indeed only to have fellowship. For love is a bond of perfection where she dwells, she does not work a partial but a complete and entire fellowship (*Gemeinschaft*)."

comrade in faith, how can anyone be willing to say that in such a one even a speck or drop of Divine love is present?

It is only after one makes such a comparison that one is able to properly locate the Haffner tract in the spiritual history of Anabaptism. For it is certain without a doubt that the Anabaptist movement as a whole lived from its great proclamation of the great love. Rudolf Wolkan has demonstrated this so masterfully from their hymns in his two books, *Lieder der Wiedertäufer* (1903), and *Die Hutterer* (1918), and has illustrated it with so many splendid characteristics out of his examples that it will no doubt suffice merely to refer to his work here. But how manifold nevertheless this conception of love has been understood. The love which Hans Haffner understood (and with him possibly the other Philippite Brethren?) is thoroughly different from the love which, for example, the well-known Hänsel Schmidt, or Raiffer (executed at Aachen, 1558), hymns:

Die Liebe wird auch erkennet, bei Wort, Leben und Tat,
Der sich Gott ganz ergibet, Christi Geist in ihm hat,
Der hat die Gemeinschaft allezeit, wie Christus hat bewiesen,
Er als ein Glied am Leib.

Liebe Brüder und Schwestern, ihr Kinder Gottes rein,
Lasst uns nach der Liebe allzeit streben fein,
Dass wir in ihr, und sie in uns allzeit erfunden werde,
Sonst ist alles umsonst.[11]

Die wahre Gottesliebe, die da Gott selber ist,
Tut das Werk in ihm üben, jetzt und zu aller Frist.
Dass er mit allen Frommen schon das Zeitliche mag verlassen,
Und in Gemeinschaft stehen.[12]

The love which is meant here does not soon exhaust itself with the giving of alms and it is not fulfilled only because God "commanded" it. The love which is here sung is much more the constructive principle of the entire life, which drives and compels the lover to fellowship (*Gemeinschaft*). It is much more than a single deed, since it is really the basic principle and foundation of all life and work. In a certain sense "resignation" takes the place of this "love" in our tract, but even here one can see the characteristic differences of teaching (and therefore also of life) of the two groups. With Haffner resignation means primarily only to assume something unpleasant and difficult, the mortification

---

11 *Lieder der Hutterischen Brüder* (Scottdale, 1914). 564–67. The entire forth hymn has love as its theme.
12 *Lieder*, 577.

of the flesh, as for example to forsake father and mother, while according to the Hutterite conception this is indeed a part of resignation, but naturally does not exhaust the concept. For this is (for example with Ulrich Stadler) the "free and willing heart" that has renounced the world, sin, and the devil, and the striving and struggles to attain perfection through service, that is the fellowship of the saints.

We may perhaps summarize as follows. With Haffner (whether this is true of all the Philippite Brethren cannot be asserted) the merely negative ascetic element in love and resignation is dominant in that the redemptive value of mortification of the flesh is emphasized. With the Hutterian Brethren on the contrary, who quite generally have experienced the love–magnifying power of communism of goods, the more positive content of this basic concept comes to the foreground in all their confessions. The meaning of these basic conceptions is positive, while the renunciation phase is only the unavoidable obverse of fellowship. The inner life of the Hutterian Brethren was no doubt able to last so long primarily because of this, and it is not impossible that on the other hand the essential weakness of the Philippite Brethren lay in the dominance of the ascetic teaching. For even if during certain brief and difficult periods in history suffering overshadows all the constructive life, the suffering attitude is nevertheless ultimately overcome and outshone by the love and fellowship which is liberative and which alone produces life. This fact is of course not contraried by the deep formulation which our tract presents of the two types of conception of God, namely that it is not sufficient to accept God, only as a gift in His grace, but that one should much more, yea, above everything approach Him "in the way of suffering" (*leidenderweis*). The Hutterites, as well as all other Anabaptists, held similar views on this point.

It is therefore clear according to our analysis, and will no longer seem remarkable, that the Hutterites could not understand this rather classic writing by Haffner. This is probably also the reason that it has been handed down in only one manuscript. Nevertheless the little booklet on the whole presents us with an excellent picture of Anabaptist thinking and living, especially out of the earlier period of the movement which has not yet been clearly understood. For this reason it is a considerable enrichment of our knowledge of the dogmatic literature of the Philippite group.

SOURCE: *Mennonite Quarterly Review*, V (1931), pp. 87–99.

LEONHARD SCHIEMER AND HANS SCHLAFFER TWO TYROLEAN ANABAPTIST MARTYR–APOSTLES OF 1528

Leonhard Schiemer

Leonhard Schiemer of Vöklabruck, Upper Austria, who died a martyr on January 14, 1528, at Rattenberg on the Inn, Tyrol, has only recently been recognized as an outstanding leader of the very beginning of the Anabaptist movement. He belongs to the line of South German Anabaptists roughly characterized by the names Hans Denck and Hans Hut, to which group also Hans Schlaffer, Ambrosius Spittelmaier, and Hans Nadler belonged. They all represent a stronger spiritualistic emphasis in their Christian faith than the Swiss Brethren. The "outer word" alone does not suffice for a true understanding, Schiemer would say; rather the true light of the Holy Spirit is needed which shines in our heart.

Of his life some details are known from his *Bekanntnus*,[1] which he submitted to his judge in January 1528. He was brought up at Vöklabruck and Vienna by God–fearing parents, and desired to enter the Catholic priesthood. But when he found little godliness in the life and teaching of the priests he joined the Barefoot Friars (Franciscans), noted for their piety. But again he found nothing but strife and hypocrisy; finally, having tried this life for six years he fled from the monastery at Judenburg, Styria. A kind citizen of that city gave him some clothing and a guilder for his needs. Now he began to wander about: first he went to Nürnberg where he learned the tailor's trade (and probably met some of the leading men of the Radical Reformation). Thence he went to Nikolsburg, Moravia, to hear Hubmaier's teachings—having vigorously opposed them in his former days. From here he turned to Vienna to learn more about true Christianity from Hans Hut. He related that the assembly "in the Kärntnerstrasse" was greatly embarrassed when he entered, suspecting him to be a spy. After two days of talks, however, he accepted believers' baptism from Oswald Glaidt in the spring of 1527. From Vienna he went to Steyr, the industrial city in Upper Austria, known for its

---

1 Lydia Müller, ed., *Glaubenszeugnisse oberdeutscher Taufgesinnter* (Leipzig, 1938) (Hereafter cited as *Glaubenszeugnisse*, I), 80f.

great readiness to receive radical ideas. Here he stayed for a time, earning his living by his trade and baptizing many converts to the new faith. The brotherhood made him a preacher (*Leermeister*) and soon sent him into many lands (Salzburg, Bavaria, Tyrol) to spread his new message. Although he was well aware that several monasteries in Austria were trying to apprehend him as a renegade monk he obeyed his call without hesitation, and was caught in the city of Rattenberg on the Inn (in the documents always written Rotenburg), November 25, 1527, scarcely six months after his conversion. In Rattenberg, he claims, he had worked only one day, and yet he signs one of his epistles to the local brotherhood as "your unworthy bishop." We cannot completely reconstruct the story of that Rattenberg Anabaptist congregation, but there is little doubt that Schiemer's influence was tremendous, in spite of the fact that he was in prison until his execution by the sword seven weeks later, January 14, 1528. The district judge Bartholomeus Angst was most lenient to his prisoner,[2] allowing brethren to go in and out and to give him paper and ink to write as much as he wanted. Thus these seven weeks are among the most fruitful ones in the long and bitter story of South German and Tyrolean Anabaptism. His writings were soon collected in a pamphlet or booklet presumably for the local congregation, but they found wide distribution afterwards in Moravia, Germany, and Switzerland. The Hutterites as well as Pilgram Marpeck and his group were greatly indebted to this outstanding Anabaptist teacher.

At one time Schiemer tried to escape[3] but was caught again. Now his imprisonment was made harder. Torture and hunger made him miserable in the flesh, and the dread of death made him shudder. But he gained new strength by the thought, "If I did not place all my confidence in the Lord, I would fall; but the Lord is my comfort and my confidence; he forsakes none who trusts Him."[4] The government in Innsbruck urged Judge Angst to greater rigor and requested the speeding up of the case. Schiemer was condemned to death by fire in accordance with the mandates of King Ferdinand, but the sentence was moderated to beheading and burning the corpse afterwards. "After him about seventy others testified to their faith in Rattenberg," writes the *Hutterite Chronicle*, thus demonstrating the amazing spiritual vitality of this "Schiemer congregation."

The writings produced by Schiemer in prison are found in numerous Hutterite codices (best perhaps in the oldest one extant, 1566, now at a Bruderhof in Montana) and, surprisingly, also in the *Kunstbuch* of 1562, which originated in the Marpeck group. The numbering and counting of these writings is not easy because the items are sometimes written together and sometimes separated, sometimes considered as "epistles" and sometimes

---

2 *Geschichts–Bücher*, 61.
3 *Glaubenszeugnisse*, I, 76.
4 *Loc. cit.*

taken as tracts or sermons. Their tremendous appeal and effectiveness in the shaping of the Anabaptist genius and tradition cannot be doubted. Fortunately, the majority of Schiemer's writings have been published by Lydia Müller;[5] others will follow in *Glaubenszeugnisse*, II[6] and in the forthcoming edition of the *Kunstbuch*. The list is roughly as follows:

1. *Eine hübsche Erklärung der 12 Artikel des christlichen Glaubens*, contained in an epistle to the church in Rattenberg (*Glaubenszeugnisse*, I, 44–58; *Kunstbuch*, No. 10). The oldest codex of the Hutterites (1566) has this item too, supplemented by two pages containing a remarkable diagram of four circles: /the Will of God/Adam/Creature/Christ/, plus accompanying text (not yet published).

2. *Was die Gnad sey. Eine Vorred*, and a tract "Concerning Threefold Grace." The term *Vorred* means with the Hutterites always "sermon" but at this place it might also mean "introduction" (*Glaubenszeugnisse*, I, 58–71; *Kunstbuch*, No. 9). This is a real gem of Anabaptist writing. In the article concerning "The Second Grace" there is a lengthy insertion called *Auslegung des Vater Unser*, a paraphrase of the Lord's Prayer (to be reissued parallel with a similar piece by Hans Langenmantel in *Glaubenszeugnisse*, II). In the *Kunstbuch* this item runs over without interruption into item

3. *Vom Fläschl* (*Glaubenszeugnisse*, I, 72–74), concluded by a lengthy epistle to the congregation of Rattenberg, dated December 4, 1527 (*Glaubenszeugnisse*, I, 74–77). The *Kunstbuch* has *Fläschl* and epistle all under No. 9. It might be said that Schiemer was never more profound and close to the spirit of the great medieval mystics than in this item. The ensuing epistle is more personal; the writer suddenly interrupts his "*Lehr*" (instruction) by being overwhelmed by his predicament and now wants to pour out his troubled mind to his brethren.

4. *Von der Tauff im Neuen Testament*, also called *Von dreyerlei Tauff* (namely, by the Spirit, by water, and by blood, very much a counter piece to the *Dreyerlei Gnad* above, No. 2; *Glaubenszeugnisse*, I, 77–78). The *Kunstbuch* includes this item in No. 10 (see above, item 1) as a sort of appendix. The Hutterite codices call this item "the third epistle by Leonhard Schiemer," apparently meaning the third item which Schiemer sent from prison. The term "epistle" is not quite correct as this item does not contain personal communications. The *Kunstbuch* presents these four items as 9 and 10.

5. *Trostbrief an einen schwachen Bruder*. In many Hutterite codices but not in the *Kunstbuch* or in Müller.

---

5 See footnote 1.
6 Lydia Müller and Robert Friedmann, eds., *Glaubenszeugnisse oberdeutscher Taufgesinnter*, II (to be published at Gütersloh in 1962) hereafter cited as *Glaubenszeugnisse*, II).

6. *Ein wahrhaft kurz Evangelium, heut der Welt zu predigen*, found only in the *Kunstbuch*, to be published in *Glaubenszeugnisse*, II, a rather short piece, a kind of sermonette.

7. *Ein Bekanntnus vor dem Richter zu Rotenburg* (most likely January 1528) (*Glaubenszeugnisse*, I, 80–81; not in the *Kunstbuch*), a brief biography with a concluding apologetic paragraph.

These are the known items of Schiemer's work, all produced for his Rattenberg brethren during the seven weeks of his imprisonment. The writer of this article, however, is inclined to ascribe to Schiemer also a number of anonymous items found in Hutterite codices, usually following Schiemer's "epistles" and apparently serving a similar purpose—organizing the Rattenberg church and giving it guidance, direction, and order.

8. *Ordnung der Gemein, wie ein Christ leben soll*. In the *Hutterite Chronicle* (*Geschicht–Buch*,[7] 60–61), inserted by the writer of the Chronicle for 1529 without much argument taken most probably again from the afore–mentioned (hypothetical) booklet of Schiemer's writings.[8] It is a skeleton church discipline, a true model of Anabaptist thought concerning ordering life in the congregation, much shorter than the Schleitheim articles of the same year (1527), only laying the groundwork for all future attempts in the same direction. Most likely Schiemer drew it up tentatively in order that the Brethren of the incipient congregation might have guidance after his death.

9. 9 to 12 are anonymous tracts of similar purpose. One is a catechism; the rest contain more or less moral instruction.[9] The *Lieder der Hutterischen Brüder* (1914, p. 19) assigns all these items expressly to Schiemer.

Besides these writings several hymns are likewise ascribed to Schiemer:

1. "Dein heilig statt hond sie zerstört" (*Glaubenszeugnisse*, I, 82–83, after Beck, 58–59, note);

2. "Wir bitten dich, ewiger Gott, neig zu uns deine Ohren" (*Ausbund*, No. 31); here the author is named Leonard Schöner whence the *Martyr's Mirror* may have taken the name; also in *Lieder der Hutterischen Brüder*, 28–29;

---

7 *Geschicht–Buch*.

8 *MQR* published an English translation of the fuller test as found in the codices: *MQR*, XXIX (1955), 162–66.

9 No. 9 *Von der Prob des Geistes*; No. 10: *Von der Kinderzucht*; No. 11: *Unterricht eines wohlgefälligen Lebens*; No. 12: *Von den bösen Weibern*, a strange warning refering to famous O. T. cases beginning with Eve, and showing the tragic consequences of trusting seducing women. At first the writer was reluctant to ascribe the tract to Schiemer, but his *Bekanntnus* (*Glaubenszeugnesse*, I, 81) refers expressly to accusations of the Tyrolean authorities that the Anabaptists had too much to do with evil women.

3. "Sollstu bei Gott dein wohnung han" (*Lieder der Hutterischen Brüder*, 28–29). According to an old codex in Esztergom this hymn is said to have been composed by Schiemer, but according to Wolkan[10] it was written by Ludwig Haetzer;
4. "Wie köstlich ist der Heilgen Tod" (Wiswedel,[11] 185, who took it from the Beck collection in Brno, file No. 45). No further reference is found.

Schiemer's Theology and Teaching

One might easily agree with Wiswedel's statement[12] that both Schiemer and Schlaffer had been strongly influenced by medieval Mysticism (while being priest or monk), in the main by Tauler and the *Deutsche Theologie* just as Hans Denck and some of the early Spiritualists had been. Christ must be born in us, we must suffer with Him, be crucified and be buried with Him, also descend into Hades with Him, in order to be raised with Him.[13] Schiemer prefers the translation "The Word became flesh and dwelleth *in* us," rather than "among" us, as we likewise believe "in" God not "on" God (German: *an Gott*), etc.[14] Justification without sanctification loses its deeper meaning,[15] countering Paul's thesis by references to Matt. 25. In such an outlook naturally the old problem of "the inner and outer Word" becomes a most urgent issue, although this emphasis on the inwardness of God's Word never leads to a quietistic enjoyment but rather to an active witnessing and following of Christ.[16]

This becomes perhaps most impressive in the beautiful small tract *Vom Fläschl*: "A reply to those who say we drink something from a small flask, of which the devil himself does not know what it contains." Very well, says Schiemer, let it be called a flask. But the drink in it is nothing but a contrite, crushed, and sad heart, pounded by the mortar of the cross. The grapes in it grew in God's vineyard and were pressed under the press of tribulation. From such a flask Christ drank on the cross. And as a flask is narrow at the top but wide at the bottom, thus is also the way of salvation: once a man has overcome all agony and tribulation the flask gets wide and he receives God's comfort and consolation.

Schiemer teaches three kinds of grace: the first is the Word given us by the Father as a divine light (the law). This divine light in man shows him what sin is (*anzeigen was sind sey oder nit*). Although this light is the same in all

---
10 Rudolf Wolkan, *Die Lieder der Wiedertäufer* (Berlin, 1903), 12.
11 Wilhelm Wiswendel, *Bilder und Führergestalten aus dem Täufertum*, Vol. II (Kassel, 1930) (hearafter cited as *Bilder*, II).
12 *Bilder*, II, 184.
13 *Glaubenszeugnisse*, I, 53.
14 *Ibid.*, p. 61.
15 *Ibid.*, p. 78.
16 Cf. Wiswedel, "The Inner and the Outer Word," *MQR*, XXVI (1952), 171–91.

men, not all accept it in the same way.[17] The second grace is Christ or divine righteousness (*Gerechtigkeit*). The first light is our taskmaster (*Zuchmeister*), preparing us for the other light which is Christ (apparently Christ *in us*). But in order to see this second light one needs to go through the "furnace of suffering" (Luther: *Feuer der Trübsal*, Eccl. 2:5, also I Peter 1:7, "gold tested by fire"; the Anabaptists changed the word into *Schmelzofen der Gelassenheit*), *denn der ungecreutzigte christ ist wie ein unprobiertes erz*.[18] In other words, an untested faith is no faith at all. Thus the second grace might also be called "the cross." The third grace, finally, is a grace of joy and rejoicing. It is the promise of the Holy Spirit and His glory. While the life of the "world" begins merrily but ends sadly, the life of a God–fearing man has a sad beginning but eventually the Holy Spirit comes to him and anoints him with the oil of unspeakable joy.

As there are three kinds of grace there are also three kinds of baptism, well known from the Scriptures themselves: the first baptism is with the Holy Spirit, the second is with water, and the third with blood. Baptism with water is a confirmation of faith and an inner covenant with God. "When one has written a letter he seals it. But no one would seal a letter without knowing what it contains. Whoever baptizes a child acts like a man who seals an empty letter."[19]

It would be an attractive task to search for the spiritual roots of these teachings. Herbert Klassen in his study of Hut[20] strongly suggests that many a thought of Schiemer, Schlaffer, Ambrosius Spittelmaier, and others goes back to this dynamic and dedicated leader, as far as we are able to reconstruct his doctrines. This is most likely correct. But it is certainly also true that a great many of these ideas are derived from Schiemer's own spiritual experiences, condensed as they were into the unbelievably brief span of perhaps nine months. The wide use of his writings throughout the Anabaptist brotherhood, including Pilgram Marpeck, and the unique heroism of the Rattenberg congregation (seventy–two martyrs within a few years) give vivid testimony to the spiritual force of these tracts, suggesting that also the sixteenth century knew something of the charismatic and pneumatic experiences of the apostolic church.

II. Hans Schlaffer

Hans Schlaffer, like Leonhard Schiemer, had a short but highly significant career as an early Anabaptist preacher and leader in the Bavarian–Austrian area, and died a martyr at Schwatz, some five miles from Rattenberg in the

---

17 *Ibid.*, p. 63.
18 *Ibid.*, pp. 67, 68; the repetition of this idea is characteristic.
19 *Ibid.*, p. 79.
20 To be published in *MQR*, XXXIII (1959).

Tyrol, on February 4, 1528. The *Hutterite Chronicle*[21] calls him "a highly gifted man." His "Account" (*Verantwortung*) before the magistrate of Schwatz in 1527[22] states that he had entered the Catholic priesthood in 1511 and served in Upper Austria. With the coming of Luther he began to preach the pure Gospel but soon was forbidden to do so. In 1526 he resigned his priesthood, realizing that "it was the estate of a false prophet." For a time (1526–27) he stayed with the Protestant Lord Zelkin at his castle Weinberg near Freistadt, Upper Austria. It was either then or still earlier that he had come into contact with Anabaptists, most likely with Hans Hut. It is not known when or by whom he was baptized, but Grete Mecenseffy[23] shows how heavily the Anabaptist congregation of Freistadt leaned on Schlaffer, who followed more or less the line of Hut. In any case he left the area, beginning a period of wandering, the sequence of places being not quite clear. He visited Nikolsburg in 1527 where he heard the dispute between Hubmaier and Hut, which happened prior to Hut's coming to Upper Austria. He may have been converted to Hut's ideas on that occasion and returned temporarily to Freistadt, establishing an Anabaptist congregation there; but it is also possible that he was in Nikolsburg even before he came to Lord Zelkin. In any case Freistadt soon became an unsafe abode, and he then went to Bavaria. First he went to Augsburg where he met Jakob Wideman and again Hans Hut; he may have been present at the "Martyr Synod" of Augsburg. Next he went to Nürnberg where he met Hans Denck and Ludwig Haetzer in September 1527,[24] "two excellent, in God learned men"; finally he went to Regensburg where he met Oswald Glaidt and Wolfgang Brandhuber, two more of the then leading men in the growing Anabaptist movement.

From Regensburg he turned south to the Inn Valley of Tyrol, to Brixlegg and Rattenberg, where he had some relatives. But after a brief stay due to sickness he went on toward Hall on the Inn for the winter. On his way he attended a meeting of Anabaptists in the mining city of Schwatz on the Inn on December 5, 1527. There he was seized by the police and imprisoned in the near–by Frundsberg castle, together with the brother Linhard Frick (or, as the *Kunstbuch* calls him, Funck). He was brought before the magistrate and submitted a written *Verantwortung* which was sent to the provincial government in Innsbruck. His defense was very dignified: he had sought nothing evil but only divine truth; nothing was further from his mind than rebellion. Children, he contended, should not be baptized, for "they were the Lord's as long as they were in innocence, and they would not be damned." The Innsbruck government sent instructions to Judge S. Capeller for conducting the case. The statements of the prisoners would be sent to the authorities

---

21 *Geschicht–Buch*, 44 f.
22 *Glaubenszeugnisse*, I, 115–21.
23 Grete Mecenseffy, "Die herkunft des oberösterreichischen Täufertums," *Archiv für Reformations–geschichte*, XLVII (1956), 252–59.
24 Walter Fellmann, *Hans Denck, Religiöse Schriften* (Gütersloh, 1956), 18.

in Bavaria who also wanted to try these men. Orders were further given to convene the court with twelve jurymen to pass sentence on the two prisoners. At the same time a secret report should be made by the judge on the attitude of the jurymen, as it was known that some of them did not approve of death in such cases. Finally the death sentence was pronounced and Schlaffer and Frick were beheaded at Schwatz on February 4, 1528.

Schlaffer left nine writings, all well preserved in numerous Hutterite codices. His long prayer written in the night before the execution is also found in the *Kunstbuch* of 1561 as No. 12. Of these writings only one rather short piece was composed while Schlaffer was still free, most likely in Freistadt, for the local brotherhood; it is a sort of shortened paraphrase of Hut's *Vom Geheimnus der Tauff* (Mecenseffy). All the other writings were written in prison between Dec. 6, 1527, and Feb. 3, 1528, in slightly more than eight weeks. These are the writings:

1. *Kurzer Bericht eines christlichen Lebens* (also *Kurzer Bericht und Lehr eines rechten christlichen Lebens*); it is made up of the "Hut paraphrase" (*Glaubenszeugnisse*, I, 94–96) and two prayers (*ibid.*, 96–98).[25] Already in the first document we recognize Schlaffer's greatest potential: his profound gift of praying or communicating with his God.

2. *Ein einfältiger Unterricht zum Anfang eines gotseliges Lebens*, again introduced by a beautiful lengthy prayer (*Glaubenszeugnisse*, I, 84–94). This tract, written Dec. 19, 1527, likewise reveals clearly Schlaffer's dependence on Hut.[26]

3. *Kurze und einfältige Vermahnung von der Kindertauff, und wie derselbige nit mag beibracht werden aus Heiliger Schrifft*. It was written Jan. 2, 1528 (*Glaubenszeugnisse*, I, 98–105).

4. *Brief an einen schwachen Bruder, Antwort auf etliche Fragstück*, also Jan. 2, 1528 (*Glaubenszeugnisse*, I, 105–10).

5. *Von der Art und Gestalt Christi, was er geistlich und leiblich sey geformieret* (unpublished, found in Canadian Hutterite codices).

6. *Bekandtnus und Verantwortung dem Richter zu Schwatz schriftlich Uberantwortet*, no date (*Glaubenszeugnisse*, I, 110–15)

7. *Die andere Verantwortung: Antwort auf [fünf] Fragstück vor dem Richter* (*Glaubenszeugnisse*, I, 115–21). This account was apparently first given orally before the judge, and later written down by Schlaffer for his brethren.

8. *Ein Bericht seiner Verantwortung vor der Obrigkeit getan an seine Geschwistriget im Herren zugeschickt, Pfingstag vor Pauli Bekehrung*, January 25, 1528 (*Glaubenszeugnisse*, I, 121–25). This is another

---

25 *Geschichts–Bücher*, 651.
26 *Glaubenszeugnisse*, I, 85.

summary of Schlaffer's defense. He informed his brethren (perhaps the congregation of Schwatz) that the authorities in Innsbruck had falsified his written statement (No. 6), completely changing its meaning; for that reason he wanted to inform his brethren about what he had actually written. Thus we have three different documents (Nos. 6 to 8) in which Schlaffer gives account of the major ideas of South German Anabaptism as it had evolved at that time.

9. *Ein einfältig Gebet*, also called *Gebet, Bericht und öffentlich Bekanntnus, Hans Schlaffer Testament und eigen Bekanntnus gegen Gott*, written February 3, 1528, in the night before his execution. This is found in the *Kunstbuch* No. 12, and in many Hutterite codices.[27] In the typescript copy in the Goshen College Library this prayer covers eighteen pages; in a closely written Hutterite codex (1566) it covers eight leaves. This prayer is no doubt one of the most profound and moving documents in the entire German devotional literature. Like Augustine in his Confessions he talks to God at great length about his life and thoughts, strengthening his mind during the agonizing hours before his death. It is most likely here that Schlaffer's greatest power is to be found and also his greatest contribution to Anabaptist tradition.

Schlaffer composed also two hymns: "Ungnad begehr ich nit von dir," No. 32 in the *Ausbund*, and pp. 22–23 in *Lieder der Hutterischen Brüder*; the hymn was also circulated as a pamphlet in 1527, and reprinted in 1550 and 1551 in Nürnberg; "Herr Got, mein ewiger Vater" (with the acrostic "Hanns Schlaffer") in *Lieder der Hutterischen Brüder*, 21–22; it was written in the last hours of his life, either before or after the above prayer.

Schlaffer's Teachings

Schlaffer's main ideas were taken from Hans Hut, often to the point of verbatim borrowing. But this was nothing unusual in those days (compare Marpeck and Rothmann); what really mattered was the particular emphasis or slant given to the ideas. In all Schlaffer's writings we meet the same spiritualistic or pneumatic atmosphere as in those of Schiemer, Ambrosius Spittelmaier, Hans Nadler, and other men connected with Denck and Hut. "Even if Christ had died a hundred times, it would avail nothing if the spiritual Christ is not preached also."[28] "Who ever descends into Hades with Christ, that is *in* Christ, will also be led out of Hades by God."[29] Pilgram Marpeck some twenty years later liked to indulge in speculation of this kind in exactly the same way.

---

27 Also *Geschichts–Bücher*, 652, has a very inadequate version of the prayer.
28 *Bilder*, II, 197, quoted from a copy in the Beck collection, file 46, in Brno.
29 *Glaubenszeugnisse*, I, 96.

Schlaffer is aware that suffering marks the genuine Christian in the "world," and his writings abound in such thoughts. "All Scriptures speak of nothing but of the suffering of the elect, from Abel to the apostles; that is why the lamb has been killed ever since the beginning of the world."[30] "Who ever suffers in the flesh stops sinning."[31] And in the Account: "Here I stand as a lamb which does not open its mouth as it is being slaughtered, to which may Christ…grant me strength and help."[32] "Only he who follows Christ is a Christian." Of particular appeal is a short passage in his first *Bericht und Lehr* where he speaks of the *Tiefe Christi*, meaning Christ's lowliness (*Niedrigkeit*) and resignation. "It might also be called Hell, that a man could imagine himself deserted by God and all creatures. This lowliness (*Tiefe*) is the sign of Jonah. Into this lowliness one has to enter if one wants to be saved in Christ."[33] This is a thought which was repeated twenty years later nearly verbatim by Pilgram Marpeck in his "Epistle to the Brethren in the Grisons, Appenzell and Alsace," February 1, 1547, dealing with *Von der Tiefe Christi*.[34]

Grete Mecenseffy[35] compared this entire tract of Schlaffer[36] with the Confession of the Freistadt Anabaptists[37] and Hut's *Vom Geheimnus der Tauff*, and found a near identity of all three, at least in certain sections. She thinks that the major ideas were borrowed from Thomas Müntzer, Hut's first spiritual awakener, but this remains a debatable question. Rather one could think of the influence of late medieval Mysticism as the true root of this line of tradition. In any case it remains a "gospel of the cross" which became particularly real as this cross was being experienced in the agony and dread of death.

In his "Letter to a Weak Brother" Schlaffer tries to answer certain scruples of that brother concerning difficult doctrinal issues; his reaction here might be called again typically Anabaptist. "One should not worry too much," he writes, "concerning certain secrets as if it would hurt you not to grasp their meaning. Rather one should take into captivity all thought and reason in obedience to Christ (II Cor. 10:5).[38] This answer is found time and again in Anabaptist sources.[39] On the delicate issue of the meaning of the Trinity, Schlaffer answers again quite typically for pneumatic Anabaptism: "God is neither this nor that.[40] But Schlaffer does not deny the truth of the Trinity; in fact he defends it to the best of his ability.

---

30 *Ibid.*, p. 88.
31 *Ibid.*, p. 89.
32 *Ibid.*, p. 124.
33 *Ibid.*, p. 96.
34 *Kunstbuch*, No. 35; see Heinold Fast, "Pilgram Marbeck und das oberdeutsche Täufertum," *Archiv für Reformationsgeschichte*, XLVII (1956), 235.
35 See note 23.
36 *Glaubenszeugnisse*, I, 94–96.
37 A. Nicoladoni, *Johannes Bünderlin* (Berlin, 1893), 250–52.
38 *Glaubenszeugnisse*, I, 107.
39 See Friedmann, "Reason and Odedience," *ME*, IV.
40 *Ibid.*, p. 108. Here Lydia Müller refers to a stanza of a hymn by Ludwig Haetzer which says exactly the same thing and must have been known to Schlaffer.

Leonhard Schiemer and Hans Schlaffer

Schlaffer and Schiemer are usually mentioned together, and rightly so. They both had been Catholic clergymen, had become true apostles of budding Anabaptism, both pursuing mainly the Denck–Hut line. Both died as martyrs within the span of two and a half weeks not more than five or six miles apart in the Inn Valley. Both left a valuable legacy to their brethren, who kept their memory and also their teachings alive. Schiemer was no doubt more the "bishop" who cared father-like for his congregation or church; Schlaffer never had one to care for. His accounts and tracts are rich sources of instruction and of strength, but his most lasting contributions are his numerous prayers. No other Anabaptist ever produced documents of this kind as profound and spiritual as Schlaffer.

SOURCE: *Mennonite Quarterly Review*, XXXIII (1959), pp. 31–42.

SHORTER SKETCHES OF OUTSTANDING LEADERS

PETER RIEDEMANN, 1506–56

Peter Riedemann (Rideman, Rydeman, Ryedeman), (1506–56), was a Hutterite bishop, missionary, and outstanding doctrinal writer, by some called the second founder of the Hutterite brotherhood. Because of his height he was also called "the tall Peter," and because of his first imprisonment in Gmunden, Upper Austria, was also known as "Peter of Gmunden."

Riedemann was born in 1506 in Hirschberg, Silesia, Germany, where he learned the shoemaker's trade. In 1529 he is encountered for the first time, imprisoned in Gmunden for his Anabaptist faith. Apparently he had previously joined the Anabaptist Brethren in Upper Austria, where Hans Hut and later Wolfgang Brandhuber had been active as missioners, mainly around the cities of Linz, Steyr, and Gmunden 1527–29. Riedemann had been ordained as *Diener des Wortes* in 1529. During his three years' imprisonment (1529–32) Riedemann wrote his first great doctrinal work, *Rechenschaft unseres Glaubens geschrieben zu Gmunden im Land ob der Enns im Gefencknus*, a work of deeply spiritual qualities, which placed Riedemann doctrinally very near to his contemporary brethren Hans Schlaffer and Leonhard Schiemer. (A complete publication of this work is planned for the second volume of *Glaubenszeugnisse*, to be published in the *Täuferakten* Series in 1962.) Even though Riedemann at the time of writing this work had not yet joined the Hutterites, they have faithfully preserved this "Account of Our Faith" in numerous manuscript books. Besides its main part, this work contains also two separate pieces of great beauty not strictly belonging to the confession proper:

1. *Wie man das Haus Gottes bauen soll und was Haus Gottes sei*, and
2. *Von den sieben Pfeilern an diesem Hause* (Proverbs 9:1).

In 1532 Riedemann escaped from prison. He worked first with the Brethren in Linz, but soon thereafter joined the Hutterite brotherhood in Moravia, then still in its formative years. In 1533 he was sent out for the first time as a missioner (*Sendbote*) into Franconia, to spread the Anabaptist message. On his way he visited the remnants of the older Anabaptist groups in Upper Austria, inviting them to join the group in Moravia.

In 1533–37 he was again jailed for the sake of his faith in Nürnberg, but little is recorded of him in this period. In July 1537 he was released from prison upon his promise not to preach in Nürnberg, and he now returned home to Moravia, again via Upper Austria. Here he met the remnants of the Philippite Brethren and took them into his care as if he were their bishop. Four epistles from his hand (1537–39) written to these Philippite Brethren in Linz, Steyr, and Gmunden, and two more (1537–38 and 1540) to other Philippites in Germany (Württemberg, Palatinate, etc.) are still extant. These epistles give a strong impression of pastoral care for this almost leaderless group, some of whom later joined the Hutterites in Moravia.

About 1532, prior to the above journey, Riedemann married an Anabaptist sister Katharina, called familiarly "Treindl." Among his many letters there are six very lovely ones sent to his "marital sister." In 1539 the Brethren sent him again on a mission trip to Hesse mainly to straighten out an unpleasant affair with Hans Both, a friend of Melchior Rinck and a former Philippite. At Holzhausen Riedemann composed an important epistle. Returning in the same year 1539, he arrived at the brotherhood a few days after the unfortunate government raid at Steinabrunn, Lower Austria. Several letters of comfort written to the imprisoned in Falkenstein are extant, which again show Riedemann as a true pastor, loving and full of concern. Two months later he was again on his way to Hesse through Austria, Tyrol, Württemberg, and Swabia (Lauingen), visiting all the groups he could reach. In Hesse he seems to have been very successful, since large numbers (perhaps as many as ninety or one hundred) were now making their way to Moravia. Some of these newly won members were imprisoned in Württemberg en route; Riedemann comforted them too in the genuine fashion of a shepherd.

Not long thereafter, most likely toward the end of February 1540, Riedemann himself fell into the hands of the authorities of Hesse and was chained in a dark and severe prison in Marburg. It should be noted that Philip of Hesse did not permit Anabaptists to be put to death. The numerous letters written by Riedemann during this imprisonment (1540 to early 1542) show that his condition was soon eased. He was permitted to help the jailer by making shoes; then he and another brother were transferred to the near-by castle of Wolkersdorf, where the administrator (*Vogt*) was sympathetic to Anabaptist ideas and somewhat ashamed of all the imprisonment. Riedemann now had full freedom of movement, but he felt obligated to remain at the castle. His activities were manifold. He received visitors from Hesse and from Moravia (his old friend Hans Gentner, a former Philippite from Austria, but now a Hutterite, was sent to consult him concerning a difficult case at home), and he continued to dispatch newly won brethren and sisters to Moravia. In 1541 his correspondence became more sparse; it may be assumed that at that time he was working on his great doctrinal work, the *Rechenschaft*. One of the letters (No. 21) indicates that his main motive for writing this Confession was to inform Philip of Hesse about the true beliefs and viewpoints of the Anabaptists. (This fact was not known heretofore.) Since he had full leisure, the book became rather lengthy and carefully worked out. More trouble in the Moravian brotherhood and the death of the *Vorsteher* (bishop) Hans Amon in February 1542 prompted the Brethren to ask him to come home if he could do so without hurting his conscience.

Late in February 1542 Riedemann was back in Moravia, where after Hans Amon's death Leonhard Lanzenstiel was chosen *Vorsteher* of the brotherhood. Riedemann was now made co–bishop, and this cooperation worked out very well. Lanzenstiel was more of a practical man, while Riedemann was the great spiritual teacher and leader. From now until his death in 1556 Riedemann remained with the brotherhood, leading it forcefully through years of severe persecution and trial. In 1545 the brotherhood presented to the lords of Moravia a petition which can safely be assigned to Riedemann's hand. A copy of the *Rechenschaft* of 1540 was enclosed with this appeal.

The years 1547–51 brought the severest persecution which the brotherhood had to endure before their total expulsion from Moravia in 1622. The Brethren were homeless as hounded game, moving hither and thither, and digging underground tunnels (called *lochy* in Czech) as temporary abodes. Many fell away, but the strong core remained loyal. In fact, the group was augmented by newcomers from Silesia (former Gabrielites). One of Riedemann's letters of this period was addressed to these Silesian Brethren and spoke frankly about their suffering. One can almost feel the strong spiritual forces that bound the brotherhood together in those days, Riedemann, Lanzenstiel, and Walpot being responsible leaders. The *Rechenschaft* may well have added to the strength of their conviction, as the church now had available a statement which was well argued and documented by not less than 1,800 Bible references. One last letter by Riedemann (of 1549–50) was addressed to those brethren who were now scouting for new and safer homes east of the Carpathian Mountains in (then Hungarian) Slovakia.

In December 1556 Riedemann died on the Bruderhof of Protzka, Slovakia, at the age of fifty, having been a minister of the Divine Word for twenty–seven years, and having suffered in prison for nine years. The *Hutterite Chronicle* contains a lengthy obituary, in which all his achievements are listed, with the comment, "For he was rich in all divine secrets and the gift of the spiritual language issued forth from him like a spring which gushes over. All souls who heard him gained peace.... On his deathbed he comforted his brethren with the words of Ezra 8:3 and 9" (presumably IV Ezra). Shortly before his passing he composed the hymn "Quitt, ledig, los hat uns gemacht Christus vom Tod, des Teufels Macht" (*Lieder der Hutterischen Brüder*, p. 516).

Riedemann's written work is quite considerable. It may be classified in three divisions: doctrinal writings, epistles, and hymns.

a. The **Doctrinal writings** comprise two large works:
1. the *Gmundener Rechenschaft* (1529–32), one of the strongest expressions of early Anabaptism, biblicistic, yet thoroughly spiritual (well called "Biblical spiritualism," as over against the general spiritualism of the Sebastian Franck type);
2. the great *Rechenschaft unseres Glaubens*, written in 1540–41, one of the few books ever to have been printed by the Hutterian Brethren, published in 1565. To this day it has remained the basic doctrinal statement of the Hutterites.

b. **The Epistles**. Next to nothing was known about Riedemann's epistles until recently. Wolkan refers to them as "a major source of our knowledge of the Hutterite doctrinal position," but only four epistles were incorporated in the Chronicle and were thus known to him. As far as could be ascertained, only one manuscript codex (at a Bruderhof in Montana) and several recent copies of it contain a nearly complete collection of these most valuable documents, thirty-four in number (six of which are addressed to "Treindl"). To them must be added the epistle to the lords of Moravia (*Landesherren*) of 1545, mentioned above. The present biographical sketch has been partly drawn from the contents of these epistles. They express a deep and concrete Christian faith, a genuine brotherly love, and a pastoral concern for the fellow brethren and sisters, whom he calls his "dear little children." No prison or persecution could stop him in these acts. The epistles will be published in full in a *Täuferakten* publication in the near future.

c. **Hymns**. The *Lieder der Hutterischen Brüder* (Scottdale, 1914) contain (pp. 450–537) forty-five hymns by Riedemann. One additional hymn, "O Herr, wie reichlich tröstest du," composed in 1529, was discovered by Elias Walter, the editor of the *Lieder*, after the publication was out, and another, the "Glaubensbekenntnis" (*Ausbund*, No. 2): "Wir glauben all an einen Gott," is likewise ascribed to Riedemann, even though the Brethren think it was composed by Siegmund Wiedemann. Hymn 37 in the *Ausbund*, "Komm Gott Vater vom Himmel," is likewise by Riedemann (*Lieder*, p. 483), composed while imprisoned in Gmunden in 1529, which praises the martyr death of Hans Langenmantel. It is possible that still more hymns were written by this outstanding man. Rudolf Wolkan, who carefully studied these hymns (*Lieder*, pp. 185–206), considers Riedemann the greatest Hutterite hymn writer. The hymns are found in numerous Hutterite codices in both Europe and America.

One may safely say that the fact that the brotherhood weathered the critical years of 1545–51 and kept its spiritual testimony so high that they could continue unspotted until far into later centuries was due not least to the work of this man, a true bishop of his flock. His writings are preserved in numerous codices and are still being copied by the Hutterian Brethren in America.

SOURCE: *Mennonite Encyclopedia*, IV, pp. 326–28.

ULRICH STADLER, d. 1540

Ulrich Stadler (d. 1540), a Hutterite leader, was one of the strongest personalities among first generation Anabaptism, next to Riedemann the best theological thinker of the Moravian groups, he was a man with stern conceptions of true discipleship. He was born in Brixen, Tyrol, and became a mining official in Sterzing. In the early 1520's he turned Lutheran, but soon joined the Anabaptists of Sterzing. When persecution became unbearable, he moved to Moravia (date not known). At first he became a member of the Austerlitz Bruderhof, which (when a group of Tyroleans left it for Auspitz) came under the leadership of Jakob Wiedemann in 1531. In 1535, when persecution also set in in Moravia, Stadler and his co–worker Leonhard Lochmaier, together with a group of Austerlitz Brethren, sought refuge in Poland. Two Bruderhofs were established there under his supervision in 1535–37: in Ladomir in Podolia (south of Volhynia) near the Galician border and in Krasnikow (in the sources Krasnicktau) in Lodomeria, then a small independent principality in the Volhynian area. A letter "To the Authorities, in Poland" shows that he encountered much tribulation here too, in spite of the renowned tolerance of Polish nobles. In 1537, when persecution in Moravia had ceased, he and Lochmaier returned there with about one hundred persons, surviving many dangers on this return march. In Bucovic, east of Austerlitz, he established a Bruderhof of his own. At that time Hans Amon was the *Vorsteher* of the Hutterites and their only leader; Stadler visited him and after long talks organically joined the Hutterite brotherhood. He then serves as the *Vorsteher* of the Bucovic Hutterite settlement from 1537 until his death in 1540.

Stadler's numerous writings can be found in many Hutterite codices both in Europe and in America. Their numbering is difficult since pieces are put together or separated as the copyist felt moved. Here is the list as complete as possible:

1. *Vom lebendigen Wort und geschriebenen, ein kurzer Unterschied und Bericht.*

2. *Eingang ins Christentum*, written in the form of an epistle: "Unsern herzlieben Brüdern und Geschwistrigeten, wo sie seind nach Gottes Willen, zu Handen."
3. *Was der Tauff sei...auch vom Bundt unsres Herrn Jesu Christi mit seiner Braut*;
4. *Gott der gnädige und langmütige Vater....*

Two church regulations:
1. *Eine liebe Unterrichtung Ulrich Stadlers der Sünden halben, auch des Ausschlusses und wie er darin steht, auch der Gemeinschaft der Güter halben.*
2. *Was die Gemeinschaft Christi heisst in seinem Leib und Blut, eine Ordnung im Haus Gottes.* This piece contains also a section: *Vom ehelichen Stande—sechs Artikel.*
3. Four epistles "geschrieben von Ladomir in Podolien gen Krasnicktau auf Grenz Polen":
   a. *An den Bruder Michael, von der Erbsünde, ein kurzer und doch gründlicher Bericht*;
   b. *Ein ander Sendbrief über die Erbsunde, Red und Widerred*;
   c. *Ein Sendbrief den Fremdlingen und Bilgramen geen Crasnicktau Polln, am Lichtmess 1536* (February 2);
   d. *Ein kurzer Mahnbrief.*

Stadler's Teachings
  A. Theological Issues:
   1. **Original Sin.** Stadler is one of the very few Anabaptists ever to discuss this doctrine. He knows that the term itself cannot be found in the Scriptures. Although he strongly pleads for a life of purity ("Be pure as newborn babes," I Peter 2:2), he condemns those who think that life without sin is possible. Man, however, can fight the tendencies toward sin, if only he allows the spirit to dominate and to discipline the flesh. Tribulations are the disciple's way to this end. "Whatever does not come out of faith, is sin."
   2. **Inner and Outer Word.** Stadler might be called the foremost authority on this central issue of early Anabaptism, having written a special tract on this subject (item 1 above). One might call his position "Biblical Spiritualism," something distinctly different from both "pure" Spiritualism and later legalism. Also in his second tract above he stresses the primacy of the inwardness of Christ in the believer.

B. **The Church:**
1. **Community of Goods.** Stadler's tract "Von der Ordnung der Heiligen" (above, No. 5) might be regarded as the classical expression of this idea of full Christian sharing in the brotherhood–church. It is an original contribution of high spirituality, quite independent of Jacob Hutter's teaching on the point. Stadler's main argument here is the idea of *Gelassenheit*, a term more often used by him than by any other Anabaptist (except perhaps Haffner). Of a true disciple of Christ he expects a "free, detached, resigned heart," which has died to the world and is dedicated alone to the Lord and the brethren. He stresses time and again that a life of that kind needs rigid discipline, quite in accord with his idea of purity and fighting sin.
2. **The functions of the "Servant of the Lord"** (*Diener des Herren*), Stadler's term for *Vorsteher* or "bishop." The classical exposition of his concept of such a leader and shepherd is found in his paragraph concerning excommunication: "The servant ought to have the power to punish all self–willed, disobedient members." One gets the strong impression that his conception of leadership approximates that of a prior or abbot of a medieval monastery. His ascetic ideals fairly correspond to such a life, with the exception of married life.
3. **Married Life.** Few Anabaptists have dealt more often and more thoroughly with this theme than Stadler. In his tract *Vom ehelichen Stande*—six articles he begins with the motto: "Whoever lacks the gift of chastity [meaning the ability to stand lifelong celibacy] ought to marry according to the will of God." Somewhere else he states that "God will wink at our marital work (*Gott aber sihet durch die finger unsers zerstörüchen leibs willen im eelichen werk*)…for the sake of the children, and He will not count it against us, if it is performed in the fear of the Lord"—a typically puritanical thought. In two of his epistles he elaborates further on this topic, which certainly was a foremost one in a brotherhood–church as strict as the Hutterites.
4. Finally the over–all **ordering of the church**, the **church discipline or regulation**, again a major concern for a leader of Stadler's stature. We know two such *Gemeindeordnungen* from his pen (items 5 and 6, the latter still unpublished), forerunners of Riedemann's much larger work of 1541. No details can be offered here; that he sets an ascetic ideal as his model goes almost without saying. A man who wants to discipline his flesh has, of course, not too much appreciation of "*Geschleck und gute bissen*

und trünklein." But no work should ever be construed as proof of sinlessness. In all our doings we are always under temptation and must never slacken in our "good fight." If we continue in it, however, we may eventually be saved from "eternal death."

No other Hutterite brother is known to have expressed so radical a viewpoint as Stadler. The numerous copies, however, of his writings prove the high regard for teachings of this kind, which later Hutterites called "sharp preaching."

SOURCE: *Mennonite Encyclopedia*, IV, pp. 607–8.

HANS SCHMID, d. 1558

Hans (Hänsel) Schmid, also called Hans Raiffer, probably because he was born in the Tyrolean village of Raiffach, was a Hutterite leader and martyr (d. 1558), successful missioner, composer of hymns, writer of letters and doctrinal tracts, a strong and leading personality, one of the noblest representatives of the second period of Anabaptism. The data of birth and conversion are not known. In 1548 (a period of severe persecution in Moravia) he was made minister and four years later was confirmed in this office. Soon thereafter he began his successful mission work in Germany: in 1555 he was in Hesse (district of Nidda), in 1556 in the Rhenish Palatinate around Kreuznach and Worms, where he won over a group of "Swiss Brethren" to the Hutterite way after long and serious debates, in 1557 he worked along the Lower Rhine and around Aachen, winning the important Swiss Brother Hans Arbeiter and other Swiss Brethren, most of whom now moved to Moravia like those from Kreuznach. Next his work led him into the Eifel district of Western Germany and again to Aachen. Here, on Jan. 9, 1558, during a meeting, he was surprised by city authorities and together with five brothers and six sisters (all of the former Hans Arbeiter group) he was imprisoned.

On the events between January 9 and the day of his execution, October 19, there is much detailed information thanks to the thirty–five extant letters and the fifteen hymns written in prison, which material the *Chronicle* used for its graphic account. Raiffer had cherished some hope of finding leniency at the hands of the City Council, but of the twelve Anabaptists imprisoned five men were finally executed, the sixth recanted and was thereupon released (he returned to Moravia, repented, and was reaccepted by the Brethren), and the six women were flogged and driven out of the city. At one time all twelve were allowed to be together from 4 a.m. to 10 p.m., but then were separated again in different prisons. They sang overly loud as often as they could to comfort each other, and they wrote letters to each other between their confinements, as well as letters to the Rhineland Brethren and also those in Moravia. Schmid was badly racked but remained steadfast, defending his faith courageously and helping others to do likewise. Of his thirty-five letters from prison fifteen were addressed to his "marital sister" (wife), Madlen (Magdalena), in Moravia. Apparently messengers could communicate freely with the prisoners. A wealthy woman in Aachen sent them extra food, but Schmid refused it unless she would change her mind and allegiance. All attempts to persuade him failed as they did with nearly all Anabaptists; accordingly the city authorities finally had to obey the imperial mandates issued by the "new" emperor Ferdinand I. In October 1558, all five brethren were publicly strangled and then burned.

Of this unusually strong personality we get a vivid picture from his numerous writings, which places him on the level of Peter Riedemann.

Letters

The letters are found in many Hutterite codices, which proves their popular appeal. Of the thirty-seven letters the thirty-five written in Aachen are described above. Seventeen of these are scheduled to be published in a forthcoming volume of Anabaptist epistles edited by the present writer. One letter (perhaps of 1557), written to Romies Caltenburg and dealing with the Incarnation, is extant in a codex in Bratislava. Schmid discussed this topic several times, repeating more or less the Nicene creed. One letter of 1555 (now in Darmstadt) written to the Tentmeister of Nidda contains a defense against slander and a sort of summary of Anabaptist teaching.

Doctrinal Writings

Of Schmid's doctrinal writings the following are known:

A. *Eine Rechenschaft vom Abendmahl und seiner rechten Bedeutung*, written in prison in Aachen and sent to his fellow prisoners as well as to the Brethren in Moravia, obviously a repetition of his oral defense before the authorities. This document has two parts:

   a. a defense of the Zwinglian theology of the Lord's Supper (the symbolical interpretation);

   b. *Vom rechten Gebrauch...*, which explains the idea of community (*Gemeinschaft*) both with Christ and with the Brethren.

B. *Brüderliche Vereinigung zwischen uns und etlichen Schweizer Brüdern* (1556), containing the debate with Lorenz Huef and others at Kreuznach, a statement of the Hutterite position in seven articles in which the main differences from the Swiss Brethren position are formulated. Andreas Ehrenpreis reprinted this piece in his *Sendbrief* of 1652. The article concerning marriage and divorce is very informative, and so is the one concerning ministers and their special honors, etc.

C. One year later (1557) Schmid discussed seventeen articles with Hans Arbeiter, the titles of which are named but their contents not published. Here we find also two theological items: Concerning Original Sin, and Concerning the Incarnation of Christ. One may safely assume that Schmid's views coincided with those of Riedemann.

Hymns

The *Lieder der Hutterischen Brüder* (pp. 551–611) contains fifteen hymns by Hans Schmid (hymn No. 3 is not by Schmid but about him), and six hymns by his co–prisoners, most of them of great beauty and depth. Wolkan (pp. 211–28) discusses them at great length, reprinting five of them in full, and claiming that with Schmid and Riedemann Hutterite hymn composition reached its climax. Wiswedel (p. 99, note 5) claims that Schmid composed twenty–four hymns, but does not report further. One hymn is printed by Wackernagel (*Kirchenlied*, III, p. 812). One hymn, "O herre Gott vom Himmelreich merck auff und sieh die worte…," composed by Schmid and Jörg von Ingenheim, is found in the Anabaptist hymnal *Ein Schon Gesangbüchlein*. The main theme of all these hymns is love, obedience to God, community, and *Gelassenheit*, a key attitude of the Anabaptists. Of particular beauty is hymn No. 4, "Fröhlich so wollen wir singen," a deeply felt praise of Christian love. Many a hymn shows the typical Anabaptist acrostic—a hidden message composed by the first words of each stanza.

The names of the brethren who were martyred with Schmid are Heinrich Adam, Hans Weckh, Matthias Schmied, and Tillman Schneider.

SOURCE: *Mennonite Encyclopedia*, IV, pp. 462–63.

KLAUS FELBINGER, d. 1560

Klaus Felbinger (also called *Schlosser*, meaning "Locksmith," after his trade), was an outstanding Hutterite martyr who died in 1560 in Landshut, Bavaria, Germany. We know nothing of his origin and earlier life. The Hutterite chronicles give his name for the first time when he was chosen *Diener des Worts* (preacher) in Moravia in 1558. Soon afterwards he was sent as a missionary to Bavaria, most likely his native country, together with a brother. But in 1560 the two men were seized near Neumarkt in Lower Bavaria, and soon thereafter brought in chains to Landshut, a well–known fortress and castle. Here they were kept in the dungeon for over ten weeks. The Catholic clergy vainly tried all means of persuasion to make him recant. Then he was racked to the point where even the executioner pleaded for him. But Felbinger still remained firm in his faith. From prison he sent two extensive epistles (*Sendbriefe*) home to the brotherhood in Moravia, in which he gives a detailed report of his many debates with the clergy and other officials, and from these documents we learn his extraordinary knowledge of the Bible and his skill in defending his position. His opponents were obviously amazed. Two learned clergymen came expressly from Munich to convert him, but it was of no avail. Their rational theology was one thing, his living faith in Christ and His commandments another. At the end we read in one of his epistles the following episode: "You cannot convince me," said Felbinger to his inquisitors, "for you do not stand in the Truth, and therefore I intend to stay in the simplicity of Christ." To this the chancellor answered, "I do not think that you are so simple. [Note that the word 'simplicity' is here used in a double meaning. Felbinger means plainness, absence of sophistication, while his opponent thinks of ignorance.] I think there is not one in a hundred who could defend himself as well as you do. For I do not think of you as a fanatic (*Schwärmer*) as are found everywhere and have no reason for their beliefs." To this Felbinger added, "God made him admit this, a comfort for me" (Zieglschmid, *Chronik*, p. 402). Felbinger had also drawn up as a brief tract, his *Confession of Faith* (or *Rechenschaft*) which he submitted to the lords of Landshut. But they were not willing to deal leniently with sectarians. The mandates were applied, and on July 19, 1560, he was beheaded in Landshut, together with his brother–companion.

His Confession as well as his epistles circulated widely among the Brethren and did not fail to strengthen them in their faith. When the Hutterite brother Veit Grünberger was examined in Salzburg in 1573, he had this to say: "They may do with us as they wish. We will bear it with endurance, for I have carefully read the *Rechenschaft* of Klaus Felbinger and of Hans Mandel, more than once, so that I know that our faith is well founded in God's Scriptures."

We have from Felbinger these two epistles:
a. *Sendbrief an Leonhard Sailer*, 1560 (published by Loserth, "Zur Geschichte der Wiedertäufer in Mähren," *Ztscht f. Allg. Gesch.* I, 1884, 451–54);
b. *Ein Sendbrief Klaus Felbingers geschrieben aus seiner Gefenknus an die Gemein Gottes in Mähren im 1560. Jahr.*) Published by Loserth in "Der Communismus der mährischen Wiedertäufer," *Arch. f. österr. Gesch.* LXXXI, 1894, 292–310.) This epistle contains the details of his debates, and is strongly dogmatic.

There exists also his confession, *Abgeschrift des Glaubens welchen ich, Klaus Felbinger, zu Landshut den Herrn daselbst für mich und statt meines mitgefangenen Bruders zugestellt habe* (this is his *Rechenschaft oder Verantwortung*). This document has not yet been published but exists in several Hutterite codices.

Felbinger is also the author of five well-known hymns, four of which are published in the *Lieder der Hutterischen Brüder* (Scottdale, 1914), 11, 647–49, and (out of place) pp. 441–46. The fifth hymn is known only from European codices.

SOURCE: *Mennonite Encyclopedia*, II, pp. 320–21.

KASPAR BRAITMICHEL, d. 1573

Kaspar Braitmichel (d. 1573), also called Kaspar Schneider because he was by trade a tailor, was the first chronicler of the Hutterian Brethren in Moravia. Born in Silesia like his fellow brother Peter Riedemann, he joined the Hutterite brotherhood during its hardest time, in the 1530's, perhaps as early as 1533. In 1538 he was chosen *Diener der Notdurft* (deacon). In the following year he was captured during a religious service at Steinabrunn together with 150 others and taken to nearby Falkenstein castle (Lower Austria), whence all the Brethren were sent to Trieste for work on Venetian galleys. He managed somehow to escape, and then returned to Moravia or rather to adjoining Slovakia, where new Bruderhofs had just been established. In 1548 he was chosen by lot to be *Diener des Wortes* (preacher) of the Holitsch Bruderhof. Later on he seems to have moved back to Austerlitz in Moravia, which then was the center of the entire brotherhood. This move was perhaps due to his alert interest in the history of the group and his fine gift for writing. Perhaps he became the clerk of the *Vorsteher* or the archivist of the brotherhood. In Austerlitz he died in peace in 1573.

Braitmichel was the beginner of the official church chronicle of the Hutterites called the *Geschicht-Buch*, which work he must have started toward the end of his life, during the period of the outstanding *Vorsteher* Peter Walpot. He begins this work with an elaborate summary of church history "from the beginning of the world" to the year 1520, taken chiefly from Sebastian Franck's *Chronica*. Then he continues his story up to the year 1542. In his signed preface he apologizes that he could not carry his work further due to his poor eyesight and other physical frailty. Yet we have also another chronicle from his hand, now in the library of the Hungarian Primate at Esztergom, Hungary (described as Codex I in Beck's *Geschichts-Bücher*), which runs again "from the beginning of the world" up to 1534 (the first seventy leaves). This chronicle served perhaps as a preliminary experiment in such annalistic activities, and may later have inspired the larger enterprise of the official *Chronicle*. In two other Hutterite codices one finds a short report of historical nature, *Wie die Brüder von dem Gabriel* (i.e., Ascherham) *sich mit uns vereinigt haben...* (in 1545), also drawn up by Braitmichel, who most likely had been present at these negotiations and may even have taken the minutes of this event. This brief account was later incorporated into the *Great Chronicle* (Zieglschmid, *Die Aelteste Chronik*, pp. 250–57) by the continuer of Braitmichel's work, the brother Zapff. In addition, two epistles from Braitmichel's hand have been preserved, one sent in 1568 to the brother Leonhard Dax and his fellow sufferers in prison at Alzey, Palatinate, the other containing an admonition to repentance, sent to Silesia, his home country where the Gabrielite Brethren lived. All this indicates that he filled an important position in the leadership of the brotherhood. Four hymns written by him are found in the *Lieder der Hutterischen Brüder* (1914, pp. 98–101, 175–78, 647–703): "Merkt auf, herzliebe Brüder mein" (12 stanzas); "O Herre Gott vom Himmelreich" (53 stanzas); "Christliche Art, Eifer und Trieb" (30 stanzas); and "Ich schrei zu dir, O Herre Gott" (8 stanzas).

SOURCE: *Mennonite Encyclopedia*, I, p. 402.

PETER WALPOT, 1521–78

Peter Walpot (Walbot),1521–78, was a bishop of the Hutterian Brethren in Moravia during their Golden Age, one of the outstanding leaders of the brotherhood, a creative writer and organizer, a stern and upright character, who did much to bring the brotherhood to that spiritual and moral height which attracted many converts during the second half of the sixteenth century. He was a Tyrolean, born near Klausen, south of the Brenner Pass. When eight years old he was present when George Blaurock was executed for his faith in Gufidaun near Klausen. He seems to have turned Anabaptist at an early age (like many other Tyroleans), for in 1542 he was already a minister (*Diener des Worts*) in Moravia. By profession he was a cloth-shearer (*Tuchscherer*), whence he was often called "Peter Scherer." From now on he participated in all the major activities of the brotherhood; e.g., in the important debate between the Gabrielites and the Hutterites in 1545. It appears that Walpot was particularly well-read, not only in the Scriptures, but also in church history and in contemporary polemics and apologetics. He is probably the author of the remarkable *Fünf Artikel des grössten Streites zwischen uns und der Welt*, a summary of the most significant theological and practical positions of the Hutterites in which they differed from the "world," a tract apparently derived from the earlier debate with the Gabrielites. From now on the Hutterites had not only Riedemann's *Rechenschaft* but also these *Fünf Artikel* to give an account of their faith and life.

In 1546 Walpot and his wife were active in Silesia "in the work of the Lord," apparently among the remnants of the Gabrielites, once going as far as Danzig. After Riedemann's death (1556) Walpot was the uncontested spiritual leader of the brotherhood. When, in 1557, Lutheran theologians at Worms published their condemnation of Anabaptism in the *Prozess wie es soll gehalten werden* (also called *Bedenken*), only the Hutterites replied (even though they were more remote from the controversy than any other Anabaptist group), and this reply became known as *Handbüchlein wider den Prozess*.... It is a fine and highly spiritual apology of Anabaptism. To be sure, it was circulated anonymously and was approved by the entire brotherhood, but there can be no doubt that it was Walpot who formulated the points of defense and of emphasis.

In 1565, when the bishop of the brotherhood, Leonhard Lanzenstiel, died, Walpot was elected the new bishop, both of Moravia and adjacent Slovakia. He filled this office for the next thirteen years (1565–78) with much energy and wisdom. While he had seen great hardship in Moravia during the 1540's, now a time of peaceful development had set in. There was no longer any persecution in Moravia (the Counter-Reformation did not come to that country until the end of the century) and the brotherhood spread and flourished, numbering at that time 30,000 baptized souls. The administrative center was the Bruderhof at Neumühl, where the bishop resided. The Brethren could now afford to have one of their most precious books printed, Riedemann's *Rechenschaft*, very likely by an itinerant journeyman printer by the name of Vollandt at the Neumühl Hof, where Walpot was instrumental in this enterprise.

The activities of this excellent man must have been manifold indeed. Missioners were sent out into all German lands (as far as Denmark) and into Switzerland. Many newcomers had to be assimilated, and the discipline at home had to be carefully watched and regulated lest the community deteriorate. A wealth of epistles from this period have survived, written to the missioners abroad "in the name of the entire brotherhood," encouraging and comforting them in their hard work. No doubt most of these were drafted by the bishop himself. Kaspar Braitmichel now began the first draft of what gradually became *Das grosse Geschicht-Buch* (*Great Chronicle*), assisted by Walpot. An enormous correspondence was brought in almost daily by returning Brethren (no other mail was ever used), and had to be read before the assembled Brethren and answered. Economic and social questions both in Moravia and Slovakia had to be solved; e.g., the relationship to the manorial lords and to the larger cities (many a farmer in Moravia noted with envy the thriving colonies and their enterprise). There were also the schools of the brotherhood to be managed, and on inspection Walpot found many things that needed attention. A model "school regulation" and a notable "address to the schoolmasters," November 15, 1568, remarkably modern for the sixteenth century, both by Walpot, have been preserved.

In the late 1560's and early 1570's, some Polish Unitarians visited the Moravian Bruderhofs several times, in fact at one time (1569?) several young Poles volunteered to live for one whole year in the Bruderhofs in order to learn how to run such a collective large–scale enterprise. (They were disappointed and became severely critical, since such a Bruderhof is possible only on the basis of a specific attitude, foreign to the Poles.) These visits resulted in an exchange of letters of unusual interest; Walpot's epistles to the Poles were inserted into the Chronicle.

The Protocol of the Frankenthal Colloquy of 1571 claims that a certain Peter Scherer and two other Brothers attended this occasion; Wolkan and Hege assumed that this was Peter Walpot. Yet neither a Scherer nor a Walpot is listed as participating in the debate in any conspicuous way, and Walpot did not even respond when Dathenus asked whether Hutterites were present.

During the 1570's Walpot also drew up a catechism for the children (still in use today), several prayers for children, and also some hymns to be learned in school.

With Swiss Brethren of the Rhine area a lively correspondence developed, the most important epistle being the letter addressed to the Swiss Brethren of Modenbach on the Rhine in 1577, in which the distinguishing points between Hutterites and Swiss Brethren were again formulated and defended. In an earlier paper by this writer also the anonymous tract *Anschlag und Fürwenden* was attributed to Walpot, but more recent research has shown that it was drawn up by Leonhard Dax, doubtless with Walpot's full approval. Dax, a former Catholic priest and versed in the Latin language, soon became an important assistant to Walpot in all matters of theology and literary polemics.

The most important contribution of this busy man was still to come: the elaboration of the Hutterite program of 1545–47, i.e., the "Five Articles." Now in more peaceful times Walpot could develop the ideas of this program by adding ample Biblical and church historical references, and by elaborating on each point. Thus there developed a large work (far larger than the *Rechenschaft*) of basic nature, the anonymously written *Ein schön lustig Büchlein etliche Hauptartikel unseres christlichen Glaubens*, etc., briefly called *Das grosse Artikelbuch*, dated 1577. That it was authored by Walpot is beyond doubt; in fact one eighteenth–century copy (now in Montana) expressly names him as the writer. And yet it was more the result of the work of the brotherhood as a whole than was, e.g., Riedemann's *Rechenschaft*, which was written in the lonely prison in Hesse. Some twenty–three old copies of the sixteenth and seventeenth centuries still extant, and many new ones, give evidence of the continued interest of the brotherhood in this work.

On January 30, 1578, Walpot died, not without having first addressed all the elders of his church assembled around his bed. The *Chronicle* contains this last address, and then adds a special paragraph of praise and gratitude. "He was a loyal shepherd," the Chronicle says, "an outstanding teacher (i.e., preacher), and a godly ruler, etc."

Besides the tracts and epistles mentioned above, Walpot also composed two hymns (*Lieder der Hutterischen Brüder*, pp. 737–39). He was probably the author of the earliest known sermons of the brotherhood. Although these early sermons are anonymous, the dates indicate that this bishop was the author.

Walpot's richly filled life gave new strength and direction to the brotherhood. He was perhaps less "spiritual" (pneumatic) than Riedemann, but he was nevertheless the true continuer of the ideas of Jakob Hutter. Obedience to the Word of God, resignation (*Gelassenheit*) in all things secular, and loyalty to the great cause of Anabaptism—these are the forces which moved the life and activities of this outstanding Anabaptist brother.

SOURCE: *Mennonite Encyclopedia*, IV, pp. 880–81.

JOHANNES WALDNER, 1749–1824

Johannes Waldner, 1749–1824, a Hutterite chronicler of the eighteenth century, was born near Villach, Carinthia, of Lutheran parents, with whom he migrated on the order of Empress Maria Theresa to Transylvania in 1755, along with other Lutherans. Here the entire Carinthian exile group joined the Hutterites and became the very soul of a revitalization of the brotherhood. In his later years he wrote his recollections, the *Denkwürdigkeiten*, as a sort of continuation of the old Hutterite chronicle, the *Geschicht–Buch*. Thus grew a remarkable new book, the *Klein–Geschichtsbuch der Hutterischen Brüder* (first printed in 1947). Waldner wrote the story only to the year 1802; the remainder to 1947 was done by other writers. In this work he mentioned his own experiences at different places.

In 1767 Waldner shared the dramatic flight of the brotherhood across the mountains into Rumania (Walachia) and all of their subsequent hardships until the Brethren found a new home in Ukraine, first in Vishenka, later in Radichev. In 1782 he was elected preacher, and in 1794 *Vorsteher* of the entire brotherhood. In 1818 an unfortunate conflict arose as one group wished to give up the principle of community of goods. Waldner insisted on continuing this time–honored principle in spite of all external difficulties. "I would rather die at the stake than to abandon the old practice" (p. 423). Thus a split occurred and Waldner moved to a new place near by called Neudorf. In 1824 he died at the age of seventy–five.

Waldner began writing his *Denkwürdigkeiten* in 1793, but he prefaced this personal story by a brief recapitulation of Hutterite history as found in the larger chronicle and amplified it by records otherwise unknown. This resulted in a brilliant history of the Hutterites, more condensed than the older *Great* (Braitmichel) *Chronicle*, yet full and rich. Johann Loserth, who read this work for the first time about 1930, considered Waldner an outstanding history writer, with a unique skill in making events live.

But this revival of the interest in history was only secondary to Waldner's more central achievements. His main concern was the revival of the old and genuine spirit of the Hutterites as it had been at the time of the great bishop Andreas Ehrenpreis (d. 1662). A major avenue to this end was the collection and rewriting of the old sermons which at Waldner's time had almost been forgotten. New sermon books were produced by Waldner and his co-workers, taken from old sermon notebooks. Waldner also incorporated excerpts from these sermons into the *Klein–Geschichtsbuch* (pp. 204–21). This made an invaluable inheritance for the Brethren, which has continued alive to this day, and which is the very center of all their piety. Waldner also renewed the old *Gemeindeordnungen* and insisted on their observance. In short, he became the rejuvenator of the brotherhood at a time when it was particularly difficult to continue the tradition. That the Hutterites could survive so strongly through the ages (after the conclusion of the heroic first century) is due mainly to the work of three outstanding men: Ehrenpreis, Waldner, and Elias Walter.

SOURCE: *Mennonite Encyclopedia*, IV, pp. 876–77.

ELIAS WALTER, 1861–1938

Elias Walter Jr. (1862–1938) was a Hutterite bishop and leader of the Dariusleut. He was born in Russia and came to America in 1874 as a boy of twelve when the family of Darius Walter settled at the Wolf Creek colony in South Dakota. He was ordained preacher in 1898, and served in this capacity for forty years; in 1928 he was elected bishop of the Dariusleut. He was among the first to establish a Bruderhof in Canada (1898), and he himself migrated as the first Hutterite minister to Canada in 1918 when the harshness of the United States government during World War I drove the Brethren away from South Dakota. He then settled in the Stand–Off Colony in southern Alberta, near Lethbridge, where some of his descendants still live.

In 1888 Elias Walter came into contact with John Horsch, forming a friendship which proved most profitable to both. It was through Horsch that the European world first learned of the existence of the Hutterites in America. In 1889 Walter discovered the original Hutterite Chronicle (*Geschicht–Buch*) at a neighboring colony of Hutterian Brethren who had come from Russia. This Chronicle he copied not less than three times; one copy he sent later to Rudolf Wolkan in Vienna, who published the book in 1923. The title page bears as publication place Vienna and Stand–Off Colony.

Walter was a man of the greatest dedication to a revival of the old, genuine Hutterite spirit. Not since Johannes Waldner, who died in 1824, had the brotherhood had a leader like Elias Walter. Without Andreas Ehrenpreis in the seventeenth century, Waldner in the eighteenth, and Walter in the nineteenth and twentieth centuries, modern Hutterianism would be almost unthinkable. Walter was a man of indefatigable activity, a bishop in the true sense of the word, concerned at all times for the spiritual needs not only of the Dariusleut but of all Hutterites in both good and bad days. In his lifetime he copied innumerable volumes of Hutterite literature: twenty–one sermon books, twelve epistle books, the *Handbüchlein wider den Prozess*, a commentary on the Book of Revelation, the Article Book, and many more. He also began the compilation of a fairly comprehensive catalog of all Hutterite writings, which is of inestimable value for present–day scholarship.

In 1902 Walter published Riedemann's great *Rechenschaft* at Berne, Ind., using the rare copy of the library of the University of Chicago as his source. In 1914 he established a real precedent when he published the *Lieder der Hutterischen Brüder* at Scottdale, Pa., since then the generally accepted hymnal of all Hutterites. This work is based on the compilation of three old hymn codices of the sixteenth and seventeenth centuries. In 1919 he published the *Gesangbüchlein...meistens aus alten Handschriften gesammelt* (Scottdale), containing other hymns than the 1914 edition, but smaller in size. In 1920 he published Andreas Ehrenpreis' *Sendbrief...brüderliche Gemeinschaft, das höchste Gebot der Liebe betreffend* at Scottdale. In 1923 the *Geschicht–Buch* (see above) appeared, as did the *Geschichte der zwölf Patriarchen*, a smaller volume also edited by Walter.

In 1930 Eberhard Arnold, who made his first contact with him in 1926, came to America, visited all colonies, and was finally ordained preacher by Elias Walter at Stand–Off Colony. Arnold then also received from Walter a number of most valuable old codices of former centuries as well as a number of sermon books.

One special aspect of Walter's activities was his bookbindery at Stand–Off Colony. Here he bound for practically all the Hutterite preachers their (handwritten) sermon books. He bound also the Chronicle in innumerable copies, as well as hymn books, tracts, etc., all with great skill and care. His son continues this activity.

Elias Walter was married to Elizabeth Hofer (1886). They were blessed with a large family, seven daughters and three sons. The youngest son, Jacob (b. 1910), was elected preacher after his father's death in 1928 and is still serving in this capacity.

John Horsch and Elias Walter carried on a long and fruitful correspondence until Walter's death. Horsch was the actual editor of all the manuscripts which were printed at Berne and Scottdale. Along list of titles of the (hitherto unknown) codices is published in Horsch's *Kurzgefasste Geschichte der Mennoniten–Gemeinden. Nebst einem Verzeichnis der Literatur der Taufgesinnten* (Elkhart, 1890). Horsch was also the liaison with Wolkan in Vienna. When the United States draft laws during World War I caused difficulties for the Hutterites, it was Elias Walter who represented the Hutterites in negotiations in Washington, and it was John Horsch who served as a go–between. A considerable file of Walter–Horsch correspondence has been preserved in the Goshen College Historical Library. The oldest Hutterite Epistle Book, a codex of 1566, existing at one Hutterite Bruderhof, was sent to Horsch in Elkhart in 1888, who published a considerable number of epistles from it in the *Herold der Wahrheit* (1888–89).

A series of articles by Elias Walter under the title, "Wie kamen die Hutterischen Brüder nach Amerika?" appeared in the *Mennonitische Blätter* for 1908, pp. 49 f., 53–55, 61–63, 70, and 87–89.

SOURCE: *Mennonite Encyclopedia*, IV, pp. 882–83.

THE OLDEST KNOWN HUTTERITE CODEX OF 1566

A Chapter in Anabaptist Intellectual History

Original Anabaptist writings of the sixteenth century are relatively rare even though of prime importance for a proper appreciation of the movement. Besides these, there are only secondary sources by, in most cases, unsympathetic outsiders, or court and archival records, which completely lack the spirit of what Anabaptism really stood for. Only in Moravia something of an Anabaptist archive or historical library was built up during the rather peaceful years of 1560–1590 at the residence of the head bishop (*Vorsteher*), called the Neumühle.[1] Here apparently careful records were kept of everything pertaining to the brotherhood: all incoming letters (from brethren on mission or in prison) as well as careful copies of all outgoing epistles, the annals or church records (such as ordinations, appointments, deaths, and other important community events), and a fairly rich library of devotional literature, theological and otherwise, for the most part of Anabaptist origin. This last named section was fortunately not at all narrowly conceived. It contained not only practically everything produced by the Hutterites themselves, such as Riedemann's *Rechenschaft* or the great *Article Book*,[2] and all the numerous confessions and defenses of Brethren at trials anywhere in German lands, tracts of all kinds, *Ordnungen* (regulations), and hymn collections, but it contained also writings of friends and forerunners, such as the complete works of Balthasar Hubmaier (printed, hence never copied in Hutterite codices), the Schleitheim Confession, and similar early documents,[3] also the *Vermahnung* (or *Taufbüchlein*) by Pilgram Marpeck (reproduced anonymously), parts of Menno Simons' writings, even a tract by a Philippite brother, all the writings of such leaders as Hans Denck, Hans Hut, Michael Sattler, Leonhard Schiemer and Hans Schlaffer, Hans Langemantel and Jörg Hauck von Juchsen, also well-known books such as Sebastian Franck's *Chronica*, Eusebius' *Church History*, and the writings

---

1 See article "Neumühl," *ME*, III.
2 See article "Article Book," *ME*, I.
3 See Robert Friedmann, "The Schleitheim Confession and Other Doctrinal Writings of the Swiss Brethren in a Hitherto Unknown Edition," *MQR*, XVI (1942), 82–98.

of Flavius Josephus. It is even possible that Latin books were available in this strange library, such as the pseudo–Clementine epistles, published in Latin by Sichem in 1526 and translated for the Brethren by Leonhard Dax, a former Catholic priest. This was truly the "Golden Age" of Anabaptism which founded such a center in Moravia. Nothing comparable has become known from any Swiss, German, or Dutch Anabaptist group, even though the Netherlands eventually also established full toleration toward the end of the sixteenth century.

Not much is known of this Neumühl center, but at least a few Brethren are known to have been gifted in writing and recording who might have conceived such an 'Anabaptist Historical Library,' for example, Peter Walpot (d. 1578), the efficient *Vorsteher* of 1565–78, Leonhard Dax (d. 1574), and Caspar Braitmichel (d. 1573),[4] one of the oldest and most experienced members of the brotherhood, a born "historian" and collector. It is this last-named brother to whom we owe the idea of a *Geschicht–Buch* or *Chronicle* and its execution at least to the year 1542; this is learned in part from the preface of the *Great Chronicle*. The concept may have occurred to him when he first hit upon the idea of a combination devotional reader for the Brethren of his Bruderhof. To make the untapped treasures of that "archive" available to them not only to strengthen them but also to inform them of their origin and the reason for their particular stand in the face of an opposing and tempting "world"—that was certainly a royal idea. Of course, printing such materials was out of the question. Only Riedemann's *Rechenschaft* was once printed (probably in an edition of perhaps not more than one hundred copies), presumably as an experiment simply because a journeyman printer happened to pass through the Neumühl Bruderhof. (We call it an "experiment," since the Brethren did not want the spread of their literature to outside areas; but the Catholic priest Fischer, the archfoe of the Brethren in Moravia, managed to secure a copy.) Otherwise the Brethren in all their history up to 1900 had almost nothing printed (save two small exceptions). Their literature was and to a large extent still is a manuscript literature. It is still today the pride of a Hutterite preacher in South Dakota or Alberta to show the visitor on his book shelves twenty, thirty, even sixty handwritten volumes of their tracts, hymns, and sermons.

To sum up: It is the conjecture of this writer that it was Caspar Braitmichel who first decided to produce such a combination "codex" (manuscript book), written beautifully in two colors (black, with red for titles, page headings, and paragraph beginnings), on good strong paper, and bound solidly in embossed leather, closed by two brass clasps. In the course of about one century the number of such precious codices (usually written in exemplary penmanship) must have reached one thousand if not more; even today three to four hundred are known both in the Old World and in America. It is further

---

4   See the pertinent articles in *ME*.

my conjecture that because of the success of this new devotional literature Braitmichel decided to try his hand with the production of a Chronicle of the brotherhood, including the "prehistory" of the entire movement—taken to a large extent from Sebastian Franck's *Chronica*.[5] But much was added out of Braitmichel's own knowledge, such as, for instance, the story of Petrus Olivi, the Franciscan Spiritual of the thirteenth century;[6] thus the book as a whole gives the impression of a solidly original work. Its value as a source of information is inestimable. To cite only one instance: the classical story of the first adult baptism in Zürich on January 21, 1525 (Grebel, Blaurock, Manz), is known to us exclusively through this Braitmichel chronicle. When and how he got this bit of information is not recorded, but since Braitmichel had been a Hutterite brother since the early 1530's, and since many Swiss Brethren either had joined the Hutterites in Moravia or had at least come into contact with them,[7] it may be assumed that Braitmichel's source was personal hearsay, possibly deriving from George Blaurock, as H. S. Bender supposes. In another instance, when the Gabrielites joined the Hutterites in 1545, a conversation (*Religionsgespräch*) preceded this decisive step, and Braitmichel was probably not only present at these negotiations but kept the minutes (*Protokoll*) of these talks, now incorporated in the Chronicle.

Thus out of recollections of more than forty years and with the help of all kinds of documents, the text of the Chronicle gradually developed—to give future generations information about roots and reasons for their being "brothers."

Thus it is my impression that a devotional reader came first, and right after it the beginning of the Chronicle, around the years 1566–70. That this chronicle survived (in two nearly identical copies) is well–nigh miraculous considering the vicissitudes of Hutterite history. They are still carefully preserved and in part copied by the present–day Brethren, who brought a large library of such codices with them when they left Russia in the 1870's to settle in South Dakota (and after 1918 in Canada). Many items of their former libraries (nearly every Bruderhof had one) were taken away by the Austrian authorities from 1695–1700 on. During the reign of Maria Theresa (1740–80) wholesale confiscations took place. Wagon loads of manuscript books and Bibles were carried away in Slovakia by Jesuits (at a time when elsewhere the Jesuits were no longer recognized, in fact had as an order been dissolved by the pope), and either stored in Jesuit college libraries (e.g., in Skalitz, Slovakia, which library was later incorporated into the library of the University of Budapest), or given to the nearest parish priest to deal with at his pleasure. Some of these books were taken to Bratislava (Cathedral library), some to Esztergom–Gran (library of the archbishop and primate of

---
5 See article "Chronica," *ME*, I.
6 See Friedmann, "A Hutterite Book of Medieval Origin," *MQR*, XXX (1956), 65–71.
7 See article "Swiss Brethren in Moravia," in *ME*, IV.

Hungary), but many were simply destroyed, often burned as being "without value" as heretical books. We do not know how many were thus eliminated.

Nevertheless a considerable number of these old books were preserved, most likely by those who had formerly lived in Transylvania. On their great trek to Rumania, Ukraine, and South Russia (1767 ff.), they carried them along as their most precious heirlooms. Thus we find today both in the United States and in Canada (and in part also in Paraguay, with the Society of Brothers) a valuable array of such books, little read nowadays to be sure, but reverently preserved. They are the personal property of single brothers, in fact the only "private" property they have, and a complete list of them is not easily established. If a brother dies he bequeaths his "old" books to whomever he pleases. Unfortunately such books can also be found today with people formerly connected with the Hutterites, but now living on their own. (Thus, for instance, a precious Riedemann codex is reported on a farm near Freeman, S.D., the property of a family formerly Hutterite. The Krimmer Mennonites also count a considerable number of former Hutterites among their members.)

In my own endeavor to establish a catalog of all these valuable documents as complete as possible I visited a great number of these American and Canadian Bruderhofs, but did not succeed in completely ferreting out all originals still extant.[8] While doing this work I heard of one particularly old and rich codex containing unique material, which was known to many and copied several times by the late bishop Elias Walter.[9] I soon learned that it had also been known to John Horsch through his friendship with Walter, and some first information had been published by Horsch in the *Herold der Wahrheit* in 1888.[10] It was also known to Eberhard Arnold, the founder of the Society of Brothers, who mentioned this codex in his footnotes to the unfinished publication of the Hutterite *Klein–Geschichtsbuch* (1933), naming it appropriately "Codex Braitmichel." But now no one knew where this remarkable book might be, even though everyone knew about it. Finally, after about a year's search, one kind brother gave me a clue and soon I got the confirmation that the codex was safe in a colony in northern Montana. Naturally I had to see it, traveling 1700 miles, and I want to acknowledge gratefully the splendid reception and hospitality at this Montana Bruderhof, where a cottage was made available to me that I might study the book undisturbed.

There was, however, a small disappointment: the original leather binding no longer exists because it was worn out. Some thirty or forty years ago the book was rebound, and for that reason lacks somewhat that quaint and

---

8   It is hoped that this *Catalog* will one day be published in the German language together with a complete listing of the entire Hutterite literature of sixteenth and seventeenth centuries.
9   See article "Elias Walter," *ME*, IV.
10   John Horsch in *Herold der Wahrheit*, 1888, p. 165.

beautiful external appearance of similar codices. To acquaint the reader now with this book, we shall try to describe it as completely as possible.

The title, carefully written, reads as follows: *Epistel Buech, mit fleisz geschriben von vilen streitern und zeugen gottes, allen frumen zum trost. Sambt einem ordentlichen register, etc.* The date at the bottom of the page says DMLXVI, which suggests that this is possibly the oldest Hutterite codex in existence (the *Kunstbuch* of Jörg Maler antedates it by five years: 1561). The claim that Braitmichel was the compiler is only a conjecture (first made by Eberhard Arnold), but it has much in its favor, even though the codex itself shows different scribal hands at work—nothing unusual with Hutterites. The book is of quarto size and contains 16 un-numbered and 625 numbered leaves (1,282 pages). It is in perfect condition—in spite of its age of nearly four hundred years. It is written in typically Hutterite sixteenth-century penmanship (ink), sometimes rather small, but always clearly legible. Titles, page headings, and the beginning of each chapter are written in red ink. The book is written in two columns (making roughly 2,400 columns, not including the "Register," or Table of Contents). Many items are preceded by a short summary of the contents by the compiler. The alphabetic "Register" at the beginning is by no means complete, and the following listing is not taken from it but from direct inspection. The book reveals an amazing variety, presenting not less than forty-two different writers or groups of writers, each one usually represented with several items. A number of items are presented anonymously—as is customary in Anabaptist literature—but the context allows certain conclusions. Here is the listing:

2 Timo am 3.

Jacob Hutter: Sechs Episteln, einschliesslich der an den Landeshauptmann von Mähren, 1535, fol. 1–34, and 119, 120;

[Anonymous]: Ein Sendbrief geschriben anstatt der ganzen Gemeinde und Bruderschaft an die Herre des Landes zu Mähren, gesandt im Jahre 1545 (NB. Fälschlich Jakob Huter zugeschrieben), fol. 35–42.

Hans Amon: Drei Episteln an Jörg Fasser und Lienhard Sailer nach Mödling, 1536;

Epistel an die Gefangenen auf Falckenstein, 1539;

Drei Episteln an die Brüder in Triest und auf dem Meer;

Epistel an die Geschwistriget zu Gostal;

Brief an die lieben Schwestern und Kranken zu Steinabrunn (these nine letters fol. 42–63; two more epistles fol. 135–37).

Jeronimus Käls, Michael Seifensieder, and Hans Oberecker: Eight epistles and "Ein schönes Lied," fol. 63'–78' and fol. 138–51. (The hymn is "Ich freu mich denn, O Vater mein, in meinem Elend jetzt vorhanden.")

Six brothers: Lamprecht Gruber, Hans Beck, Lorentz Schuester, Hänsel Planer, Peter, sein Knecht, Hänsel Thaler: Drei Episteln 1532 an die Ältesten der Gemeinde gesandt von Stertzing im Etschland aus der Gefanckhnuss, fol. 79–82.

Thomas Waldhauser: Epistel an die Brüder zu Brünn, 1528, fol. 83–86.

Kuentz Füechter: Epistel an die Gemein im Etschland, gesandt aus der Gefanckhnuss zu Stertzing, 1532, fol. 86–88.

Offerus Griesinger, sambt seinem mitgefangen Bruder Leonhard (Lochmaier): Vier Briefe aus dem Gefängnis zu Brixen, fol. 89–112.

Wilhelm Grissbacher: Ein Brief aus der Gefanckhnuss, 1535, fol. 113–14.

Hans Donner und Hans Seidel: Ein Brief aus Sankt Veith in Kärnten, 1538, fol. 115–16.

Hans Peckh und seine mitgefangenen Brüder: Zwei Briefe aus dem Gefängnis zu Guffidaun, fol. 117–18, 124–25.

Jörg Wagner: Eine schöne Epistel (story of his martyrdom), auch seine Artikel und sein Verhör, 1527 (In Codex erroneously "1537." This is no letter but a report by an eyewitness), fol. 121–124.

Ludwig Fest: Ein Brief aus dem Gefängnis zu Schwatz in Tirol, 1533, fol. 126–27.

Leonhard Roth: Epistel dem Bruder Abraham und denen, die bei ihm in Einigkeit des Geistes gesamblet sind, geschrieben aus der Gefanckhnus (1540), fol. 128–30.

Gefangene Brüder auf Falckenstein: Brief an die Gemein Gottes in Mähren (1540), fol. 131–34.

Hans Amon (see also above): Sendbrief an Walser Mayr, Justina und Endln, etc., fol. 135–36;

Sendbrief an Leonhard Schienbacker, fol. 136–37.

Jeronimus Käls (see above): Sendbrief an Hans Amon, 1536;
Rechenschaft Jeronimus, Michel Behem und Hans Oberrekker, aus Ihren Banden und Gefencknussen (fol. 144–46);

Die acht Epistel an die Kinder Gottes zu Auspitz in der Schul (all this): fol. 138–51.

Jörg Fasser und Leonhard Sailer (or Lanzenstiel): Neun Episteln an die Gemein Gottes in Mähren, gesandt aus dem Gefängnis zu Mödling, 1536, fol. 152–62, and fol. 172–96.

Klein Michel (Michael Seifensieder or Behaim, of Bohemia): Drei Episteln aus seinen Banden in Wien an die Gemeinde Gottes in Mähren, fol. 163–67, 168–72 (see also above fol. 71–72).

Stoffel Aschelberger: Vier Episteln an die Brüder zu Znaim, etc., gesandt von Falckenstein, 1540, fol. 197–99.

Hans Schlaffer: Die zwei Verantwortungen, 1527, schriftlich überantwortet (Antwort auf die Fragen getan vom Richter), fol. 200–6;

Ein einfältiger Unterricht zum Anfang eines christlichen Lebens (enthält auch die Fragen der Taufe halben), fol. 206–12;

Testament und eigen Bekanntnus gegen Gott, ein ainfaltiges Gebet durch ainen gefangenen armen Brueder im Herren, zu Schwatz geurtelt und betrübt bis in den Todt. Datum Schwatz, Montag nach Lichtmess dises gefährlichsten 28. Jars, fol. 212–19 (This is the longest prayer ever composed by an Anabaptist, one of the most profound prayers ever written down in the agony of imminent death.);

Folgt nun ein kurzer Bericht: Anfang eines christlichen Lebens, auch Gebet und Danksagung, fol. 219–20;

Kurtz und einfältige Vermahnung von der Kindertaufe, am 2. Tag January im 1528 Jahr, fol. 221–24;

Brief an einen Bruder, Antwort auf etliche Fragstücke, fol. 225–27;

Ein Bericht seiner Bekanntnus und Verantwortung vor der Obrigkeit getan, an seine Geschwistriget im Herren zugeschrieben. Geschrieben am Pfingstag vor Pauli Bekehrung, A.D. 1528, fol. 227–30.

Leonhard Schiemer: Eine Epistel an die Gemein zu Rottenburg [ie., Ratten–berg, darin eine hüpsche Erklärung der XII Stücke christlichen Glaubens begriffen, fol. 232–39. (Fol. 231 does not exist.) Fol. 240 contains a diagram (see later), 240' a brief meditation (see later);

Was Gottes Gnad sei, fol. 241–42;

Eine Epistel Leonhard Schiemers an die Gemein zu Rottenburg am Inn, 1527 Jahr, Von dreierlei Gnad (the section "Von der andren Gnad" has also a remarkable paraphrase of the Lord's Prayer), fol. 242–55;

Folgt nun Vom Fläschl, fol. 251'–53 (one of the finest pieces ever written by an Anabaptist). Datum: Zu Rottenburg am Inn in meinen Banden), am Pfingstag nach Andre, A.D. 1527;

Von der Tauff im Neuen Testament, ganz klärlich entdeckt und erklärt durch den Bruder Leonhard Schiemer, fol. 256–58;

Ein Bekanntnus, 14. tags Januaris 1528, fol. 258–59;

Ein schöner Trostbrief an einen schwachen Bruder, fol. 260–63;

Eine Geschicht beschehen zu Glatz in der Schlösing. Clement Adler, der is in den Götzentempel gangen und hat den Pfaffen geheissen still zu sein, fol. 263–64 (a most mysterious affair).

(Leonhard Schiemer ?): Ein feiner oder schöner Artikel von der Prob des Geistes, in Frag und Antwort, auch Gegenred (a sort of catechism, most likely for the Rattenberg church), fol. 264'–71;

Fogt ein schöner, klarer Unterricht oder Unterweisung eines gottseligen oder Gott wohlgefälligen Lebens, fol. 272–76;

Nun folgt ein Artikel, Exempel von den bösen, gottlosen Weibern und was die Schrift darvon sagt, fol. 276–81;

Allhie nachfolgt ein schöner Artikel, nämlich Lehr, Vermahnung oder Warnung von den bösen Weibern, wie die Geschrift darvon sagt, fol. 281–86;

Folgt ein Artikel Von der Kinderzucht und was die Heilige Schrift sagt, fol. 286'–99.

Ulrich Stadler: Ein kurzer Unterricht Ulrich Stadlers der Sünd halben, auch des Ausschlusses und wie es darin steht; auch der Gemeinschaft der zeitlichen Güter halben, wider die, so des Herren Werk, Band und Strick schelten, mit wahrhaftiger Zeugnus der heiligen Geschrift, fol. 301–4;

Von der Gemeinschaft der Heiligen, fol. 304'–5';

Von der Ordnung der Heiligen in ihrer Gemeinschaft und Leben, mit den Gütern ihres Vaters allhie in ihrer Wohlfahrt in dem Herzen, fol. 305'–8;

Die Epistel an die Gemein zu Crasnicktau, gesandt von Ladomir aus Podolien, 1536, fol. 308–9;

Eine andere Epistel, auch der Gemein zu Crasnicktau gesandt, fol. 309–10.

Michael Sattler: Brüderliche Vereinigung etzlicher Kinder Gottes, sieben Artikel betreffend (1527), fol. 310–15;

Epistel an die Gemein Gottes zu Horb, fol. 315–18;

Die Artikel und Handlung Michael Sattlers, 21. Mai 1527, fol. 318–21.

Claus Felbinger: Abgeschrift des Glaubens, etc. (hard to read), fol. 321–31;

Sendbrief aus seiner Gefangenschaft an Leonhard Sailer, geschrieben am St. Johannistag, fol. 333–35;

Ein ander Sendbrief (concerning his trial), fol. 336–48.

Brüder auf dem Mör (ie., the Falckenstein prisoners, now in Trieste or on their way to Genoa, 1540): Rechenschaft und Zeucknhuss unsres Glaubens, darumb wir Trübsal und Gefenckhnuss dulden und leiden, was uns Gott zugeschickt umb solcher Bekanntnus willen, die wir tun mit Wort und Tat, fol. 349–58.

Die gefangenen hingeführten Brüder zum Mör: Sendbrief, 1539, fol. 359–61.

Peter Rideman: 24 Episteln (1537–49), fol. 362–434; Rechenschaft und Bekanntnus des Glaubens, geschrieben zu Gmunden in Oesterreich (1529–32), fol. 435–60.

Antony Erdtfordter: Urlaubsbrief an die zu Clagenfurt, 1538, fol. 461–79.

Johannes Landtsperger (active 1527–29): Selections from his printed works, without titles:

Der allmächtige, ewige Gott hat erstlich durch Mosen und Propheten geboten, etc. (including the parable Wie ein Zimmerman ein Haus ganz und gar verfertigt);

Ceremonien oder Sitten im Alten Testament;

Das Gesetz (a) der Werke und des Lebens, (b) der Sünde und des Todes, (c) des Geistes und des Glaubens;

Ein kurzer Begriff und Auslegung, was denn sei die vier Tier Apoca. IIII, mit der Weissagung der vier Zahlen, die hin und wieder in der Geschrift gefunden werden, fol. 480–83.

Hans Langenmantel: Ein gründlicher Unterricht von der greulichen Mess, fol. 484–99;

Hernach folgt christliches und pabstliches Abentmal, Vergleichung und Widerspiel;

Vom Nachtmal des Herren, aus Matthäus, Markus, Lukas, Paulus, fol. 484–99 (this entire item is also called "Vom Abendmahl");

Verantwortung des Nachtmahls oder Brotbrechens, fol. 499–502;

Ein göttliche und gründliche Offenbarung von dem wahrhaften Wiedertauff, mit götlicher Wahrheit angezeight, 1527, fol. 502–14;

Eine schöne Auslegung des Vater Unser, fol. 514'–18 (might be compared with Leonhard Schiemer's similar paraphrase above, fol. 494–550).

Hans Denck: Was geredt sei, dass die Geschrift sagt, etc. fol. 518–28.

Hänsel Schmid: 17 Episteln aus dem Gefängnis zu Aachen, 1558, fol. 529–75 (the first epistle is extremely long, fol. 529–40);

Rechenschaft vom Abendmahl Christi und seiner rechten Bedeutung, unchristlicher Gebrauch, gemacht durch Hänsel Schmidt aus seiner Gefenckhnuss zu Aach, fol. 575–80.

Heinrich Adam, auch genannt Kramer: Drei Sendbriefe aus Aachen, 1558, fol. 580–83.

Franz Wälsch (ie., Francesco della Sega): Ein Sendbrief aus Venedig, 8. September 1563, fol. 583–85.

Hans Mändel oder Klein Hänsel: Drei Episteln, 1551 und 1561, fol. 586–600;

Glaubensbekanntnus dreier Mannspersonen: Hans Mändel, Eustachius Kotter und Jörg Rack, 1561, fol. 602–9.

Hänsel Hueter (ie., Mang): Brief an seine eheliche Schwester Gredl, aus Sundthofen im Algey, fol. 610–13.

Conrad Schuster (ie., Heinzemann): Ein Sendbrief von Wien aus der Gefenckhnuss an die Ältesten der Gemein Gottes zu Märhern (1559), fol. 614–17.

Caspar Braitmichel: Ein Bussbrief in die Schlesing an seinen Vetter Casper, Datum Märhern, den December (no year), fol. 618–25.

This volume seems to have been the prototype of all later similar Anabaptist codices (with the exception of the *Kunstbuch* which slightly precedes our book), a complete devotional library in itself, leading and guiding the Brethren at home and on their hazardous missionary trips. Here they learned what their faith really meant, existentially to be sure, and not only intellectually. The inclusion of so many early tracts (those prior to 1530)

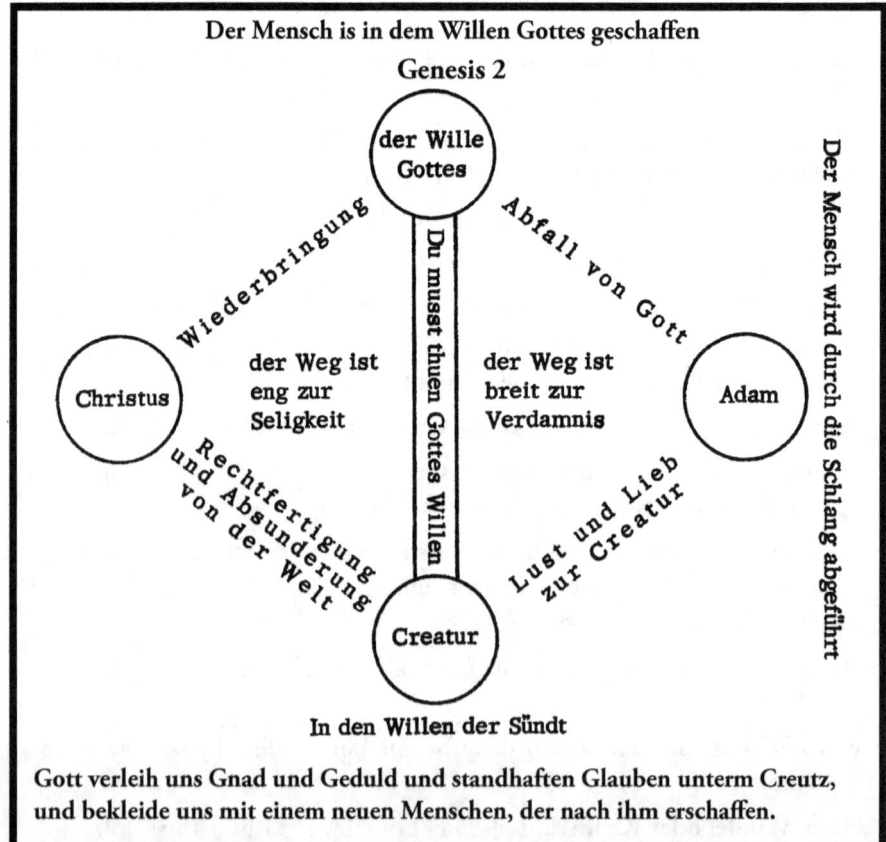

seems to have made this book particularly valuable, even though most of them have been known from other sources as well.

But this generalization is not true in every regard. For instance, nowhere else do we find all the tracts of Leonhard Schiemer united in this way, besides a number of unknown items interpreted as instructions (written in prison) for the budding Rattenberg community.[11] Of particular interest appears to me one page at the conclusion of Schiemer's *Eine hüpsche Erklärung der XII Stücke christlichen Glaubens*, which carries a remarkable diagram summarizing at a glance the central doctrine of Anabaptist life (fol. 240). [See diagram on 302.]

This diagram is followed on the next page (fol. 240') by a brief meditation on silence:

Stillschweigen: Ein christlich gottförchtiger Mench schweigt bis zu seiner Zeit / weiss wol wenn es Zeit ist, darumb dass die Zeit bös und gefärlich ist / keins vertraut seim Nächsten / soll sich auch keiner auff ein Fürsten verlassen / verwar die Thüer deines Mundts / verdore die, die in deiner Schoss liegt / Ursach, der Sohn wird den Vater verunehren, die Tochter wird die Muetter sich lauen / darumb sagt der Weise Mann (Eccl. 3): Schweigen hat sein Zeit / Reden hat sein Zeit / also musst ein Zeit schweigen bis zur verordneten Zeit / do der Herr die Fürsten zu Schandten macht.

Geist gebürt [gebiert] *Forcht*, die Forcht Gottes gebürt rechte Erkanntnus, gebürt rechte Lieb, wie Johannes sagt. Das wir haben erkannt und der Lieb geglaubt / Ungefärbte Lieb gebürt einen bewerten Glauben / Die Lieb glaubt alles / Und dergleichen: die Lieb ist eine Erfüllung des Gesetzes. / Der mich liebt, der hält meine Worte / die Gott lieben, denen dienet es alles zum Besten / ein erfahrener Glaub kann sich alles Guets zu Gott verstehen / auch ganz ergeben / Waget alles, das er hat und vermag / Glaub gebürt Rechtertigung / Rechtfertigung gebürt Erleuchtung oder Herrlich–Machung / Herrlich–Machung gebürt Jesu Christo gleich zu werden.

The section of Leonhard Schiemer's writings is introduced on folio 241 by the following paragraph:

Allhie sein etliche schöne Artikeln und Geschriften nach Grund der Wahrheit gestellt und gemacht von treuen und frummen Zeugen der Wahrheit. Erstlich manicherlei schöne Artikel vom lieben Brueder Leonhard Schimer, samtlich einer feinen Vorred anfencklich.

A likely assumption is that all these and a few more pieces had been collected by the valiant Rattenberg church (which had more than seventy

---
11 See article "Rattenberg," *ME*, IV.

martyrs during a rather brief history) and put together in a booklet, the great inheritance from their first "bishop." This booklet was then brought to Moravia when congregational life became impossible in the Tyrol. The items: "Prob des Geistes" (a catechism), "Unterweisung eines Gott wohlgefälligen Lebens," the strange item "Von den bäsen Weibern und was die Geschrift dazu sagt," and the educational tract, "Von der Kinderzucht" (fol. 264'– 99), here anonymously presented, seem to have originated with Leonhard Schiemer, who while awaiting his fate was anxious to give his "children" as much guidance and advice as possible. This is not only the impression of the present writer but also of the late Bishop Elias Water, who, in his edition of the *Lieder der Hutterischen Brüder* (Scottdale, 1914), page 19, lists all these anonymous tracts as the work of Schiemer. It certainly adds a great deal to our picture of this outstanding early Anabaptist leader and martyr.[12]

That Schiemer's contemporary brother Hans Schlaffer was a great master of prayer becomes also strikingly clear from this codex, which has all his prayers (especially his long one written in the night before his execution, fol. 212–19) in such a form that the value becomes immediately evident.[13]

The most valuable part, however, of the entire codex seems to be found in folios 362–434: the complete collection of Peter Riedemann's 34 epistles, found nowhere else, an inestimable source not only for our appreciation of this great leader but also for our knowledge of the background of his *Rechenschaft* of 1541, and in general for the history of Anabaptism *ca.* 1537–49, including the story of the little known Philippites.[14] It is somewhat strange that no other Hutterite codex contains these epistles[15] in view of the high esteem in which this outstanding leader was held throughout all Hutterite history. There is but one surprising slant to this topic: the compiler of the codex did not also connect the collective missive No. 2, dated 1545 (fol. 35–42) with Riedemann. Although written in the name of the entire brotherhood to the *Landeshauptmann* (governor) of Moravia, there can be little doubt that it was conceived and written by Riedemann, at that time the only brother able to write such an epistle.[16]

This then is the codex. It is most gratifying that the opportunity arose to microfilm it in 1958 at the Mennonite Historical Library of Goshen College, where it also will be re–enlarged and printed positively, thus making available to scholars a wide range of original Anabaptist sources of the highest order.

SOURCE: *Mennonite Quarterly Review*, XXXIII (1959), pp. 96–107.

---

12 See Friedmann, "Leonhard Schiemer and Hans Schlaffer, Two Early Anabaptist Martyrs," *MQR*, XXXIII (1959), 31–42.
13 Some of these prayers will be published in the forthcoming volume by Lydia Müller and Robert Friedmann, *Glaubenszeugnisse deutscher Täufer*, II (Gütersloh, 1962); more material of this kind is planned for the next volume of the *Täuferakten*, the *Briefe der Täufer*.
14 The article "Riedemann," in *ME*, IV is in part based on this collection of epistles.
15 The entire collection of Riedemann letters will be published in the planned volume of *Briefe*.
16 Joseph Beck published parts of this letter in his *Geschichts–Bücher* as an anonymous epistle.

A COMPREHENSIVE REVIEW OF RESEARCH ON THE HUTTERITES 1880–1950

The names of the three outstanding Austrian scholars stand at the beginning of the modern study of Hutterite thought and life. **Joseph von Beck** (1815–87), Johann Loserth (1846–1936), and Rudolf Wolkan (d. 1927). They discovered, or rediscovered, the rich original sources of the Hutterites (their handwritten books), and immediately recognized their tremendous significance far beyond their relevance for a relatively small sectarian movement. During a long industrious life Beck collected an enormous amount of original material in Austrian and Hungarian libraries and archives. Out of this material he composed, somewhat mosaic–like, the original story of this amazing brotherhood. His *Geschichts–Bücher der Wiedertäufer in Oesterreich–Ungarn* (Vienna, 1883), with its countless enlightening footnotes, is still a major basis for our knowledge of Hutterite life. To be sure, his material was much richer than that utilized in this volume; it also required more historical integration than he was inclined to produce. Thus hundreds of boxes of handwritten transcripts, mainly of Hutterite manuscript books (codices), were left as his estate (*Nachlass*).

The task of bringing this material to life fell to **Johann Loserth**, Professor of Modern European History at the University of Graz, Styria. From 1890 to 1930 this most capable historiographer of the Hutterites brought forth a wealth of books and studies which may be called truly classical.[1] It is to him that we owe most of our knowledge of Hutterite life and thought.

Though himself a Catholic, he concentrated with great sympathy and understanding upon these unique people. He combined a very dynamic use of all sources available with a fine intuition. After having utilized most of Beck's material, he turned it over to the Moravian Landesarchiv at Brno (Brünn), now Czechoslovakia. This so–called Beck collection (Beck's *Nachlass*) may be called almost exhaustive, including even the most far–fetched source material; unfortunately some of its files are nearly illegible due to Beck's poor penmanship. All transcripts are handwritten.[2]

---

1 The article "Loserth," *ML*, II, 693, contains a fairly complete list of Loserth's studies regarding the Austrian Anabaptists.
2 Described by Harold S. Bender, in the *MQR*, XXIII (1949), 105–7, "Anabaptist Manuscripts in the Archives at Brno, Czechoslovakia."

Rudolf Wolkan, Professor of German Literature at the University of Vienna, was the first European scholar to rediscover the living Hutterites here in America. (John Horsch, who contacted the Brethren as early as 1890 or even before, was instrumental in this rediscovery.) Neither Beck nor Loserth (prior to 1908) knew anything about them. Wolkan made his name first known by his *Lieder der Wiedertäufer* (Berlin, 1903), a volume still unsurpassed in genuine enrichment of our knowledge, important not only for Anabaptist hymnology but also for a new, clear–cut distinction between the three main groups of Anabaptists, the Swiss Brethren, the Dutch Mennonites, and the Austrian Hutterites. The unique story of the *Ausbund* was here told for the first time. In 1923, Wolkan published the *Geschicht–Buch der Hutterischen Brüder*, using a transcript of the original manuscript which Beck thought to be lost, but which actually had been carefully kept by the Brethren during all their pilgrimages. The language of this 1923 edition is somewhat modernized, thus changing the flavor of the original text. In spite of this new and well–prepared publication, Beck's older edition did not become obsolete, due to the extraordinary scholarly apparatus which no researcher ever can do without. Wolkan published also a descriptive book on the Hutterites (*Die Hutterer*, Vienna, 1918), in which for the first time the existence of a continuation of the "Great" Chronicle (called "the Small Chronicle") was mentioned. Its author, Johannes Waldner (d. 1824), is named here for the first time, too. A transcript of this smaller chronicle, the *Klein–Geschichtsbuch*, made in Canada, was on Loserth's desk for many years; economic reasons alone prevented its publication by this master of Anabaptist history. Yet Loserth's last greater paper of 1930 gives an excellent summary of the contents of the new chronicle.[3] From personal talks with Loserth about 1930, I can affirm that he was deeply impressed by the personality of Johannes Waldner, whom he judged to be one of the finest historiographers he had ever read. And yet Waldner was an unskilled man, a peasant by background.

All these three men worked with love and untiring devotion in this field. It seems almost as if an earnest student, once he has come into contact with this unique religious material, will never give it up completely. Those who studiously delved into these testimonies could not help being fascinated; after a while they became a part of this fellowship of devoted research men. I have hardly met any of them who remained completely indifferent, even if the religious attitude of the Brethren appeared strange at first and far from their own ideas.

Beck's collection is still the greatest mine of knowledge to be tapped. In spite of the fact that the transcripts are handwritten only, a microfilming of this treasure of more than one hundred files (with thousands of sheets), would provide American scholars with a permanent stock of original Anabaptist material. It is the intention of the present writer to prepare an exhaustive

---

3   Loserth, "Decline and Revival of the Hutterites," *MQR*, IV (1930), 93–112.

description of all these manuscript books from which these transcripts were taken. Prior to World War II these codices were kept in European libraries and archives, but now it is feared that quite a few of them might be lost for ever.

Among the historians of the Reformation at the beginning of this century it was primarily **Heinrich Böhmer**, Professor of Church History at the University of Leipzig, who stimulated a new interest in the hidden story of the Anabaptists. A strangely ambivalent love and dislike drew him to Thomas Müntzer, the Christian revolutionary. Böhmer developed the totally wrong idea that Anabaptism in general had its origin with this remarkable man Müntzer. Accordingly, he instructed the students of his seminar to do their research in this misleading direction. Nevertheless, he aroused the interest of his colleagues for these "stepchildren" of the Reformation, and prompted a number of excellent monographs in this new field of church history.[4] One of his students was **Dr. Lydia Müller**, whom he had urged to go to Slovakia and Hungary to make firsthand studies of the remnants of the Hutterite colonies and of the manuscripts in the different archives. The results of this research are two books by Dr. Müller, *Der Kommunismus der mährischen Wiedertäufer* (Leipzig, 1928), and *Glaubenszeugnisse oberdeutscher Taufgesinnter* (Leipzig, 1938), the first of a planned two–volume edition of Hutterite texts. It is true that there is much bias and slant in these books, mainly in the first one (in this regard Dr. Müller differed much from Loserth and Wolkan), and Mennonite scholars will criticize her for that. Yet much good material has been assembled and digested, valuable for every student of Hutterite lore. The *Glaubenszeugnisse* (Vol. I) is a very fine collection of Hutterite tracts, epistles, and confessional accounts; unfortunately too much had to be presented in a condensed and abbreviated form, which spoils the very meaning of these documents. Thus this volume cannot be called the "standard" edition of this material; yet, up to now it is the only source edition available, and as such much in demand. As I understand, the manuscript of Volume II was prepared completely by Dr. Müller, who was killed during the war by a bomb, and the manuscript is now in the hands of her nephew, Pastor Ludwig Milner at Würzburg, and will be published soon. A microfilm copy is deposited in the Goshen College Library.

The Verein für Reformationsgeschichte during the 1920's pursued a great plan: every bit of Anabaptist source material, such as mandates of the authorities, records of Anabaptist trials, epistles and other writings of Anabaptist origin, and so on, was to be published in a large series of text volumes. The first volume of this series came out in 1930; it was Gustav Bossert's source volume on *Herzogtum Württemberg* (Leipzig, 1930). It

---

4 Here is a list of monographed works out under his guidance: Ecke, *Schwenckfeld und der Gedanke einer apostolischen Reformation* (1911), Neuser, *Hans Hut* (1913), Sachsse, *Hubmaier* (1914), L. Müller, *Der Kommunismus der mährischen Wiedertäufer* (1928), and A. Lohmann, *Zur geistigen Entwicklung Thomas Müntzers* (1931).

contains an extensive section of Hutterite sources, namely, the complete text of the numerous epistles of the Hutterite brother Paul Glock between 1563 and 1569, taken in full from Beck's collection. It is thus far the largest source publication of Hutterite epistles.

It was in the year 1923 that I myself came in contact with Hutterite manuscript books for the first time, handed over to me by Rudolf Wolkan (Vienna). For the next few years he guided all my work in this new field; it was an unforgettable experience. The result was a paper, "Die Briefe der Österreichischen Täufer," published in 1929 in the *Archiv für Reformationsgeschichte*, XXVI.[5] This study of the unique epistolary literature of the Hutterites has found fairly wide attention, since it opened a new world of Christian testimonies, hitherto overlooked. The similarity to the epistles of the New Testament is striking. In 1930 and 1931 another large research study of mine was published. "Eine dogmatische Hauptschrift der Hutterischen Täufergemeinschaften in Mähren," *Archiv für Reformationsgeschichte*, XXVIII/XXIX. Peter Walpot, the Hutterite *Vorsteher* in the Golden Age of the brotherhood (1565–78), was identified as the probable author of this remarkable confessional document. The study of its sources and background was particularly rewarding for a greater appreciation of Hutterite thought and theology. A small paper of mine, "Die Habaner in der Slovakei," published in the *Wiener Zeitschrift für Volkskunde*, XXXII (1927), gave a folkloristic picture of what has remained of Hutterism in Europe. "Habaner" is the name of those Brethren who in the eighteenth century had been converted by force to Catholicism and thus could stay unmolested at their Bruderhofs (colonies).[6] The small Anabaptist tract, "Concerning the True Soldier of Christ" (1534), was published in the *Mennonite Quarterly Review*, 1931, so to say as a by-product of my research in Hutterite literature. The original of this tract is lost today; it was the only known tract from the Philippite Brethren in Moravia who first sang the hymns later collected in the *Ausbund*.

Strange contacts were achieved. Czech scholars in Moravia and Silesia, even in Prague, began to show interest in some aspects of Hutterite research. **Dr. Karel Czernohorsky** must be credited with the finest publication concerning Hutterite handicraft, mainly their ceramics and pottery. A copy of his main work is in Goshen College library; it is written in Czech language but with a German "resumé" and many beautiful plates.[7] The able former director of the Moravian Landesarchiv in Brno (Brünn), which preserves the Beck collection, **Dr. Franticek Hruby**, published—partly upon a casual suggestion on my part—the results of his research also in the German

---

5 An English translation of this paper appeared in the *MQR*, XX, (1946) 147–77, "The Epistles of the Hutterian Brethren, 1530–1650, a Study in Anabaptist Literature."

6 An English summary of this paper may be found in the *Proceedings of the Fifth Annual Conference on Mennonite Cultural Problems*, held at Freeman, South Dakota, August 1946, pp. 61–66.

7 In my brief essay, "Christian Love in Action—the Hutterites," in *Mennonite Life*, July 1946, pp. 42, 43, four samples of this lost art of ceramics are reproduced from Czernohorsky's book.

language, entitled *Die Wiedertäufer in Mähren* (Leipzig, 1935). This book is particularly valuable for its use of new Czech source material dealing with the economic side of the Hutterite existence, mainly in Moravia. It shows that almost every noble estate in this territory prided itself on its splendid Hutterite pieces of ceramics.

One of the most enlightening studies in the history of Anabaptist ideas was produced by **Ethelbert Staffer** under the title, "Märtyrertheologie und Täufertum," published in the *Zeitschrift für Kirchengeschichte*, LII (1933).[8] It demonstrates as one of the central ideas of Anabaptism the principle of "the suffering church" in this world; naturally Hutterite material provided the author with a major part of his proof texts.

Next we turn to the work of the Baptist preacher **Wilhelm Wiswedel**, a research scholar of high rank. The material which he found in the Beck collection of the Moravian Landesarchiv thoroughly captivated him. That was in the 1920's, in 1950 he is still continuing this type of work. His excellent *Bilder und Führergestalten aus dem Täufertum* (2 vols., Kassel, 1928 and 1930),[9] unites solid scholarship with most appealing presentation. Naturally, these studies shed also new light on many phases and aspects of Hutterite life. The manuscript of Volume III is ready for print, and is to be published soon in Kassel, Germany, with American aid. Wiswedel also published a number of excellent research papers, of which only the more important ones shall be mentioned here. "Das Schulwesen der Hutterischen Brüder," *Archiv für Reformationsgeschichte*, 1940, uses the outstanding addresses of Peter Walpot concerning education, 1568, his school discipline, 1578, and other material which proves that Hutterite elementary education in the sixteenth century was definitely of a superior nature.[10]

"Gabriel Ascherham und die nach ihm benannte Bewegung," *Archiv für Reformationsgeschichte*, 1937, deals with an early schism among the Moravian Anabaptists and their final unification.

"Die Nikolsburger Artikel," *Zeitschrift für Bayrische Kirchengeschichte*, 1938, is particularly important because it proves once for all that these articles of ill repute, accusing the Hutterites of anti-trinitarian leanings, were a forgery (made in Augsburg), and had nothing to do with any Anabaptist group.

"Die alten Täufergemeinden und ihr missionarisches Wirken," *ARG*, XL (1943), and XLI (1948), makes use of a rare Hutterite manuscript, called

---

8 An English translation of this study appeared in the *MQR*, XIX (1945), 179–214, under the title, "The Anabaptist Theology of Martyrdom."

9 An extensive review of the first two volumes, by the present writer, may be found in the *MQR*, XIV (1940), 187–92.

10 Cf. Harold S. Bender, "The Hutterite School Discipline of 1578 and Peter Scherer's Address of 1568 to the Schoolmasters," *MQR*, V (1931), 231–44 (based upon a study by W. Salinger, in a German educational journal, 1901). The Wiswedel study discussed here contains also a Hutterite catechism (*Kinderlehre*) of 1620. This piece would deserve an English translation.

by Beck "codex ritualis," which contains the liturgy, so to say, used by the Brethren on the occasion of the sending out of the Brethren "missioners" into the four corners of the German–speaking land. It is well known that the Hutterites were possibly the most aggressive group among the Anabaptists regarding missionary work (or was it rather proselytizing?). This was first stressed by Johann Loserth, and more recently restudied by Franklin H. Littell (see later). Many more articles by Wiswedel are published in the *Sendbote*, the magazine of the German Baptists in America (Cleveland), and a new series is announced to appear soon, again dealing in the main with Hutterite material and Hutterite doctrines.[11] Since this magazine, however, is not easily available, no further details are quoted here.

In connection with its great *Täuferakten* publication program, the Verein für Reformationsgeschichte made extensive plans toward a comprehensive edition of the Hutterite material. A committee was established to take care of this enterprise. The late **Hans von Schubert**, Professor of Church History at the University of Heidelberg and president of the Verein, was chairman; Johann Loserth (then 84) was named honorary adviser, while Dr. Lydia Müller (Leipzig), Dr. Paul Dedic (Graz), and I (Vienna) were named the scholarly workers who had to collect, transcribe, and edit the entire material available. Three or more volumes were scheduled. Dr. Müller's work, the tracts and doctrinal writings of the Hutterites, was at least partly published in 1938 (*Glaubenszeugnisse*). My own assignment concerned the epistolary literature of the Brethren. The unhappy conditions of Europe after 1933, however, prevented any completion of this plan. Today, the transcripts of about sixty Hutterite epistles (about one fifth of all epistles extant), prepared at that time, are kept in custody at Goshen College for possible later publication. **Dr. Paul Dedic** was to ransack all Austrian archives for records of trials, mandates, and other governmental documents. The material thus collected was tremendous; many thousands of documents were assembled and transcribed, a surprise even to the expert. But it could never be published. And now, 1950, the bad news comes to us that Dr. Dedic passed away recently. It may be assumed that his material went to the Landesarchiv of Styria, in Graz, for safekeeping, since Dr. Dedic worked at this place for the last ten years. Fortunately, he was able to publish at least some results of his arduous research: the *Mennonite Quarterly Review*, 1939, brought from his pen the fine study, "Social Background of the Austrian Anabaptist." It opens a new aspect and thus happily supplements all the earlier studies in Hutterite lore. With the coming of Nazism and the war, research nearly collapsed. There was very good intention on the part of the Verein für Reformationsgeschichte, but nothing could be published after 1938. Whether the Hutterite material of the *Täuferakten Kommission* will ever

---

11 Pastor Wiswedel writes me (April 1950) that a study of his, entitled "Die Reformation geht noch fort," will soon be published in the *Sendbote* (organ of the German Baptists in the U. S., Cleveland), dealing with the teachings of the Anabaptists concerning the New Testament concept of the church (*Gemeinde*), and likewise concerning baptism, Lord's Supper, discipline, mission to the unbelievers, etc.

come to light is quite uncertain in spite of the lively interest of historians of the Reformation period in this new field. Dr. Müller and Dr. Dedic are dead; Pastor Wiswedel is now 73; I myself have moved to the United States where German source publications are not likely to be carried out.

However, we cannot leave the old continent without mentioning two or three doctoral dissertations in our field deserving highest attention. The first one is by a certain **Dr. Franz Heimann** whose whereabouts could never be ascertained.[12] His Ph.D. dissertation entitled *Die Lehre von Kirche und Gemeinschaft in der Hutterischen Täufergemeinde,* 1927 (ms. at the University library, Vienna), is a first rank study of Hutterite thoughts and practices. Dr. Heimann starts with the question whether Peter Riedemann, author of the great *Rechenschaft* of 1545, was influenced to any great extent by the writings of Balthasar Hubmaier (d. 1528). The answer that this influence was but minimal, and that what was truly original with the Hutterites must be regarded as a product of their own genius, is but a minor part of Heimann's findings. More important are the positive formulations regarding the spiritual principles involved. Goshen College is fortunate enough to have a typescript copy of this dissertation, and it is hoped that it can be published in translation in the not too distant future.

Another dissertation is of quite recent origin. **Dr. Hans Georg Fischer**, a Lutheran minister of Vienna, Austria, wrote his thesis on *Jacob Huter, ein Bild evangelischer Frömmigkeit aus dem 16. Jahrhundert* (1949), submitted to the Evangelical Theological Faculty of the University of Vienna. This paper consists of three parts: the life of Jakob Hutter, the theology of Hutter, and the full text of the eight existing epistles of this leader, brought together in this way for the first time. The most original part is, of course, the second one which advances our grasp of Anabaptist theology very much. The Hutterites in America are anxious to have this first complete biography of their leader printed, and the Historical Committee of the General Conference Mennonites is considering its publication (ed. Dr. C. Krahn, Bethel College). There is hope that the second part will also be published in an English translation in the *Review* in 1951. Dr. Fischer has shown unusual enthusiasm for the Anabaptist vision, and there are indications that it will be he who will carry on the torch of Hutterite research in Europe, especially in Austria.

A third doctoral thesis dealing with *Das Täufertum im Tiroler Unterlande* by **Dr. E. Widmoser** (ms. Un. Libr. Innsbruck, Tyrol.) centers around the Anabaptist trials in Tyrol during the sixteenth century. This subject proved to be less profitable for the advancement of our knowledge of the Hutterite story. The author studied many court records, but the result is somewhat monotonous, and offers not too much beyond what was already known through Loserth's great study on the Anabaptists in Tyrol (1892/93).

---

12   In spite of my earnest endeavor, Dr. Heimann is the only scholar in the field whom I could never contact even though he graduated not long after myself from the same university.

We now turn to the advancement of Hutterite research in the United States. The elder historian of both Mennonitism and Hutterite life here is no doubt **John Horsch** (d. 1941). As already mentioned above it was he who first brought about a contact with the Hutterites in Canada, mainly with the very active *Vorsteher* Elias Walter of Stand–Off Colony, near MacLeod, Alberta, Canada. That was as early as 1890 or even before. Horsch knew the text of both the larger and the smaller chronicle of the Hutterites, and he used both sources for his excellent monograph., *The Hutterian Brethren, a Story of Loyalty and Martyrdom* (Goshen, 1931). It is an important book, very well written and well documented, the first comprehensive study of the Hutterites in the English language. Horsch had contact with practically every scholar in the field of Anabaptistica, and this fact helped greatly the promotion of further research. From time to time, the *Mennonite Quarterly Review* published valuable Hutterite material. Harold S. Bender, for instance, translated a German study concerning the school system of the Brethren, entitled "The Hutterite School Discipline of 1578 and Peter Scherer's Address of 1568 to the Schoolmasters," *Review*, 1931. This preceded W. Wiswedel's related paper of 1940. He likewise translated Paul Tschetter's diary of 1873 (when this brother came over from Russia to find new land), again *Review*, 1931.[13] Also my own paper, "Concerning a True Soldier of Christ, a Hitherto Unknown Tract of the Philippite Brethren in Moravia" (1534), was published in Bender's translation in the *Review*, 1931. Other papers in translations in the Review, are the one by Paul Dedic (1939), by Ethelbert Staffer (1945), and my study on the Hutterite epistles (1946).

Perhaps I may be permitted to enumerate at this place briefly my own contributions in the field of Hutterite lore since my coming to Goshen College in 1940. The Chapter VIII of my book, *Mennonite Piety Through the Centuries* (Goshen, 1949), deals with "Discussions Between the Hutterite Brethren and the Moravians," using in the main T. Th. Müller's stimulating research study on this subject, published in 1910, in the *Zeitschrift für Brüdergeschichte*. In my paper, "Encounter of the Anabaptists and Mennonites with Anti–Trinitarianism" (*Review.*, 1947), the strange contacts of the Hutterite Brethren with members of the (Socinian) Polish Church are further discussed, with some new material hitherto overlooked.[14] In the same context belongs also the shorter paper, "Reason and Obedience, an Old Anabaptist Letter of Peter Walpot (1571) and Its Meaning" (*Review*, 1945), in which the idea of the filial obedience of an earnest Christian toward the commandments of God is argued about and placed in opposition to the more sophisticated theology of the Unitarians. This idea of obedience to the Word of God is, no doubt, one of the main pillars of Anabaptism. It presupposes a certain simplicity (*Einfalt*) of the mind.

---

13 The German original of Paul Tschetter's Diary appeared in the *Klein–Geschischtbuch*, 571–606.

14 Some new material concerning these contacts became known through E. M. Wilbur's great work, *A History of Unitarianism* (Harvard Press, 1946). This material is written in the Polish language, and would certainly deserve a translation.

"The Adventures of a Hutterite Brother in Turkey, 1607–1710," appeared in the *Review*, 1942, taking its material from a rare Hutterite source now most likely lost.

A section from the *Klein–Geschichtsbuch* provided the material for a paper entitled, "An Anabaptist Ordinance on Nonresistance, 1633" (*Review*, 1951); it is my hope that this recent study will stimulate more discussions of the background and the arguments of this basic Anabaptist–Mennonite principle of nonresistance. The Anabaptist literature on this subject is not yet well known.

An illustrated popular article on the Hutterites in *Mennonite Life*, 1(1946), "Christian Love in Action—The Hutterites," has found quite sympathetic attention. It represents a brief summary of things Hutterite worth knowing.

The entire scope of Hutterite lore was the main theme of the Fifth Annual Conference on Mennonite Cultural Problems, held at Freeman, South Dakota, in August 1946. The *Proceedings* contain much good material (lectures and discussion), yet the brochure is hard to find in any library. Bethel College still has a stock of it.

A new and very productive worker in the field in America came from a most unexpected quarter, namely, that of Germanistic language research. Professor **A. J. F. Zieglschmid** (1903–50), then teaching at Northwestern University, Evanston, Illinois, discovered on his European trip of 1938 almost the same manuscripts which before him Beck, Loserth, Wolkan, Müller, and Friedmann had studied. (They are kept in Slovakian and Hungarian libraries and archives). At first these writings were to him just interesting sources of early *Neuhochdeutsch* with a Bavarian slant, and he brought transcripts of these sources along for possible publication. (See *Review*, January and April issues, 1941, and October 1943). But soon he caught fire. He sensed that there was more to this material than its mere quality of a philological monument. He visited the Hutterite colonies in South Dakota, lived with the Brethren for weeks, and gained their confidence. The result of this contact is truly remarkable: two large volumes published and a third large one in manuscript. *Die älteste Chronik der Hutterischen Brüder* (Philadelphia, 1943) is a diplomatic edition of the Great Chronicle of the Brethren, and comprises 1050 pages. Four years later, *Das Klein–Geschichtsbuch der Hutterischen Brüder* (Philadelphia, 1947) was published, a complete edition of the Small Chronicle, with a total of 860 pages. It contains the above-mentioned text by Johannes Waldner up to 1802, a first edition of high value, and then its continuation compiled by the editor from many sources, up to 1947—a rich material in more than one regard. Zieglschmid's industry and gift for finding relevant material is truly amazing.[15] The Appendices of the *Klein–Geschichtsbuch* (pp. 501–683) provide us again with first-rate source material, otherwise unobtainable. A complete collection of the unique *Gemeinde–*

---

15 See my extensive review in *MQR*, XXII (1948).

Ordnungen, 1651–1873, deserve here particular mention. (All this material was taken from handwritten sources preserved through the centuries by the Brethren). Another great enhancement of the volume is an almost complete bibliography of Hutterite studies and sources, with 374 items. The volume concludes with a well–rounded subject index, again a first in this field, which will prove invaluable for future research.

It is most tragic that Zieglschmid's premature death in 1950 prevented him from publishing his third large volume, a revised and greatly enlarged edition of the *Hutterisches Liederbuch*. (The typescript of about 4500 pp. is now kept in the Mennonite Church Archives, Goshen, Ind.) It is our hope that it can be published posthumously together with Zieglschmid's research in the history of the tunes, and a musicologist's transcript of the tunes themselves. Zieglschmid published also a valuable German paper in our field, "Die ungarischen Wiedertäufer bei Grimmelshausen" in *Zeitschrift für Kirchengeschichte*, June 1940,[16] which summarizes his findings of his European research trip, 1938.[17] Two further documentary articles appeared in the *Mennonite Quarterly Review*: "Unpublished Sixteenth Century Letters of the Hutterian Brethren" (January and April 1941) and "A Song of the Persecution of the Hutterites in Velke Levary" (July 1943). The first article presents five letters of 1527 to 1535, the second a historical hymn of 80 stanzas reporting the defection in 1725 of a Hutterite community to Catholicism. No doubt, Zieglschmid contributed much to make the name of the Hutterites known among scholars of all kinds, and his source publications will remain much in use. Several articles of his in the *American–German Review* (1942) were welcome popularizations of the theme.

Occasionally an academic dissertation or thesis in this country is devoted to Hutterite life. In 1924, **Bertha W. Clark** published in the *Journal of Political Economy* (University of Chicago) her excellent study, "The Hutterian Communities," based on personal contacts during a prolonged stay with the brethren. She was primarily interested in the economic principles of the group, but soon understood that there is more to it than a merely "economic" community of goods. In 1939, **L. E. Deets** wrote a Ph.D. dissertation at Columbia University entitled, *The Hutterites, a Study in Social Cohesion*, again based on first–hand investigations. He concentrated upon the sociological aspect of Hutterite life (first study 1931), lived for some time in the colonies, but unfortunately lacked some deeper insight into the spiritual roots of this kind of life. Thus he does not reach far beyond the popular "case" study type, without major advancement in our knowledge of Hutterite principles.

---

16 Zieglschmid published an excerpt of this paper in *Publ. of Mod. Language Assn.* (*PMLA*), December 1939, pp. 1031–40.

17 An erroneous hypothesis concerning the "Brethren from Thessalonica," who once came to Moravia to visit the Hutterites, was cleared up by Friedmann in his paper, "Encounter of the Anabaptists and Mennonites with Anti–Trinitarianism," *MQR*, XXII (1948), 147, note 28. These men were in all likelihood Socinian refugees from Venice who had found relative safety in Turkey.

In 1930, **D. E. Harder** wrote an M.A. thesis for Bethel College under the title, *The Hutterian Church*. I have not seen this paper and assume that it has never been published.

At present **Dr. Joseph W. Eaton** of the Department of Sociology and Anthropology, Wayne University, Detroit, is engaged in another case study regarding Hutterism, which is subsidized by the U.S. Health Service. Dr. Eaton and collaborators are set to find out the reasons why there is such excellent mental health in spite of much intermarriage. It is well known that mental cases are exceedingly rare among the Brethren, thus belying all sociological assumptions. Fortunately, Dr. Eaton has a fine grasp of the spiritual conditioning of the life of the Brethren, and he is inclined to give high credit to these intangibles. The work is going on at the present time and the results will be published in some near future. All told, it seems that such a study represents but a marginal contribution to Hutterite lore, though it may contribute to the solution of the American mental health problem.

A particular paragraph should be devoted to the work of **Dr. Franklin H. Littell**, formerly of the University of Michigan, and now in Germany serving the Religious Affairs Branch of the American government. His Ph. D. thesis (under Professor R. H. Bainton, Yale) deals with *The Anabaptist View of the Church* (1946). It places the idea at the "Restitution" of the primitive church in the very center of Anabaptist theology. A great deal of the source material used for this work is taken from Hutterite testimonies such as, e.g. Lydia Müller's *Glaubenszeugnise*. Though the treatment is comprehensive and general, taking Anabaptism as a large whole the Hutterites yet loom very large in Dr. Littell's book. And that not only because this source material is more ample and readily available but more so because the strongly organized Hutterite church can be taken as a master example for this idea of "restitution."[18] As I understand, the book will soon be published in a series edited by the American Church Historical Society. Needless to say, Dr. Littell is thoroughly familiar with the entire vast literature in this field, and in warm sympathy with this "Left–Wing" group of the Reformation time. The *Review* has published two enlightening related essays by Dr. Littell, one in January 1947, entitled, "The Anabaptist Theology of Missions," and another one in January 1950, entitled, "The Anabaptist Doctrine of the Restitution of the True Church." Both are well documented from about the same sources as mentioned above. The former study, on the theology of missions, deals in the main with "The Great Commission" which the Anabaptists in general felt as their central concern, and which the Hutterites in particular followed with never–ending zeal and aggressiveness. Hence the growth of their church in Moravia. We know something about their zeal through the study by

---

18 It is, for instance, well known that the Hutterites base their specific doctrine of community of goods on the similar practice of the early church in Jerusalem (Acts 4). See the discussion on this point in the Freeman, S.D., *Proceedings*, 1946.

Wilhelm Wiswedel mentioned above. Dr. Littell gives further evidence of this phenomenon, calling the Hutterites outright "a missionary community." The second study, on the idea of restitution repeats somewhat his greater work, developing in detail the implications of such program or vision.

A minor, though interesting, detail of the Hutterite settlement in America has found attention in a study by **Professor K. J. Arndt**, "The Harmonists and the Hutterians."[19] From it we learn that between 1875 and 1885 these communistic settlers, sometimes called Rappites offered a helping hand to the newly immigrated Hutterites, both in Dakota and also in a settlement experiment in Penneylvania. An elaborate correspondence is still extant and may one day be published by Dr. Arndt.

Publication of Hutterite source material is naturally one of the most urgent requirements for any deeper appreciation of this group as well as of all Anabaptists. We cannot talk about the Hutterites, or for that matter about Anabaptists in general, without knowing their literature, their confessions, epistles, tracts, defense, etc. True, some material has been published, but much more is still pending. Zieglschmid's Chronicles, Müller's *Glaubenszugnisse*, Bossert's bulky volume (Württemberg) are to us just suggestions of what still could and should be done. Lydia Müller's second volume, Zieglschmid's Hutterite hymnal (*Liederbuch*), Dr. Dedic's Austrian archive material are a few items of this kind. Peter Riedemann's great *Rechenschaft unseres Glaubens* (1545), published for the last time as a private printing by the Eberhard Arnold group in 1938, has been translated into English and is being brought out in the fall of 1950 by the (English) Hutterite Brethren, Wheathill Bruderhof, Bridgnorth, Shropshire, England. It represents a most welcome document of Anabaptist thought, now available in English. But still more is needed. I myself am hoping to be able to publish the Hutterite epistles as far as they are available. The present collection comprises about sixty epistles, and some more might still he added from new sources; but there is hardly any chance to publish all epistles extant (about three hundred). An English "Reader" of Anabaptist texts is, no doubt, the most urgent desideratum. The younger generation of scholars in this country will need translated material for their further interpretation. When and how this will be done is at present a moot question. We would truly need a "Foundation" to carry out such large plans, paralleling the German *Täuferakten* publication.

One side of Hutterite activities has not found any attention thus far—their preaching. What Dr. Roy Umble has achieved for present–day Mennonitism, namely, an expert study of preaching in the Mennonite Church, its contents and its forms, should also be tried with the Hutterites, who follow an older (seventeenth or eighteenth century) tradition of reading their sermons from time–honored sermon collections. The existence of these

---

19 Karl J. Arndt, " The Harmonists and the Hutterians," *American–German Review*, X (August 1944). The main content of this study is repeated in *Klein–Geschichtsbuch*, 461–64.

Vorreden (sermons) was not known at all until recently; most likely they would yield quite valuable insights into the spiritual life of the group, to be sure not exactly of the original pattern but of that of later centuries. The *Klein–Geschichtsbuch* contains (pp. 204–21) a good collection of such *Reden*, in the main dealing with the decay of the brotherhood and what should be done to check it (order, tradition). Another subject never under scrutiny is the medical knowledge of the Hutterian Brethren. It is well known that they had excellent physicians and surgeons among them; one Georg Zabel was called to the court of Emperor Rudolph II in Prague in 1581 (and he actually cured the emperor); another physician, Balthasar Goller, accompanied the imperial ambassador Count Herberstein on his journey to Constantinople (1608–9), and so on. They had popular barbers and surgeons who were much in demand among the Moravian aristocracy. A wealth of medical recipes has survived which are still in use. (One is by Pilgram Marpeck). The transcript of an *Arznei Handbüchl* (medical manual) of 1635 is awaiting publication.

But above all the major issue in all Anabaptist research at the present time centers around the not yet fully formulated "theology of Anabaptism:" namely, the ideas of the Anabaptists concerning sin and salvation, the kingdom of God on earth, the concept of the church, the justification for nonconformity, etc., perhaps even the question of community of goods. Hutterite material should prove particularly valuable and best suited to guide us in the appreciation of Anabaptist life and dedication. The *Review* issue of January 1950 contains such a first attempt, and Hutterite ideas are amply quoted therein. Still more will be done in the near future, as we hope. A new interest is awakened among the younger generation of Mennonite scholars. And it seems as if this interest is not merely academic. The Anabaptist spirit is still alive, and the Hutterite witnessing has something significant to add to this spirit.

SOURCE: *Mennonite Quarterly Review,* XXIV (1950), pp. 353–63.

AFTERWORD TO THIS EDITION
"But the Hutterites in Particular!"

More than any other Anabaptist scholar and Christian believer, Robert Friedmann was the one to unveil the innermost workings, spirit and thought of the faith community that came to be known as the Hutterites.[1] He did it, not only as a scholarly pursuit, but also out of personal interest, indeed, conviction! As he himself states:

> It was really a sort of fateful decision, which I made while I was still a student at the university, to study the Anabaptist writings of these sixteenth-century people who, as I learned very soon, were the Hutterites. What captivated my interest immediately was this kind of genuineness, or as we say today, authenticity, of these epistles. They were genuine Christian existential documents, testimonials which profoundly gripped me right at the very beginning.[2]

The impact of these Hutterian writings would ultimately lead Friedmann from the Jewish tradition to Christian baptism.

And so, in 1923 Robert Friedmann discovered Anabaptism. He never lost this fundamental focal point in history. It became his main scholarly pillar, and so remained up to his death in 1970, half a century later. And here, his leanings were definitely with the Hutterites. How often did I hear Robert Friedmann exclaim, "But the Hutterites in particular!"

Friedmann furthermore ascertained throughout his life that Anabaptism held a genuinely unique place in all of Christian history:

> ...[T]he Anabaptists were for me the only phenomenon in the entire two thousand years of church history where the idea of Gospel–Christianity, if I may call it this way, was realized, and in particular among the Hutterites, because the Hutterites had the fortunate situation of living in Moravia where they could develop this system of Anabaptist living, while the other ones were always

---

1 "...[N]o one did as much research and publishing on Hutterite life as [Robert Friedmann] did. He is the unchallenged master in the reconstruction of Hutterite life from the sixteenth to the eighteenth centuries." Walter Klaassen, "Robert Friedmann as Historian," in *Mennonite Quarterly Review* 48 (April 1974), 133.

2 Robert Friedmann, in "Conversations with Robert Friedmann," ed., Leonard Gross, *Mennonite Quarterly Review* 48 (April 1974), 149.

persecuted and had very little chance of really developing their ideas of a true brotherhood. In that regard I would say the Hutterites are different.³

Friedmann saw Christianity, as lived out by the Anabaptists, as a living faith—as he called it, an "existential" faith. He then went on to describe this living Christianity, again in his own words:

> ...Anabaptism is existential Christianity. And its...main royal idea is the idea of the kingdom of God which is not only a promise to come but in a nuclear way is already here among the brotherhood—namely a work of peace and harmony and mutual love. The brotherhood is, so to speak, a little nucleus of the kingdom of God in the here and now. And that is, maybe, what gives such an enormous strength, an existential strength, to these epistles and other documents of the Hutterites, and of course, of other [Anabaptist] writers as well—but the Hutterites in particular because the Hutterites could produce such an enormous amount of literature.⁴

* * * * *

We owe a world of gratitude to that friend of the Hutterites, Robert Friedmann. I thank him for his loving attention to Anabaptist history, for his carefully–researched windows into its poignant essence and spirit. His incredibly sharp eye now allows us to experience the living character of sixteenth–century Anabaptism in general, and Hutterianism in particular—an existential character emanating the vision and courage of the early Christians that defies systematic definition and at best can only be described. And although it is impossible to recreate or reincarnate the movement at least in its sixteenth–century manifestations, it is certainly there for anyone who has the eyes and ears, the mind and spirit, to perceive it. There was indeed something substantial, spiritual and cohesive within the movement which helped to give Anabaptism its "punch." In its vision of a peaceable community of gathered disciples of Jesus there was power, but without coercion. There was at times conscious disregard for human law, in obedience to the higher law of love. There was the fulfillment of peace within a called–apart kingdom—in a nuclear fashion to be sure, yet genuine, by transcending the kingdoms of this world. Friedmann was absolutely sure these ideas were sixteenth-century reality among bodies of witnesses called Anabaptists—above all, among the Hutterites who held all things common. To be sure, the reality was never

---

3 Ibid., 147.
4 Ibid., 173. The "Robert Friedmann Memorial Issue" of the *Mennonite Quarterly Review* (April, 1974), brings together a wealth of information on Friedmann, along with an extensive bibliography of his writings.

perfect. It was a vision sought after but only incompletely attained here on earth, but it was a reality which nonetheless supplied the moving force behind what Friedmann described as Anabaptism.

If Friedmann is correct in saying that a reincarnation of that Anabaptism of yore is impossible, the question arises, "Why study Anabaptism?" Why come to terms with the historical realities that once had been? Friedmann himself provides a clue to the answer in his own life and intellectual synthesis. The questions which arose out of the Reformation movement in general and in the broad Anabaptist movement in particular are our questions, usually posed more realistically than questions we might pose by just confining ourselves to the present. Furthermore, how the various Reformation groups and movements answered questions provides us with a profound clue to answers for today. Their confusion is also ours. This is the relevant carry–over from one generation to another, which unfortunately can be, and often is, largely overlooked by now–oriented intellectuals and philosophers.

But is there more carry-over than this? Maybe, Friedmann would say. But as he constantly affirmed, the Spirit must be at work within the group, and the timing—this all-important, eschatological timing—must be right. We disciples must gather and then wait, expectantly! (Acts 1)

Leonard Gross
Goshen, Indiana
February 2010

KEY TO SYMBOLS AND ABBREVIATIONS IN FOOTNOTES

ME—Mennonite Encyclopedia, 4 vols. (Scottdale, 1955–59)

ML—Mennonitisches Lexikon, 4 vols. to letter S (Weierhof and Frankfurt, later Karlsruhe, 1913–)

MQR—Mennonite Quarterly Review (Goshen, 1927–)

Geschichts–Bücher—Josef von Beck, *Die Geschichts–Bücher der Wiedertäufer in Oesterreich–Ungarn...* (Vienna, 1883)

Geschicht–Buch—*Geschicht–Buch der Hutterischen Brüder*, edited by Rudolf Wolkan (Vienna, 1923)

Aelteste Chronik—*Die älteste Chronik der Hutterischen Brüder*, edited by A. J. F. Zieglschmid (Philadelphia, 1943)

Klein–Geschichtsbuch—*Das klein–Geschichtsbuch der Hutterischen Brüder*, edited by A. J. F. Zieglschmid (Philadelphia, 1947)

Communismus—Johann Loserth, "Der Communismus der mährischen Wiedertäufer im 16. und 17. Jahrhundert, Beiträge zu ihrer Geschichte, Lehre, und Verfassung," *Archiv für österreichische Geschichte*, LXXXI (1894), 135–322

ARG—Archiv für Reformationsgeschichte

A CHRONOLOGICAL BIBLIOGRAPHY OF THE CHIEF WRITINGS OF ROBERT FRIEDMANN

A. Articles in German in European Journals

"Die Habaner in der Slowakei," *Wiener Zeitschrift für Volkskunde*, XXXII, 1927 (reprint, 11 pages, illustrated).
"Die Briefe der österreichischen Täufer, ein Bericht," *ARG*, XXVI (1929, 30–38, and 161–187, with exhaustive bibliography). (A condensed English version appeared in *MQR*, 1946.)
"Vernunft und Gehorsam, ein alter Täuferbrief und sein Sinn," *Mennonitische Blätter*, LXXVI (1929), 44–47. (The same article appeared also in English in the *MQR*, 1945.)
Review of Wilhelm Wiswedel, *Bilder und Führergestalten aus dem Täufertum*, I and II, in *Mennonitische Blätter* (1929), 113–114, and *ibid.* (1932), 2–4 (The same review appeared also in English in the *MQR*, 1940.)
"Eine dogmatische Hauptschrift der hutterischen Täufergemeinschaften in Mähren," *ARG*, XXVIII (1931), 80–111, and 207–240 (Ergänzung der Bibliographie," *ibid.*, 240–241); XXIX (1932), 117.
"Von einem wahrhaften Ritter Christi, ein bisher unbekannter Traktat aus den Kreisen der philippischen Brüder in Mähren," *Zeitschrift für Kirchengeschichte*, Dritte Folge II, Vol. LI (1932) 524–535. (The same article appeared also in English in the *MQR*, 1931.)
"Über Thomas Müntzer (Ein Sammelreferat)," *Mitteilungen des Instituts für österreichische Geschichtsforschung*, XLVII (1933), 90–97.

B. Articles in the *Mennonite Quarterly Review*

Concerning the True Soldier of Christ. 5:87–99, April 1931.
Anabaptism and Pietism. 14:90–128 April 1940; 14:149–169, July 1940.
Spiritual Changes in European Mennonitism, 1650–1750. 15:33–45, Jan. 1941.
Dutch Mennonite Devotional Literature from Peter Peters to Joannes Deknatel, 1625–1753. 15:187–207, July 1941.

The Schleitheim Confession (1527) and Other Doctrinal Writings of the Swiss Brethren in a Hitherto Unknown Edition. 16:82–98, April 1942.

The Devotional Literature of the Swiss Brethren, 1600–1800. 16:199–200, Oct. 1942.

Adventures of an Anabaptist in Turkey, 1607–1610. 17:73–86, April 1943

Mennonite Prayer Books. 17:179–206, Oct. 1943.

On Mennonite Historiography and on Individualism and Brotherhood. 18:117–122, April 1944.

The Devotional Literature of the Mennonites in Danzig and East Prussia to 1800. 18:162–173, July 1944.

Reason and Obedience. 19:27–40, Jan. 1945.

The Epistles of the Hutterian Brethren. 20:147–177, July 1946.

John Horsch and Ludwig Keller. 21:160–174, July 1947.

Additional Comments on Loserth's Study on Carinthia. 21:248–251, Oct. 1947.

Faith and Reason: The Principles of Mennonitism Reconsidered, in a Treatise of 1833, Tr. and ed. by R. Friedmann. 22:75–93, April 1948.

The Encounter of Anabaptists and Mennonites with Anti–Trinitarianism. 22:139–162, July 1948.

Anabaptism and Protestantism. 24:12–24, Jan. 1950.

A Comprehensive Review of Research on the Hutterites, 1880–1950. 24:353–363, Oct. 1950.

A. J. F. Zieglschmid, an Obituary. 24:364–365, Oct. 1950.

An Anabaptist Ordinance of 1633 on Nonresistance. 25:116–127, April 1951.

Peter Riedemann on Original Sin and the Way to Redemption. 26:210–215, July 1952.

Hutterite Physicians and Barber–Surgeons (additional notes). 27:128–136, April 1953.

A Communication to the Editor: A Critical Discussion of H. W. Meihuizen's Study, "Spiritual Trends and Movements Among the Dutch Mennonites of the 16th and 17th Centuries." (27:259–305 Oct. 1953) 28:148–154, April 1954.

Christian Sectarians in Thessalonica and Their Relationship to the Anabaptists. 29:54–69, Jan. 1955; addenda, 30:78, Jan. 1956.

Claus Felbinger's Confession of 1560. 21:141–161, April 1955; Addenda, 30:78, Jan. 1956.

The Oldest Church Discipline of the Anabaptists. 29:162–166, April 1955; Correction. 32:236–238, July 1958

The Anabaptists Answer Melanchthon: (II) Some Further Studies Pertaining to the *Handbüchlein* of 1588, 29:223–231, July 1955.
A Hutterite Book of Medieval Origin, 30:65–71, Jan. 1956.
Economic Aspects of Early Hutterite Life, 30:259–266, Oct. 1956.
An Example of the Spirit of Early Anabaptism, 30:289, Oct. 1956.
A Notable Hutterite Document: Concerning True Surrender and Christian Community of Goods, Translated by Kathleen E. Hasenberg (Introduction by Robert Friedmann). 31:22–62, Jan. 1957.
Thomas Müntzer's Relation to Anabaptism, 31:75–87, April 1957.
The Philippite Brethren: A Chapter in Anabaptist History, 32:270–297, Oct. 1958.
Leonhard Schiemer and Hans Schlaffer: Two Tyrolean Anabaptist Martyr-Apostles of 1528, 33:31–42, Jan. 1959.
The Oldest Known Hutterite Codex of 1566: A Chapter in Anabaptist Intellectual History, 33:96–108, April 1959.
The Doctrine of Original Sin as Held by the Anabaptists of the Sixteenth Century, 33:207–215, July 1959.
Hutterites Revisit European Homesteads: From the Diary of David Hofer, 33:305–322, Oct. 1959.
Jakob Hutter's Last Epistle to the Church in Moravia, 1535, 34:37–47, Jan. 1960.
An Epistle Concerning Communal Life: A Hutterite Manifesto of 1650 and Its Modern Paraphrase, 34:249–274, Oct. 1960.
A Newly Discovered Source on the Transmigration of the Hutterites to Transylvania 1621–24, Edited text. 35, July 1961.

C. Articles in English in Other American and European Journals

"Conception of the Anabaptists," *Church History*, IX (1940), 341–365.
"The Mennonite Historical Library of Goshen College," *The American German Review*, IX (1942), 12–14 (illustrated).
"Recent Interpretations of Anabaptism," *Church History*, XXIV (1955), 132–151.
"The Christian Communism of the Hutterite Brethren," *ARG* (1955), 196–208.
"Progress in Anabaptist Studies: A Comprehensive Review 1955–57," *Church History*, XXVII (1958), 72–76.
"The Doctrine of the Two Worlds," in C. F. Hershberger, *The Recovery of the Anabaptist Vision* (Scottdale, 1957), 105–118; "The Hutterian Brethren

and Community of Goods," *ibid.*, pp. 83–90. (The second item is a reprint of a part of the study in *ARG*, 1955.)

In *Mennonite Life*
"Christian Love in Action," I (1946), 38–43 (illustrated).
"Of Hutterite Books," VII (1952), 81–83.
"Wilhelm Wiswedel—His Service to Anabaptist Appreciation," X (1955), 41–44 (illustrated).
"Hutterite Pottery or Haban Fayences," XIII (1958), 147–152 (182) (illustrated).
"More About Habaner Pottery," XIV (1959), 129–130 (illustrated).
"Anabaptism in the Inn Valley," XV (1960), 109–114 (illustrated).

D. Books Published or in Preparation

Mennonite Piety Through the Centuries, its Genius and its Literature (Studies in Anabaptist and Mennonite History, No. 7), Mennonite Historical Society, Goshen, Ind., 1949 (287 pp.)

Glaubenszeugnisse oberdeutscher Täufer, II, by Lydia Müller and Robert Friedmann. To be published by the Verein für Reformationsgeschichte about 1962 in the *Täuferakten* series (about 700 pages of Anabaptist sources with introductions).

Die Schriften der Huterischen Täufergemeinschaften. (Österreichische Akademie der Wissenschaften, Philosophisch-Historische Klasse Denkschriften, 86. Band), Hermann Böhlaus Nachf., Wien, 1965. (179 pp.)

E. Articles in the Mennonite Encyclopedia

For a complete list see *MQR*, XXXV, July 1961.

BIOGRAPHICAL SKETCH

Robert Friedmann was born June 9, 1891, into a liberal Jewish family in Vienna, Austria. Following his education as an engineer in the Technical University of Vienna, 1908-14, he studied history and philosophy at the University of Vienna, 1920-24, securing a Ph. D. in 1924. He then taught at Gymnasiums in Vienna 1925-38.

He began his Anabaptist studies in 1929, when he was commissioned by the *Verein fur Reformationsgeschichte* to edit a volume of Hutterite epistles. In 1939 he left Austria, reaching the United States via England the same year. At Goshen, he converted to the Mennonite faith and expanded his substantial oeuvre about the history of Anabaptism and especially about the history of the Hutterites for the rest of his life.

Robert Friedmann was Honorary Fellow at Yale Divinity School in 1940, and Research Fellow in Anabaptist Studies at Goshen College 1940-43. For a part of the latter period he was Visiting Lecturer at Goshen College. He was an assistant editor of the *Mennonite Encyclopedia*, 1947-59, responsible for the former Austro-Hungarian territories and the Hutterian Brethren.

From 1945 up to his retirement, he was Professor of History and Philosophy at Western Michigan University at Kalamazoo, Michigan. During this period, he was also an Associate Editor of the *Mennonite Quarterly Review*.

Robert Friedmann died in 1970.

www.ingramcontent.com/pod-product-compliance
Lightning Source LLC
Chambersburg PA
CBHW071855290426
44110CB00013B/1151